Final Report of the Thirty-ninth Antarctic Treaty Consultative Meeting

ANTARCTIC TREATY
CONSULTATIVE MEETING

Final Report
of the Thirty-ninth
Antarctic Treaty
Consultative Meeting

Santiago, Chile
23 May - 1 June 2016

Volume I

Secretariat of the Antarctic Treaty
Buenos Aires
2016

Published by:

Secretariat of the Antarctic Treaty
Secrétariat du Traité sur l' Antarctique
Секретариат Договора об Антарктике
Secretaría del Tratado Antártico

Maipú 757, Piso 4
C1006ACI Ciudad Autónoma
Buenos Aires - Argentina
Tel: +54 11 4320 4260
Fax: +54 11 4320 4253

This book is also available from: *www.ats.aq* (digital version)
and online-purchased copies.

ISSN 2346-9897
ISBN (vol. I): 978-987-4024-22-0
ISBN (complete work): 978-987-4024-18-3

Contents

VOLUME I

VOLUME II

PART II. MEASURES, DECISIONS AND RESOLUTIONS (Cont.)

4. Management Plans

ASPA No 116 - New College Valley, Caughley Beach, Cape Bird, Ross Island

ASPA No 120 - Pointe-Géologie Archipelago, Terre Adélie

ASPA No 122 - Arrival Heights, Hut Point Peninsula, Ross Island

ASPA No 126 - Byers Peninsula, Livingston Island, South Shetland Islands

ASPA No 127 - Haswell Island

ASPA No 131 - Canada Glacier, Lake Fryxell, Taylor Valley, Victoria Land

ASPA No 149 - Cape Shirreff and San Telmo Island, Livingston Island, South
    Shetland Islands

ASPA No 167 - Hawker Island, Princess Elizabeth Land

PART III. OPENING AND CLOSING ADDRESSES AND REPORTS

1. Opening and Closing Addresses

Welcoming Address by the Minister of External Relations Heraldo Muñoz Valenzuela

2. Reports by Depositaries and Observers

Report of the USA as Depositary Government of the Antarctic Treaty and its Protocol

Report of Australia as Depositary Government of CCAMLR

Report of Australia as Depositary Government of ACAP

Report of the UK as Depositary Government of CCAS

Report by the CCAMLR Observer

Report of SCAR

Report of COMNAP

3. Reports by Experts

Report of IHO
Report by WMO
Report by IPCC
Report of ASOC
Report of IAATO

PART IV. ADDITIONAL DOCUMENTS FROM ATCM XXXIX

1. Additional Documents

Abstract of SCAR Lecture
Presentations at the Special Working Group on the 25th. Anniversary of the
Protocol on Environmental Protection

2. List of Documents

Working Papers
Information Papers
Background Papers
Secretariat Papers

3. List of Participants

Consultative Parties
Non-consultative Parties
Observers, Experts and Guests
Host Country Secretariat
Antarctic Treaty Secretariat

Acronyms and Abbreviations

ACAP	Agreement on the Conservation of Albatrosses and Petrels
ASMA	Antarctic Specially Managed Area
ASOC	Antarctic and Southern Ocean Coalition
ASPA	Antarctic Specially Protected Area
ATS	Antarctic Treaty System or Antarctic Treaty Secretariat
ATCM	Antarctic Treaty Consultative Meeting
ATME	Antarctic Treaty Meeting of Experts
BP	Background Paper
CCAMLR	Convention on the Conservation of Antarctic Marine Living Resources and/or Commission for the Conservation of Antarctic Marine Living Resources
CCAS	Convention for the Conservation of Antarctic Seals
CCRWP	Climate Change Response Work Programme
CEE	Comprehensive Environmental Evaluation
CEP	Committee for Environmental Protection
COMNAP	Council of Managers of National Antarctic Programs
EIA	Environmental Impact Assessment
EIES	Electronic Information Exchange System
HSM	Historic Site and Monument
IAATO	International Association of Antarctica Tour Operators
ICAO	International Civil Aviation Organization
ICG	Intersessional Contact Group
IEE	Initial Environmental Evaluation
IHO	International Hydrographic Organization
IMO	International Maritime Organization
IOC	Intergovernmental Oceanographic Commission
IOPC Funds	International Oil Pollution Compensation Funds
IP	Information Paper
IPCC	Intergovernmental Panel on Climate Change
IUCN	International Union for Conservation of Nature
MPA	Marine Protected Area
NCA	National Competent Authority
RCC	Rescue Coordination Centre
SAR	Search and Rescue

SCAR	Scientific Committee on Antarctic Research
SC-CAMLR	Scientific Committee of CCAMLR
SGMP	Subsidiary Group on Management Plans
SOLAS	International Convention for the Safety of Life at Sea
SOOS	Southern Ocean Observing System
SP	Secretariat Paper
UAV	Unmanned Aerial Vehicle
UNEP	United Nations Environment Programme
UNFCCC	United Nations Framework Convention on Climate Change
WMO	World Meteorological Organization
WP	Working Paper
WTO	World Tourism Organization

PART I
Final Report

1. Final Report

Final Report of the Thirty-ninth Antarctic Treaty Consultative Meeting

Santiago, Chile, May 23 – June 1, 2016

(1) Pursuant to Article IX of the Antarctic Treaty, Representatives of the Consultative Parties (Argentina, Australia, Belgium, Brazil, Bulgaria, Chile, China, the Czech Republic, Ecuador, Finland, France, Germany, India, Italy, Japan, the Republic of Korea, the Netherlands, New Zealand, Norway, Peru, Poland, the Russian Federation, South Africa, Spain, Sweden, Ukraine, the United Kingdom of Great Britain and Northern Ireland, the United States of America, and Uruguay) met in Santiago from 23 May to 1 June 2016, for the purpose of exchanging information, holding consultations and considering and recommending to their Governments measures in furtherance of the principles and objectives of the Treaty.

(2) The meeting was also attended by delegations from the following Contracting Parties to the Antarctic Treaty which were not Consultative Parties: Belarus, Canada, Colombia, Malaysia, Monaco, Portugal, Romania, Switzerland, Turkey and Venezuela.

(3) In accordance with Rules 2 and 31 of the Rules of Procedure, Observers from: the Commission for the Conservation of Antarctic Marine Living Resources (CCAMLR), the Scientific Committee on Antarctic Research (SCAR) and the Council of Managers of National Antarctic Programs (COMNAP) attended the meeting.

(4) In accordance with Rule 39 of the Rules of Procedure, Experts from the following international organisations and non-governmental organisations attended the meeting: the Antarctic and Southern Ocean Coalition (ASOC), the International Association of Antarctica Tour Operators (IAATO), the International Hydrographic Organization (IHO), the International Panel on Climate Change (IPCC) and the World Meteorological Organization (WMO).

(5) The Host Country Chile fulfilled its information requirements towards the Contracting Parties, Observers and Experts through the Secretariat Circulars, letters and a dedicated website.

Item 1: Opening of the Meeting

(6) The meeting was officially opened on 23 May 2016. On behalf of the Host Government, in accordance with Rules 5 and 6 of the Rules of Procedure, the Head of the Host Government Secretariat, Ambassador Patricio Powell, called the Meeting to order and proposed the candidacy of Ambassador Alfredo Labbé, General Director of Foreign Policy, as Chair of ATCM XXXIX. The proposal was accepted.

(7) The Chair warmly welcomed all Parties, Observers and Experts to Chile. He noted the importance of the Antarctic Treaty System as a cooperation mechanism between states, highlighting its evolution over the past 55 years since the Antarctic Treaty entered into force. Ambassador Labbé further noted the new environmental challenges that Parties faced in cooperatively governing and protecting the Antarctic, and hoped that ATCM XXXIX would be a fruitful and constructive meeting.

(8) Delegates observed a minute of silence in honour of the passing of Mr David Wood and Dr Malcolm Laird. Mr Wood, a Canadian-Australian citizen, was a helicopter pilot who had participated in several National Antarctic Programme expeditions and had worked for many years with the Australian Antarctic Division. Dr Laird, from New Zealand, participated in his first expedition to Antarctica in 1960. He was a recipient of the Polar Medal and contributed to significant geological mapping of the Ross Sea region.

(9) The Hon. Heraldo Muñoz Valenzuela, Minister of Foreign Affairs of Chile, joined the meeting along with the Minister for National Defence, Hon. José Antonio Gómez Urrutia, and the Undersecretaries for both Departments. Minister Muñoz warmly welcomed delegates, noting that ATCM XXXIX marked the 55th anniversary of the entry into force of the Antarctic Treaty. While acknowledging that international cooperation in Antarctica pre-dated the Treaty, he highlighted that, since its signature, the Treaty had provided a model of effective international cooperation. He emphasised Chile's commitment to strengthening the Antarctic Treaty System and to developing Antarctic science, and reported that it was constructing an International Antarctic Centre with a focus on logistical support in Punta Arenas, to be

completed in 2019. Noting that the Antarctic Peninsula had registered a three-degree temperature increase in the last 50 years, he underlined the implications of Antarctic warming for the entire planet and the importance of continued Antarctic climate studies. Minister Muñoz underlined the importance of focusing on the conservation of the Antarctic environment, and stressed that Chile believed that Parties should work towards a representative system of marine protected areas. He noted that Parties were united by a long and shared history in Antarctica, and recalled the extraordinary operation, led by Chilean pilot Luis Pardo, who rescued the survivors of Ernest Shackleton's expedition in 1916. Minister Muñoz remarked that the many challenges still facing Antarctica should be addressed jointly and, noting the large concentration of stations in the Antarctic Peninsula, highlighted the potential for further synergy between them. He stated that this was important for enhancing science and reducing the human footprint in Antarctica. Finally, he wished Parties a fruitful meeting and encouraged them to keep working towards the protection of Antarctica.

Item 2: Election of Officers and Creation of Working Groups

(10)   Ms Xiao-mei Guo, Head of Delegation of China, Host Country of ATCM XL, was elected Vice-chair. In accordance with Rule 7 of the Rules of Procedure, Dr Manfred Reinke, Executive Secretary of the Antarctic Treaty Secretariat, acted as Secretary to the Meeting. Ambassador Patricio Powell, head of the Host Country Secretariat, acted as Deputy Secretary. Mr Ewan McIvor of Australia acted as Chair of the Committee for Environmental Protection.

(11)   Three Working Groups were established:

- Working Group 1 on Policy, Legal and Institutional Issues;
- Working Group 2 on Operations, Science and Tourism; and
- Working Group 3 on the 25th Anniversary of the Protocol on Environmental Protection.

(12)   The following Chairs of the Working Groups were elected:

- Working Group 1: Dr René Lefeber from the Netherlands;
- Working Group 2: Mr Máximo Gowland from Argentina and Professor Jane Francis from the United Kingdom;
- Working Group 3: Ambassador Francisco Berguño from Chile.

Item 3: Adoption of the Agenda and Allocation of Items

(13)   The following Agenda was adopted:

1. Opening of the Meeting
2. Election of Officers and Creation of Working Groups
3. Adoption of the Agenda and Allocation of Items
4. Operation of the Antarctic Treaty System: Reports by Parties, Observers and Experts
5. Report of the Committee for Environmental Protection
6. Operation of the Antarctic Treaty System
    a. Venezuela's request to become a Consultative Party
    b. General Matters
7. Operation of the Antarctic Treaty System: Matters related to the Secretariat
8. Liability
9. Biological Prospecting in Antarctica
10. Exchange of Information
11. Education Issues
12. Multi-year Strategic Work Plan
13. Safety and Operations in Antarctica
14. Inspections under the Antarctic Treaty and the Environment Protocol
15. Science Issues, Scientific Cooperation and Facilitation
16. Implications of Climate Change for Management of the Antarctic Treaty Area
17. Tourism and Non-Governmental Activities in the Antarctic Treaty Area, including Competent Authorities Issues
18. 25th Anniversary of the Protocol on Environmental Protection
19. Preparation of the 40th Meeting
20. Any Other Business
21. Adoption of the Final Report
22. Close of the Meeting

(14)   The Meeting adopted the following allocation of agenda items:

- Plenary: Items 1, 2, 3, 4, 5, 19, 20, 21, 22.
- Working Group 1: Items 6, 7, 8, 9, 10, 11, 12.

- Working Group 2: Items 13, 14, 15, 16, 17.
- Working Group 3: Item 18

(15) The Meeting also decided to allocate draft instruments arising out of the work of the Committee for Environmental Protection and the Working Groups to a legal drafting group for consideration of their legal and institutional aspects.

Item 4: Operation of the Antarctic Treaty System: Reports by Parties, Observers and Experts

(16) Pursuant to Recommendation XIII-2, the Meeting received reports from depositary governments and secretariats.

(17) The United States, in its capacity as Depositary Government of the Antarctic Treaty and its Environment Protocol, reported on the status of the Antarctic Treaty and the Protocol on Environmental Protection to the Antarctic Treaty (IP 42). In the past year, there had been one accession to the Treaty and no accessions to the Protocol. For the Treaty, Iceland had deposited its instrument of accession on 13 October 2015. The United States noted that there were currently 53 Parties to the Treaty and 37 Parties to the Protocol.

(18) Parties congratulated Iceland on its accession to the Antarctic Treaty. Noting that this year marked the 25th anniversary of the Environment Protocol, several Parties expressed their hope to see further accessions this year, and encouraged other Parties thinking of acceding to the Protocol to do so.

(19) Australia, in its capacity as Depositary for the Convention on the Conservation of Antarctic Marine Living Resources (CCAMLR), reported that there had been no new accessions to the Convention since ATCM XXXVIII. It noted that there were currently 36 Parties to the Convention (IP 44).

(20) Australia, in its capacity as Depositary for the Agreement on the Conservation of Albatrosses and Petrels (ACAP), reported that there had been no new accessions to the Agreement since ATCM XXXVIII, and that there were 13 Parties to the Agreement (IP 43). It noted that feedback from the Fifth Meeting of Parties was held in Spain from 4 to 8 May 2015 indicated that a number of countries are progressing towards accession to ACAP. Australia highlighted that ACAP shared the conservation objectives of other instruments of the Antarctic Treaty System and encouraged all Parties which were not members of ACAP to consider joining the Agreement.

(21)   The United Kingdom, in its capacity as Depositary of the Convention for the Conservation of Antarctic Seals (CCAS), reported that it had not received any requests to accede to the Convention, or any instruments of accession since ATCM XXXVIII (IP 2). The United Kingdom encouraged all Contracting Parties to CCAS to submit their returns on time.

(22)   The Executive Secretary of CCAMLR provided a summary of outcomes of the Thirty-fourth Annual Meeting of CCAMLR which was held in Hobart, Australia, from 19 to 30 October 2015 (IP 5). It was chaired by Mr Dmitry Gonchar (Russian Federation). Twenty-three Members, two Acceding States and twelve Observers from non-government including industry organisations participated. Key outcomes of interest to the ATCM included the implementation of the Arrangement for the release of CCAMLR vessel monitoring system (VMS) data to support search and rescue (SAR) efforts in the CAMLR Convention Area – an initiative started at a SAR workshop held in association with ATCM XXXVI. Noting that the outcomes of the CCAMLR Scientific Committee (SC-CAMLR) from 2015 would be presented to CEP XIX, he reported on: the harvest of toothfish and krill under CCAMLR-regulated fisheries in the 2014/15 season; continuing work in relation to marine protected areas; the lowest incidental mortality of seabirds in CCAMLR fisheries ever reported; climate change; capacity building initiatives for early career scientists; and the outcomes of a CCAMLR Symposium to mark the 35th anniversary of the adoption of the Convention, co-chaired by Chile, Australia and the USA, which was held in Chile, 6 to 8 May 2015.

(23)   SCAR presented IP 20 *The Scientific Committee on Antarctic Research (SCAR) Annual Report 2015/16 to the Antarctic Treaty System*, and referred to BP 2, which highlighted some recent scientific publications by the SCAR research community since the last ATCM that could be of interest to the delegates. SCAR highlighted several examples of its activities including participation in the Antarctic Roadmap Challenges project in 2015. This initiative, led by COMNAP, represented the second step of the SCAR Antarctic and Southern Ocean Science Horizon Scan. Both initiatives are the topic of the SCAR Science Lecture at this year's ATCM (BP 3). Through wide consultation, including with COMNAP, SCAR developed the SCAR Code of Conduct for Activity in Terrestrial Geothermal Areas in Antarctica (WP 23). SCAR also highlighted its participation in the meetings 'Antarctica and the Strategic Plan for Biodiversity 2011-2020: The Monaco Assessment' (see IP 38) and the '2015 UNFCCC COP21' in Paris. SCAR also highlighted the awarding of several fellowships, including the 2015 Tinker-Muse prize

to Dr Valérie Masson-Delmotte of France. SCAR prepared an update of the Antarctic Climate Change and the Environment Report (IP 35) and provided a progress report regarding Geoconservation (IP 31) in advance of a full report on this issue to the CEP in 2018.

(24) SCAR indicated that the 34th SCAR Delegates Meeting and the Open Science Conference would be held in Kuala Lumpur, Malaysia on August 20. At this conference SCAR would be hosting a 'Wikibomb' as a way of increasing the visibility of female Antarctic researchers and helping to encourage girls around the world to pursue science careers. SCAR also reported that it was working on plans for the XII SCAR Biology Symposium in July 2017 in Belgium, and the POLAR2018 Conference to be held in Davos, Switzerland jointly with the International Arctic Science Committee. SCAR also noted that Dr Jenny Baeseman had been appointed as the new SCAR Executive Director.

(25) COMNAP introduced IP 10 *Annual Report for 2015/16 of the Coucil of Managers of National Antarctic Programs (COMNAP)*, and stated that it was now an international association of 30 National Antarctic Programmes and three observer programmes. COMNAP convened a number of workshops this year including the Sea Ice Challenges, Antarctic Roadmap Challenges (ARC) and would soon convene the Search and Rescue (SAR) Workshop III, as per ATCM Resolution 4 (2013). Published outcomes from the Sea Ice and the ARC workshops are available to download from the COMNAP website. The COMNAP report highlights a number of ongoing projects. Of particular note are the Station Infrastructure Catalogue project which is a comprehensive database of Antarctic facilities in order to improve information sharing for scientific collaboration; the ARC project which was a community effort which identified critical technology, infrastructure and access requirements of the Antarctic research community for the mid to long term future and the development status and cost of those critical requirements; the Unmanned Aerial Systems (UAS) Working Group which has drafted a UAS handbook for discussion.

(26) In relation to Article III-2 of the Antarctic Treaty, the Meeting received reports from other international organisations.

(27) The IHO presented IP 4 *Report by the International Hydrographic Organization* (IHO), which focused on the limitations of hydrographic knowledge in Antarctica and the consequent risks to scientific and maritime operations. The IHO reiterated that 90 per cent of Antarctic waters remained unsurveyed and that this posed serious risks for maritime incidents. It urged Parties to ensure that all their vessels used depth sensors and made

this information available to hydrographic offices to improve hydrographic mapping. The IHO encouraged Parties to participate in the next meeting of the Hydrographic Committee on Antarctica (HCA), to be held in Tromsø, Norway, from 28 to 30 June 2016, and to contribute effectively to its activities in accordance with Resolution 5 (2014). It stated that the location of the meeting had changed to Norway due to the earthquake that struck Ecuador in April. It further expressed its solidarity with Ecuador for the loss and damage suffered, and thanked Norway for its willingness to host the meeting.

(28) Argentina stated that in the next three years it intended to finalise charts in the areas of Marguerite Bay, the South Orkney Islands, and Seymour Island (Marambio), completing this way the nine charts it was committed to before the IHO.

(29) WMO presented IP 11 *WMO Annual Report 2015-2016*, which described its activities during the period. WMO noted the global temperature in April 2016 was the highest April temperature recorded since temperature recording began in 1880, and that this was the twelfth consecutive month in which this phenomenon had been observed. WMO remarked that this created a strong impetus for Parties to take action on climate change. It remarked that, in May 2015, the World Meteorological Congress approved Polar and High Mountain activities as one of the seven WMO priorities for 2016 - 2019, and noted its positive engagement with Antarctic Treaty Parties in the area of climate research.

(30) IPCC presented IP 116 *Recent Findings of IPCC on Antarctic Climate Change and Relevant Upcoming Activities*, which identified information within its Fifth Assessment Report relevant to the Antarctic area. IPCC reported on its acceptance of an invitation from COP 21 of the United Nations Framework Convention on Climate Change (UNFCCC) to prepare a Special Report on Impacts of Global Warming of 1.5°C above pre-industrial levels by 2018. The IPCC welcomed Parties' participation in the scoping meeting for the Special Report that would be held in August 2016 in Geneva. The IPCC also noted, at its 43rd session, that it had approved the preparation of a Special Report on climate change, desertification, land degradation, sustainable land management, food security, and greenhouse gas fluxes in terrestrial ecosystems and a Special Report on climate change and oceans and the cryosphere. IPCC thanked Monaco for providing financial support for the Special Report on Climate Change and Cryosphere, and noted that the scoping meeting would be held sometime in November or December 2016. The IPCC invited all governments to nominate experts to assist in the preparation of the Special Reports.

(31) ASOC presented IP 123 *Report of the Antarctic and Southern Ocean Coalition*. ASOC noted its participation in several intersessional contact groups (ICGs) and attendance at meetings relevant to the Antarctic environmental protection in the last year. ASOC stated that it was encouraged to see that so many Parties had declared their ongoing commitment to the spirit of the Environment Protocol. It highlighted the 25th anniversary of the Protocol, and its ban on mineral resource activities as an opportunity to celebrate and reflect. ASOC hoped that the bold and forward thinking of Parties in the past could help inspire those making decisions affecting Antarctica and the Southern Ocean in the next 25 years.

(32) IAATO presented IP 112 IAATO *Overview of Antarctic Tourism: 2015-16 Season and Preliminary Estimates for 2016-17*. Noting that it too was celebrating its 25th anniversary in 2016, IAATO reaffirmed its mission to advocate and promote environmentally safe and responsible visitation to the Antarctic Treaty area. It noted that all commercial SOLAS passenger ship operators conducting tourism activities in the Antarctic Treaty Area were currently members of IAATO, with one exception: a Japanese flagged non-IAATO vessel that cruised the Antarctic Peninsula in January 2016, without making any landings. IAATO reported that the 2015/16 season saw a total of 38,478 visitors, an increase of approximately five per cent compared to the previous season.

Item 5: Report of the Committee for Environmental Protection

(33) Mr Ewan McIvor, Chair of the Committee for Environmental Protection, introduced the report of CEP XIX. The CEP had considered 38 Working Papers and 51 Information Papers. In addition, 5 Secretariat Papers and 4 Background Papers had been submitted under CEP agenda items. The Chair of the CEP highlighted the items on which the CEP had agreed specific advice to the ATCM, but encouraged Parties to review all parts of the CEP Report.

Strategic Discussions on the Future Work of the CEP (CEP Agenda Item 3)

(34) The Chair of the CEP advised that the Committee had considered a report by Argentina on the ICG established at CEP XVIII to develop a publication on the 25th anniversary of the Environment Protocol. The Committee had agreed to advise the ATCM that it had: endorsed the publication on the occasion of the 25th anniversary of the Protocol on Environmental Protection to the Antarctic Treaty and agreed to forward it to the ATCM for consideration;

and recommended that the publication be launched on 4 October 2016, on the occasion of the actual anniversary of the signing of the Protocol, making use of the dissemination mechanism identified during the ICG and any other mechanisms that emerge following the CEP discussions.

(35) The Chair of the CEP further noted that the Committee had updated its Five-year Work Plan to incorporate actions that arose during the meeting.

Operation of the CEP (CEP Agenda Item 4)

(36) The Chair of the CEP advised that the Committee had considered environment-related elements of a report by Australia on the ICG established at ATCM XXXVIII to review information exchange requirements. The Committee had agreed to advise the ATCM that it had recommended specific changes to: the items of information exchange on contingency plans for oil spills and other emergencies; and items of information exchange on IEEs and CEEs.

(37) The Committee had also considered WP 10, submitted by Australia, Japan, New Zealand, Norway, SCAR, Spain and the United States, which reported on the operation of the Antarctic Environments Portal. The Committee reaffirmed the importance of the development of the Portal as a reliable, unbiased information source, to be used on a voluntary basis, to support its discussions. The Committee also agreed to give further consideration to additional topics for information summaries to include in the Portal, future management of the Portal, and how to identify representatives to serve on the Editorial Group.

(38) Reflecting on the importance of science based policy in the Antarctic area, the Meeting expressed support for the development of the Antarctic Environments Portal, and hoped the Portal would be a vehicle to enhance cooperation between the CEP and ATCM. As the Portal focused on the priorities of the CEP, the Chair of the CEP noted that Parties could also inform the future content of the Portal by suggesting topics for summaries. The Meeting welcomed the growing contributions from scientists and the CEP, and the role of the Antarctic Environments Portal in supporting the CEP to perform its key function to provide advice on the implementation of the Environment Protocol.

(39) New Zealand encouraged all Parties to adopt a best practice approach to the information exchange requirements of the Protocol. New Zealand recalled Resolution 3/2015 regarding the Antarctic Environments Portal and

welcomed the recommendation from the CEP/SC-CAMLR Joint Workshop encouraging the use of the Portal.

(40) While recognising its utility, Argentina noted the need for a greater openness and representativeness in contributing to the contents of the Antarctic Environments Portal, and looked forward to making contributions to strike this balance.

Cooperation with other Organisations (CEP Agenda Item 5)

(41) The Chair of the Committee advised that the Committee had considered the report of the Joint CEP/SC-CAMLR workshop on Climate Change and Monitoring held in Punta Arenas, Chile, on 19 and 20 May 2016. The Committee had agreed that the workshop had been valuable in further enhancing the cooperation and information sharing between the two committees. The CEP had also recognised the importance of monitoring progress on implementation of the workshop recommendations, and welcomed the advice that work already underway or planned in the near future by SCAR was consistent with the priorities in the Climate Change Response Work Programme (CCRWP).

(42) Noting that the ATCM Multi-year Strategic Work Plan prioritised consideration of the workshop's outcomes, the Committee had agreed to advise the ATCM that it had welcomed the report of the Joint CEP/SC-CAMLR Workshop on Climate Change and Monitoring and had endorsed its recommendations.

(43) Australia stressed the importance of climate change research and monitoring through SCAR, Integrating Climate and Ecosystem Dynamics (ICED) and Southern Ocean Observing System (SOOS) as reflected in the CEP Report, and noted that it would be useful to provide resources to these programmes to support the shared objectives of the CEP and SC-CAMLR. Norway cited its work with the Russian Federation in the Barents Sea to integrate a balanced view of the ocean into the planning of all human activities. It considered the joint efforts and collaborations would be a precursor to the development of integrated ocean management within the Antarctic Treaty System.

(44) The Meeting thanked the convenors of the workshop and, recalling the first Joint CEP/SC-CAMLR Workshop held in 2009, commended the CEP for promoting understanding of the mutual goals of the CEP and SC-CAMLR, climate change and environmental monitoring. The Meeting noted that it was a good example of the value of cooperation between different components

of the Antarctic Treaty System, and highlighted the utility of integrating the significant and valuable scientific monitoring work of SCAR and other specialist bodies into the work of the Antarctic Treaty System.

Climate Change Implications for the Environment: Strategic approach (CEP Agenda Item 7)

Strategic Approach

(45)   The Chair of the CEP reported that the Committee had welcomed a suite of papers that highlighted the importance of understanding and addressing the environmental implications of climate change, and would contribute to its work in that regard through the CCRWP. The CEP Chair also noted that many of the environment-related recommendations arising from the 2010 Antarctic Treaty Meeting of Experts (ATME) on Climate Change and Implications for Antarctic Management and Governance had been incorporated into the CCRWP.

Implementation and Review of the Climate Change Response Work Programme

(46)   The Chair of the CEP reported that the Committee had: reviewed progress against the actions identified in the CCRWP agreed at CEP XVIII and adopted under Resolution 4 (2015); discussed options for managing the CCRWP and supporting its implementation; and updated the CCRWP. The Committee had welcomed the offers by SCAR and WMO to provide reports to CEP XX on their research and monitoring activities relevant to the CCRWP, and agreed to request relevant external programmes including the SOOS and ICED to provide similar information about how their activities could contribute.

(47)   Noting the ATCM's request in Resolution 4 (2015) to receive annual updates on implementation of the CCRWP, the Committee had agreed to advise the ATCM that: steps were already being taken to address several tasks/actions identified in the CCRWP for 2016; it had agreed to encourage National Antarctic Programmes, SCAR, WMO, and relevant external expert organisations to support and facilitate the research and monitoring activities identified in the CCRWP; it had updated the CCRWP to reflect actions undertaken and to incorporate other minor modifications; and it had agreed to convene informal intersessional discussions to support further consideration at CEP XX of the best means for managing and supporting implementation of the CCRWP.

(48) The Chair of the CEP also noted that the Committee had reflected on the importance of incorporating high quality and up-to-date scientific advice into its deliberations on the environmental implications of climate change in the Antarctic Treaty area, and had agreed that it would be valuable to have a direct means of drawing on the expertise of the IPCC. With reference to Rule 4c of the CEP Rules of Procedure adopted under Decision 4 (2011), the Committee agreed to propose that the ATCM approve the IPCC as an Observer to the CEP.

(49) The Meeting commended the CEP's focus on the CCRWP, and encouraged the CEP to continue its work on innovative mechanisms to implement the work programme. The Meeting agreed to consider the progress against the CCRWP annually and to add this item to its Multi-year Strategic Workplan. The Meeting welcomed the WMO contributions to the Committee. The Meeting supported the CEP's efforts to encourage National Antarctic Programmes, the WMO, and other experts, to support and facilitate monitoring activities identified in the CCRWP.

(50) The Meeting endorsed the IPCC to be admitted as an Observer to the CEP (Decision 1 (2016) Observers to the Committee for Environmental Protection), and looked forward to its contribution in the future. The IPCC sincerely thanked the delegations, and urged all Parties to contribute to its scoping meeting for its Special Report on the Ocean and Cryosphere to be held in Monaco in December 2016.

Environmental Impact Assessment (EIA) (CEP Agenda Item 8)

Draft Comprehensive Environmental Evaluations

(51) The Chair of the CEP reported that the Committee had considered the draft CEE prepared by Italy for proposed construction and operation of a gravel runway in the area of Mario Zucchelli Station, Terra Nova Bay, Victoria Land, Antarctica, the report of an ICG led by France to review the draft CEE, and papers submitted by Italy presenting further information as an initial response to points raised by the ICG. The Committee had welcomed Italy's commitment to respond to the issues raised and, should it decide to proceed with the proposed activity, had encouraged Italy to take into account the Committee's advice when preparing the required final CEE.

(52) The CEP had agreed to advise the ATCM that the draft CEE generally conformed to the requirements of Article 3 of Annex I to the Protocol on Environmental Protection to the Antarctic Treaty. If Italy decides to proceed

with the proposed activity, additional information or clarification should be provided in the required final CEE, as set out in WP 21 to this meeting, in order to facilitate a comprehensive assessment of the proposed activity. The information provided in the draft CEE supported the conclusion that the impacts of constructing and operating the proposed gravel runway were likely to be more than minor or transitory, and the draft CEE was generally clear, well structured, and well presented, although improvements to some of the maps and figures were recommended.

Other EIA Matters

(53) The Chair of the CEP reported that the Committee had considered several papers containing information relevant to understanding and managing the environmental aspects of the use of unmanned aerial vehicles (UAVs) in Antarctica. It had acknowledged the benefits of UAVs for supporting research and monitoring, noted the continuing need for scientific understanding of the environmental impacts of UAV use and, in this regard, looked forward to receiving a summary of the state of knowledge regarding the impacts of UAVs on wildlife from SCAR at CEP XX. Noting that the ATCM was also considering UAV use in Antarctica, the Committee had agreed to advise the ATCM that it recognised the usefulness of the COMNAP Guidelines for Certification and Operation of Unmanned Aerial Systems in Antarctica (WP 14). The Committee had also recognised the need to develop guidance on the environmental aspects of UAVs, and that it would initiate at CEP XX work to develop such guidance.

(54) The Meeting thanked the CEP for its advice on UAVs, welcomed COMNAP's guidelines and looked forward to SCAR's advice to help the Parties take advantage of a useful technology in a safe and environmentally sound manner.

(55) The United Kingdom noted the discussion on UAVs touched on issues relevant to both the CEP and the ATCM, and suggested that in the future consideration could be given to holding joint sessions between CEP and ATCM experts to discuss matters of joint interest, such as CEEs, inspections and UAVs.

(56) The CEP Chair expressed support for taking a more cooperative approach to issues of common interest between the ATCM and CEP, and noted there would be utility in ATCM representatives engaging with their CEP colleagues on the planned CEP intersessional discussions regarding UAVs.

(57) The CEP Chair reported that the Committee had considered a report by Australia and the United Kingdom on the ICG established at CEP XVII

(2014) and continued at CEP XVIII (2015) to review the Guidelines for Environmental Impact Assessment in Antarctica. Following further minor amendments made during the meeting, the Committee had finalised the revision of the Guidelines. The Committee had also considered the broader policy and other issues raised during the intersessional work, noted that they called for careful consideration, and thanked the United Kingdom for its offer to work with interested Members to develop a paper to support further discussion of these issues at CEP XX.

(58) Following consideration of the report of the ICG established to review the Guidelines for Environmental Impact Assessment in Antarctica, the Committee had endorsed a revision to the Guidelines and agreed to continue its work on broader policy considerations. Noting that the existing Guidelines were adopted under Resolution 4 (2005), the Committee had agreed to forward to the ATCM for adoption a draft Resolution to revise the Guidelines.

(59) The Meeting adopted Resolution 1 (2016) Revised Guidelines for Environmental Impact Assessment in Antarctica, and highlighted the importance of the Guidelines for the ongoing implementation of the Protocol.

(60) Reflecting that the EIA was one of the most important tools of the Protocol, the United Kingdom encouraged the CEP to keep the ATCM advised on its deliberations on broader policy and other EIA issues. New Zealand also noted it had been ten years since the Guidelines had been updated, and urged Parties to consider updating such tools more regularly to support the implementation of the Protocol.

Area Protection and Management Plans (CEP Agenda Item 9)

Management Plans

(61) The CEP Chair reported that the Committee had considered papers that presented eight revised management plans for Antarctic Specially Protected Areas (ASPAs). The Committee had also agreed to advise the ATCM that the existing management plan for ASPA 166 Port-Martin, Terre-Adélie, should be extended for a further period of five years.

(62) The Chair of the CEP also noted the Committee had recalled its discussion at CEP XIV (2011) in considering a paper by the United Kingdom presenting the results of monitoring at ASPA 107 Emperor Island. Following careful consideration, and with the support of the United Kingdom, the Committee had decided, however, that the ASPA status should be maintained for a further

five years. The Committee had also encouraged other Members to provide any relevant monitoring data to assist with this further assessment.

(63)   The Committee had discussed the value of developing guidance for the Committee's consideration of proposals to de-designate ASPAs, and welcomed Norway's offer to lead work to inform further consideration of this issue at CEP XX.

(64)   The CEP Chair also reported that the Committee had considered a paper reporting on informal intersessional discussions led by China on its proposal to designate an Antarctic Specially Managed Area (ASMA) to protect the scientific and environmental values in the Dome A area. The Committee had welcomed China's offer to lead further informal intersessional discussions to consider management options for Dome A.

(65)   The Meeting celebrated the successes of the Subsidiary Group on Management Plans (SGMP) in supporting the efficiencies of the CEP, and welcomed the development of management plans to support area protection. Highlighting the prioritisation of the issue in the CCRWP, New Zealand urged the CEP to continue to prioritise developing representative areas of each biogeographic region, and areas likely to provide refuge to species at risk.

(66)   The Meeting welcomed Spain becoming a co-manager of ASPA 126.

(67)   Accepting the CEP's advice, the Meeting adopted the following Measures on Protected Areas:

- Measure 1 (2016) *Antarctic Specially Protected Area ASPA No. 116 (New College Valley, Caughley Beach, Cape Bird, Ross Island): Revised Management Plan.*

- Measure 2 (2016) *Antarctic Specially Protected Area ASPA No. 120 (Pointe-Géologie Archipelago, Terre Adélie): Revised Management Plan.*

- Measure 3 (2016) *Antarctic Specially Protected Area ASPA No. 122 (Arrival Heights, Hut Point Peninsula, Ross Island): Revised Management Plan.*

- Measure 4 (2016) *Antarctic Specially Protected Area ASPA No. 126 (Byers Peninsula, Livingston Island, South Shetland Islands): Revised Management Plan.*

- Measure 5 (2016) *Antarctic Specially Protected Area ASPA No. 127 (Haswell Island and Adjacent Emperor Penguin Rookery on Fast Ice): Revised Management Plan.*

- Measure 6 (2016) *Antarctic Specially Protected Area ASPA No. 131 (Canada Glacier, Lake Fryxell, Taylor Valley, Victoria Land): Revised Management Plan.*

- Measure 7 (2016) *Antarctic Specially Protected Area ASPA No. 149 (Cape Shirreff and San Telmo Island, Livingston Island, South Shetland Islands): Revised Management Plan.*

- Measure 8 (2016) *Antarctic Specially Protected Area ASPA No. 167 (Hawker Island, Princess Elizabeth Land): Revised Management Plan.*

(68) The Meeting also agreed to extend the existing management plan for ASPA 166 Port-Martin, Terre-Adélie for a further period of five years.

Historic Sites and Monuments

(69) The CEP Chair reported that the Committee had recalled its decision at CEP XVIII (2015) that future proposals for new designations of Historic Sites and Monuments (HSM) should be put on hold until further guidance was established on approaches to protection of historic heritage in Antarctica. The Committee had considered a number of papers on this issue, and agreed to forward one proposal for a modification to the List of Historic Sites and Monuments to the ATCM for approval by means of a Measure.

(70) Accepting the CEP's advice, the Meeting adopted Measure 9 (2016) *Revised List of Antarctic Historic Sites and Monuments: Incorporation of a historic wooden pole to Historic Site and Monument No 60 (Corvette Uruguay Cairn), in Seymour Island (Marambio), Antarctic Peninsula.*

(71) The Committee had agreed to defer two proposals for additions to the List of HSMs for further consideration following the development of guidance on approaches for the protection of historic heritage in Antarctica: Historical pre-1958 remains in the vicinity of Marambio Station; and Antarctic King Sejong Station History Gallery. The Committee had agreed that the interim protection afforded to pre-1958 sites in accordance with Resolution 5 (2001) would apply to the historical remains in the vicinity of Marambio Station.

(72) The Committee had agreed to establish an ICG to work during the 2016/17 and 2017/18 intersessional periods with the aim of developing guidance material for Parties' assessment of conservation approaches for the management of Antarctic heritage objects.

(73) The Meeting considered that management of heritage was an important part of Annex V, and welcomed the CEP's planned development of further guidance

material based on the most relevant conservation approaches. Norway noted with appreciation the CEP's prioritisation of heritage management issues and underlined the importance of developing policies for the Antarctic Treaty System in this area. The United Kingdom encouraged the involvement of heritage experts with and without Antarctic backgrounds to share best practice. Argentina noted its interest in contributing to discussions, and highlighted the need to continue to offer special temporary protection to sites that needed it.

Site Guidelines

(74) The Chair of the CEP mentioned that the Committee had considered proposed Site Guidelines prepared by Ukraine, the United Kingdom, the United States, Argentina and IAATO for Yalour Islands, Wilhelm Archipelago, and proposed Site Guidelines prepared by the United Kingdom, Chile and IAATO for Point Wild, Elephant Island. The Committee had agreed to forward the following new Site Guidelines to the ATCM for adoption: Yalour Islands, Wilhelm Archipelago and Point Wild, Elephant Island.

(75) The Meeting welcomed the work of the CEP on the development of Site Guidelines, noting it was useful work that minimised the risk of impacts from visitors to those sites. During the Meeting, Ecuador and Spain noted that the Committee supported the recommendation that the lower track in Barrientos Island should remain closed; and that the Committee encouraged Ecuador and Spain to continue the long term monitoring to assess the recovery of vegetation on both tracks to provide future reports on its status. Australia commended, in particular, the cautious and considered approach of the CEP to the management of Barrientos Island.

(76) The Meeting considered and approved two new Site Guidelines by adopting Resolution 2 (2016) *Site Guidelines for Visitors*.

Other Annex V Matters

(77) The Chair of the CEP noted the Committee had considered a paper by the United Kingdom proposing a revision of the Guide to the presentation of Working Papers containing proposals for Antarctic Specially Protected Areas, Antarctic Specially Managed Areas or Historic Sites and Monuments to facilitate the collection of additional information on how proposed protected areas fit within systematic environmental-geographical framework tools. Following discussion, the Committee had agreed to advise the ATCM that it recommended revising 'Template A: Cover sheet for a Working

Paper on an ASPA or ASMA' appended to the 'Guide to the presentation of Working Papers containing proposals for Antarctic Specially Protected Areas, Antarctic Specially Managed Areas or Historic Sites and Monuments' adopted under Resolution 5 (2011) to include new and revised questions.

(78) The Chair of the CEP noted that the Committee had considered a paper by SCAR presenting the *SCAR Code of Conduct for Activity within Terrestrial Geothermal Environments in Antarctica*, and recognised the value of the Code of Conduct for supporting the planning and conduct of activities in terrestrial geothermal areas to minimise risks to the high scientific and environmental values of such areas. The Committee had endorsed the Code of Conduct, and agreed to forward to the ATCM for approval a draft Resolution on encouraging the dissemination and use of the Code of Conduct.

(79) Accepting the CEP's advice, the Meeting adopted Resolution 3 (2016) *Code of Conduct for Activity within Terrestrial Geothermal Environments in Antarctica*. The Meeting congratulated SCAR for its work on the Code of Conduct.

(80) The CEP Chair also noted the Committee had thanked Birgit Njåstad (Norway) for her excellent work as SGMP convenor for the previous four years, and appointed Patricia Ortúzar (Argentina) to the role of SGMP convener.

(81) The Meeting also sincerely thanked Birgit Njåstad for her work as SGMP convenor, and congratulated Patricia Ortúzar for her appointment as the SGMP convener.

(82) In highlighting the importance of MPAs and challenges in processing the information required to implement an MPA, Argentina thanked ASOC for its assistance in capacity building regarding MPA data processing for members of its National Antarctic Directorate and Argentine Antarctic Institute.

Conservation of Antarctic Flora and Fauna (CEP Agenda Item 10)

Quarantine and Non-native Species

(83) The CEP Chair reported that the Committee had considered a report by the United Kingdom on the ICG established at CEP XVIII (2015) to review the CEP Non-native Species Manual. The Committee had endorsed the revised Manual, which had been comprehensively reviewed and revised by the ICG, and had agreed to incorporate a series of actions recommended by the ICG into its Five-year Work Plan under the priority 1 issue Introduction of Non-native Species. The Committee had endorsed a revision to the CEP Non-native Species Manual. Noting that the current version of the Manual

had been adopted under Resolution 6 (2011), the Committee had agreed to forward to the ATCM for adoption a draft Resolution to revise the Manual and encourage its dissemination and use.

(84) Accepting the CEP's advice, the Meeting adopted Resolution 4 (2016) *The Committee for Environmental Protection Non-native Species Manual.*

Inspection Reports (CEP Agenda Item 12)

(85) The CEP Chair reported that, under this agenda item, the Committee had considered papers reporting on inspections conducted by China during December 2015, had welcomed the general findings that the six inspected stations were in compliance with the Environment Protocol; and had considered papers reporting on inspections conducted by Argentina and Chile during February 2016, and welcomed the general findings that the five inspected stations were in satisfactory compliance with the requirements of the Environment Protocol.

Election of Officers (CEP Agenda Item 14)

(86) The CEP Chair noted that the Committee had thanked Birgit Njåstad of Norway for her outstanding work as CEP Vice-chair for the past four years. The Committee had also elected Patricia Ortúzar of Argentina as CEP Vice-chair and had elected Mr Ewan McIvor (Australia) to serve a second two-year term as CEP Chair.

(87) The Meeting congratulated Mr McIvor on his appointment for a second term as Chair of the CEP. It also thanked Dr Polly Penhale of the United States, Vice-chair of the Committee, for her continuing support of the Chair of the CEP, and congratulated Patricia Ortúzar of Argentina on her appointment as Vice Chair of the CEP.

(88) The Meeting warmly thanked Birgit Njåstad of Norway for her involvement and outstanding work as CEP Vice-chair during the last four years.

Preparation for Next Meeting (CEP Agenda Item 15)

(89) Norway thanked the Committee for their excellent work and noted the need to further discuss a meeting structure that ensures sufficient time for Parties to consider the CEP Report and the CEP advice.

(90) The Chair of the CEP noted that the Committee had adopted a Preliminary Agenda for CEP XX, reflecting the agenda for CEP XIX.

(91)   The Meeting thanked Mr McIvor for his comprehensive report of the work of the CEP, and for his inspired leadership of the CEP.

Item 6: Operation of the Antarctic Treaty System: Venezuela's request to become a Consultative Party

(92)   Venezuela informed the Meeting that following current guidelines it had formally submitted a request for Consultative status to the depositary government of the Antarctic Treaty. It also noted that it had been a Non-consultative Party since 1999, and had been engaged in scientific activity in the Antarctic without interruption since 2008.

(93)   Japan and Ecuador supported the request of the Bolivarian Republic of Venezuela for Antarctic Treaty Consultative Status. Japan insisted that an increase in Consultative Parties directly contributes to dissemination of the principles of the Antarctic Treaty and the Protocol on Environmental Protection to the Antarctic Treaty. Japan welcomed Venezuela becoming a Consultative Party. Japan expressed its hope to continue to undertake work in Antarctica in cooperation with other Parties.

(94)   Welcoming Venezuela's contribution to Antarctic research, the Meeting encouraged Venezuela to continue developing its plans and strategies for attaining Consultative status. Several Parties offered to assist Venezuela in achieving this objective.

(95)   Several Parties suggested a set of criteria should be developed against which to determine whether it was appropriate to grant a Party Consultative status.

(96)   The Meeting recalled the Guidelines on notification with respect to Consultative Status adopted by ATCM XIV, as well as Decision 4 (2005) on the same subject adopted by ATCM XXVIII, and agreed that it would be useful to review the existing Guidelines and consider whether there was a need for additional or updated guidance on the conditions to be satisfied by a Party seeking Consultative status.

(97)   The Meeting decided to establish an ICG on Criteria for Consultative Status with the following terms of reference:

- review the existing procedure for obtaining Consultative Party status, including Decision 4 (2005);
- review the Guidelines on notification with respect to Consultative status;

- consider whether additional or updated Guidelines would provide further clarity regarding the granting of Consultative Party status as per Article IX, paragraph 2, of the Antarctic Treaty, which requires that a "Contracting Party demonstrates its interest in Antarctica by conducting substantial scientific research activity there, such as the establishment of a scientific station or the despatch of a scientific expedition";
- consider other recommendations for Contracting Parties wishing to obtain Consultative Party Status; and
- report to the ATCM.

(98) It was further agreed that:

- only Consultative Parties would be invited to provide input;
- the Executive Secretary would open the ATCM forum for the ICG and provide assistance for the ICG; and
- Chile, New Zealand and Uruguay would act as co-convenors.

Item 6b: Operation of the Antarctic Treaty System: General Matters

(99) The United Kingdom introduced WP 5 *Revision of the 'Guide to the presentation of Working Papers containing proposals for Antarctic Specially Protected Areas, Antarctic Specially Managed Areas or Historic Sites and Monuments'*, noting that the paper had been introduced in CEP under agenda item 9e, Area Protection and Management Plans - Other Annex V Matters. The paper had proposed some revisions to Template A.

(100) The Meeting noted that revisions to the guide had been approved by the CEP. The Meeting adopted Resolution 5 (2016) *Revised Guide to the presentation of Working Papers containing proposals for Antarctic Specially Protected Areas, Antarctic Specially Managed Areas or Historic Sites and Monuments*.

(101) The United Kingdom introduced WP 7 *ATCM Rules of Procedure relating to Intersessional Consultations*, prepared jointly with the United States. The paper highlighted the lack of clarity and guidance to the Executive Secretary on which contact persons each Consultative Party considered were the most appropriate to be contacted during a formal intersessional consultation. The proponents proposed that the ATCM consider: whether it was appropriate for the Executive Secretary to deem contact persons nominated under Recommendation XIII-1 as those designated by the Consultative Party

pursuant to Rules 46 and 47 of the ATCM Rules of Procedure; whether to advise the Executive Secretary that for the purposes of Rules 46 and 47 of the Rules of Procedure, it was the Representative (*ie*, Head of Delegation) and their Alternate who should be deemed the designated contact; and whether to advise the Executive Secretary to request specific advice from each Consultative Party to maintain a separate list of contact persons pursuant to Rules 46 and 47.

(102) The Meeting thanked the United Kingdom and the United States and noted the importance of good communication during intersessional consultations, for which the identification of a reliable contact point was necessary. The Meeting decided that the relevant paragraphs of the Rules of Procedure of the Antarctic Treaty Consultative Meeting would be updated (see Decision 2 (2016) *Revised Rules of Procedure for the Antarctic Treaty Consultative Meeting*). The Meeting agreed that each Party would notify the Executive Secretary of their Representative and any Alternate Representatives in accordance with revised Rule 46(a) within two weeks of the closure of the ATCM.

(103) Australia introduced WP 19 *Enhancing awareness of the Antarctic Treaty Parties' work through the earlier public release of the ATCM Report*. Australia proposed that Consultative Parties agree to make a preliminary version of the report of each ATCM publicly available via the Secretariat website within three months of the Meeting. This would be consistent with the timing for public availability of Measures, Decisions and Resolutions, and would assist in enhancing general awareness of the Parties' important work on governing and managing the Antarctic Treaty area. The paper suggested changes to the Procedures for the Submission, Translation and Distribution of Documents for the ATCM and the CEP.

(104) Parties welcomed Australia's paper and saw value in releasing a draft version of the Report within three months of the meeting. Several Parties highlighted the benefit of releasing a preliminary Report at the same time as the timing of the publication of the Measures, Decisions and Resolutions, and noted the public interest in ATCMs.

(105) In response to questions from Parties, the Executive Secretary stated that a preliminary Report would not result in higher costs and that only editorial changes were made after the adoption of the Final Report at each ATCM. The Executive Secretary further noted that translations into all four Treaty languages and expert proofreading would be completed before the publication of the preliminary Report. The final formatting and layout were features that were more time intensive.

(106) The Meeting agreed that a preliminary version of the Report should be released within three months of the meeting. The Meeting decided that the relevant paragraphs of the Annex *Procedures for the Submission, Translation and Distribution of Documents for the ATCM and the CEP* contained in the Rules of Procedure of the Antarctic Treaty Consultative Meeting and the Committee for Environmental Protection, would be updated (see Decision 2 (2016) *Revised Rules of Procedure for the Antarctic Treaty Consultative Meeting*).

(107) The United States introduced WP 38 *Confirming Ongoing Commitment to the Prohibition of Mining Activity in Antarctica, other than for Scientific Research. Antarctic Mining Ban*, jointly sponsored with Argentina, Australia, Belgium, Chile, the Czech Republic, Finland, France, Germany, Italy, Japan, the Republic of Korea, the Netherlands, New Zealand, Norway, Poland, South Africa, Spain, Sweden, the United Kingdom and Uruguay.

It indicated that this proposal was offered in light of the 25th anniversary of the Protocol. The best-known part of the Protocol is the prohibition on activities related to mineral resources under Article 7, otherwise known as the mining ban. This obligation, to which all Protocol Members ascribe, is often misunderstood. The mining ban does not expire in 2048; it can only be reconsidered at that point. This misunderstanding can be addressed, at least in part, by adopting a Resolution. This is also a moment when, at the 25th anniversary, Parties can reaffirm their commitment to Article 7, given its importance in the context of environmental protection.

(108) The Meeting warmly welcomed the paper and draft Resolution. Parties recognised Article 7 as a pillar of the Protocol on Environmental Protection and reiterated their strong commitment to the protection of Antarctica and its environment for future generations.

(109) The Meeting noted there was widespread misconception and misunderstanding regarding an expiry date of Article 7 and the prohibition on mining activity in Antarctica. Several Parties highlighted the need to ensure more publicity was given to reaffirming the continued prohibition of mining activities in the Antarctic beyond 2048.

(110) Noting that a Resolution was required and following further discussion, the Meeting adopted Resolution 6 (2016) *Confirming Ongoing Commitment to the Prohibition on Antarctic Mineral Resource Activities, other than for Scientific Research. Support for the Antarctic Mining Ban*.

(111) The Russian Federation introduced WP 39 rev. 1 *On "openness" of the gateway to the Antarctic*. Noting that most ships and air routes to the Antarctic passed

via the southern sea ports and airports that served as gateways to the Antarctic, the Russian Federation called on Parties in charge of operations in those sea ports and airports to consider the problem described in the paper regarding transit travel of participants of National Antarctic Programmes to and from Antarctica. It invited Parties to find a positive solution to the matter.

(112) Following discussion and noting the concerns regarding transit travel of participants of National Antarctic Programmes, Parties in control of gateway transit points responded positively, stating that they were willing to resolve the issue of transit problems for other National Antarctic Programmes, and if need be, on a case by case basis.

(113) Norway introduced WP 50 *Improving interaction between CEP and ATCM*, jointly prepared with Australia. Parties were invited to consider whether an agreement could be reached: that documents would only be submitted to either the CEP or ATCM; that documents that were submitted to both the ATCM and CEP clearly outlined what questions should be discussed by the ATCM and CEP respectively; that Chairs could coordinate their plans for the agenda in advance; that Chairs could review papers as they are submitted and, as appropriate, could invite the author(s) to redirect their paper to another part of the meeting; and to update the Secretariat's Manual for the submission of documents to the ATCM and the CEP to include general guidance on these matters.

(114) Parties emphasised the need to strengthen the relationship between the CEP and ATCM. Several Parties expressed concern that by preventing papers being submitted jointly to both CEP and ATCM the system would lack flexibility, and that in some cases the designation of papers to both was necessary. Coordination between Chairs of each Group was recognised as an important factor in determining the best use of available time during the meeting. Parties noted that an annotated agenda was already used in the CEP and asked that a similar approach be adopted for the other Working Groups, with earlier availability of this and the summary of papers to better facilitate preparation for the sessions.

(115) The Meeting agreed that documents submitted to both the ATCM and CEP should, where possible, clearly indicate what questions or issues should be discussed respectively by the ATCM and CEP, providing Chairs with the opportunity to more fully discuss and coordinate their plans for the agenda in advance. It further agreed that Working Group Chairs should review papers as they are submitted and, as appropriate, invite the author(s) to redirect their paper to another part of the Meeting. It was agreed that it

would be useful for the Chairs to coordinate their plans for the agenda in advance of each ATCM. Following further discussion, the Meeting agreed that these suggestions would be reflected in a revision to the Annex to the Rules of Procedure for the Antarctic Treaty Consultative Meeting entitled *Procedures for the Submission, Translation and Distribution of Documents for the ATCM and the CEP*. The Meeting adopted Decision 2 (2016) *Revised Rules of Procedure for the Antarctic Treaty Consultative Meeting (2016)*.

(116) The Meeting discussed the merits of having annotated agendas for each Working Group. Parties agreed it would be beneficial for all meeting participants to have an annotated agenda and summary of papers, circulated by the respective ATCM Working Group Chairs and Secretariat, in preparation for the meeting. This would assist efficiency and allow for a coordinated sequence of discussion between the ATCM and CEP. The Executive Secretary confirmed that this could be done in conjunction with the Chairs of the respective Working Groups. The Meeting agreed to reflect this in the *Secretariat Programme 2016/2017*.

(117) The United Kingdom noted that it would be useful for the work of the ATCM to receive a report from the Antarctic Treaty Secretariat listing those Measures that are currently not yet in force. It was agreed that the Antarctic Treaty Secretariat would produce a Secretariat Paper using information contained in the report from the Depositary Government on the status of those Measures, but preferably being more "user friendly". Parties emphasised that the information contained in the Secretariat Paper should be factual and neutral in nature. The Meeting agreed to reflect this in the Secretariat Programme 2016/2017.

(118) ASOC presented IP 79 *An Unprecedented Achievement: 25 Years of the Environmental Protocol*. ASOC reflected on the positive outcomes of the Protocol on Environmental Protection and encouraged Parties to take Protocol implementation further. In welcoming the paper, Parties noted that the Protocol was a keystone of the Antarctic Treaty System. Its strength lay in the fact that it was designed to adapt to changing circumstances, having the legal flexibility to address contemporary environmental issues.

Item 7: Operation of the Antarctic Treaty System: Matters related to the Secretariat

(119) The Executive Secretary introduced SP 3 rev. 1 *Secretariat Report 2015/16*, detailing the Secretariat's activities in the Financial Year 2015/16 (1 April

2015 to 31 March 2016). He reported that, following an invitation for the submission of proposals for translation and interpretation services for ATCM XXXIX, a three-year contract was awarded to the company ONCALL, Australia. He noted that the Secretariat had organised a literature competition for students from schools in Argentina and Chile on the occasion of the commemoration of the 25ᵗʰ anniversary of the Environment Protocol.

(120) The Executive Secretary updated the Meeting on issues related to coordination and contacts, information technologies, publication of the Final Report of ATCM XXXVIII, public information, personnel and financial matters. He noted that there were no changes in Secretariat personnel during the 2015/16 period. In relation to the Electronic Information Exchange System (EIES), improvements had been made and he encouraged Parties to submit their reports in a timely manner. He advised that contributions from Brazil and Ukraine had been delayed and invited these Parties to send their payments as soon as possible.

(121) The Executive Secretary introduced SP 4, *Secretariat Programme 2016/17.* This outlined the activities proposed for the Secretariat in the Financial Year 2016/17 (1 April 2016 to 31 March 2017). He referred to WP17 *Report of the intersessional contact group established to review information exchange requirements*, and noted that the Secretariat would implement the requested changes. On staffing matters, the Executive Secretary proposed the promotion of Ms Anna Balok and Ms Viviana Collado to salary level G4, pursuant to Regulation 5.5 of the Staff Regulations.

(122) The Executive Secretary also introduced SP 5 *Five Year Forward Budget Profile 2016-2020*, which provided the Secretariat's budget profile for the period 2016-2020. He noted that the budget profile showed no major changes and maintained a zero nominal increase in contributions in that period. He stated that in this five year period, no increase of salaries had been requested.

(123) The Meeting thanked the Executive Secretary for these detailed reports and acknowledged the important work undertaken by the Secretariat in supporting the general governance of Antarctica. Some Parties encouraged payments of arrears to be addressed as soon as possible by the Parties concerned.

(124) Following further discussion the Meeting adopted Decision 3 (2016) *Secretariat Report, Programme and Budget.*

(125) Chile introduced WP 42 *Revised Procedure for Selection and Appointment of the Executive Secretary of the Secretariat of the Antarctic Treaty*, prepared jointly with Argentina and the United States. Chile noted that because the current Executive Secretary's term would expire in August 2017, an

appropriate procedure for the selection and appointment of a new Executive Secretary needed to be put in place. This would enable the Meeting to appoint a new Executive Secretary at ATCM XL in Beijing, China.

(126) The Meeting welcomed this proposal. In response to queries from some Parties on the proposed selection criteria and procedures for ranking candidates, Chile assured the Meeting that the proposed procedure was the same as that used at ATCM XXXII. Following further discussion, Chile confirmed that the selection of the successful candidate would be by consensus. The Meeting agreed to clarify in the Decision that applicants should provide a CV together with the standard application form.

(127) The Meeting adopted Decision 4 (2016) *Procedure for Selection and Appointment of the Executive Secretary of the Secretariat of the Antarctic Treaty*.

Item 8: Liability

(128) The United States, as Depositary Government of the Antarctic Treaty and its Protocol on Environmental Protection to the Antarctic Treaty, confirmed that 12 Consultative Parties had communicated their approval of Annex VI.

(129) Parties provided updated information on the status of their ratification of Annex VI, and implementation of Annex VI in domestic legislation. Of the Parties who had approved Annex VI (Australia, Finland, Italy, the Netherlands, New Zealand, Norway, Peru, Poland, the Russian Federation, South Africa, Spain, Sweden and the United Kingdom), five reported that they were applying domestic legislation implementing Annex VI pending the entry into force of Annex VI (Finland, the Netherlands, Norway, the Russian Federation and Sweden).

(130) Several Parties reported that they were in the process of implementing Annex VI in domestic legislation. Some Parties indicated implementation might be completed within the current legislative period.

(131) Some Parties expressed their concern over the general lack of progress made towards the entry into force of Annex VI.

(132) The Meeting agreed to continue to monitor implementation of Annex VI.

(133) Parties that had already approved Annex VI to the Protocol, as well as those that had implemented or were in the process of implementing Annex VI into their domestic legislation, offered to share their experiences with other Parties and were encouraged to do so via the Electronic Information Exchange System (EIES).

(134) With regard to insurance issues, the Executive Secretary advised the Meeting that the International Oil Pollution Compensation Funds (IOPC Funds) had been invited to attend this ATCM. Having initially accepted the invitation, the IOPC Funds had later declined.

(135) The United Kingdom noted that the International Group of Protection and Indemnity Clubs (IGP&I) had shown an interest in liability issues for Antarctica and regularly discussed these matters. It was suggested that the secretariat of the International Group of Protection and Indemnity Clubs (IGP&I) could provide advice regarding shipping activities and that this might be appropriate for the next ATCM. IAATO noted that it could take this discussion forward with its members.

(136) The Meeting requested the Executive Secretary to renew its invitation to the IOPC Funds and to invite the London P&I Club to attend a future ATCM, and to inform those bodies that the ATCM would welcome their input and advice on issues relating to insurance under Annex VI of the Protocol.

Item 9: Biological Prospecting in Antarctica

(137) Recalling Resolution 7 (2005) *Biological Prospecting in Antarctica*, Resolution 9 (2009) *Collection and Use of Antarctic Biological Material*, and Resolution 6 (2013) *Biological Prospecting in Antarctica*, Belgium encouraged Parties to report on their activities related to biological and genetic resources in Antarctica. It reminded Parties that issues related to biological prospecting were being addressed in other international forums, including the United Nations, and stressed the importance of making collective progress in the ATCM on this issue.

Item 10: Exchange of Information

(138) Australia introduced WP 17 *Report of the Intersessional Contact Group Established to Review Information Exchange Requirements*. It reminded Parties that some changes and clarifications to information exchange requirements were agreed to by ATCM XXXVIII and reflected in Decision 6 (2015). That Meeting had identified outstanding items which were addressed by the ICG. Australia reported that the ICG: undertook discussion to review the information currently required to be exchanged, focusing in particular on the items described as requiring attention by ATCM XXXVIII; considered

whether there was continued value for Parties to exchange information on these items; considered whether some of them needed to be modified, updated, differently described, made mandatory (where currently described as optional) or removed; considered the timing of information exchange for these items; considered how each item should best fit into the category of pre-season, annual and permanent information; and considered whether the information could be better exchanged through other mechanisms (for example those operated by COMNAP).

(139) Japan appreciated Australia's initiative for the ICG to improve the current EIES. Among the information exchanged, that of research plans would be especially important for international research collaboration which is encouraged by Article III of the Treaty. With consultation with other forums like SCAR, COMNAP, CCAMLR and each Party's research committee, it should contribute to a safe and streamlined research operation in the Antarctic, international research collaboration, and sharing of research platforms including Antarctic stations and vessels. Japan expressed its intention to continue working with this ICG for EIES.

(140) The Meeting welcomed the work of the ICG, acknowledging Australia's role in leading discussions during the intersessional period, and recognising that information exchange was an important pillar of the Antarctic Treaty System. While highlighting the usefulness of the EIES, some Parties noted that its effectiveness depended largely on active participation and encouraged Parties to engage proactively in its use.

(141) Noting the CEP's advice on the exchange of information on environmental matters, the Meeting decided to update the Annex to Decision 6 (2015). The Meeting adopted Decision 5 (2016) *Exchange of Information*. The considerations relating to the amendments to the information exchange requirements, annexed to the Decision, are contained in Appendix 4 to this Report. The Meeting noted that if there were outstanding issues regarding the functioning of the EIES they would be considered at the next ATCM.

(142) Brazil presented IP 74 *Regulations and Procedures for Vessels Proceeding to Antarctica*, which referred to regulations established by the Brazilian government pertaining to ships and citizens proceeding to Antarctica from Brazil. Brazil also presented IP 75 *Reconstruction and Foundation Stone of the New Brazilian Station in Antarctica*, regarding the rebuilding of the Comandante Ferraz Antarctic Station, damaged by fire in 2012. Brazil noted that due to reconstruction efforts, resources for conducting its scientific activities were constrained, and requested Parties' cooperation and

solidarity to support its scientists. Finally, Brazil introduced IP 73 *XXXIV Antarctic Operation*, which reported on the XXXIV Antarctic Operation (OPERANTAR XXXIV). The vessels *Almirante Maximiano* and *Ary Rongel* departed for Antarctica from the Naval Base of Rio de Janeiro in October 2015 and returned in March 2016.

(143) The following paper was also submitted under this item:

- BP 7 *Measures under the Protocol on Environmental Protection to the Antarctic Treaty: Implementing Legislation of the Kingdom of the Netherlands* (Netherlands).

Item 11: Education Issues

(144) Bulgaria introduced WP 24 *First Report on the Intersessional Contact Group on Education and Outreach*, jointly prepared with Belgium, Brazil, Chile, Portugal and the United Kingdom. The ICG recommended that the ATCM: recognise the usefulness of the Forum on Education and Outreach; advise the Parties to promote use of the Forum to provide information of their activities related to Education and Outreach; assess key international activities/events related to education and outreach that Parties could engage; promote the use of educational materials already available in the Forum; promote the use of the Forum to engage more Parties on Education and Outreach; look into assessing other reliable sources of educational materials; and advise the Parties to promote not only Antarctica and Antarctic research through their Education and Outreach Activities but the Antarctic Treaty and Environment Protocol itself. Bulgaria highlighted the active participation in the forum of Parties, Experts and Observers.

(145) The Meeting thanked Bulgaria for leading the ICG and emphasised the importance of education and outreach activities. Some Parties commented on their own national efforts to promote Antarctic-related education and outreach. IAATO thanked the Parties for extending an invitation to participate in the ICG. Several Parties expressed a desire for the ICG's work to continue, and encouraged others to participate in ICG discussions. The Meeting recognised the usefulness of the Forum on Education and Outreach, and encouraged Parties to make use of the Forum, including for the listing of international activities and events, as well as of educational materials already available on the Forum. Parties were also encouraged to provide translations in Treaty languages of such educational materials.

(146) Spain introduced WP 20 *Enhancing Antarctic Education and Outreach Visibility*, jointly prepared with the United Kingdom, Belgium, Bulgaria, Chile, Italy, and Portugal. The paper emphasised the importance of achieving the objectives set out in Measure 1 (2003) on the dissemination of information on the Antarctic Treaty System. It also proposed the creation of a section within the Secretariat website to allow interested Parties to access education and outreach materials designed for the general public. The proposal involved the voluntary participation of Parties, with appropriate disclaimers to make clear that Parties' contributions were solely reflective of the views of each participating Party. The education and outreach section of the website would allow interested Parties to share their education and outreach activities, including links to their respective pages of existing projects and materials.

(147) The Meeting thanked the proponents for their paper. In response to a concern that the disclaimer regarding the neutrality of Parties' contributions would not be clear enough, the United Kingdom clarified that the section of the Secretariat website dedicated to education and outreach would link to individual Parties' websites and would not itself contain individual Parties' material. It was suggested that the proposal be further considered by the ICG on Education and Outreach.

(148) The Meeting agreed to continue the ICG on Education and Outreach for another intersessional period, and agreed to the following terms of reference:

- foster collaboration at both the national and international level, on Education and Outreach;

- identify key international activities/events related to education and outreach for possible engagement by the Antarctic Treaty Parties;

- share results of educational and outreach initiatives that demonstrate the work of Antarctic Treaty Parties in managing the Antarctic Treaty area;

- emphasise ongoing environmental protection initiatives that have been informed by scientific observations and results, in order to reinforce the importance of the Antarctic Treaty and its Protocol on Environmental Protection;

- promote related education and outreach activities by Experts and Observers, and encourage cooperation with these groups;

- discuss the possibility for creation of an Antarctic Education and Outreach section at the ATS website; and

- monitor and share information about educational and outreach activities related to the 25th Madrid Protocol anniversary celebrations undertaken in 2016.

(149) It was further agreed that:

- Observers and Experts participating in the ATCM would be invited to provide input;
- the Executive Secretary would open the ATCM forum for the ICG and provide assistance to the ICG; and
- Bulgaria would act as convener and report to the next ATCM on progress made in the ICG.

(150) Portugal presented IP 7 *POLAR WEEKS: an Education and Outreach Activity to Promote Antarctic Science and the Antarctic Treaty System*, prepared jointly with Brazil, Bulgaria, France and the United Kingdom. The paper introduced POLAR WEEKS, an education and outreach activity undertaken by the Association of Polar Early Career Scientists and Polar Educators International. POLAR WEEKS aimed to bring together polar scientists, educators and their students in order to share information about the polar regions, and promote the Antarctic Treaty System from an educational perspective. It noted that POLAR WEEKS had been used as a tool to promote educational activities in several Treaty nations, and that examples demonstrated POLAR WEEK's educational impact.

(151) Colombia presented IP 25 *Campaña Educación Marítima "Todos somos Antártida" Programa Antártico Colombiano*. This paper outlined the activities of Colombia's "We are all Antarctica" education and outreach campaign. The campaign aimed to raise awareness of Antarctica in Colombia, particularly within the scientific and educational communities. The activities included workshops, documentaries, courses, seminars and conferences.

(152) The Russian Federation presented IP 67 *Russian Initiative on Declaring 2020 the Year of Antarctica*. The paper took into account the enormous historical-geographical and political importance of the 200th anniversary of the discovery of Antarctica by various explorers. The Russian Federation encouraged all Parties to join the proposal for declaring 2020 the Year of Antarctica and to take part in preparations and holding special events on the occasion of the anniversary.

(153) Chile presented four papers: IP 87 *Educational Program "Polar Scientist for a Day": Opening an Antarctic Laboratory for the Children*; IP 89 *Antarctic Stories: A seed of Identity*; IP 90 *New educational map of Antarctica using Augmented Reality*; and IP 98 *XV Encuentro de Historiadores Antárticos Latinoamericanos: "Rescatando el Pasado para Entregarlo a las Futuras Generaciones"*. Chile highlighted their work done on education issues, such as an educational map of Antarctica, the publication of a children's book inspired by Antarctic science, a children's educational programme and a workshop on Antarctic history.

(154) Chile also presented IP 88 *Antarctic Dialogues Chile – Bulgaria: Art and Culture*, jointly with Bulgaria. This paper reported on joint activities related to art and polar culture organised in Punta Arenas by the Chilean Antarctic Institute and the Bulgarian Antarctic Institute.

(155) Chile also presented IP 99 *EAE & JASE Expedición Antártica Escolar/ Joint Antarctic School Expedition*, prepared jointly with the United States. This paper provided information on an educational science expedition for high school students and teachers during the 2015-2016 Antarctic season, organised by the Chilean Antarctic Institute and the National Science Foundation (NSF) of the United States.

(156) The following information papers were also submitted and taken as presented under this agenda item:

- IP 17 *Libro Digital: Aprendemos en la Antártida* (Venezuela).
- IP 19 *Video 15 años de Venezuela en la Antártida* (Venezuela).

(157) The following background paper was submitted under this agenda item:

- BP 4 *The book Belarus in Antarctic: On the Tenth Anniversary on the Beginning of Scientific and Expeditional Research* (Belarus).

Item 12: Multi-year Strategic Work Plan

(158) The Meeting considered the Multi-year Strategic Work Plan adopted at ATCM XXXVIII (SP 10). It considered how to take each priority item forward in the coming years, and whether to delete current priorities and add new priorities.

(159) The Meeting agreed to insert the following new priority items:

- the implementation of the CEP's Climate Change Response Work Programme (CCRWP);
- joint inspections;
- modernisation of Antarctic stations in the context of climate change (with additional advice provided by COMNAP);
- hydrographic surveying in Antarctica; and
- visitor site monitoring.

(160) The Meeting also agreed to continue work on maritime and aviation safety, requesting the Secretariat to engage in the intersessional period with ICAO and IMO.

(161) The IHO Representative suggested that it would be useful to examine in much more detail the impact of the status of hydrographic surveys and nautical charts covering Antarctic waters. It was proposed that the IHO consider organising a seminar similar to the one offered at ATCM XXXI held in Ukraine in 2008. Chile and Ecuador supported consideration of the IHO proposal. The Meeting agreed to insert a new priority relating to hydrographic surveying in Antarctica, and agreed to consider the issue in 2018.

(162) Belarus proposed that the dedicated discussion on UAV use listed in the Multi-year Strategic Work Plan should distinguish between unmanned aerial vehicles and cabled and remotely-operated autonomous underwater unmanned vehicles. The Meeting agreed that COMNAP should first report on the use of autonomous underwater unmanned vehicles by National Antarctic Programmes.

(163) Noting some Parties' concerns with the current implementation of the Multi-year Strategic Work Plan, and following the approach taken by the CEP, the Meeting agreed that: the Secretariat would prepare a Secretariat Paper annexing the previous year's Multi-year Strategic Work Plan; each Chair would raise the Multi-year Strategic Work Plan in relation to the closing of each Agenda Item; and each Chair would only populate the Items of the Multi-year Strategic Plan that related to his or her Agenda Items. The Meeting also noted that the decision to populate annotated agendas at the next meeting would permit the ATCM to consider the issues in a more structured manner.

(164) After discussion, the Meeting adopted Decision 6 (2016) *Multi-Year Strategic Work Plan for the Antarctic Treaty Consultative Meeting.*

Item 13: Safety and Operations in Antarctica

Safety

(165) COMNAP presented IP 52 *Search & Rescue (SAR) Workshop III*, which provided information on the upcoming COMNAP SAR Workshop III, co-hosted by Instituto Antártico Chileno (INACH) and DIRECTEMAR Chile, on 1-2 June 2016, Valparaiso, Chile. The overarching objective of the workshop would be to continue improving SAR coordination and response in Antarctica as a follow-up from the 2008 and 2009 workshops. Registrations indicated that there would be a total of 54 participants including representatives from all five of the Rescue Coordination Centres (RCCs) which have SAR coordination and response responsibilities over portions of the Antarctic Treaty area, National Antarctic Programmes, IAATO, CCAMLR and others. COMNAP would make available the outcomes from the workshop.

(166) The United States presented IP 37 *Search and Rescue (SAR) Initiatives Affecting Antarctica*, which provided an overview of four international initiatives that had significant impact on SAR response requirements and capabilities as well as on equipment used by SAR services, National Antarctic Programmes and commercial industry. The evolving nature of both SAR and the human presence in the Antarctic Treaty area required continued collaboration and coordination of all stakeholders to ensure that Antarctic SAR operations remained efficient and effective. The United States provided further detail on the following four international SAR initiatives: the International Code for Ships Operating in Polar Waters (Polar Code), noting it will enter into force on 1 January 2017; the Global Aeronautical Distress and Safety System (GADSS); the Medium-altitude Earth Orbit Search and Rescue System (MEOSAR); and the Antarctic SAR Workshop.

(167) COMNAP thanked the United States for IP 37 which contained important SAR-related information and noted that the keynote speaker at the COMNAP SAR Workshop III would be from the International Cospas-Sarsat Secretariat, which would present information on the MEOSAR System mentioned in IP 37. COMNAP would make the MEOSAR information available after the workshop.

(168) Chile presented IP 94 *Search and Rescue cases in the Antarctic Peninsula area, season 2015/2016*, which summarised the SAR actions provided by Chile's Search and Rescue Service (MRCC) for the 2015/16 period. While noting that there had been no cases of SAR incidents, it reported on

seven medical evacuations. Chile emphasised that the increasing activities of logistics, science and tourism in the Antarctic Peninsula would lead to more incidents of this nature that were likely to affect National Antarctic Programmes in the region.

(169) The Meeting thanked COMNAP, the United States and Chile for presenting their papers, and stressed the value of SAR operations and international cooperation in Antarctica. Several Parties underlined the importance of further discussing issues relating to safety in Antarctica and commended COMNAP for its leadership in organising the SAR workshop.

(170) The IHO welcomed SAR initiatives and stressed that the availability of nautical charts was a key factor for reducing risk in maritime operations. It suggested that it would be useful to have advance access to information on locations where operations would take place, enabling the IHO to focus its efforts towards those areas.

(171) CCAMLR reported that, in its efforts to support SAR activities, it had recently signed an agreement with the five MRCCs operating in the Antarctic, to implement a system for MRCCs to access vessel monitoring system (VMS) data quickly.

(172) The United Kingdom thanked several Parties for assisting with a medical evacuation undertaken by the British Antarctic Survey from Halley Station during the previous winter season, particularly acknowledging the support provided by Norway, and the support offered by Argentina and Chile. It reported that the operation had been successful and that the casualty had since recovered. The Russian Federation thanked Chile for providing medical assistance to one of its staff members who had been evacuated to Punta Arenas, and emphasised that it was a good example of how combined efforts among Parties could save lives. Australia thanked Parties for their condolences on the passing of Mr David Woods, highlighting the assistance received from China and India. Australia also expressed its thanks to Japan, the United States and China for their assistance following the grounding of the Aurora Australis near Mawson Station, and noted that their assistance was characteristic of the spirit of cooperation found in Antarctica.

Operations: Air

(173) COMNAP introduced WP 14 *The COMNAP Unmanned Aerial Systems-Working Group (UAS-WG)*, reminding the Meeting that the Working Paper had already been discussed in the CEP but that discussion had focused

on environmental issues related to the topic of UAVs. The UAS-WG had developed and provided the Antarctic UAS Operator's Handbook. COMNAP noted that UAV is a tool that has many benefits: science support, operations, logistics, safety to human life, including that no humans are involved on-board the UAVs, and in situations such as deployment to understand sea ice conditions in advance of vessel movement into ice areas. UAVs reduce overall environmental impact for science support by reducing the use of fossil fuels and their associated emissions. COMNAP noted that the UAS Handbook presented is an evolving document. COMNAP recommended that the ATCM support the usefulness of the Handbook and encouraged Parties to give consideration to the non-mandatory guidance the Handbook provided. COMNAP noted that the Handbook should be viewed as a living document and that as UAVs technologies evolved, so should the recommendations and appendices included in the document.

(174) The Meeting thanked COMNAP for the Working Paper, noting the usefulness of the UAS Operator's Handbook. The Meeting expressed overall support for the use of UAVs for scientific purposes and underlined their benefits both for science and other operations in Antarctica. Many Parties acknowledged that additional research was required in relation to the safety risks and environmental impacts of UAV use. Some Parties stated that they had already adopted national regulations on the use of UAVs and that it was important for national legislations to be aligned with the work undertaken by the ATCM. Several Parties encouraged COMNAP to continue working on the development of the Handbook.

(175) Spain presented IP 28 *Operación de UAV/RPAS en la Antártida: Normativa aplicada por España*, which reported on the Spanish Polar Committee policy on the use of UAVs and Remotely Piloted Aircraft Systems (RPAS) in scientific and technical work to be applied during the Spanish Antarctic Campaign. It noted that this policy was based on existing Spanish regulations and on COMNAP's guidance on UAV use. Spain recognised the work undertaken by COMNAP.

Operations: Maritime

(176) ASOC presented IP 82 *Progress on the Polar Code*, which provided a brief update on progress to protect the Southern Ocean from the risks associated with vessels operating in the region. ASOC recommended that the Antarctic Treaty Parties should collaborate with colleagues attending IMO's Maritime Safety Committee's 96th Session, to ensure that there was widespread

support at MSC 96 for Phase 2 (Step 2) of work on the Polar Code. It also advised that the Parties consider the threats from shipping activities and environmental protection measures which remained outside of the Polar Code, prioritise them and take action. It further advised Parties to review the potential opportunities for reducing the risks of collisions and groundings and protecting vulnerable areas through the use of IMO measures. ASOC stated that Parties should monitor continuing work on the Polar Code to ensure the resulting rules met the standards set by the Environment Protocol, including Annex IV.

(177) Argentina presented IP 109 *XVIII Combined Antarctic Naval Patrol 2015-2016*, which outlined the activities of the 18th Combined Antarctic Patrol, carried out jointly with Chile between November 15th and March 31st 2016. The main purpose of the Patrol was to execute search and rescue operations and assistance with navigation incidents, but also included environmental protection tasks in Antarctica, cooperation with National Antarctic Programme logistics, medical assistance and provision of meteorological navigation data. Argentina also presented IP 110 *Incorporation of new units to maritime SAR and protection of the marine environment operations in the Antarctic area*, which reported on the acquisition of four new naval units by the Argentine Navy, which will assist in the Combined Antarctic Patrol with Chile.

(178) Chile presented IP 93 *Chilean Aids to Navigation in the Antarctic Peninsula*. It provided a historic overview of the Support Net for Maritime Navigation by Chile, which had guaranteed safety in navigation around the Antarctic Peninsula and facilitated contact among bases, stations and refuges located in Antarctic territory. It also presented IP 95 *Guides and Recommendations made by Chile for Diving Activities in the Antarctic*, and urged Parties to consider the establishment of common security criteria for diving and preparation of those involved (stations, companies and tourism operators) for emergency situations. Chile also presented IP 97 *Cooperation of the Hydrographic and Oceanographic Service of the Chilean Navy (SHOA) in the Manufacturing of Nautical Cartography in the Antarctic Area (Program 2010-2020)*, which outlined the programme of hydrographic surveying in Antarctica by Servicio Hidrográfico y Oceanográfico de la Armada de Chile (SHOA), initiated in 2010 and to be concluded in 2020.

(179) Colombia presented IP 50 *Contribución de Colombia a la Seguridad Marítima en la Antártica*, its contribution to maritime safety in Antarctica through the development of simulation models of sea ice and oil spills and a hydrographic

component for updating international nautical charting. It was noted that the project results supported the conduct of scientific research in Antarctica and Colombia's next expedition to Antarctica in 2016/17, where Colombia will continue to develop studies of inter-annual variability of waves and sea level, advances in understanding of oceanographic and meteorological conditions in the Gerlache Strait and the acquisition of bathymetric data. Colombia, through its Maritime Authority, has applied for admission as a member of the Antarctic Hydrographic Commission (CHA).

(180) New Zealand encouraged further participation in the development of the Polar Code and noted that it was important for all Parties to be fully engaged in matters concerning the environmental impact of SOLAS and non-SOLAS vessels.

(181) The Russian Federation presented IP 68 *Russian hydrographic studies in the Southern Ocean in the season 2015-2016*, which provided an overview of Russian hydrographic studies in the Southern Ocean from 1956 to 2016, onboard the ships *Georgy Sarychev, Faddey Bellingshausen, Admiral Vladimirsky* and *Akademik Fedorov*.

(182) The IHO congratulated Colombia, Chile and the Russian Federation for their work in advancing international hydrography and invited all Parties to cooperate with hydrographic services to preserve the safety of human life and the marine systems. It further invited Russian authorities to submit the results of their work to the IHO.

Operations: Stations

(183) Belarus presented IP 22 *Formation of Belarusian Antarctic infrastructure-modern state and prospects*, which summarised the infrastructure activities undertaking during the 2006-2015 period, of eight seasonal Belarusian Antarctic expeditions. Belarus also informed the Parties about the construction of the first facility of the Belarus research station in Antarctica in December 2015 to February 2016 and it underscored that the top priorities for Belarus in Antarctica for 2016-2020 will be furthering the development of the research stations infrastructure, conducting scientific research, environmental protection activities, environmental monitoring in Antarctica, and expanding and furthering international scientific and logistical cooperation. Belarus thanked the Russian Federation and India for providing logistical support and assistance.

(184) Germany reiterated its thanks to Chile for continued logistic support, noting several positive interactions between the Chilean Antarctic Base General

Bernardo O'Higgins and the German Antarctic Station GARS O'Higgins, located thirty metres away.

(185) The following papers were also submitted and taken as presented under this item:

- IP 30 *Modernisation of GONDWANA-Station, Terra Nova Bay, northern Victoria Land* (Germany). This paper reported on the modernisation of Gondwana Station carried out in the 2015/16 season to improve working conditions, increase the station's maintenance feasibility and operating efficiency, and considerably reduce the station's environmental impact and human footprint. Germany acknowledged Italy and the Republic of Korea for their support in the modernisation of its station.

- IP 47 *Upgrade of the SANAE IV Base Systems* (South Africa). The paper highlighted South Africa's plans to implement a comprehensive upgrade of some of the base systems at its SANAE IV base.

- IP 110 *Recuperación de la infraestructura y mejoramiento medioambiental para la Base O'Higgins. Un esfuerzo nacional para mejorar el apoyo a la investigación científica antártica* (Chile).

(186) The following papers were also submitted under this item:

- BP 9 *Australia's New Antarctic Icebreaker* (Australia).

- BP 10 *Polish sailing yacht accident at King George Island (Antarctic Peninsula) – update on the successful rescue operation* (Poland).

- BP 11 *Aplicación del Plan de Manejo Ambiental en la Estación Maldonado* (Ecuador).

- BP 12 *Seguridad en las operaciones ecuatorianas en la Antártida* (Ecuador).

- BP 13 *XX Campaña Ecuatoriana a la Antártid*a (Ecuador).

- BP 14 *Uso de drones para la generación de cartografía en la Isla Greenwich – Antártida* (Ecuador).

- BP 16 *Generación de cartografía oficial en el sector de la Isla Greenwich-Punta Fort William-Glaciar Quito-Punta Ambato, e Islas Aledañas* (Ecuador).

- BP 18 *Refugio Antártico Ecuatoriano (RAE): Desarrollo y aplicación de eco-materiales en el proyecto y construcción de un prototipo habitable de emergencia* (Ecuador).

Item 14: Inspections under the Antarctic Treaty and the Environment Protocol

(187) China introduced WP 22 *Inspection undertaken by the People's Republic of China in accordance with Article VII of the Antarctic Treaty and Article XIV of the Protocol on Environmental Protection*, and referred to IP 48 *Report of the Antarctic Treaty Inspections undertaken by the People's Republic of China in accordance with Article VII of the Antarctic Treaty and Article 14 of the Environmental Protocol: April 2016.* The paper reported that China had designated seven observers to undertake inspections of the stations of the Russian Federation, the Republic of Korea, Uruguay and Chile on King George Island between 25 and 28 December 2015. China presented a number of general recommendations as a result of the inspections. China thanked the inspected Parties for their assistance and warm reception during the inspections.

(188) The Meeting congratulated China on its successful inspections, and Parties whose bases were inspected welcomed the recommendations outlined in China's thorough inspection report.

(189) Argentina introduced WP 44 *General Recommendations from the Joint Inspections Undertaken by Argentina and Chile under Article VII of the Antarctic Treaty and Article 14 of the Environmental Protocol* jointly prepared with Chile. Argentina also referred to IP 72 *Report of the Joint Inspection Programme Undertaken by Argentina and Chile under Article VII of the Antarctic Treaty and Article 14 of the Environmental Protocol* also jointly prepared with Chile. This paper reported on the joint Antarctic Treaty inspections undertaken between 16 and 18 February 2016 that involved five Antarctic stations and one refuge. The paper described the methodology used for the inspections and presented a number of general recommendations as a result of this activity, underscoring the value of previous inspection reports, current updated information from EIES, as well as a completed Checklist A ("Permanent Antarctic Stations and Associated Installations", set forth in Resolution 3 (2010)), prepared by station leaders at the time of the inspection.

(190) The Meeting thanked Argentina and Chile for the comprehensive report of their joint inspections. Those Parties whose stations were inspected welcomed Argentina and Chile's recommendations.

(191) The Meeting reaffirmed that inspections in Antarctica are a valuable aspect of the Antarctic Treaty System. Parties noted that inspections and their

subsequent recommendations were worthwhile and useful in improving facilities and procedures as well as compliance with the Protocol's environmental provisions at Antarctic stations.

(192) Some Parties expressed the view that greater cooperation and information was needed to facilitate a more efficient inspection process and underscored the value of joint inspections having balanced teams of observers. It was noted that stations in close proximity to each other and easily accessible were repeatedly inspected. It was further noted that frequent inspections placed a burden on those stations, and potentially disrupted scientific programmes. In preventing duplication of inspections, and in ensuring other stations were inspected, it was suggested that more information on past inspections was necessary. Some Parties suggested that the EIES be more widely used and be appropriately provided with current and complete information by Parties. It was further suggested that the Secretariat prepare a complete list of all Antarctic facilities on its website, together with details of previous inspections (by year and inspecting Party), with links to the relevant inspection reports (recognising that this would require inspection reports to be split into separate files for each facility).

(193) The United States noted the importance of the inspections regime and while noting the burden that inspections cause and its attempt to give a two days' advance notice of inspections, it was necessary to keep in mind the Parties have a right under the Antarctic Treaty and Protocol to carry out inspections and no advance notice was legally required. Moreover, it was up to individual Parties to determine which stations or areas in Antarctica they wished to visit.

(194) The broader availability of information was also considered important in making inspections more streamlined. Access to past reports would ensure that past recommendations had been considered during subsequent inspections. Argentina mentioned that COMNAP's Station Infrastructure Catalogue, once completed, will be a useful resource in preparing for inspections.

(195) The Meeting urged Parties to keep updated the information on Antarctic stations in the EIES.

(196) The Republic of Korea presented IP 102 *Rethinking Antarctic Treaty inspections; patterns, uses and scopes for improvements*, which proposed the development of a new, more cooperative model whereby inspections were conducted in a more collaborative and inclusive manner, with different Parties contributing in unique ways.

(197) The Meeting thanked the Republic of Korea for presenting the paper and for raising interesting questions in relation to inspections under the Antarctic Treaty and the Environment Protocol. Many Parties highlighted that the mechanism of inspections was a fundamental component of the Antarctic Treaty System and expressed a will to further enhance collaboration and participation. Some Parties reaffirmed that the right of each Contracting Party to conduct inspections is enshrined in the Treaty. Any recommendations on the conduct of inspections could not undermine the right to conduct inspections set out in the Treaty and the Protocol. Other points raised on this matter focused on how multilateral inspections could take place more effectively, how the inspection mechanism could be made more consistent, and the importance of enhancing information exchange.

(198) The Meeting agreed to establish an ICG to consider the practice of conducting inspections under the Antarctic Treaty and the Environment Protocol with the aim of:

- describing the practice of inspections under Article VII of the Antarctic Treaty and Article 14 of the Environment Protocol;
- exchanging views on the practice of conducting such inspections and exploring options to enhance the effective organisation of inspections, including the promotion of cooperation in conducting inspections, as appropriate;
- providing a report, including any agreed recommendations, to Working Group 2 at ATCM XL.

(199) It was further agreed that:

- Observers and Experts participating in the ATCM would be invited to provide input;
- the Executive Secretary would open the ATCM forum for the ICG and provide assistance for the ICG; and
- the Netherlands, the Republic of Korea and the United States of America would act as co-convenors and report to the next ATCM on the progress made in the ICG.

(200) The following papers were also submitted under this item:

- BP 5 *Follow-up to the Recommendations of the Inspection Teams on Maitri Station* (India).
- BP 15 *Preparación de la Estación Ecuatoriana "Pedro Vicente Maldonado" para la Inspección Ambiental* (Ecuador).

Item 15: Science Issues, Scientific Cooperation and Facilitation

Science Cooperation and Strategy

(201) COMNAP presented IP 51 *COMNAP Antarctic Roadmap Challenges (ARC) Project Outcomes*, which provided a summary of the critical technologies, infrastructure and access requirements in order to support future Antarctic research, such as that identified in the SCAR Horizon Scan project. The ARC project is a community effort that will require international collaboration to deliver. Full results of the project are published and can be downloaded from the COMNAP website.

(202) SCAR congratulated COMNAP for undertaking and leading this very important initiative.

(203) Portugal informed the Meeting of a mini-symposium that would take place during the upcoming SCAR Open Science Conference in Kuala Lumpur, which aimed to highlight the relevance of the science carried out by the international community of Antarctic scientists under SCAR, to the Antarctic Treaty System, including the Environment Protocol.

(204) Portugal presented IP 8 *Assessment of trace element contamination within the Antarctic Treaty area*, jointly prepared with Chile, Germany, the Russian Federation and the United Kingdom. This paper outlined the assessment of trace elements in soil and moss samples collected from Fildes Peninsula and within ASPA 150 Ardley Island. It reported that samples from some areas of Fildes Peninsula that had been subject to long-term and ongoing human activity showed enrichment of trace elements, compared to background levels. The authors encouraged Parties to share their monitoring data from across the Antarctic Treaty area to help inform future monitoring research and policy development.

(205) France presented IP 26 *POLAR.POD: Observatory of the Southern Ocean - An unprecedented international maritime exploration and data exchange*, which described POLAR.POD, a private initiative led by French explorer Jean-Louis Etienne. Noting that the Southern Ocean was under-surveyed by traditional observation methods, France explained that POLAR.POD aimed to complement the array of current research instruments with a large capacity to host oceanographic and atmospheric sensors with all the data being freely available to the scientific community. It further reported that the floating station would be operated by wind power, producing zero emissions and no impact on Antarctic waters. There were already more than 100 researchers

from around the world engaged in the project and any interested Parties could participate.

(206) In response to a query by the United Kingdom related to the legal definition of the POLAR.POD, France clarified that it would be classified as a vessel.

(207) SCAR presented IP 32 *Report on the 2015-2016 activities of the Southern Ocean Observing System (SOOS)*, which reported on the SOOS Five-Year Implementation Plan and provided some key milestones and activities conducted during the 2015/16 period. SCAR thanked Australia for its support in hosting the SOOS secretariat.

(208) Chile presented IP 84 *Cooperación Científica Chile – Corea (Ciencia KOPR-I-NACH)*, which reported on the activities conducted at the First Scientific Workshop Chile-Republic of Korea, in Punta Arenas in February 2016. It also presented IP 85 *Programa Nacional de Ciencia Antártica de Chile: Análisis crítico 2000-2015*, which reported on progress achieved by the National Programme of Antarctic Science of Chile over the past 15 years, and IP 86 *Seminarios Científicos en Base Escudero: creando espacios para la colaboración científica en Antártica*, which reported on scientific seminars which took place at the base Professor Julio Escudero, Fildes Peninsula, in 2015 and 2016. It also presented IP 91 *Ilaia. Information for International Collaboration beyond the South*, which reported on the journal *Ilaia*, created in 2014 with the objectives of facilitating information exchange between the National Antarctic Programmes and promoting scientific international collaboration.

(209) Australia presented IP 111 *Australian Antarctic Strategy and 20 Year Action Plan*. Australia outlined some key elements of the strategy and plan, which included the acquisition of a new world-class research and resupply Antarctic icebreaker that would replace the Aurora Australis; consolidation of new and stable funding to support an active Australian Antarctic programme; the aim of establishing Australia's position of science leadership in Antarctica to support a robust and effective Antarctic Treaty system; and efforts to build Tasmania's status as the premier East Antarctic Gateway for science and operations.

(210) Romania presented IP 124 rev. 1 *Proposal for a Cooperation of Romania with Argentina and Australia in Antarctica* and IP 125 rev. 1 *Prospectives of Romania cooperation with Australia in Antarctica*, which reported on proposals for scientific collaboration with Australia and Argentina in both West and East Antarctica.

(211) The Republic of Korea presented IP 21 *Report from Asian Forum of Polar Sciences to the ATCM XXXIX*, which reported on developments in the Asian Forum for Polar Sciences (AFoPS) since ATCM XXXVIII. Recalling that AFoPS had existed for 11 years and was dedicated to polar research and cooperation, it outlined the organisation's plans for the next decade, designed to further develop and strengthen cooperation in polar sciences among its five Members (China, India, Japan, Malaysia, and the Republic of Korea). The Republic of Korea also noted that AFoPS has a growing number of observers including Thailand, Indonesia, Philippines, Vietnam and Sri Lanka.

(212) The Russian Federation presented IP 66 *Solution of the problem of influence of Freon clathrate hydrates in the drilling fluid on lake water purity in the deep borehole at the Russian Vostok station.* Noting concerns raised by the formation of clathrate hydrates in ice core drilling fluids, the Russian Federation presented the results of experiments conducted at the Petersburg Institute of Nuclear Physics. These found that ecologically clean penetration into the surface layer of Lake Vostok using silicone fluid at the boundary of lake water inhibited the formation of clathrate hydrates.

(213) It was noted that Parties should encourage the international community of experts in the area of subglacial sampling to collaborate and engage with this issue in order to achieve the best scientific advice possible.

(214) Japan presented IP 117 *Japan's Antarctic Research Highlights 2015–16*, which reported on research activities carried out by the Japanese Antarctic Research Expedition (JARE) in the Japanese Antarctic Syowa Station area. Japan highlighted three aspects of its programme: PANSY, the largest atmospheric radar in Antarctica at Syowa Station, which started full system operation to conduct the first international campaign observation based on a combination of general circulation model simulations and simultaneous observations by several Mesosphere, Stratosphere, and Troposphere/Incoherent Scatter (MST/IS) radars around the world; intermediate ice core drilling to reconstruct past climate variations in Dronning Maud Land; and geomorphological and geological field surveys in the central Dronning Maud Land for reconstructing past variability of the Antarctic ice sheets. Japan thanked Norway for supporting its activities in the Troll Station area.

(215) Colombia presented IP 24 *II Expedición Científica de Colombia a la Antártica Verano Austral 2015/2016 "Almirante Lemaitre"*, which presented the main results of the Second Colombian Scientific Expedition to Antarctica in 2015/16, an increase in the number of research projects of 9 to 15. It also presented IP 46 *Programa de Investigación en Mamíferos Marinos*

Antárticos: Con especial atención hacia Cetáceos Migratorios a aguas colombianas, using satellite tagging techniques, and IP 49 *III Expedición Científica de Colombia a la Antártica Verano Austral 2016/2017 "Almirante Padilla"*, on the Third Colombian Scientific Expedition to Antarctica in 2016/2017. Colombia thanked Argentina, Chile, Ecuador and Italy for supporting its expeditions.

(216) Malaysia presented IP 63 *Malaysia's Activities and Achievements in Antarctic Research and Diplomacy*. The paper reported on Malaysia's activities and achievements in Antarctic research and diplomacy, such as scientific research conducted, support to scientific initiatives, the hosting of Antarctic meetings, and international collaborations with other National Antarctic Programmes.

(217) The following paper was also submitted and taken as presented under this item:

- IP 40 *United Kingdom's Antarctic Science: Summary of British Antarctic Survey Science Priorities 2016-20*. This paper provided an overview of the science priorities of the British Antarctic Survey.

Expeditions

(218) Ukraine presented IP 29 *The experience of a joint Ukrainian-Turkish Expedition to the Antarctic Vernadsky Station* in 2016 jointly prepared with Turkey. This paper reported on the first Joint Ukrainian-Turkish Antarctic Expedition 2015/16. The activities took place at the Vernadsky Antarctic Station and surrounding areas. The Ukraine noted that the experience may be of interest to Non-consultative Parties that did not maintain Antarctic stations but strived to conduct "substantial scientific research activity" as a prerequisite for the attainment of Consultative status. Turkey thanked Ukraine for its support and cooperation during the expedition.

(219) Australia presented IP 54 *Australian Antarctic Science Programme: highlights of the 2015/16 season*, which highlighted Australia's achievements in relation to its Antarctic Strategic Science Plan. These achievements included: ice sheet studies under the ICECAP II project; the major marine science research voyage on the Kerguelen Axis; the Glacial Isostatic Adjustment research in East Antarctica; and the use of a remotely operated underwater vehicle used to measure physical and biological properties of fast-ice. The programme had a strategic research focus designed to inform Australia's environmental policy and conservation management, and made contributions to global issues through international bodies.

(220) Chile presented IP 96 *Monitoreo Ambiental en Bahía Fildes. Programa de Observación del Ambiente Litoral de Chile (P.O.A.L.)* This paper highlighted the work of the Chilean Navy on marine environmental monitoring to assess trends of certain contaminants in the framework of the Coastal Environment Observation Program of Chile.

(221) The following papers were also submitted under this item and taken as presented:

- IP 16 *Boletín Antártico Venezolano* (Venezuela). This paper discussed the Venezuelan Antarctic Report, in which it celebrated 15 years of the country's adherence to the Antarctic Treaty. The report described the main initiatives such as scientific expeditions and research, technological and informative materials, and the international collaboration that supported these efforts.

- IP 18 *IX Campaña Venezolana a la Antártida* (Venezuela). This paper presented information about the 9th Venezuelan Campaign to Antarctica, based on bilateral collaboration with the Instituto Antártico Chileno (INACH). The campaign was considered successful and is expected to be concluded in 2019.

- IP 55 *Belgian Antarctic Research Expedition BELARE 2015-2016* (Belgium). This paper presented the activities carried out at the Princess Elisabeth Station during the 2015-2016 season. The Belgian Polar Secretariat will directly manage the Princess Elisabeth Station and the Belgian Antarctic Research Expeditions and recently successfully organised the campaign BELARE 15-16.

Climate

(222) WMO presented IP 13 *The Polar Challenge: towards a new paradigm for long-term under-ice observations.* WMO noted that, despite advances in numerical modelling, the reliability of long-term climate change predictions in the Antarctic and Arctic was severely limited by the lack of systematic in situ observations of and beneath the sea-ice. The World Climate Research Programme and the Prince Albert II of Monaco Foundation were jointly promoting, together with other co-sponsors, a Polar Challenge to reward the first team to complete a 2000 kilometre continuous mission with an Autonomous Underwater Vehicle (AUV) under sea ice. WMO remarked that the competition would run from 2016 until at least 2019 and that registration was welcome anytime during that period. WMO encouraged Parties' involvement.

(223) WMO also presented IP 14 *Polar Regional Climate Centres and Polar Climate Outlook Fora (PRCC – PCOF)*. It noted that WMO Regional Climate Centres (RCCs) were centres of excellence that operationally generated regional climate products including climate monitoring and prediction in support of regional and national climate activities. WMO was interested in views concerning an Antarctic scoping workshop, as has been developed for the Arctic and high mountain regions, engaging the user, research, and operational communities. The workshop could explore shared objectives at the technical level and a better understanding of the necessity for, and desired form and function of, a Polar Regional Climate Centre.

(224) WMO presented IP 15 *The Year of Polar Prediction*. Noting that significant knowledge gaps in observational coverage and process understanding existed at the poles, WMO has initiated major efforts to address the lagging environmental forecasting capabilities in the region. A key element of these activities was the Year of Polar Prediction (YOPP), with a Core Phase from mid-2017 to mid-2019. YOPP's mission is to enable a significant improvement in environmental prediction capabilities for the polar regions and beyond, by coordinating a period of intensive observing, modelling, prediction, verification, user-engagement and education activities. Although more focused in scope, WMO noted that YOPP built on the legacy of the International Polar Year. An International Coordination Office for Polar Prediction was hosted at the Alfred Wegener Institute, in Bremerhaven, Germany. WMO referred Parties to the YOPP website for further details: *http://www.polarprediction.net*.

(225) WMO presented IP 34 *The Antarctic Observing Network (AntON) to facilitate weather and climate information*, prepared jointly with SCAR. Noting that Antarctica was a very data sparse area of the world, WMO remarked that AntON consisted of manned and automatic weather stations currently in operation in Antarctica and the sub Antarctic islands. WMO recommended the Treaty Parties note the need for the AntON and its associated metadata in accordance with WMO practices; notify the AntON (*AntON@wmo.int*) if there were any changes regarding stations/platforms in the Antarctic region where meteorological data were collected; provide to the AntON whenever possible the metadata concerning which information was collected at each site or ship that related to meteorology and related (eg, snow depth) data; and ensure aircraft operating in Antarctica provide meteorological observations, either through AMDAR or by compiling such information into bulletins and transmitting them to their local WMO Information System/GTS centre.

(226) The Meeting thanked WMO for its suite of papers and welcomed the contributions. Parties were reminded to supply weather and climate information to WMO collaborations wherever possible.

(227) The Russian Federation presented IP 70 *Current Russian results of studies of climate variability at present and in the past.* This paper presented the Russian Antarctic Expedition's contributions to environmental state monitoring in the Antarctic. Meteorological, upper-air, oceanographic and satellite observations of Antarctic sea ice are a permanent element of activity of the Russian Antarctic stations and, in recent years, they have been supplemented by automated weather stations, borehole monitoring observations of the state of permafrost layer and monitoring of global albedo by astronomical methods. The Russian Federation noted that the findings indicated that the tendency for warming in the subsurface layer of the atmosphere is accompanied by the increasing extent of sea ice in the Antarctic area. Multi-directionality of these natural processes indicated the existence of a complex structure of cause-effect mechanisms determining climatic changes. Given the poor climate monitoring network in the Antarctic area, the materials on the assessment of global albedo of the planet could serve as the most informative data on the assessment of climate variability.

(228) The following papers were also submitted under this item:

- BP 1 *Scientific and Science-related Cooperation with the Consultative Parties and the Wider Antarctic Community* (Republic of Korea).
- BP 6 *Twenty years of Ukraine in Antarctica: main achievements and prospects* (Ukraine).
- BP 17 *Niveles de concentración de metales pesados y efectos del cambio climático en macrohongos y macrolíquenes, estación Maldonado-Antártida* (Ecuador).
- BP 19 *Desarrollo del Programa Nacional Antártico del Perú* (Peru).
- BP 20 *Actividades del Programa Nacional Antártico de Perú Periodo 2015 – 2016* (Peru).

Item 16: Implications of Climate Change for Management of the Antarctic Treaty Area

(229) SCAR presented IP 35 *Antarctic Climate Change and the Environment 2016 Update.* In addition to reporting on the physical effects of climate change on the environment, the update also detailed research on the biological and

ecological impacts of these changes. The document built on the material in the Antarctic Climate Change and the Environment (ACCE) report, which was published by SCAR in 2009, with an update of the key points appearing in 2013 and annual updates provided to the ATCM.

(230) IPCC presented IP 116 *Recent Findings of IPCC on Antarctic Climate Change and Relevant Upcoming Activities*. This paper reported on the Contribution of Working Group I to the Fifth Assessment Report (AR5) of the IPCC, which concluded that the Antarctic ice sheet was losing mass, with the average rate of ice loss higher over the 2002-2011 period than before. It also found that floating ice shelves around the Antarctic Peninsula continued a long-term trend of retreat and partial collapse in response to changing atmospheric temperatures. It further reported the preparation of two additional Special Reports, including one on Climate change, oceans and the cryosphere.

(231) WMO presented IP 12 *WMO Climate-related Activities in the Antarctic Region*. This paper updated Parties on relevant Antarctic climate-related activities undertaken by the WMO. These activities included the provision of various climate services for the Antarctic region, and climate research projects involving ice sheet mass balance and sea level, the Southern Ocean and sea ice, permafrost, model inter-comparisons and downscaling experiments, polar climate predictability, and melting ice and global consequences.

(232) Parties thanked SCAR, IPCC and WMO for their contributions, and noted the importance of scientific reporting to the Meeting. It was noted that scientific reporting should be tailored to policy makers. Ecuador expressed its concerns about climate change impacts on its country and offered additional assistance to continue climate observations in Antarctica. Australia noted that it was conducting a review of its risk assessment of the impacts of climate change on Australian Antarctic infrastructure, and that it stood ready to assist other countries in conducting similar risk assessments.

(233) The United Kingdom presented IP 41 *The Future of Antarctica Forum*, which was jointly submitted and co-sponsored by Argentina, ASOC and IAATO. The paper reported on the outcomes of the first Future of Antarctica Forum that was convened by the US-based science and educational organisation Oceanites, Inc. and held from 28 February to 9 March 2016 in the Antarctic Peninsula.

(234) The United Kingdom noted that this Forum was held 10 years after the UK led the first Site Guideline tour and that it was extremely useful to look at changes to various sites, particularly in light of climate change-induced

effects that have been detected in the rapidly warming western Antarctic Peninsula. A range of discussions had taken place during the Forum, with major Antarctic stakeholders present, including representatives from the tourism and fishing industries, who actively engaged in discussions and made it clear that they have shared objectives.

(235) Importantly, all stakeholder participants agreed on the importance of continued monitoring of the sensitive Antarctic Peninsula region and challenged Oceanites, because of the Antarctic Site Inventory's 22-year history monitoring this region, to 'distinguish the direct and interactive effects of climate change, fishing, tourism, and national operations on ecosystems in the Antarctic Peninsula region for improved environmental management'.

(236) Oceanites accepted the challenge to bring together and analyse relevant data, with assistance from the Forum participants, and with encouragement to keep the ATCM informed as this effort proceeds. In particular, with assistance from IAATO and the Association of Responsible Krill harvesting companies (ARK), it hoped that analyses could assist management of the krill fishery in the vicinity of penguin breeding and foraging locations.

(237) ASOC was pleased to participate in the Forum and found it valuable to have informal discussions with a variety of Antarctic stakeholders. They considered that it would be useful for the project proposed by Oceanites to move forward so that the impact of human activities in the Peninsula region could be better understood.

(238) IAATO noted how pleased it was to participate in the Forum (and that one of its member companies helped facilitate logistics for the Forum) and that it greatly valued having this Forum that allows for discussion by a wide range of stakeholders on the evolution of the Antarctic Treaty system in the 21st Century. IAATO further emphasised that evidence-based environmental management was extremely valuable, that it was encouraged by the potential of the work being undertaken, and that it would continue to support the Forum and Oceanities' work going forward.

(239) ASOC presented IP 78 *Antarctic Climate Change, Ice Sheet Dynamics and Irreversible Thresholds: ATCM Contributions to the IPCC and Policy Understanding*. It highlighted a report by the International Cryosphere Climate Initiative titled "Thresholds and Closing Windows" that addressed the risks of irreversible cryosphere climate change. To maximise the potential for avoiding such irreversible impacts in the Antarctic, ASOC remarked that it was imperative that the Antarctic scientific community communicate the

most recent and accurate research to governments and policy makers through participation in IPCC assessment reports and a rapid assessment report in coordination with SCAR.

(240) Referring to SP 7, the United Kingdom noted that the Secretariat had not sought substantive input from ICAO or IMO during the intersessional period, but had simply invited them to attend the ATCM. The United Kingdom suggested that a more detailed and substantive request be made to the Secretariat in the next Multi-year Strategic Work Plan, to ask it to engage with ICAO and IMO about the discussions of the ATCM on matters pertaining to aviation and maritime safety, and to invite both bodies to provide written responses with information about their work which may have relevance to the work of the ATCM.

Item 17: Tourism and Non-Governmental Activities in the Antarctic Treaty Area

Review of Tourism Policies

(241) New Zealand introduced WP 28 *Report of the Intersessional Contact Group 'Developing a Strategic Approach to Environmentally Managed Tourism and Non-Governmental Activities'*, jointly prepared with India. It noted that the ICG had identified priority areas and gaps within the existing tourism management framework which had been recognised in previous ICGs and Working Papers addressing tourism (*eg*, ATCM XXXI - WP 51, ATCM XXXII - WP 10 and Resolution 7 (2009), ATCM XXXVII - WP 24 and ATCM XXXVIII - IP 104 rev.1). The ICG report described the general themes discussed by the group, and recommended that the ATCM: consider its report; agree to work to develop a common vision of Antarctic tourism at ATCM XL; conduct a comprehensive review of progress in implementing the recommendations of the 2012 CEP Tourism Study, and agree to a Multi-year Work Plan to implement outstanding areas of work focused on tourism. New Zealand emphasised the need for the Parties to agree on a common vision for the development of tourism in Antarctica in order to better consider effective measures that were able to manage its continued growth and diversification, and invited Parties to provide input regarding specific elements of the strategic vision for consideration at ATCM XL.

(242) The Meeting thanked New Zealand and India for leading the ICG and for identifying some of the fundamental issues and challenges related to tourism

activities in Antarctica. Recognising that Antarctic tourism would continually evolve, it noted the difficulty of forecasting its potential future implications. The Meeting agreed that there was a need to be proactive and develop a forward pathway to address issues relating to tourism. The Meeting agreed the value of developing a common strategic approach to Antarctic tourism management, with several Parties pointing out that Resolution 7 (2009) *General Principles of Antarctic Tourism* offered a general framework for such an approach. Several Parties emphasised the need to further enhance existing tourism management mechanisms, including its adequate supervision and enforcement and its systematic monitoring; others considered that existing regulations related to tourism were, at this point, potentially sufficient to adequately manage it if implemented fully. In this respect, it was emphasised that Site Guidelines for Visitors had proven to be successful. Although some Parties suggested the possibility of adopting a quota or some other form of system to regulate and limit tourism numbers, others felt this was not necessary. Some Parties felt it was more important to focus now on specific actions and on how to improve existing procedures, rather than general discussions. The Meeting commended IAATO for its contributions and efforts in this regard.

(243) Several Parties expressed concern about the potential increase of mass tourism and the diversification of activities, particularly those related to extreme adventure tourism. It was noted that many of these activities posed a serious risk to human life, including to the SAR teams that might be required to assist in rescue operations and could also disrupt National Antarctic Programme activities. It was further pointed out that these activities may also have the potential to cause impacts on the Antarctic environment. In this regard, several Parties considered the possibility of restricting authorisations for land-based adventure tourism.

(244) The United States indicated that it was possible that new tools or regulations covering tourism might be appropriate if it can be clearly demonstrated that these are needed. However, in its view, a balanced approach is needed, taking into account that tourism is a legal and acceptable activity. While IAATO makes a strong contribution in helping manage tourism, ultimately it is for the Parties to provide regulation. In the United States' view, a focus on environmental protection and ensuring safety should form the basis for developing a strategic approach to tourism.

(245) Recalling Resolution 7 (2014), several Parties underlined the importance of bringing Measure 4 (2004) into force, and encouraged Parties to do

so. Several Parties noted the need for better communication between National Competent Authorities. Some Parties also noted that although tourism was a legitimate and accepted activity, it should operate within a framework of outreach and education. Parties further noted the need to take a precautionary approach; the importance of addressing the cumulative effects of tourism; and the need to develop effective and systematic ways of on-site monitoring as well as that of authorised expeditions. Finally, some Parties suggested implementing a new taxation system for tourists travelling to Antarctica, as a way of generating collective income that could be used to enhance environmental protection and study the environmental impacts of tourism. The Meeting noted that the CEP was currently doing work on Recommendation 3 of the 2012 CEP Tourism Study in relation to site sensitivity; however, to prepare for next year's work on this issue, the Meeting asked the Secretariat to provide an update on the current state of recommendations of the 2012 CEP Tourism Study, and about the feasibility of implementing the database referred to under Recommendation 1. It was noted in this regard that notwithstanding information by IAATO there is no comprehensive and accurate picture of Antarctic tourism.

(246) IAATO presented IP 106 *Towards Developing a Strategic Approach to Environmentally Managed Tourism and Non–Governmental Activities: An Industry Perspective*. This paper aimed at identifying priority questions and gaps related to Antarctic tourism. In particular, it stressed the importance of implementing the agreements of previous ATCMs, such as Measure 4 (2004) and Measure 15 (2009), into national legislations. While valuing Recommendation XVIII-1 (1994) as a cornerstone, IAATO noted that it was not yet in force and suggested that the ATCM might consider updating the Guidelines for those organising and conducting tourism and non-governmental activities in the Antarctic to take into account agreements since 1994. IAATO highlighted that the goal of its strategy is to conduct safe and responsible tourism in Antarctica. It also noted the importance of ensuring careful assessment of new tourist activities prior to them taking place, so as to avoid more than minor or transitory impacts, and rejected the notion of permanent structures solely in support of non-governmental activities in Antarctica. IAATO also suggested that there could be value in periodically conducting a full "Strengths, Weaknesses, Opportunities and Threats (SWOT) analysis" of tourism and non-governmental activities within Antarctica.

(247) The United Kingdom introduced WP 11 *Antarctic Treaty Party nationals engaging with unauthorised non-Governmental expeditions to Antarctica*. During the Special Working Group on Competent Authorities, held during

ATCM XXXVIII (2015), it was suggested that further consideration should be given to the issue of Antarctic Treaty Party nationals who participate in unauthorised activities in Antarctica (ATCM XXXVIII Final Report, paragraph 287). The United Kingdom presented WP 11 to stimulate discussion on whether the ATCM should develop a more clear and consistent position on individuals participating in unauthorised activities in Antarctica who were not the operators or organisers of such activities. The United Kingdom suggested that there were lessons to be learned from the action taken by CCAMLR in 2009, when it adopted Conservation Measure 10-08 Scheme to promote compliance by Contracting Party nationals, which recognised that nationals from CCAMLR Contracting Parties may support or engage in illegal, unreported and unregulated fishing activities, using vessels flagged to states which were not licensed to fish under CCAMLR. The United Kingdom further noted that the ATCM might consider whether and how it might be possible to encourage Consultative Parties to undertake actions to verify if their nationals were engaged in unauthorised activities or expeditions in Antarctica; and, if appropriate, to provide for adequate measures to be taken against such individuals.

(248) The Meeting thanked the United Kingdom for the paper and recognised the importance of this complex issue. Several Parties shared details regarding their national regulations and how they apply to nationals participating in unauthorised activities in Antarctica. Some Parties reported how such actions presented practical difficulties, especially with nationals participating in activities organised by and operated from other Parties. Most Parties considered that, given the complexities involved in pursuing individuals within their jurisdiction participating in unauthorised activities, the operators and/or organisers of such activities in Antarctica should be held legally accountable, whilst recognising that this meant that individuals participating in such activities would face no legal penalty in most cases. The Meeting agreed it was useful to share among the Parties their experiences and progress made regarding the prosecution of individuals within their jurisdiction that engage in illegal activities in Antarctica, highlighting the need to improve information exchange between Competent Authorities. Some Parties noted that loopholes must be avoided with respect to effective prosecution.

(249) The United States introduced WP 41 rev. 1 *Consideration for Non-governmental and Tourism Activities Involving Combined Air and Cruise Transportation to Antarctica*. Based on information provided by IAATO, this paper noted that there was a need to consider the environmental and safety issues that may be associated with the observed increase in combined air and

cruise transportation to the Antarctic. This relatively new facet of tourism presented challenges both due to the potential for increased visits to certain sites and due to the involvement of multiple Competent Authorities in the various components or segments involved in a single fly-cruise expedition. In the United States' view, the reduction in time needed for each voyage might raise considerations regarding the environmental impacts and safety of increased ship traffic, the length of time spent by ships in the Antarctic between port calls, and the associated passenger landings in and around King George Island and the Antarctic Peninsula. As a result, the United States believed that there might be a benefit in reviewing communication and coordination among the multiple Parties involved in fly-cruise activities. This communication could ensure a more complete environmental impact assessment process and could identify other considerations such as safety. The United States also considered that recommendations from its WP 25 *Benefits of Communication among Competent Authorities for Tourism and Non-governmental Activities* were linked to those in WP 41 rev. 1.

(250) The Meeting thanked the United States for submitting this useful paper on an important topic with significant environmental and safety issues. Several Parties noted the importance of considering this issue in light of discussions related to the strategic approach to tourism.

(251) Some Parties expressed concern regarding the authorisation of these combined expeditions, noting that in many cases there were at least two Parties involved in the permitting process and that this could lead to unexpected gaps in the assessment of activities, for instance during the transfer between different modes of transport. They also highlighted the difficulty for Competent Authorities to properly assess these cases, as they only received partial information about the entire activity and could not therefore examine it as a whole.

(252) There were also concerns regarding the potential future development of air and cruise activities, including some logistic aspects such as the bunkering, provisioning and resupplying of vessels; the management of waste; and considerations related to air traffic control. Concerns related to the increase of cumulative impacts and the EIA implications were also expressed. Concern was also expressed regarding the possibility that air transport might exponentially increase tourism in Antarctica, resulting in a need for larger planes, which could additionally demand the enlargement of current infrastructures and landing strips. Some Parties noted that although air and cruise tourism was increasing, it was a risky business model for operators,

due to its high reliance on weather conditions. The Meeting underscored the importance of enhancing communication and information exchange between Competent Authorities, especially when tourism and non-governmental activities involved multiple Antarctic Treaty Parties.

(253) IAATO reported that although the increase in activities involving combined air and cruise transportation was significant, particularly when compared to other tourism types, it was still a small segment of the market. It was noted by some Parties that this may not be the case in the future. IAATO noted that it had established a working group to stimulate cooperation and communication in this area. It reaffirmed that currently there were a number of practical considerations with air access, as it was highly dependent on weather conditions and the limitations of the runway, and noted that during the previous season a very low percentage of operators had achieved their expected return flight schedules. It finally reported that the Chilean operator DAP had recently joined IAATO.

(254) Germany presented IP 36 *Antarctic Tourism Study: Analysis and Enhancement of the Legal Framework*, which evaluated the legal regulatory framework for Antarctic tourism and proposed amendments in the light of future developments. It noted that the study had identified a range of lacunas and shortcomings in the existing regulatory framework for tourism, which lacked mechanisms to effectively address its impacts. It then proposed to use the full potential of already existing instruments and regulations within the ATS, as well as a range of recommendations to improve its regulation capacity. It suggested the prohibition and limitation of certain types of tourism.

(255) The Meeting thanked Germany for submitting this valuable paper and for the efforts put into the annexed commissioned study, which was considered a very useful input for discussions, particularly around the development of a strategic approach to tourism.

(256) The following paper was also submitted and taken as presented under this item:

- IP 118 *Assessing New Activities Checklist* (IAATO). This paper presented a checklist for assessing new activities, which was adopted during the IAATO 2016 Annual Meeting.

Competent Authorities

(257) The United States introduced WP 25 *Benefits of Communication Among Competent Authorities for Tourism and Non-governmental Activities,* which

suggested how effective communication and coordination among multiple Competent Authorities could promote appropriate EIAs and proper national permitting or authorisation for non-governmental and tourism activities. It noted that when one or more expeditions involving multiple Parties' authorisation were disconnected from a regulatory perspective, there was danger of encountering gaps and mistakes in the process, and emphasised that in those cases Competent Authorities would specially benefit from fluent communications.

(258) Norway introduced WP 35 *Communication mechanisms: National Competent Authorities,* jointly prepared with France, the Netherlands, New Zealand and the United Kingdom. Recalling that the Special Working Group on Competent Authorities issues at ATCM XXXVIII had concluded that there was a need to develop several instruments/processes to enhance communication between Competent Authorities, Norway proposed the establishment of a contact list for competent authorities and relevant RCCs on the ATS website. It was also proposed that a discussion forum for Competent Authorities be established on the ATS website, based on the same interface as the ATCM and CEP forum. Norway highlighted the need for an easy, updated and transparent system, noting that current contact lists were not updated.

(259) The Meeting thanked the papers' proponents and showed broad support for their proposals. It noted the need for effective communication between Competent Authorities, particularly in cases where operators from more than one Party were involved in permitting or authorising an activity; in reporting illegal activities; and in cases where Parties authorised activities that could have a direct impact on another Party.

(260) The Meeting discussed how best to improve coordination and communication among Competent Authorities. It noted that it was not always clear which Competent Authorities were responsible for permitting or authorising a proposed non-governmental activity, and highlighted the complexities that arose when, for example, at least two Competent Authorities had been contacted regarding authorisation of the same activity. Several Parties reported actual cases that helped to illustrate such complexities. Noting that activities were at times defined as one activity or a compilation of smaller, distinct sub-activities, the Meeting highlighted the importance of ensuring that all aspects of an activity were considered appropriately while, at the same time, avoiding unnecessary duplication.

(261) The Meeting considered that early communication among Competent Authorities could help to resolve many issues with regards to tourism and non-governmental activities before they escalated. It recalled Resolution 3 (2004), which encouraged Parties to exchange information about activities involving potential implications for other Parties; to consult relevant Parties as appropriate during the process of evaluating activities and, where applicable, prior to any decision to authorise the activity or permit to proceed. This Resolution also recommended nomination to the Secretariat of a single contact point for information about tourism and non-governmental activities in Antarctica. The Meeting noted the importance of Parties implementing the recommendations in this Resolution.

(262) The Meeting agreed to set up a contact list of Competent Authorities on the ATS website, which would be simple to find and publicly available. It also tasked the Secretariat with circulating an electronic annual reminder to Parties to update the Competent Authorities' contact details.

(263) The Secretariat informed the Meeting that it had the capability and flexibility to organise the contacts database to include detailed information on Competent Authorities' contact points in accordance with Parties' suggestions. It was noted that the Secretariat required further clarification and details from Parties with respect to the specific requirements of any changes to the website. The Secretariat also highlighted that it was ready to provide the Meeting with any information requested and considered relevant for further discussions.

(264) The Meeting agreed to create a sub-forum on the Secretariat website, where Competent Authorities could exchange information on authorisations, permits and other relevant information on tourism matters. There was also agreement regarding the need to improve clarity of and access to the National Contact Point information list on the Secretariat website.

Trends and Patterns

(265) The United Kingdom introduced WP 34 *Data Collection and Reporting on Yachting Activity in Antarctica in 2015-16* jointly prepared with Argentina, Chile and IAATO. This paper consolidated information from the United Kingdom, Argentina, Chile and IAATO relating to yachts sighted in Antarctica, or indicating an intention to travel to Antarctica, during the 2015-16 season. The report noted that of the 41 yachts that were sighted in, or reported an intention to sail to, Antarctica during the 2015-16 season,

just less than half were IAATO members; 16 were non-IAATO members, but had Party authorisation to travel to Antarctica; one vessel was sighted in Antarctica having been denied authorisation; two were understood to have not had Antarctic authorisation; and the authorisation status of a further four yachts remained unclear.

(266) The Meeting thanked the United Kingdom, Argentina, Chile and IAATO for their work in providing the report on yachting activity. Parties were encouraged to use the EIES as it made verification and identification of vessels easier, and facilitated access to the often complex information requirements faced by Competent Authorities. The Meeting thanked the Secretariat for the summarised EIES report tool and searchable information on yacht activity on the Antarctic Treaty Secretariat website.

(267) In the case of unidentified and unverified yacht arrivals in Antarctica, some Parties provided clarifications, while others noted that they were still seeking further information about nationals or nationally flagged vessels before they could take action. Parties also expressed a willingness to ensure that each incident of unauthorised yachting activity was suitably investigated. Several Parties reiterated the value of a clear Competent Authorities contact list in monitoring yachting.

(268) The Meeting noted that, even with the full cooperation and collaboration of Competent Authorities, some yacht owners and operators continued to circumvent current regulations and management measures. There was unanimous rejection of unauthorised yacht activities in Antarctica, particularly of yacht owners and operators who intentionally exploited technicalities in order to avoid scrutiny of their operations.

(269) IAATO presented IP 104 rev. 1 *Patterns of Tourism in the Antarctic Peninsula Region: a 20-year analysis*, prepared jointly with the United States. It identified three major tourism trends: that tourism activities had focused on a very small number of mostly ice-free sites covering a total area of 200 hectares; that tourism numbers would likely grow in new non-English speaking markets; and that Antarctic tourism was strongly influenced by global socio-economic forces and as such future projects should take into account such impacts. IAATO also presented IP 105 *Report on IAATO Operator Use of Antarctic Peninsula Landing Sites and ATCM Visitor Site Guidelines, 2015-16 Season*, which provided estimates of Antarctic tourism from IAATO operators for the 2016/17 season, statistical data from the post visit reports for the recently concluded 2015/16 season, and an overview of patterns of tourism of the Antarctica Peninsula region.

(270) The Meeting thanked IAATO and the United States for the information provided, and noted with interest the outcomes of IAATO's 20-year analysis. In response to a query, IAATO affirmed that the highly concentrated nature of tourism in Antarctica facilitated the management of visited sites, through close monitoring and tools such as site guidelines. IAATO also confirmed that a number of sites were now regularly reaching peak daily visitor numbers.

(271) Following discussion on the need to improve visitor site monitoring, the Meeting agreed to include this as an item in its Multi-year Strategic Work Plan. The Meeting agreed to task the CEP with developing a series of 'best estimate' trigger levels to assist in guiding monitoring efforts, as outlined in Recommendation 7 of the 2012 CEP Tourism Study.

(272) Argentina introduced IP 108 *Report on Antarctic Tourist flows and cruise ships operating in Ushuaia during the 2015/16 austral summer season*. This paper reported on the numbers of passengers and vessels leaving the port of Ushuaia for Antarctica in the 2015/16 season. The report included the number of cruises, passengers' nationalities, the average number of crew by vessel, the personnel in charge of cruises, and vessels' registrations. The conclusions pointed to a slight growth in the number of passengers, vessels and cruises for the 2015/16 season.

(273) IAATO introduced IP 112 *IAATO Overview of Antarctic Tourism: 2015-16 Season and Preliminary Estimates for 2016-17*. IAATO provided estimates of Antarctic tourism from IAATO operators for the 2016-17 season and the statistical data from the post visit reports for the recently concluded 2015-16 season. It noted that passengers from the United States, Australia, and China made up the largest contingent of visitors. These numbers reflected only those travelling with IAATO member companies and did not include those individuals taking part in research projects that were being supported by IAATO operators.

(274) The following paper was also submitted and taken as presented under this item:

- IP 92 *Taller Nacional de Turismo Antártico, Punta Arenas, 5 de abril 2016. [National Workshop on Antarctic Tourism, Punta Arenas, April 5, 2016]* (Chile). This paper presented the results of the National Workshop on Antarctic Tourism, held at the Instituto Antártico Chileno, in Punta Arenas. The discussion enabled the sharing of institutional perspectives, the evaluation of the current status of tourism activities and its future trends, and the establishment of national priorities for Antarctic tourism.

Sites

(275) France presented IP 1 *Reinstalling the memorial plaque of "Le Pourquoi Pas?" on Petermann Island (Charcot's cairn 1909, HSM 27)*, jointly prepared with IAATO. France reported that after being alerted that the memorial at the HSM 27 with the list of the crew of Jean-Baptiste Charcot's vessel had been found on the ground, it had established a plan in collaboration with IAATO to reinstall the plaque. They carried out the work successfully on 13 January 2016. France thanked IAATO for its collaboration.

(276) Argentina presented IP 101 *Analysis of Management Measures of the Tourism Management Policy for Brown Scientific Station*, which provided an analysis of tourism management activities implemented in Brown Station from the 2013/14 season onward, with special emphasis on the successful results obtained in the first year of implementation of these management activities. IAATO thanked Argentina for the application of such measures at Brown Station. Argentina also presented IP 114 *Areas of tourist interest in the Antarctic Peninsula and South Orkney Islands region. 2015/2016 austral summer season*, which reported on the distribution of tourist visits to the Antarctic Peninsula and South Orkney Islands region according to the journeys made by vessels during the 2015/16 summer season, operating through the port of Ushuaia. Argentina noted that eight tourist visit areas were identified on the Antarctic Peninsula and South Orkney Islands region, highlighting that the most frequented ones were Central-West Antarctic Peninsula and South Shetland Islands, followed by the Southwest area.

(277) Belgium presented IP 56 *Developing a blue ice runway at Romnoes in Dronning Maud Land*. The paper reported on the development of a blue ice runway by a private operator at Romnoes, near the Belgian Princess Elizabeth Station, in Dronning Maud Land. It noted that the operator ALCI had expressed its intention to submit an IEE or CEE at ATCM XXXVIII, but had failed to do so. Parties questioned if the activities carried out over the last seasons in preparation of the runway were covered by a permit or authorisation from an Antarctic Treaty Party: the operator had undertaken a test flight on the runway in the 2014/15 season and preparation works were planned but stopped during the 2015/16 season. While Belgium recognised the potential merits of the project for the Belgian Princess Elisabeth Station as well as for the DROMLAN network as a whole, it considered that some concerns should be properly addressed including its potential burden and implications on the activities at Princess Elisabeth Station; the submission of a CEE, or at minimum an IEE for such a runway to be assessed by the

ATCM; the authorisation or permit system to be applied; and whether specific tourism policies would be applied for the runway. Via the paper Belgium invited other Parties to join in reflecting upon the development of the project and its possible implications, including environmental ones.

(278) The Meeting thanked Belgium for submitting this useful paper, and acknowledged the concerns it raised. It highlighted the importance of ensuring that private operators complied with existing procedures and regulations. Several Parties emphasised the need to ensure direct and transparent exchange of information among Parties and tour operators in cases like this.

(279) South Africa reported that within its national regulations it did not have the necessary procedures in force for permitting or authorising such activities, but it assured Parties that it undertook full revision of permits for NGO activities permitted by other Parties. South Africa reported that all other activities of the private operator are permitted by the Russian Federation and once it had been fully made aware of the activities undertaken in Romnoes it had reminded the private operator of the requirements of the Environment Protocol. It also noted that ALCI had confirmed it would put on hold all activities related to the runway.

(280) The Russian Federation highlighted that the DROMLAN project was inter-governmental in nature and that the performance of air operators was evaluated annually. It emphasised that for a number of reasons DROMLAN had decided that it had become necessary to develop a standby ice runway at Romnoes but that it was not intended to be a principal runway. The DROMLAN network had given its agreement for the development of the project and the test flight in the 2014-2015 season. The Russian Federation also confirmed it had been involved in the test flight as consultant for ALCI. Since the exploitation of the runway did not require any infrastructure to build, the Russian Federation considered that the runway would cause no major impact on the environment. The Russian Federation underlined its commitment to providing safe transportation in the Dronning Maud Land area.

(281) Parties exchanged further details about the development of the blue ice runway. They noted, with concern, that there were a variety of conflicting understandings about the nature of these activities and how they were authorised, and a high degree of confusion at the time of assigning responsibilities. Norway confirmed that DROMLAN had not given their approval for the project. Several Parties highlighted that, although the blue ice runway did not require infrastructure to be built, the mere landing of aircraft and offloading of passengers would have an environmental impact that should be considered. Additional concerns

raised by Parties included: the fact that for the project no necessary permits were given and that the established authorisation procedures of the ATS were not followed; the fact that no CEEs or EIAs were conducted as appropriate; that DROMLAN did not have the legal right to authorise the activity or permit such a runway to be built; the potential for the runway to be used as a tourist landing site in addition to national programme use; that no authorisation had been requested to perform the test landing; and that this case could set a worrying precedent. While some Parties suggested that this matter should be considered by the CEP, others emphasised that the ATCM was the appropriate forum for considering this issue and questioned why it had not been brought to the attention of the Meeting before.

(282) The Meeting accepted Belgium and Norway's offer to conduct further inquiries on the development of the blue ice runway before any further activities in the frame of the project would be performed and to report back to ATCM XL.

(283) IAATO presented IP 121 *IAATO Wildlife Watching Guidelines for Emperor Penguins and Leopard Seals*, which presented two new sets of IAATO wildlife watching guidelines; one for emperor penguins and one for leopard seals. It also presented a short animated briefing, which it had developed to supplement its existing Mandatory Briefing, and referred Parties to IP 107 *How to be a Responsible Antarctic Visitor: IAATO's New Animated Briefings*.

(284) The Meeting thanked IAATO and expressed its support for the development of guidelines on wildlife watching. Several Parties congratulated IAATO for the useful animation and highlighted the quality of the presentation.

Item 18: 25th Anniversary of the Protocol on Environmental Protection

(285) The chair, Ambassador Francisco Berguño, opened the Symposium to celebrate the 25th anniversary of the Environment Protocol on 30 May 2016 and welcomed participants. He recalled that ATCM XXXVIII had agreed to hold a symposium to celebrate and discuss achievements in relation to the Environment Protocol's role as the framework for advancing environmental protection in Antarctica and to focus on ensuring that the Protocol was future-proof. He thanked Norway for its role in leading preparatory work for the Symposium (WP 49, ATCM XXVIII - WP 44).

(286) The Hon. Bob Hawke, former Prime Minister of Australia, addressed the Meeting, via video, and stated that the ratification of the Environment

Protocol was a remarkable achievement of global significance. He remarked that opening up Antarctica to mining, as was being negotiated in the decade leading up to the signing of the Environment Protocol, would have been an act of vandalism on the Antarctic wilderness. He noted that, by working together, the Parties had embarked on a new course whereby the protection of the Antarctic environment, as a natural reserve devoted to peace and science, was paramount. Recalling growing global demands on mineral resources, he stated that it was the right decision to include Article 7 of the Protocol, which prohibited any activity relating to mineral resources other than scientific research. He reflected on the unique nature of Antarctica, the attributes that made it important to science, and its considerable natural wonders. He considered that Antarctica deserved the highest protection and therefore urged all Non-consultative Parties that had not yet done so to sign the Protocol. Remarking on the common misunderstanding that the ban on mining in Antarctica would expire in 2048, he called on Parties to reaffirm their commitment to a permanent ban on Antarctic mineral resource activities.

(287) The Hon. Edgardo Riveros, Vice-Minister of Foreign Affairs of Chile, addressed the Meeting and affirmed the fundamental place the Environment Protocol occupied in the Antarctic Treaty System. Noting that its negotiation and implementation initiated a new phase for the Antarctic Treaty System, which left behind expectations of mineral resources exploitation, he affirmed that Parties had made the right decision. He recalled that, when Parties met in Viña del Mar to begin negotiations in 1990 (SATCM X; SATCM XI-1), the objective was to agree an international instrument that would minimise the footprint of human activities on the continent. The resulting Protocol put the Antarctic Treaty on a path of greater environmental protection and he urged Parties to continue to renew their commitment to this path. He commended the ATCM for putting aside a full day to commemorate the 25th anniversary of the signing of the Protocol. He noted that current challenges included: the lack of public understanding of the Antarctic Treaty System as well as of the Environment Protocol's mining ban; the growing number of tourists and non-governmental visitors to Antarctica; and the slow adoption of Annex VI on liability arising from environmental emergencies. In conclusion, he urged Parties to make a firm political commitment to the Protocol as a fundamental centrepiece of the Antarctic Treaty System.

(288) Following these inaugural speeches, the Meeting adopted the Santiago Declaration on the Twenty-fifth anniversary of the signing of the Protocol on Environmental Protection to the Antarctic Treaty (see Appendix 1).

Item 1: The Protocol as a worldwide outstanding framework agreement for conservation and environmental protection

(289) Mr Evan Bloom of the United States made a presentation on 'The history, the vision behind, and impact of the Protocol'. He referred to the unique and extraordinary Antarctic environment, and its role as a world premier scientific laboratory that has contributed to our understanding of climate change in particular. The Antarctic Treaty Parties made a wise decision when they abandoned the approach under the Convention on the Regulation of Antarctic Mineral Resource Activities (CRAMRA) and decided to negotiate and adopt the Protocol. The Antarctic Treaty was never intended as an environmental protection instrument. The Convention for the Conservation of Antarctic Marine Living Resources (CCAMLR) was and is an environmental instrument, being one of the first treaties to follow the ecosystem-based approach to fisheries management, but more was needed. In 1991, just two years after setting aside CRAMRA, the ATCM agreed to the Protocol. Its cornerstone is Article 7, which bans all mineral resource activities, other than scientific research, and this was a decisive step for environmental protection. The Protocol's framework includes many other provisions and annexes addressing, *inter alia*, environmental impact assessments, waste management, and establishment of protected areas. Annex VI on liability, while not yet in force, is a unique approach to liability and reflects a practical means to protect the Antarctic environment. The Committee for Environmental Protection also plays a significant role in the Treaty system, providing key recommendations and advice. He urged the Parties to take this opportunity to look to the future and think of innovative ways to maintain the highest standards of environmental protection and stewardship. The pressures on the Antarctic environment will only increase in the future. The challenges are many - climate change, non-native species, impacts of both governmental and non-governmental activities. Threats to the marine environment are also growing and need attention, whether via the Protocol or through CCAMLR. The Madrid Protocol is an extraordinary achievement in international diplomacy. It is a regime that has delivered on its promises, despite the challenges that still remain. Mr Bloom stated that all Parties could take great pride in the anniversary of this unique agreement that has and will continue to serve the high ideals which ushered it into existence in 1991.

(290) Ms Therese Johansen of Norway made a presentation on 'The Protocol in comparison to other global and regional environmental framework agreements'. Noting its emphasis on scientific knowledge, the ecosystem approach to

management, and the framework for cooperation and coordination across many sectors, Ms Johansen referred to the Environment Protocol as the environmental pillar of the Antarctic Treaty System. Ms Johansen stated that the framework of the Environment Protocol was used as a model and as inspiration for other global and regional environmental framework agreements, including the Convention for the Protection of the Marine Environment of the North-East Atlantic (the OSPAR Convention). She stated that the institutional relationships between ATCM, CEP, CCAMLR, IMO and Competent Authorities were now tried and tested mechanisms for effective international cooperation. Ms Johansen commended the Environment Protocol, and referred to its institutional framework as the 'gold standard' of environmental protection.

(291) Mr Olivier Guyonvarch of France read a message from the Hon. Michel Rocard, former Prime Minister of France and Ambassador for the Poles. In his message, Mr Rocard noted that the 25th anniversary of the Environment Protocol was a time to renew the call for Parties to encourage more signatories to the Environment Protocol. He highlighted the values upon which the Environment Protocol was based and called on Parties to relentlessly renew these values within the Antarctic Treaty System. Ambassador Rocard further proposed an International Antarctic Day for the public dissemination of information about Antarctica.

(292) The Meeting thanked Mr Evan Bloom, Ms Therese Johansen and Mr Olivier Guyonvarch for their presentations. Parties recalled the historical context of the Environment Protocol, and commended the development of a unique and prescient framework dedicated to the protection of the Antarctic environment. Parties stated that the Environment Protocol was a pillar of the Antarctic Treaty System, and a milestone in environmental protection worthy of celebration. Several Parties recounted the earlier development of CCAMLR and CCAS and noted the role of these instruments in strengthening environmental protection in the Antarctic Treaty System.

(293) The Meeting recognised the major achievement of the ban on mineral resource activities in Antarctica, and also commended the flexibility and breadth of the Protocol's Annexes in addressing new challenges faced in Antarctica. It highlighted the importance of ensuring that the Environment Protocol remain a flexible legal instrument, adaptable to future challenges. Some Parties suggested that the slow ratification of Annex VI demonstrated challenges in adapting the Environment Protocol's framework to current and future circumstances.

(294) Noting its historical context, Parties encouraged renewed enthusiasm towards environmental protection, as was demonstrated at the signing of the Environment

Protocol. They also noted the importance of ensuring continued reliance on scientific evidence and nurturing of intergenerational scientific capacity.

Item 2: Effectiveness of the Protocol

(295) Dr Jose Retamales of Chile made a presentation entitled 'An Analysis of the Protocol on Environmental Protection to the Antarctic Treaty and its annexes'. Noting that the early phase of the Antarctic Treaty focussed on stabilising security risks to the continent, and that the second phase addressed the regulation of the resources of the continent, Dr Retamales remarked that the Protocol placed environmental protection at the centre of the Antarctic Treaty System's attention. Dr Retamales recalled that, beginning in the 1970s, scientific input into environmental assessments encouraged Parties to prioritise the EIA process in Protocol negotiations. He stressed that continued scientific and logistical collaboration was key to minimising the environmental impacts associated with human activities. Dr Retamales highlighted that the Environment Protocol facilitated the protection of all living species, including those we could not see, and remarked that scientific research and communication about biodiversity were key to a better understanding of what we needed to protect. Recognising the importance of krill as a keystone species, and as a marine living resource, Dr Retamales reported on research suggesting that krill may not survive increasing ocean acidification. He also underlined the importance of better understanding the impacts of climate change on the Antarctic environment, noting that Chile met seven of the nine markers of vulnerability to the adverse effects of climate change identified in Article 4 of the UNFCCC.

(296) Dr Aleks Terauds presented a paper entitled 'Effectiveness of the Protocol - a scientist's perspective,' on behalf of SCAR. Dr Terauds identified various present and future human activities that posed a threat to the Antarctic environment including mineral resource activities, climate change and the introduction of non-native species. He stressed the importance of the protection afforded by the Environment Protocol, from the designation of the Antarctic Treaty area as a natural reserve devoted to peace and science, to the specific protections outlined in the Annexes. He noted how SCAR had recognised the challenge of providing the Treaty with increasing scientific advice by establishing specific groups to respond more rapidly to Treaty requests, and was thus well placed to respond to the increased demands of the Protocol. Dr Terauds noted that, from a scientific perspective, the focus on environmental principles in the Environment Protocol provided

the opportunity to use science to guide activity. In this regard, he remarked that SCAR had successfully developed several codes of conduct to manage activities and assist National Antarctic Programmes with the protection of the environment, and reported on the development of guidelines and frameworks to assist the implementation of the specific challenges posed by the requirements of the Annexes. Dr Terauds concluded by reiterating the importance of the CEP, and its direct relationship with science through Parties and SCAR. He further noted that SCAR would continue to advise the CEP on priority issues in line with the requirements of the Protocol, and would strengthen its relationships with COMNAP and National Antarctic Programmes to improve scientific outputs.

(297) Dr Yves Frenot of France, as COMNAP Vice-chairman, presented on behalf of COMNAP the paper entitled 'Implementation of the Environmental Protocol – An operator's perspective on its impact on science support', co-authored with COMNAP's Chair Professor Kazuyuki Shiraishi of Japan, and COMNAP's Executive Secretary Michelle Rogan-Finnemore. Focusing on COMNAP's contribution to the development of the Protocol's requirements, he provided practical examples of COMNAP's response to the EIA and waste management requirements introduced by the Protocol. Reflecting more broadly, Dr Frenot noted that effective international collaboration might be the best environmental protection mechanism in support of the principles and ideals in the Antarctic Treaty and its Environment Protocol. He emphasised that COMNAP was already looking ahead, in particular through the Antarctic Roadmap Challenge (ARC) which identified critical technology and operational requirements in support of future science activities. Dr Frenot stressed that Parties' activities in Antarctica must be considered in the context of the safety of human life and the protection of the environment.

(298) Dr Frenot noted that even before the Protocol, SCAR and COMNAP had developed best practise guidelines on environmental assessment. Dr Frenot stressed the resource intensive obligation on National Antarctic Programmes who wish to develop infrastructure in support of science in the Antarctic, and noted how they would have to implement the activities in the manner contained within the provisions of the CEEs. Highlighting the role of COMNAP in developing the waste management reporting form Dr Frenot noted how the information gathered proved a useful insight into the scope of waste management and the different practices of various National Antarctic Programmes, including sophisticated processes for reducing, sorting and recycling waste. Dr Frenot mentioned the specific challenges posed by Article 1, Annex III of the Environment Protocol in relation to managing

or cleaning up historical waste sites, highlighting the costs, logistical difficulties, environmental risks, safety issues and political sensitivities.

(299) Dr Ricardo Roura of ASOC made a presentation on 'ENGO perspectives on the Antarctic Environmental Protocol' jointly prepared with Claire Christian of ASOC. Dr Roura noted how the Protocol's objectives, designation and principles met, in varying degrees, the principles for Antarctica promoted by Environmental Non Governmental Organisations (ENGOs) in the late 1970s and 1980s. Stressing the Protocol's implementation had been a continuum of successes and challenges, he underlined how the Environment Protocol's implementation had become a key component of most Antarctic operations, and the concepts and objectives within the Environment Protocol were shared with other Antarctic Treaty bodies. Dr Roura listed some of the successes of the Protocol including: the ban on mining (Article 7); the protection of the environment in the planning and conducting of activities (Article 3 and 8); the creation of the CEP (Article 11), the expansion of inspections to compliance with the Protocol (Article 14) and the specific Annexes on key issues of Antarctic operations and the environment. He also listed the challenges including: recognising wilderness values in most operations; applying a precautionary approach; addressing cumulative impacts of activities; increasing environmental monitoring; the lack of a comprehensive protected area regime; and the challenges in different Parties' implementation of compliance criteria. Dr Roura stressed in the next 25 years and beyond, Parties need to maintain the successes of the first 25 years and address the ongoing challenges, including more Antarctic actors and activities, growing environmental pressure on land and sea, and climate change. In concluding, Dr Roura presented two models of considering the Protocol to the Meeting: the Protocol as a set of rules on particular issues or as a guiding principle. Stressing that the Protocol needs to be more than the sum of its parts, Dr Roura urged a focus on strategic thinking to environmental protection, guided by the vision of the Protocol, and the development of greater synergies between actors, operators and instruments.

(300) Dr Kim Crosbie of IAATO made a presentation on 'The impact of the Protocol on protection of the Antarctic environment: an IAATO perspective', on behalf of IAATO. Dr Crosbie stressed the importance of the Protocol in its holistic approach to the environmental management of all activities in the Antarctic Treaty area. Reflecting that IAATO was founded the same year as the Environment Protocol was negotiated, Dr Crosbie underlined the meaningful impact of the Environment Protocol on IAATO's operations and activities, and noted that the EIA process has become useful as a common

framework for IAATO operators. Dr Crosbie also emphasised the role of the biosecurity requirements within Annex II in having a significant impact on IAATO operators. Noting IAATO's core mission is to ensure a no more than minor or transitory impact on the environment, Dr Crosbie also mentioned IAATO's goal to create ambassadors for the Antarctic area. Referring to how all IAATO operators teach their clients about the Antarctic Treaty and the principles of the Environment Protocol, Dr Crosbie underlined how visitors take these principles, and then apply them to other areas of global conservation. In concluding, Dr Crosbie commended the Parties for their ongoing work, and called attention to the pivotal role of the conservation of the Antarctic area in global conservation.

(301) The presentation by Professor Rüdiger Wolfrum of Germany was on Annex VI on Liability Arising from Environmental Emergencies. Professor Wolfrum stated that Annex VI added effective protection to the Antarctic environment and that the Environment Protocol and its Annexes had provided the blueprint for the regulations of the International Seabed Authority concerning deep seabed mining. In referring to advancements of customary international law, tribunal jurisprudence, and the International Law Commission's *Draft Articles on Responsibility of States for Internationally Wrongful Acts*, Professor Wolfrum recommended Parties debate and discuss whether Annex VI should be extended and broadened to include dependent ecosystems within the regime, rather than remain restricted to the Antarctic Treaty area. He recalled that the United Nations Convention on the Law of the Sea and its interaction with the Antarctic Treaty System was something Parties should take into consideration when considering climate change, the interdependence of environments outside the Antarctic Treaty area, and liability. He highlighted that actions of nationals were attributable to the State, despite common misconceptions about jurisdiction under the Antarctic Treaty System, and this placed further emphasis on the importance of the Environment Protocol's liability provisions. He further noted that it was another misconception that environmental damage was unable to be quantified in financial terms. Professor Wolfrum concluded that the Antarctic Treaty System should strive to remain at the forefront of international environmental law.

(302) Andrew Wright, Executive Secretary of CCAMLR, congratulated the Parties on the occasion of the 25th anniversary of the signing of the Protocol. CCAMLR noted the commitment of its Members to the effective implementation of the Environment Protocol. It stated that climate change and its implications for the Antarctic ecosystem were challenges for SC-CAMLR in accommodating precaution into the provision of scientific advice

to CCAMLR. CCAMLR noted that closer cooperation between SC-CAMLR and the CEP since 2009 had laid a solid foundation by which the two bodies could ensure the provision of the best available scientific advice to Parties and Members. CCAMLR noted that it looked forward to strengthening its relationship with the CEP to address priority science and environmental protection challenges in the future. CCAMLR encouraged Parties to focus on further strengthening scientific research programmes and increase science capacity across the Antarctic Treaty System, so as to better understand the changes impacting the Antarctic environment.

(303) Parties remarked that the effective operation of the Antarctic Treaty System depended on the cooperation of its component parts, and that the effectiveness of the Protocol depended on how well environmental principles were embedded in the work of these component parts. Parties also reflected on the importance of cooperation and interaction between Parties, Observers and Experts, intersessionally and at the ATCM, and how this should be further developed.

(304) Several Parties highlighted the importance of basing current and future management decisions on the best available scientific evidence, noting that this could be facilitated through increased scientific collaboration, capacity building, and increasing the allocation of resources to medium- and long-term science.

(305) The Meeting encouraged Non-consultative Parties to ratify the Protocol and its Annexes. It also welcomed Switzerland's announcement that it was in the process of ratifying the Environment Protocol. Japan also encouraged Non-consultative Parties to become Consultative Parties, and pointed out the importance of the need to enhance the openness and transparency of the Antarctic Treaty System.

Item 3: The Committee for Environmental Protection

(306) Mr Ewan McIvor, Chair of the Committee for Environmental Protection, made a presentation on 'The functioning of the Committee for Environmental Protection'. He noted that the CEP had the important responsibility of advising the Parties on how to best protect the Antarctic environment. Mr McIvor highlighted some challenges that had a bearing on the functioning of the CEP, including an increasing volume of work, and the need to keep pace with increased complexity of the work due to environmental changes as well as changes in human activities, and developments in environmental practices. To improve its effectiveness the CEP had introduced intersessional activities such as ICGs, subsidiary bodies and workshops; strategic planning

tools including a Five-year Work Plan with prioritised items; planning tools and guidelines for reviewing CEEs, ASMAs, ASPAs and Specially Protected Species; and close collaboration with Observers and Experts.

(307) In order to ensure that the Committee remained well-placed to serve the Parties, Mr McIvor suggested that Parties might wish to consider the following opportunities:

- Enhance the level of engagement by their representatives in annual CEP meetings and intersessional activities.
- Expand the CEP membership by encouraging further accessions to the Protocol.
- Develop the CEP representatives of the future.
- Promote and support science that is aimed at better understanding and addressing the environmental challenges facing Antarctica.
- Consider providing feedback on the Committee's priorities, especially with respect to governing and managing the Antarctic region.
- Make available financial or other resources to support CEP activities.

(308) The Meeting thanked Mr McIvor for his presentation, and welcomed his recommendations for ensuring the CEP remained well placed to serve the Parties. Noting that the CEP was the backbone of the ATCM, the Meeting agreed that it should increase its engagement with the CEP and help the Committee to manage its priorities.

(309) Some Parties also identified the need to reassess the structure of the ATCM, and determine how it might better enable the CEP to enhance ATCM discussions.

(310) Reflecting on the importance of cooperation in all aspects of Antarctic activity, several Parties cited specific examples of how working together with personnel from other National Antarctic Programmes had improved their capability. The Meeting urged Parties to adopt a more systematic exchange of personnel to enhance cooperation, understanding and knowledge transfer between Parties, particularly between more experienced Parties with more capability and new members of the Antarctic Treaty System.

Item 4: The next 25 years

(311) Mr Rodolfo A. Sánchez of Argentina made a presentation on 'The Future of Environmental Management in Antarctica' focusing on challenges to environmental management that National Antarctic Programmes would face

in coming years due to internal and external pressures. These challenges included finding ways to manage: funding constraints; the diversification of service providers using private operators; the rapid development of new technologies; climate change impacts in the Antarctic Treaty area and the potential to modify the priorities of Antarctic Programmes; large and diverse science programmes; the reliance on fossil fuel for operations; and institutional and structural inertia. Reflecting on options available to deal with future challenges, Mr Sánchez mentioned strategic options including ISO 14001 certification which would allow National Antarctic Programmes to establish objectives and goals, and subject them to continuous evaluation. He also proposed considering new technologies to improve infrastructure and reduce the human footprint on Antarctica; improve international cooperation and knowledge transfer in terms of environmental management; close the gap of implementation levels between different countries through innovative cooperation strategies; and better use tools to monitor and control Antarctic operations. Highlighting that improved technology would promote greater energy efficiency, Mr Sánchez noted that it would also open up areas of Antarctica that would not previously have been opened. In conclusion, Mr Sánchez reminded the Meeting: of the need to promote the implementation of better environmental standards, based on mutual cooperation; that environmental challenges would only be met if progress was made collectively rather than individually; and that society needed to be kept informed of Parties' activities in Antarctica and their commitment to protect the Antarctic environment.

(312) In her presentation on the future of the Environment Protocol, Ms Jillian Dempster of New Zealand recalled that the Protocol had reinforced an ambitious and strong vision for the future of Antarctica. Ms Dempster stated that the Protocol was intended to be a dynamic and interactive tool, capable of responding to challenges facing the Antarctic environment, including increasing human activity in Antarctica and climate change. She highlighted key areas that required attention by Parties when looking forward to the next 25 years. First, wise management of the Antarctic environment would be necessary to ensure that the values of the Protocol, and the values of the Antarctic area for science were not eroded. To ensure the Protocol was implemented effectively, Ms Dempster identified the need to continually update Annexes, keeping them in line with best practice, and used the example of Annex IV on the Prevention of Marine Pollution which should be considered and potentially updated to reflect entry into effect of the Polar Code on 1 January 2017. Additional annexes should also be considered to

respond to new and emerging challenges. Second, Ms Dempster highlighted the need for an enduring Antarctic Treaty System, through investing in the governance regime. She further noted that this may involve Parties requesting more and more complex tasks from the Secretariat, and would potentially require more investment in the Secretariat. She underlined that it was important to ensure the ATCM and CEP agendas remained flexible and cohesive across the various Meeting mechanisms to address the demands of new challenges and to ensure the effective governance of Antarctica. Finally, Ms Dempster stressed the responsibilities of Parties to the global community. She remarked that civil society held expectations of Parties and that Parties needed to communicate successes and challenges in a proactive manner.

(313) Looking back on the past 25 years, Ms Jane Rumble of the United Kingdom reflected on whether the Protocol would be fit for the next 25 years. She considered that the Environment Protocol was fit for purpose and, through its Annexes, could be adapted to cope proactively with change. She noted rapid changes affecting the continent such as increased global temperatures, population growth and decreasing biodiversity, as well as increased scientific, fishing, tourism and other activities in the Antarctic Treaty Area, and encouraged Parties to be proactive and forward looking in relation to the improvement of the Environment Protocol. Ms Rumble commented on several aspects of the Annexes. She welcomed the report from the United States that the revised Annex II would shortly enter into force, as this was important for ongoing work on non-native species. She noted that Annex I was a cornerstone of the Protocol, but that several Parties' domestic procedures for EIA had developed within the last 25 years beyond the requirements of Annex I. While celebrating the number of protected areas delineated and declared since 1966, she noted the need for more effective protected area management with a wide range of objectives. Finally, she highlighted that the Parties had not yet all ratified Annex VI, or the Protocol's requirement for repair and remediation. While encouraging the Meeting to celebrate the Environment Protocol, and inform stakeholders of its achievements, she urged Parties to avoid complacency and to ensure the comprehensive protection of the Antarctic environment.

(314) The Meeting thanked the presenters and noted that the full implementation of the Protocol would be essential in ensuring the Antarctic area remained a natural reserve devoted to peace and science, and highlighted the value of Parties sharing their past experiences of Protocol implementation as a way of facilitating improvements in the future. The Meeting noted that it was the future of the Antarctic environment that concerned and motivated Parties most.

Parties were committed to ensuring the Antarctic continent was passed onto future generations in the same condition, or better, than it had been received. It was therefore incumbent on Parties to the Protocol to continue to look over the horizon to identify future challenges and address them in a timely manner.

(315) Several Parties also expressed their views on how best to advance Antarctic environmental protection in the future. The United States suggested that bringing together a wide range of stakeholders in the Antarctic area would be the most potent way of making effective policy. It also encouraged Parties to continue addressing concrete issues, including through the submission of Working Papers, so that the CEP and ATCM could consider specific issues in detail. The Netherlands expressed hope that Antarctica would continue to be a wilderness in the future. It highlighted the need to focus on strengthening toolkits, and potentially introducing strategic environmental assessment, in the future. Chile urged Parties to continue promoting scientific and logistical cooperation, particularly in areas where many National Antarctic Programmes conducted science. In response to a suggestion from France, the Meeting agreed it was valuable to share the experiences of the Antarctic Treaty System in other international forums.

(316) ASOC thanked the presenters and noted that it was useful to conclude the Symposium with a discussion about the future implementation of the Protocol. Noting that Parties had broadly agreed that the Environment Protocol should be advanced and improved, ASOC highlighted the importance of finding practical ways of achieving this. It noted that the approach of looking at specific Annexes and considering how to either enhance their implementation or improve them was particularly useful. ASOC strongly encouraged Parties to bring forward specific proposals relating to individual Annexes to the next meeting. It also noted that many examples of potential proposals had been presented during the Symposium, including proposals for new protected areas, a review of the marine pollution Annex in comparison to the Polar Code, or using EIA to address post-activity monitoring. Acknowledging that there were many challenges ahead, ASOC urged Parties to be proactive and take the first steps to addressing these challenges now.

(317) Reflecting on this discussion, the presenters highlighted the value of effective knowledge management and transfer, the need to enhance international cooperation on environmental matters and outreach activities in benefit of the general public, and the importance of encouraging a more diverse participation in intersessional discussions.

Item 5: Other Matters

(318) Argentina presented WP 46 rev. 1 *Report of the Intersessional Contact Group on the Development of a Publication on the Occasion of the 25th Anniversary of the Madrid Protocol*. The ICG was created at CEP XVIII and was tasked with: establishing a small Author Group to develop the writing process for the publication; developing a neutral, brief, concise and web-based publication including visual and dynamic tools; identifying the different means of outreach for the publication; and submitting the draft publication to CEP XIX for consideration and approval. Argentina noted that the draft publication attached had been considered, revised and approved by CEP XIX.

(319) The Meeting thanked Argentina for its work in preparing the Report and for leading the ICG.

(320) The Russian Federation presented IP 69 *Preconditions for adopting the Protocol on Environmental Protection to the Antarctic Treaty*, which raised concerns that some Consultative Parties did not have the established national procedures for preliminary consideration of proposed activities in the Antarctic. It stated that this situation created conditions for using such Parties for arranging different types of non-governmental activity for those Parties who had such procedures in place. The paper stated that this problem arose due to the absence of real monitoring of such type of activity from the 'last port' countries at the transit route to the Antarctic. The Russian Federation stated that it had repeatedly raised these questions at preceding ATCMs but was not supported by all Parties of the Treaty.

(321) The following paper was also submitted and taken as presented under this item:

- IP 9 *25th Anniversary of the Protocol on Environmental Protection to the Antarctic Treaty: South African Accomplishments* (South Africa). This paper highlighted some of South Africa's main accomplishments in its commitment to the protection of the Antarctic environment.

Item 19: Preparation of the 39th Meeting

a. Date and place

(322) The Meeting welcomed the kind invitation of the Government of China to host ATCM XL in Beijing, tentatively from Tuesday, 16 May 2017.

(323) For future planning, the Meeting took note of the following likely timetable of upcoming ATCMs:

- 2018 Ecuador.
- 2019 Czech Republic.

b. Invitation of International and Non-governmental Organisations

(324) In accordance with established practice, the Meeting agreed that the following organisations having scientific or technical interest in Antarctica should be invited to send experts to attend ATCM XL: the ACAP Secretariat, ASOC, IPCC, IAATO, the International Civil Aviation Organization (ICAO), IHO, IMO, IOC, IOPC Funds, the International Union for Conservation of Nature (IUCN), the London P&I Club, UNEP, UNFCCC, WMO and the World Tourism Organization (WTO).

c. Preparation of the Agenda for ATCM XL

(325) The Meeting approved the Preliminary Agenda for ATCM XL (see Appendix 2).

d. Organisation of ATCM XL

(326) According to Rule 11 of the Rules of Procedure, the Meeting decided to propose the same Working Groups for ATCM XL as for this meeting. The Meeting agreed to appoint Ms Therese Johansen from Norway as Chair for Working Group 1 for 2017. It also agreed to appoint Professor Jane Francis from the United Kingdom and Mr Máximo Gowland from Argentina and as co-Chairs for Working Group 2 in 2017.

(327) The Meeting agreed that Working Group 1 would develop procedures for the election of chairs and co-chairs for the Working Groups.

e. The SCAR Lecture

(328) Taking into account the valuable series of lectures given by SCAR at a number of ATCMs, the Meeting decided to invite SCAR to give another lecture on scientific issues relevant to ATCM XL.

Item 20: Any Other Business

(329) In relation to incorrect references to the territorial status of the Malvinas, South Georgias and South Sandwich Islands made in documents related to this Antarctic Treaty Consultative Meeting, Argentina rejects any reference to these islands as being a separate entity from its national territory, thus giving them an international status they do not have. The Malvinas, South Georgias and South Sandwich Islands and the surrounding maritime areas are an integral part of the Argentine national territory, are under illegal British occupation and are the subject of a sovereignty dispute between the Argentine Republic and the United Kingdom of Great Britain and Northern Ireland, recognised by the United Nations.

(330) In response, the United Kingdom stated that it had no doubt about its sovereignty over the Falkland Islands, South Georgia and the South Sandwich Islands and their surrounding maritime areas, as is well known to all delegates.

(331) Argentina rejected the United Kingdom's statement and reaffirmed its well known legal position.

(332) Venezuela congratulated the Chair for the concise and gracious way in which he had conducted the meeting and thanked Ecuador and Japan for their support of Venezuela's application for Consultative Party status. Venezuela affirmed its commitment to the protection of the Antarctic environment, to the preservation of Antarctica as a continent devoted to peace, and to world peace. Venezuela stated that it would send the Antarctic Treaty Secretariat a document with information regarding its application, which Venezuela requested be distributed to the Consultative and Non-consultative Parties to the Treaty.

Item 21: Adoption of the Final Report

(333) The Meeting adopted the Final Report of the 39th Antarctic Treaty Consultative Meeting. The Chair of the Meeting, Ambassador Alfredo Labbé, made closing remarks.

Item 22: Close of the Meeting

(334) The Meeting was closed on Wednesday, 1 June at 13:31.

2. CEP XIX Report

Table of Contents

Report of the Nineteenth Meeting of the Committee for Environmental Protection (CEP XIX)

Santiago, Chile, May 23 – 27, 2016

(1) Pursuant to Article 11 of the Protocol on Environmental Protection to the Antarctic Treaty, Representatives of the Parties to the Protocol (Argentina, Australia, Belarus, Belgium, Brazil, Bulgaria, Canada, Chile, China, the Czech Republic, Ecuador, Finland, France, Germany, India, Italy, Japan, the Netherlands, New Zealand, Norway, Monaco, Peru, Poland, Portugal, the Republic of Korea, Romania, the Russian Federation, South Africa, Spain, Sweden, Ukraine, the United Kingdom, the United States, Uruguay, and Venezuela) met in Santiago, Chile, from 23 to 27 May 2016, for the purpose of providing advice and formulating recommendations to the Parties in connection with the implementation of the Protocol.

(2) In accordance with Rule 4 of the CEP Rules of Procedure, the meeting was also attended by representatives of the following Observers:

- Contracting Parties to the Antarctic Treaty which are not a Party to the Protocol: Colombia, Malaysia, Switzerland and Turkey;
- the Scientific Committee on Antarctic Research (SCAR), the Scientific Committee for the Conservation of Antarctic Marine Living Resources (SC-CAMLR), and the Council of Managers of National Antarctic Programs (COMNAP); and
- scientific, environmental and technical organisations: the Antarctic and Southern Ocean Coalition (ASOC), the International Association of Antarctica Tour Operators (IAATO), the International Hydrographic Organization (IHO), and the World Meteorological Organization (WMO).

Item 1: Opening of the Meeting

(3) The CEP Chair, Mr Ewan McIvor (Australia), opened the meeting on Monday 23 May 2016 and thanked Chile for arranging and hosting the meeting in Santiago.

(4) The CEP Chair noted that the meeting was taking place during the year that marks the 25th anniversary of the adoption of the Protocol on Environmental Protection to Antarctic Treaty, on 4 October 1991. He highlighted the important

role of the CEP in supporting the Parties to continue to achieve their shared objective of comprehensively protecting the Antarctic environment, and thanked Members and Observers for their ongoing efforts in this regard.

(5) The Chair summarised the work undertaken during the intersessional period, noting that all the actions arising from CEP XVIII with outcomes anticipated for CEP XIX had been addressed (IP 115).

Item 2: Adoption of the Agenda

(6) The Committee adopted the following agenda and confirmed the allocation of 38 Working Papers (WP), 51 Information Papers (IP), 4 Secretariat Papers (SP) and 4 Background Papers (BP) to the agenda items:

1. Opening of the Meeting
2. Adoption of the Agenda
3. Strategic Discussions on the Future Work of the CEP
4. Operation of the CEP
5. Cooperation with other Organisations
6. Repair and Remediation of Environment Damage
7. Climate Change Implications for the Environment

   a. Strategic approach

   b. Implementation and Review of the Climate Change Response Work Programme
8. Environmental Impact Assessment (EIA)

   a. Draft Comprehensive Environmental Evaluations

   b. Other EIA Matters
9. Area Protection and Management Plans

   a. Management Plans

   b. Historic Sites and Monuments

   c. Site Guidelines

   d. Marine Spatial Protection and Management

   e. Other Annex V Matters
10. Conservation of Antarctic Flora and Fauna

    a. Quarantine and Non-native Species

    b. Specially Protected Species

Item 3: Strategic Discussions on the Future Work of the CEP

(7)   Argentina introduced WP 46 rev. 1 *Report of the Intersessional Contact Group on the Development of a Publication on the Occasion of the 25th Anniversary of the Madrid Protocol*. The ICG was created at CEP XVIII and tasked with: 1) establishing a small Author Group to develop the writing process for the publication; 2) developing a neutral, brief, concise and web-based publication including visual and dynamic tools; 3) identifying the different means of outreach for the publication; and 4) submitting the draft publication to CEP XIX for consideration and approval. The ICG recommended that the Committee:

- consider the draft publication and generate a consultation mechanism between the Members, in order to complete its drafting in advance of the 25th anniversary of the signing of the Protocol;

- analyse the different ways of dissemination that arose from Term of Reference 3;

- suggest that the Members and related non-governmental organisations implement those forms of dissemination in which voluntary action was required;

- approve those forms of dissemination in which the general agreement of the Members was required; and

- start spreading the publication at the time of the anniversary of the signing of the Environment Protocol, on 4 October 2016.

(8)   Argentina warmly thanked the individuals involved in preparing the draft publication during the intersessional period, including: former CEP Chairs, Prof. Olav Orheim of Norway, Dr Tony Press of Australia, Dr Neil Gilbert of New Zealand and Dr Yves Frenot of France; current CEP Chair, Mr Ewan McIvor; as well as Mr Rodolfo Sánchez of Argentina.

(9) The Committee thanked Argentina and participants in the ICG for the excellent draft publication, especially the work of the ICG convener, Ms Patricia Ortúzar, and the authors of the publication. Following the incorporation of minor amendments suggested during the meeting, the Committee endorsed the publication.

(10) The Committee recognised the importance of communicating the values of the Antarctic Treaty and Environment Protocol to a general audience, and supported the options identified by the ICG for disseminating the publication. Some Members offered to contribute to the dissemination of the publication through, for example, the translation of the material into non-Treaty Party languages, and adapting the publication for particular audiences including children, those involved in Antarctic operations and scientists. The Committee thanked IAATO for its intention to incorporate the publication into its outreach activities. The Committee also supported the idea of holding an event to spread the publication on 4 October 2016.

CEP advice to the ATCM on a publication on the occasion of the 25th Anniversary of the Protocol on Environmental Protection to the Antarctic Treaty

(11) The Committee endorsed the publication on the occasion of the 25th Anniversary of the Protocol on Environmental Protection to the Antarctic Treaty and agreed to forward it to the ATCM for consideration.

(12) The Committee recommended that the publication be launched on 4 October 2016, on the occasion of the actual anniversary of the signing of the Protocol, making use of the dissemination mechanisms identified during the ICG and any other mechanisms that emerge following the CEP discussions.

CEP Five-year Work Plan

(13) The Committee considered the Five-year Work Plan adopted at CEP XVIII (SP 2) and, in keeping with its agreement at CEP XV (2012), briefly considered the work plan at the end of each agenda item.

(14) The Committee revised and updated its Five-year Work Plan (Appendix 1). The major changes included updates to reflect actions agreed during the Meeting, including actions arising from the Climate Change Response Work Programme (CCRWP) and the second joint workshop of the CEP and the Scientific Committee for the Conservation of Antarctic Marine Living Resources (SC-CAMLR).

(15) To assist with updating the Five-year Work Plan at future meetings, the Committee encouraged Members to identify clear links between meeting papers and actions identified in the Plan and, where appropriate for proposals suggesting future work, to provide suitable text for inclusion in the Plan.

Item 4: Operation of the CEP

(16) New Zealand introduced WP 10 *Antarctic Environments Portal,* jointly prepared with Australia, Japan, Norway, SCAR, Spain, and the United States. The paper recorded the benefits of the Portal and reviewed progress made since CEP XVIII, noting that the management of the Portal had been transferred to the University of Canterbury, Christchurch, New Zealand and that the Tinker Foundation had provided three years of external funding to support the Portal.

(17) New Zealand noted that several new articles had been published on the Portal since CEP XVIII including on: the vulnerability of marine habitats to climate change (relevant to CEP Item 9d); the Ross Seal (relevant to CEP Item 10b); changes in penguin distribution over the Antarctic Peninsula and Scotia Arc (relevant to CEP Items 10c and 11) and prediction of Antarctic climate (relevant to CEP Item 7).

(18) The Committee congratulated the proponents on progress made on the Environments Portal since CEP XVIII. It also thanked the Tinker Foundation and the University of Canterbury for their support.

(19) The Committee thanked France for its generous support with the translation of Portal content, and also thanked other CEP Members for their participation in the Editorial Group.

(20) The Committee reaffirmed the importance of the development of the Portal as a reliable information source that was apolitical and high quality, and of maximising, on a voluntary basis, the use of the information contained in the Antarctic Environments Portal to support the Committee's discussions.

(21) New Zealand responded to questions raised on: how to avoid duplication of information; how the quality and neutrality of the information would be maintained; how the proponents would ensure appropriate geographical balance in the authorship of content in the Antarctic Environments Portal; what challenges were being faced by the Antarctic Environments Portal; and to what extent the Antarctic Environments Portal was being used already. New Zealand reiterated that the Portal was unique and fulfilled a need not

currently being met by other sources. It stressed that the Portal provided peer reviewed summaries of the current state of knowledge in the peer reviewed literature and that the published articles did not express opinions, nor make recommendations. New Zealand reported that the Portal was being used widely, with 5,000 visits in the last 12 months. It remarked that attempts to ensure wide geographical representation would be ongoing, but that the voluntary nature of the contributions made this a continuing challenge.

(22) SCAR reminded the Committee that the quality of the articles published in the Portal was safeguarded through a rigorous editorial process involving a two-stage review by scientific experts as well as the Editorial Group.

(23) The Committee agreed that it would be helpful to encourage broader participation by scientists in the Antarctic Environments Portal, including ensuring appropriate geographical balance in authorship. The Committee noted a number of existing and planned summaries were of relevance to matters under discussion by the Committee. Germany suggested that information summaries be prepared on the environmental impacts of unmanned aerial vehicles (UAVs) and underwater noise.

(24) The Committee encouraged further consideration of options for the future management of the Antarctic Environments Portal, including considering whether the Antarctic Treaty Secretariat could host the Portal.

(25) The Committee supported the recommendations in WP 10 and agreed to:

- reaffirm the importance of the development of the Portal as a reliable information source that was apolitical and high quality;
- maximise, on a voluntary basis, the use of the information contained in the Portal to support the Committee's discussions;
- advise the Editorial Group on information summaries that it wished to see prepared for publication in the Portal (eg, through the Five-year Work Plan or CCRWP);
- continue to encourage scientists to work with SCAR in the preparation of articles for publication in the Portal;
- consider and make recommendations to the ATCM on options for the future management of the Portal in accordance with Resolution 3 (2015); and
- give thought as to how to identify representatives to serve on the Editorial Group.

(26) Australia introduced WP 17 *Report of the intersessional contact group established to review information exchange requirements*. The ICG was tasked to review the items of information currently required to be exchanged and to formulate recommendations on: whether there was continued value for Parties in exchanging information on these items; whether some of them needed to be modified, updated, differently described, made mandatory (where currently described as optional) or removed; the timing of information exchange for these items; how each item would best fit into the category of pre-season, annual and permanent information; and whether the information could be better exchanged through other mechanisms.

(27) Australia recommended that the Committee: 1) consider the report of the ICG with reference to the exchange of information relating to environmental matters; 2) formulate advice to the ATCM on any recommended changes; 3) identify any further work arising from the report of the ICG; and 4) give consideration to how that work might be advanced.

(28) The Committee thanked Australia for convening the ICG and welcomed the ICG report.

(29) Members raised concerns regarding the complexity and level of detail of information exchanged, and noted the need for critical examination of how the information exchange was evolving. They noted that it could be relevant to get a better feel of how actively Members use the EIES tool as an information source, considering questions such as what information Members search for, who uses the information and whether the degree of detail required at present is necessary. In highlighting inconsistency within the current EIES, some Members also stressed the importance of establishing a common standard of information exchange for all Parties and relevant organisations.

(30) The Committee considered the items of information relating to environmental matters, and concluded that:

- With regard to information exchange on 'Contingency plans for oil spills and other emergencies', the CEP agreed to recommend changes to: make clear that this requirement relates to environmental incidents; accommodate a description of the scope or coverage of the plan; ensure that provision of a link to a plan is optional; and to remove the item 'implementation report'. The CEP further noted that information can also be exchanged via an established COMNAP communication mechanism, for reporting on incidents and possible implementation of contingency plans (for National Antarctic Programme (NAP) incidents), and that the option is available of case-by-case reporting to the CEP where a contingency plan has been invoked in responding to a non-NAP incident.

- With regard to information exchanged on Initial Environmental Evaluations (IEEs) and Comprehensive Environmental Evaluations (CEEs), the CEP agreed to recommend changes to include an additional optional item of information for indicating 'the period/length of the activity'; and to modify the timing for the provision of information on IEEs and CEEs to encourage provision 'as soon as domestic processes are concluded, while maintaining the existing deadline for Parties to submit the information'. The CEP further noted that in some cases an IEE for an activity is amended, updated or otherwise modified by the Competent Authority, and that the information exchange requirements currently do not include sharing of information about such updates.

- The CEP noted that the current information exchange requirements for 'flora and fauna: taking and harmful interference', while meeting the Protocol requirement, will continue to result in data that cannot readily be collated across species, location, and years, due to the domestic permit arrangements in place for some Parties that relate to single species across multiple locations and *vice versa*.

- With regard to information exchange requirements for waste management plans, the CEP noted that further discussion of what information would be useful to the CEP, and what details might therefore be required, would best occur in the context of any future CEP consideration of waste management issues.

- With regard to information exchange on 'Waste disposal and waste management – inventory of past activities', the CEP noted that further discussion of this requirement would best occur in the context of any future CEP discussion of inventory of past activities.

- With regard to information exchange on 'Area protection and management – Visits to Specially Protected Areas (permit information)', the CEP noted that the ICG had considered the possibility of including copies of ASPA post-visit reports in the information exchange requirements, but that ASPA post-visit reports, required under management plans, will not always be in an official Treaty language. The CEP noted that further discussion of this issue in the CEP may be warranted, and encouraged interested Members to consider this issue and bring forward proposals as appropriate.

- With regard to the item 'change or damage to an ASPA, ASMA or HSM', the CEP noted that the option exists for a Party to provide information on an as-needed basis, on any reports of change or damage to an ASMA or ASPA.

CEP advice to the ATCM on the exchange of information on environmental matters

(31) The CEP recommended changes to the items of information exchange on contingency plans for oil spills and other emergencies as follows:

- modifying the description of the item to add underlined text as follows: 'oil spills and other environmental emergencies';

- adding an optional item to describe 'scope/coverage of the plan (eg, ship oil spill, station oil spill, station chemical incident, etc.)', in case this is not indicated in the title;

- retaining the item 'link', but making it 'optional'; and

- removing the item 'implementation report'.

(32) The CEP recommended changes to the items of information exchange on IEEs and CEEs as follows:

- the inclusion of an additional optional item of information, for indicating 'the period/length of the activity'; and

- modifying the timing for information on IEEs and CEEs to encourage provision 'as soon as domestic processes are concluded, while maintaining the existing deadline for Parties to submit the information'.

Item 5: Cooperation with other Organisations

(33) The SC-CAMLR Observer presented IP 6 *Report by the SC-CAMLR Observer to the nineteenth meeting of the Committee for Environmental Protection*, which focused on the five issues of mutual interest to the CEP and SC-CAMLR as identified in 2009 at the first joint workshop: a) Climate change and the Antarctic marine environment; b) Biodiversity and non-native species in the Antarctic marine environment; c) Antarctic species requiring special protection; d) Spatial marine management and protected areas; e) Ecosystem and environmental monitoring. It noted that due to ongoing changes in the environment related to climate and changes in the Antarctic food web, a range of precautionary measures might be needed to ensure that Article II of the CAMLR Convention was met. In particular SC-CAMLR agreed that attention was needed in

building long time-series and designing scientific studies that could predict or uncover changes in ecosystem function at an early stage, and that management approaches that worked in a changing climate should be adopted. SC-CAMLR considered a range of issues relating to biodiversity within spatial marine management and protected areas and noted that the CEP remained the lead-body on issues of non-native species. SC-CAMLR recognised that the current set of CCAMLR Ecosystem Monitoring Program (CEMP) parameters were providing indices of predator responses at different time and space scales and that this would benefit further development of feedback management approaches for the krill fishery. It awarded funds from the CEMP Special Fund Management Group towards a range of research initiatives related to feedback management. The full report on the 34th SC-CAMLR meeting was available at *https://www. ccamlr.org/en/sc-camlr-xxxiv.*

(34) COMNAP introduced IP 10 *Annual Report for 2015/16 of the Council of Managers of National Antarctic Programs (COMNAP)* and emphasised the items of particular relevance for CEP discussions. Firstly, the Infrastructure Catalogue project was a tool that would support greater collaboration in the Antarctic and thereby support reducing environmental impact from Antarctic science activities. This catalogue would be available by the end of 2016 on the COMNAP website. Secondly, COMNAP's work on Antarctic UAS use, as reported in COMNAP's WP 14, was an evolving project that would be revised to reflect published information on wildlife response to UAS use in the Antarctic as that information became available.

(35) SCAR presented IP 20 *The Scientific Committee on Antarctic Research (SCAR) Annual Report 2015/16* and referred to BP 2 which highlights some recent scientific publications by the SCAR research community since the last ATCM, that could be of interest for the delegates. SCAR highlighted several examples of its activities including participation in the Antarctic Roadmap Challenges project in 2015. This initiative, led by COMNAP, represented the second step of the first SCAR Antarctic and Southern Ocean Science Horizon Scan. Both initiatives are the topic of the SCAR Science Lecture at this year's ATCM (BP 3 rev. 1). Other activities include the participation, by SCAR, in a meeting of global biodiversity and Antarctic experts entitled 'Antarctica and the Strategic Plan for Biodiversity 2011-2020: The Monaco Assessment' (IP 38). Through wide consultation, including with COMNAP, SCAR also developed the SCAR Code of Conduct for Activity in Terrestrial Geothermal Areas in Antarctica, which is presented to the CEP for consideration (WP 23). SCAR also highlighted its participation in the 2015 UNFCCC COP21 in Paris, and the awarding of four fellowships,

including the new Prince Albert II of Monaco Biodiversity Fellowship and one SCAR/COMNAP fellowship. SCAR also awarded two Visiting Professorships, and again facilitated the 2015 Tinker-Muse prize which was awarded to Dr Valerie Masson-Delmotte. SCAR prepared an update of the Antarctic Climate Change and the Environment Report (IP 35) and provided a progress report regarding geoconservation (IP 31) in advance of a full report on this issue to the CEP in 2018.

(36) SCAR indicated that the 34th SCAR Delegates Meeting and the Open Science Conference would be held in Kuala Lumpur, Malaysia in August 2016. At that meeting, SCAR's synthesis of the scientific understanding of Southern Ocean acidification would be released. In addition, at this conference SCAR would be hosting a 'Wikibomb' as a way of increasing the visibility of female Antarctic researchers and helping to encourage girls around the world to pursue science careers. SCAR also reported on: the successful XII International Symposium on Antarctic Earth Sciences (ISAES) held in Goa, India in 2015; its plans for the XII SCAR Biology Symposium to be held in Belgium in July 2017; and the POLAR2018 Conference to be held in Davos, Switzerland jointly with the International Arctic Science Committee. SCAR also noted that Dr Jenny Baeseman had been appointed as the new SCAR Executive Director.

(37) The Committee thanked SCAR for facilitating its work through providing high quality advice and welcomed the opportunity to comment on SCAR's new strategic plan.

(38) Malaysia informed the Committee that the process of organising the XXXIV SCAR meeting and Open Science Conference was advancing and asked Members to encourage their scientific communities to participate.

(39) WMO presented IP 15 *The Year of Polar Prediction*. The Year of Polar Prediction (2017-2019) would aim to enable a significant improvement in environmental prediction capabilities for the polar regions and beyond, by coordinating a period of intensive observing, modelling, prediction, verification, user-engagement and education activities. It would also aim to address the lagging environmental forecasting capabilities at the poles, focusing on hourly-to-seasonal (Polar Prediction Project) and on seasonal-to-centennial (Polar Climate Predictability Initiative) time scales. The WMO also referred the Committee to the website for the Year of Polar Prediction: *www.polarprediction.net*.

(40) Supporting this WMO initiative, IAATO remarked that it would be useful to their members in implementing the IMO Polar Code. Furthermore, IAATO and France remarked that the work done during the Year of Polar Prediction

would also be useful in operational planning for difficult sea ice conditions. The Committee warmly supported the WMO initiative, noting the Year of Polar Prediction would contribute to improving the understanding of the environmental implications of climate change in the Antarctic Treaty area.

(41)   WMO presented IP 34 *The Antarctic Observing Network (AntON) to facilitate weather and climate information*, prepared jointly with SCAR. Noting that Antarctica was data sparse, WMO reflected on the importance of maximising the use of all of the meteorological and other data collected for weather, climate and other research and operational activities. Both the WMO and SCAR aimed to maximise the dissemination and use of such data through the Antarctic Observing Network (AntON), which collected metadata from participating manned and automatic weather stations currently in operation in Antarctica and the sub-Antarctic islands. In addition to keeping a list of the operational meteorological sites in Antarctica, WMO and SCAR, through the British Antarctic Survey, also monitored meteorological reports from ships operating in Antarctic waters. WMO also asked aircraft operators in Antarctica to provide meteorological observations for use in weather forecasting.

(42)   The Committee thanked the WMO and SCAR and expressed its support for the Antarctic Observing Network. Noting that meteorological observations from ships and aircraft contribute to the initiative, IAATO noted that it would continue to encourage its members to participate in the Antarctic Observing Network. The United Kingdom indicated that the British Antarctic Survey would continue its involvement in the Antarctic Observing Network.

Joint CEP/SC-CAMLR Workshop (Punta Arenas, Chile, 19-20 May 2016)

(43)   The United Kingdom and the United States introduced WP 53 *Report of the Joint CEP / SC-CAMLR Workshop on Climate Change and Monitoring, Punta Arenas, Chile, 19-20 May 2016*, prepared jointly by the co-convenors, and referred to IP 77 *Introduction from Co-Conveners of the Joint CEP/SC-CAMLR Workshop (Punta Arenas, Chile, 19-20 May 2016)*. The general scope of the workshop was to identify the effects of climate change that were considered most likely to impact the conservation of the Antarctic, and to identify existing and potential sources of research and monitoring data relevant to the CEP and SC-CAMLR, given that these were two of the five areas of common interest identified by the first joint CEP/SC-CAMLR workshop held in 2009.

(44)   The Committee thanked the workshop co-conveners, Dr Susie Grant (United Kingdom) and Dr Polly Penhale (United States) for their work

to lead the planning of the workshop, for chairing the workshop, and for quickly preparing the workshop report for consideration during CEP XIX. The Committee also expressed its gratitude to the government of Chile for hosting the workshop in Punta Arenas.

(45) The Committee agreed that the joint workshop had been valuable in further enhancing the cooperation and information sharing between the two committees on climate change, environmental monitoring, and other matters of mutual interest.

(46) Japan expressed concern about the relationship between the outcomes of the workshop and its terms of reference.

(47) Belgium and SCAR reminded the Committee of the SCAR Standing Committee on Antarctic Data Management, which is tasked with coordinating the management of data and information on behalf of the SCAR community. Belgium and SCAR also reminded the Committee of the capability of the *www.biodiversity.aq* portal and the Antarctic Master Directory to support the data sharing and exchange suggested in the report.

(48) China drew the attention of CEP Members to the importance of transparency in the collection, process and use of data and information. In relation to Recommendations 14 and 15, China also pointed out that the work of CEP and SC-CAMLR in response to climate change should focus on the whole Treaty/ Convention area or even broader, rather than on protected areas only.

(49) The Committee endorsed the 16 recommendations arising from the Joint CEP/SC-CAMLR workshop, as outlined in WP 53, and noted that the recommendations would also be considered by SC-CAMLR at its meeting later in the year. The Committee recognised the importance of monitoring progress on implementation of these recommendations.

(50) The Committee noted that Recommendations 1 to 4 are closely aligned with actions prioritised in the existing Climate Change Response Work Programme (CCRWP), and encouraged further incorporation of these recommendations into CCRWP updates and the CEP Five-year Work Plan. In relation to these recommendations, SCAR noted that work was already underway or planned in the near future, consistent with the priorities in the CCRWP.

- **Recommendation 1**: Encourage SC-CAMLR and CEP to recognise, encourage and support wherever possible the contribution that SCAR and programmes such as ICED and SOOS, as well as national programmes, can make to their work on climate change and related monitoring.

- **Recommendation 2**: Encourage the articulation of clear questions to be addressed to scientific programmes in order to obtain the best scientific advice relevant to the goals of the CEP and SC-CAMLR.

- **Recommendation 3**: Identify and convey shared climate change research and monitoring needs to SCAR, and to ICED and SOOS and other similar programmes, using the process outlined in Table 2 of WP 53.

- **Recommendation 4**: Encourage the periodic production of high level summaries of outcomes and progress made in programmes and reports such as SCAR-ACCE, ICED, SOOS, etc. in order to aid the CEP and SC-CAMLR in the understanding of the current state of knowledge and in the formation of questions to help progress work on climate change.

(51) The Committee noted that Recommendations 5 to 10 refer to actions that will facilitate the work of both the CEP and SC-CAMLR on climate change, noting that those relating specifically to SC-CAMLR will be considered during its discussions later in the year.

- **Recommendation 5**: Encourage flexibility in the composition of national delegations according to relevant agenda items, to allow SC-CAMLR, CEP and SCAR to engage in discussions on specific topics.

- **Recommendation 6**: Consider invitation of experts to CCAMLR Working Groups (particularly WG-EMM for discussions relating to climate change), including appropriate input from SCAR and programmes such as ICED and SOOS.

- **Recommendation 7**: Promote the development of young scientists by encouraging participation in the CCAMLR Scholarship and SCAR Fellowship programmes, with the specific aim of contributing research relevant to climate change.

- **Recommendation 8**: Encourage improved visibility of CCAMLR metadata to facilitate discoverability and exploration of data relevant to matters of mutual interest, particularly including CEMP data.

- **Recommendation 9**: Recognise that data sharing is not just sharing the products of research already collected, but information is also needed on future plans to collect additional data, to facilitate combined efforts and avoid duplication of effort.

- **Recommendation 10**: Encourage use of the Antarctic Environments Portal in providing policy-ready summaries on issues of mutual interest to members of both Committees. SC-CAMLR could be encouraged to request topics for inclusion, or to author summaries in due course.

(52) The Committee noted that Recommendations 11 and 12 require the development of further scientific input, and encouraged the involvement of SCAR and its associated programmes and other relevant organisations and programmes as appropriate.

- **Recommendation 11**: Recognise the importance of using common baseline information, and recommend that summary information such as SCAR Antarctic Climate Change and the Environment (ACCE) updates are submitted under climate change agenda item in both Committees.
- **Recommendation 12**: Consider further appropriate development of scientific reference areas with the objective of understanding impacts of climate change, using existing tools available to the CEP and SC-CAMLR.

(53) The Committee noted that Recommendations 13 to 15 relate to ongoing work by SC-CAMLR, and welcomed further updates on this work as it develops.

- **Recommendation 13**: Promote ongoing work led by Argentina, Chile, and including other Members, on the development of MPAs in planning Domain 1 (Antarctic Peninsula), acknowledging particular relevance to climate change research and the establishment of reference areas in this region of rapid change.
- **Recommendation 14**: Acknowledge that data from MPA planning processes will integrate and make available a significant amount of information that will improve decision-making and be relevant to the work of the CEP and SC-CAMLR on a range of other topics.
- **Recommendation 15**: Recognise that research and monitoring within CCAMLR and ATCM protected area systems will benefit from coordinated and integrated programmes within the respective regions, including the wider community of interested scientists (SCAR, ICED, SOOS, and/or national programmes).

(54) Finally, the Committee agreed on the importance of future joint meetings and intersessional communication between the CEP and SC-CAMLR.

- **Recommendation 16**: Encourage further and regular meetings between SC-CAMLR and the CEP, at least once every five years. Also encourage more frequent communication on topics of mutual interest in the intervening period before the next joint meeting, including via online forums and using remote access as appropriate.

(55) The Committee also endorsed the recommendation of the paper that further workshops should be held, at least once every five years, and encouraged

Members to engage in more frequent communication on topics of mutual interest in the period before the next joint meeting.

CEP advice to the ATCM on outcomes from the Joint CEP/SC-CAMLR Workshop on Climate Change and Monitoring

(56)   The Committee agreed to advise the ATCM that it had welcomed the report of the Joint CEP/SC-CAMLR Workshop on Climate Change and Monitoring and had endorsed the recommendations arising.

Nomination of CEP Representatives to other organisations

(57)   The Committee nominated:

- Dr Kevin Hughes (United Kingdom) to represent the CEP at the 34th SCAR Delegates Meeting to be held in Kuala Lumpur, Malaysia from 29-30 August 2016;

- Dr Yves Frenot (France) to represent the CEP at the 28th COMNAP Annual General Meeting to be held in Goa, India from 16-18 August 2016; and

- Dr Polly Penhale (United States) to represent the CEP at the 35th SC-CAMLR meeting to be held in Hobart, Australia, from 17-21 October 2016.

(58)   The following papers were also submitted under this agenda item:

- BP 2 *The Scientific Committee on Antarctic Research Selected Science Highlights for 2015/16* (SCAR).

- BP 3 rev. 1 *Abstract of the SCAR Lecture: Exploring the future of scientific research in Antarctica* (SCAR).

Item 6: Repair and Remediation of Environment Damage

(59)   The following paper was submitted under this agenda item:

- IP 76 *Environmental Remediation in Antarctica* (Brazil).

Item 7: Climate Change Implications for the Environment

7a) Strategic Approach

(60)   SCAR presented IP 35 *Antarctic Climate Change and the Environment – 2016 Update*, which provided an update on recent significant advances in the

understanding of climate change in the Antarctic Continent and the Southern Ocean. In addition to reporting on the physical effects of climate change on the environment, the update also detailed research on the biological and ecological impacts of these changes. The document built on the material in the Antarctic Climate Change and the Environment (ACCE) report, which was published by SCAR in 2009, with an update of the key points appearing in 2013.

(61) The Committee thanked SCAR for continuing to provide updates to the ACCE report, and reiterated the importance of SCAR's research activities for efforts to understand and address the environmental implications of climate change for the protection and management of the Antarctic Treaty area. The Committee also considered that the research findings presented in IP 35 reinforced the importance of the CEP's work to implement the CCRWP.

(62) WMO referred to the most recent report of the IPCC, and noted the importance of taking into account both natural and human-induced changes in order to correctly model both past and future climate. WMO stated that the increasing extent of sea ice in the Antarctic area did not contradict an overall global warming trend and is well documented in the published literature as well as the SCAR ACCE report and associated updates. Acknowledging that increasing sea ice in the Antarctic area had significant implications on science support, COMNAP referred the Committee to the report of COMNAP's Sea Ice Challenges Workshop.

(63) WMO presented IP 12 *WMO Climate-related Activities in the Antarctic Region*, an update on relevant Antarctic climate-related activities undertaken by WMO World Climate Research Programme. Noting the relevance of its work to that of the CEP, WMO highlighted its efforts to improve awareness of the general state of the Cryosphere through the Global Cryosphere Watch, improve the understanding of the predictability of polar climate, and use space agencies to observe the data-sparse polar regions.

(64) ASOC presented IP 78 *Antarctic Climate Change, Ice Sheets Dynamics and Irreversible Thresholds: ATCM contributions to the IPCC and Policy Understanding. Highlighting the significant challenge of communicating the threat of irreversible, long-term changes to the global climate system.* ASOC urged the Antarctic scientific community to contribute to the IPCC Special Report on the Implications of Global Warming of 1.5°C, and the Special Report on the Oceans and Cryosphere. ASOC recommended that Members, together with SCAR and other scientific organisations, respond in a timely fashion through a rapid assessment report.

(65) SCAR remarked that the summary of research requested by ASOC was consistent with its existing and planned research activities. SCAR further noted that it would consider how best to contribute to the IPCC Special Reports.

(66) The Committee thanked ASOC for its paper and welcomed SCAR's intention to contribute to the Special Report. It also encouraged Members to consider contributing through their own national processes.

(67) ASOC presented IP 81 *Antarctic Climate Change Report Card*, a summary of notable scientific breakthroughs and climate events related to anthropogenic climate change in the Antarctic. ASOC noted that the findings on climate change and ocean acidification were conclusive, and that climate change impacts were real and potentially significant for the Antarctic and the rest of the world. Recognising that Antarctic climate change science had been critical to understanding the impacts of global climate change, ASOC urged Members to continue to fund climate change science. Identifying the range of implications of climate change on environmental protection and management in Antarctica, including the need to establish protected areas, ASOC welcomed the work of the CCRWP.

(68) The United Kingdom presented IP 64 *Report on the activities of the Integrating Climate and Ecosystem Dynamics in the Southern Ocean (ICED) Programme*, which reported on the international multidisciplinary programme established in 2008 to improve understanding of change in the Southern Ocean and the implications for ecosystems and management.

(69) The Committee welcomed the paper and considered that the activities of the ICED programme were relevant to its work on climate change, as identified in the Climate Change Response Work Programme and as highlighted during the joint CEP/SC-CAMLR workshop.

(70) It was noted that all the useful and substantial information provided in the suite of papers on climate related issues shows the importance of continued focus on climate change as an important contributor to overall change in Antarctica, and its relevance in the context of governance and management of the continent (*eg*, through EIA processes, considering climate change risk when planning and conducting activities in Antarctic, disseminating information about Antarctic climate change to the global environmental forums, and encouraging coordination and accessibility of all climate relevant research data from Antarctica).

(71) The Committee referred to SP 7 *Actions taken by the CEP and the ATCM on the ATME recommendations on Climate Change*, and noted that many of the

ATME on Climate Change (2010) recommendations had been incorporated into the CCRWP.

7b) Implementation and Review of the Climate Change Response Work Programme

(72) The Committee reviewed the Climate Change Response Work Programme (CCRWP) agreed to by CEP XVIII and adopted as Resolution 4 (2015) (SP 2). It considered the actions identified for CEP XIX and noted that steps were already being taken to address most of these, including through the SGMP's ongoing work to develop ASMA guidance (WP 31), the intersessional work on reviewing the manual on Non-native Species (WP 13), the review of the Environmental Impact Assessment Guidelines (WP 15) and information summaries currently available and planned for the Antarctic Environments Portal. The Committee also noted that SC-CAMLR, SCAR and programmes such as the Southern Ocean Observing System (SOOS) and Integrating Climate and Ecosystem Dynamics in the Antarctic (ICED) were already undertaking activities of relevance to the CCRWP.

(73) In addition, the Committee noted that the CCRWP included several requirements for new and ongoing research and monitoring. The Committee encouraged National Antarctic Programmes, SCAR, WMO, and relevant external expert programmes to support and facilitate these research and monitoring activities.

(74) The Committee updated the CCRWP (Appendix 2), and welcomed the offers by SCAR and WMO to provide reports to CEP XX on their research and monitoring activities relevant to the CCRWP. The Committee also agreed that it should request relevant external programmes including SOOS and ICED to provide similar information about how their activities could contribute to matters identified in the CCRWP.

(75) The Committee noted that managing the CCRWP during the annual CEP meeting would likely be insufficient for achieving the necessary communication with observer and expert bodies, and agreed that a dedicated group, either in the form of regularly held ICGs, or a subsidiary body (with a convenor and dedicated participants, in accordance with Rule 10 of the CEP Rules of Procedure) would be the most effective way to involve such stakeholders in the work, as well as having a range of expertise available to follow up on the communication of the CCRWP.

(76) The Committee noted that further discussion was required on how such a dedicated group would operate, including how to work in the four Treaty

languages to ensure wide engagement of Members, noting at the same time that there is precedent for the effective operation of a subsidiary body.

(77) The Committee considered how to review and manage the CCRWP on an ongoing basis, and identified the following likely terms of reference for any mechanism established to review, update and maintain the CCRWP:

- overseeing and coordinating the communication between Members, SCAR and other stakeholders on identified actions in the CCRWP to facilitate its implementation;
- providing reports on the implementation of CCRWP to each CEP meeting;
- revising the CCRWP for the consideration of the CEP on an annual basis.

(78) The Committee noted the desirability and importance of clear and effective communication with Observer and expert organisations regarding tasks and information requests referred to them.

(79) The Committee welcomed New Zealand's offer to lead informal intersessional discussions on initiating the coordination of the CCRWP, including its communication and preparing suggested updates of the CCRWP, as well as options for establishing a subsidiary group to review and manage the CCRWP for CEP XX.

CEP advice to the ATCM on implementation of the Climate Change Response Work Programme (CCRWP)

(80) Noting the ATCM's request in Resolution 4 (2015) to receive annual updates on implementation of the Climate Change Response Work Programme, the Committee agreed to advise the ATCM that:

- steps were already being taken to address several tasks/actions identified in the CCRWP for 2016;
- it had agreed to encourage National Antarctic Programmes, SCAR, WMO, and relevant external expert organisations to support and facilitate the research and monitoring activities identified in the CCRWP;
- it had updated the CCRWP to reflect actions undertaken and to incorporate other minor modifications; and
- it had agreed to convene informal intersessional discussions to support further consideration at CEP XX of the best means for managing and supporting implementation of the CCRWP.

(81) Reflecting on the importance of incorporating high quality and up-to-date scientific advice into its deliberations on the environmental implications of climate change in the Antarctic Treaty area, including implementation of the CCRWP, the Committee agreed that it would be valuable to have a direct means of drawing on the expertise of the IPCC.

CEP advice to the ATCM on approving the IPCC as Observer to the CEP

(82) With reference to Rule 4c of the CEP Rules of Procedure adopted under Decision 4 (2011), the Committee agreed to propose that the ATCM approve the IPCC as an Observer to the CEP.

Item 8: Environmental Impact Assessment (EIA)

8a) Draft Comprehensive Environmental Evaluations

(83) Italy introduced WP 43 *Draft Comprehensive Environmental Evaluation for the construction and operation of a gravel runway in the area of Mario Zucchelli Station, Terra Nova Bay, Victoria Land, Antarctica*. This paper followed reports on Italy's plans to build a gravel runway as presented at previous CEP meetings (CEP XVIII - WP 30, CEP XVII - IP 57, CEP XVI - IP 80 and CEP XV - IP 41). It noted that the benefits obtained from the construction of the runway, including the more reliable and cost effective management of Italian scientific and logistic operations and increased safety and cooperation with neighbouring Antarctic Programmes, would outweigh its environmental impacts. Italy also provided a detailed explanation of some of the engineering aspects of the site research, including an aeronautical evaluation, a geophysical characterisation and a study of the morphology of the terrain including glacier movement.

(84) France introduced WP 21 *Report of the intersessional open-ended contact group established to consider the draft CEE for the "Proposed construction and operation of a gravel runway in the area of Mario Zucchelli Station, Terra Nova Bay, Victoria Land, Antarctica"*. France noted that ICG participants had commented favourably on several aspects of the proposed activity. The ICG advised the Committee that the draft CEE was generally clear, well structured and well presented, and generally conformed to the requirements of Article 3 of Annex I to the Protocol. It further advised the Committee that the draft CEE's conclusion, that the impacts of the proposed activity were likely to be more than minor or transitory, had been adequately supported by the information it contained. The ICG also suggested that, if

Italy decided to proceed with the proposed activity, there were a number of aspects for which additional information should be provided in the required final CEE.

(85) Italy presented IP 58 *The Initial Responses to the Comments on the Draft Comprehensive Environmental Evaluation for the construction and operation of a gravel runway in the area of Mario Zucchelli Station, Terra Nova Bay, Antarctic*a, as well as IP 61 *Initial Environmental Evaluation for the extension to the Boulder Clay site of the access road to Enigma Lake, Mario Zucchelli Station, Terra Nova Bay, Victoria Land, Antarctica*. IP 58 provided initial responses to comments made by participants in the ICG referenced in WP 21. It included a construction schedule and details regarding the staff needed as well as some information on birds and invertebrates in the area, and indicated some potential direct impacts to flora and fauna, and the non-native species risks. Italy also presented findings on the cumulative and indirect impact of the activities and provided details of mitigation measures.

(86) The Committee thanked Italy for the draft CEE and France for convening the ICG, and expressed support for the ICG's conclusions and recommendations. Noting the importance of the EIA processes as a significant component of environmental protection under the Environment Protocol, the Committee encouraged broad participation in future ICGs established to review draft CEEs.

(87) Several Members with activities and facilities in Terra Nova Bay and the wider region expressed their commitment to work in collaboration with Italy to maximise international cooperation and the scientific benefits of the proposed facility.

(88) Several Members reiterated that aspects of the draft CEE merited improvement or further attention, and questioned why the impacts of the construction of the access road to the proposed runway had been assessed by means of a separate IEE (submitted to CEP XIX under IP 61), rather than within the scope of the CEE assessment process.

(89) ASOC noted that, by increasing routes into the area, the proposed runway would create broader environmental impacts in the region. ASOC expressed its reservations about the proposal and recommended that, if the runway were built, Italy should consider protecting other areas in the region whose values were comparable to the area associated with the airstrip.

(90) The Committee welcomed Italy's commitment to respond to the issues raised by the ICG and by CEP Members and, should it decide to proceed with the

proposed activity, encouraged Italy to take into account the CEP's advice when preparing the required final CEE.

CEP advice to the ATCM on the draft CEE prepared by Italy for 'Proposed construction and operation of a gravel runway in the area of Mario Zucchelli Station, Terra Nova Bay, Victoria Land'

(91) Having reviewed the draft CEE prepared by Italy for the 'Proposed construction and operation of a gravel runway in the area of Mario Zucchelli Station, Terra Nova Bay, Victoria Land, Antarctica', in accordance with the Procedures for intersessional CEP consideration of draft CEEs, the CEP advised the ATCM that:

1) The draft CEE generally conformed to the requirements of Article 3 of Annex I to the Protocol on Environmental Protection to the Antarctic Treaty.

2) If Italy decided to proceed with the proposed activity, there were a number of aspects for which additional information or clarification should be provided in the required final CEE, as set out in WP 21 to this meeting, in order to facilitate a comprehensive assessment of the proposed activity. In particular, the ATCM's attention was drawn to the suggestions that further details should be provided regarding:

   a. the staff needed for the construction phase (number, accommodation etc.), as well as a clear schedule of work planed during the four years of construction;

   b. some aspects of initial environmental reference state, particularly invertebrates and all bird species (not only Adélie penguins and skuas), eg, through comprehensive bird mapping prior to commencement of construction;

   c. potential direct impacts to flora and fauna, the landscape and lake environments, and non-native species risks; the impacts related to the road, the quarries, dust and noise produced by construction work should be especially detailed;

   d. the inclusion of all parts of the activity in the scope of the CEE, including the construction and operation of the road to the runway site;

   e. cumulative and indirect impacts that might arise in light of existing activities and other known planned activities in the area, including logistical cooperation; and

f. mitigation measures related to fuel management, non-native species, wildlife disturbance, training of the construction crew.

3) The information provided in the draft CEE supported the conclusion that the impacts of constructing and operating the proposed gravel runway were likely to be more than minor or transitory.

4) The draft CEE was generally clear, well structured, and well presented, although improvements to some of the maps and figures were recommended.

8b) Other EIA Matters

Unmanned Aerial Vehicles (UAV)

(92) The Committee recalled that, following initial discussions at CEP XVII (2014) and in-depth discussions at CEP XVIII (2015), the Committee had agreed to consider initiating work to develop guidance on the environmental aspects of UAV use in Antarctica.

(93) COMNAP reminded the meeting of its ATCM XXXVIII – WP 22 which explored the risks and benefits of UAS use in the Antarctic, and then introduced WP 14 T*he COMNAP Unmanned Aerial Systems-Working Group (UAS-WG)* which reported on the activities of the COMNAP UAS-Working Group and included an initial version of the Antarctic UAS Operator's Handbook. COMNAP noted that the Handbook was a result of discussions from experts from 11 National Antarctic Programmes who participated in the UAS-WG, and thanked all those that had participated. It was noted that this Handbook is a living document that will be revised particularly in light of SCAR's forthcoming information on wildlife disturbance. The Handbook includes 12 recommendations to National Antarctic Programmes in their development of their own UAS operations guidelines and includes forms that might be useful for information exchange and advanced notification of UAS activities.

(94) Germany introduced WP 1 *UAV and wildlife minimum distances*, which summarised the results of recent research into the potential impacts of a micro-UAV on a small Adélie penguin colony on Ardley Island, and provided proposals for possible minimum distances for UAV use in Antarctica based on concrete disturbance experiments and in consideration of the precautionary approach recommended by the Committee when operating near wildlife. It recommended that the Committee consider the results and

recommendations of its paper in future discussions of guidelines for UAV use near wildlife concentrations.

(95) Poland presented IP 59 *UAV remote sensing of environmental changes on King George Island (South Shetland Islands): update on the results of the second field season 2015/2016.* The paper presented preliminary information on the second season of the joint Polish and Norwegian monitoring programme using fixed-wing UAVs to collect geospatial environmental data. It reported on observations regarding UAV impacts on breeding penguins and southern giant petrels, observations on penguin and pinniped population size and distribution, as well as the mapping of vegetation communities.

(96) IAATO presented IP 120 *IAATO Policies on the Use of Unmanned Aerial Vehicles (UAVs) in Antarctica: Update for the 2016/17 Season*, which reported that IAATO members had agreed to maintain the ban on recreational use of UAVs in coastal areas for the 2016/17 season. IAATO noted that, during the 2015/16 season, its operators had recorded 96 UAV flights, all of which had been approved by Competent Authorities and were for non-recreational use.

(97) The Committee thanked all Members and Observers that submitted papers to inform the CEP's discussion on environmental impacts of UAV use in Antarctica. Some Members also recalled that papers submitted to CEP XVIII on this topic continued to be relevant to this discussion.

(98) Acknowledging the scientific benefits of the use of UAVs to support research and monitoring, the Committee noted the continuing need for scientific understanding of the environmental impacts of UAV use, particularly on wildlife. The Committee recalled SCAR's generous offer to prepare a summary of the current state of knowledge regarding the impacts of UAVs on wildlife for the next meeting of the Committee, and appreciated SCAR's advice that this work was underway and progressing well.

(99) The Committee thanked COMNAP for its paper on the development of a handbook on Guidelines for Certification and Operation of Unmanned Aerial Systems in Antarctica and, noting that WP 14 would be considered further by the ATCM, expressed support for COMNAP's recommendation to encourage Parties to give consideration to the guidance in the Handbook if or when their National Antarctic Programme is planning to use UAV technologies in the Antarctic Treaty area. The Committee noted that the handbook highlighted the importance of considering the environmental impacts of UAVs through the EIA process, and agreed that it would be beneficial for the handbook to

be further developed as research and understanding of the environmental impacts of UAV became available.

(100) The Committee expressed its gratitude to Germany and Poland for providing updates on recent research of the potential impacts of UAVs, and urged Members to continue to provide updates on any research undertaken on the use and environmental impacts of UAVs. The Committee recognised the results presented in Germany's paper as a useful reference for its further discussions on developing environmental guidance for UAV use in Antarctica, while noting that additional research would be useful before establishing minimum approach distances.

(101) The Committee also thanked IAATO for its advice that IAATO members had agreed to continue their ban on the recreational use of UAVs in coastal areas.

(102) The Committee supported the establishment of an ICG to develop further guidance for managing the environmental aspects of UAV use, commencing at CEP XX, at which time SCAR's report on the impacts of UAVs on wildlife would be available.

(103) The Committee acknowledged the benefit of continued consideration of these matters, and of the guidance and research being produced to support further discussion at CEP XX. Noting that some Members had shared their experience of implementing national or Antarctic guidance for UAV use, the Committee considered this information would also be relevant to those discussions.

(104) While some Members expressed support for a suggestion raised during the meeting to ban the recreational use of UAVs in Antarctica, the Committee agreed that this matter could be given further consideration during the planned ICG. On this subject, the Committee noted that COMNAP's experience regarding the utility of carefully managed recreational use of UAVs to station staff, particularly those remaining in Antarctica over winter, would usefully inform future discussions.

CEP advice to the ATCM on unmanned aerial vehicles (UAVs)

(105) The Committee agreed to advise the ATCM that it recognised the usefulness of the COMNAP Guidelines for Certification and Operation of Unmanned Aerial Systems in Antarctica (WP 14). The Committee also recognised the need to develop guidance on the environmental aspects of UAVs, and would initiate at CEP XX work to develop such guidance.

(106) Australia introduced WP 15 *Report of the intersessional contact group established to review the Guidelines for Environmental Impact Assessment in Antarctica*, jointly prepared with the United Kingdom. The ICG had been tasked to: continue revising the Guidelines for Environmental Impact Assessment in Antarctica appended to Resolution 1 (2005) to address issues including those identified in ATCM XXXVII - WP 29 and, as appropriate, suggest modifications to the Guidelines; and record issues raised during discussions under ToR 1, which relate to broader policy or other issues for the development and handling of EIAs, and which may warrant further discussion by the CEP with a view to strengthening the implementation of Annex I to the Protocol. The ICG reached general agreement on a suggested revision of the EIA Guidelines. The ICG also identified broader policy or other EIA issues that might warrant further discussion by the CEP. The ICG recommended that the Committee consider the revised EIA Guidelines and, should agreement be reached on a final version, that the Committee convey the revised guidelines to the ATCM for adoption. The ICG also recommended that the Committee discuss how best to address the broader policy or other issues for the development and handling of EIAs, contained in Attachment C to the paper.

(107) The Committee thanked Australia and the United Kingdom for leading the ICG, and for presenting the report. Following the incorporation of minor amendments during the meeting, the Committee finalised the revision of the Guidelines for Environmental Impact Assessment in Antarctica.

(108) The Committee also considered the broader policy and other issues raised during the intersessional work, and noted that these called for careful consideration.

(109) The Committee thanked the United Kingdom for its offer to work with interested Members to develop a Working Paper to support further discussion of the broader policy and other EIA issues at CEP XX. The United Kingdom noted that, recognising comments by Members during the meeting, it would prioritise matters related to the establishment of a central repository for practical EIA guidance and resources, and updating the *Procedures for intersessional CEP consideration of draft CEEs* to include a standard term of reference on the appropriateness/adequacy of proposed mitigation measures. Several Members expressed interest in participating in the intersessional work.

CEP advice to the ATCM on the revision of the Guidelines for Environmental Impact Assessment in Antarctica

(110) Following consideration of the report of the ICG established to review the *Guidelines for Environmental Impact Assessment in Antarctica*, the Committee endorsed a revision to the Guidelines and agreed to continue its work on broader policy considerations. Noting that the existing Guidelines were adopted under Resolution 4 (2005), the Committee agreed to forward to the ATCM for adoption a draft Resolution to revise the Guidelines.

(111) The Republic of Korea presented IP 45 *Renovation of the King Sejong Korean Antarctic Station on King George Island, South Shetland Islands* in which the Committee was informed of planned renovations to its station, which will include the reconstruction of summer accommodation and laboratories and structural alterations to enhance the building's safety, durability and usability. It also planned to install a solar power system and replace existing fuel tanks with double skinned tanks. The IEE document for the proposed activities would be submitted to the Ministry of Foreign Affairs for approval in the coming year.

(112) Referring to its inspection of the facilities (WP 29), China remarked that the King Sejong Korean Antarctic Station was a good scientific platform and expressed support for the planned renovations.

(113) New Zealand presented IP 53 *A tool to support regional-scale environmental management*, which introduced a research programme, led by Landcare Research, to develop a tool to support broader scale environmental management. The proposed management tool would facilitate regional scale assessments of activities and impacts while allowing variations in environments to be more readily accounted for in assessments. New Zealand invited Members to attend an informal workshop on the development of the tool at the conclusion of the XXXIV SCAR Open Science Conference, to be held in Kuala Lumpur, Malaysia (27 August 2016).

(114) Welcoming New Zealand's initiative, the United Kingdom remarked that it recognised the benefit of applying this tool in other areas of Antarctica.

(115) Ecuador presented IP 122 *Licencia Ambiental de la Estación Científica Pedro Vicente Maldonado*. The Committee was informed that in August 2015 the Ecuadorian Antarctic Institute received the Environmental License for the Pedro Vicente Maldonado Scientific Station from the environmental authority of the Ecuadorian government. It also reported that, in order to

keep the license, the station has to undergo mandatory biennial audits on the application of the Environmental Management Plan for the station, also approved by the aforementioned authority. This plan has nine components that aim to protect both the environment and the station's personnel, and is subject to updates and improvements.

(116) The following papers were also submitted under this agenda item:

- IP 3 *Application of air dispersion modelling for impact assessment of construction/operation activities in Antarctica* (Belarus).

- IP 30 *Modernisation of GONDWANA-Station, Terra Nova Bay, northern Victoria Land* (Germany).

- IP 56 *Developing a blue ice runway at Romnoes in Dronning Maud Land* (Belgium).

- SP 6 rev. 1 *Annual list of Initial Environmental Evaluations (IEE) and Comprehensive Environmental Evaluations (CEE) prepared between April 1ˢᵗ 2015 and March 31ˢᵗ 2016* (ATS).

Item 9: Area Protection and Management Plans

9a) Management Plans

   i) *Draft Management Plans which have been reviewed by the Subsidiary Group on Management Plans*

(117) The convener of the Subsidiary Group on Management Plans (SGMP), Birgit Njåstad (Norway) introduced WP 31 *Subsidiary Group on Management Plans – Report on 2015/16 Intersessional Work (Norway)*, on behalf of the SGMP. The convener thanked all active participants in the SGMP for their hard work and reminded the Committee that all Members were welcome to join the SGMP. In accordance with terms of reference 1 to 3, the Group had been prepared to consider the following five draft Antarctic Specially Protected Area (ASPA) management plans referred by the CEP for intersessional review:

- ASPA 125: Fildes Peninsula, King George Island (25 de Mayo) (Chile).

- ASPA 144: Chile Bay (Discovery Bay), Greenwich Island, South Shetland Islands (Chile).

- ASPA 145: Port Foster, Deception Island, South Shetland Islands (Chile).

- ASPA 146: South Bay, Doumer Island, Palmer Archipelago (Chile).
- ASPA 150: Ardley Island, Maxwell Bay, King George Island (25 de Mayo) (Chile).

(118) The SGMP advised the CEP that since the proponent had not been able to progress the review of these management plans during the intersessional period, the SGMP was not able to give further advice and complete the review process.

(119) Chile informed the Committee that it anticipated submitting revised versions of the five management plans to the SGMP for review in the next intersessional period.

   ii) *Revised draft Management Plans which have not been reviewed by the Subsidiary Group on Management Plans*

(120) The Committee considered revised management plans for eight ASPAs. In each case, the proponent(s): summarised the suggested changes to the existing management plan; noted that it had been reviewed and revised with reference to the *Guide to the Preparation of Management Plans for Antarctic Specially Protected Areas* (the Guide); and recommended its approval by the Committee and referral to the ATCM for adoption. The Committee also considered a proposal from France to extend the existing management plan for ASPA 166 Port Martin for a further five years:

   a. WP 2 *Revised Management Plan for Antarctic Specially Protected Area No. 149 – Cape Shirreff and San Telmo Island, Livingston Island, South Shetland Islands* (United States).

   b. WP 3 *Revised Management Plan for Antarctic Specially Protected Area No. 122 – Arrival Heights, Hut Point Peninsula, Ross Island* (United States).

   c. WP 4 *Revised Management Plan for Antarctic Specially Protected Area No. 126 – Byers Peninsula, Livingston Island, South Shetland Islands* (United Kingdom, Chile and Spain).

   d. WP 18 *Revision of the Management Plan for Antarctic Specially Protected Area (ASPA) No. 167 Hawker Island, Princess Elizabeth Land* (Australia).

   e. WP 26 *Revision of the Management Plan for Antarctic Specially Protected Area (ASPA) No. 116: New College Valley, Caughley Beach, Cape Bird, Ross Island* (New Zealand).

f. WP 27 *Revision of the Management Plan for Antarctic Specially Protected Area (ASPA) No. 131: Canada Glacier, Lake Fryxell, Taylor Valley, Victoria Land* (New Zealand).

g. WP 36 *Revised Management Plan for ASPA No. 120, Pointe-Géologie Archipelago, Adélie Land* (France).

h. WP 37 *Revised Management Plan for ASPA No. 166, Port-Martin, Adélie Land. Extension Proposal for the Existing Plan* (France).

i. WP 40 *Revised Management Plan for Antarctic Specially Protected Area N°. 127 "Haswell Island" (Haswell Island and Adjacent Emperor Penguin Rookery on Fast Ice)* (Russian Federation).

(121) With respect to WP 2 (ASPA 149) and WP 3 (ASPA 122), the United States noted that only minor changes to the existing management plans were proposed. Revisions had been made in consultation with international stakeholders, and amendments included editorial improvements relating to the description of the protected area and improvements to maps.

(122) With respect to WP 4 (ASPA 126), the United Kingdom noted that only minor changes were made to supporting information in the management plan, and a reference to the Antarctic Conservation Biogeographic Regions added. The United Kingdom and Chile also proposed that Spain be recognised as a co-managing Party for ASPA 126.

(123) With respect to WP 18 (ASPA 167), Australia reported that only minor amendments were proposed to the management plan. Changes included updated population estimates for the southern giant petrel colony and a modification to section 7 specifying that overflights by aircraft, including unmanned aerial vehicles, in the Area were prohibited unless approved by a permit.

(124) With respect to WP 26 (ASPA 116) and WP 27 (ASPA 131), New Zealand noted that minor revisions were proposed to the management plans, which had been updated in consultation with scientists and environmental managers who have worked in the Areas.

(125) With respect to WP 36 (ASPA 120), France explained that it had made significant editorial changes in various sections, but the substance of the management plan was not significantly modified. Changes included rewording of section 2 for clarity, modifying various maps and adding a general description of the area including fauna and geological information.

With respect to WP 37 (ASPA 166), France explained that recent sea ice conditions in the region had continued to prevent safe access to the site, which remained valuable for the conduct of archaeological research. It therefore suggested that the management plan be extended for five years without any changes.

(126) With respect to WP 40 (ASPA 127), the Russian Federation reported that only minor changes were made to the management plan, including reference to the presence of the Lönnberg skua (Catharacta antarctica) in the area (IP 71).

(127) The Committee approved all of the revised management plans that had not been reviewed by the SGMP.

(128) The Committee also approved the extension of the existing management plan for ASPA 166 Port Martin for a further five years.

(129) The Committee supported the proposal in WP 4 that Spain be recognised as co-managing Party for ASPA 126, with the United Kingdom and Chile.

iii) New draft management plans for protected/managed areas

(130) No new draft management plans for protected/managed areas were submitted.

CEP advice to the ATCM on revised management plans for ASPAs

(131) The Committee agreed to forward the following revised management plans to the ATCM for approval by means of a Measure

#	Name
ASPA 116	New College Valley, Caughley Beach, Cape Bird, Ross Island
ASPA 120	Pointe-Géologie Archipelago, Terre Adélie
ASPA 122	Arrival Heights, Hut Point Peninsula, Ross Island
ASPA 126	Byers Peninsula, Livingston Island, South Shetland Islands
ASPA 127	Haswell Island (Haswell Island and Adjacent Emperor Penguin Rookery on Fast Ice)
ASPA 131	Canada Glacier, Lake Fryxell, Taylor Valley, Victoria Land
ASPA 149	Cape Shirreff and San Telmo Island, Livingston Island, South Shetland Islands
ASPA 167	Hawker Island, Princess Elizabeth Land

(132) The Committee also agreed to advise the ATCM that the existing management plan for ASPA 166 Port-Martin, Terre-Adélie, should be extended for a further period of five years.

iv) Other matters relating to management plans for protected/managed areas

(133) The United Kingdom introduced WP 9 *The Status of Antarctic Specially Protected Area No. 107 Emperor Island, Dion Islands, Marguerite Bay, Antarctic Peninsula*, which noted that the Area had been designated for special protection since 1966 to ensure the protection of its emperor penguin breeding colony. At CEP XIV, the United Kingdom had alerted the Committee that its scientists had cast doubt over the continued existence of the colony (ATCM XXXIV - WP 18) and the Committee supported the United Kingdom's suggested approach to delay revision of the ASPA management plan for five years to enable the status of the colony to be confirmed. Subsequent monitoring work identified no substantial recovery of the earlier emperor penguin colony and aerial and automatic photography had shown only a few intermittent appearances of a few likely non-breeding emperor penguins. Following the United Kingdom's reassessment of the Area's suitability for ASPA status using the tools in Article 3 of Annex V, and given that the Area lacked any other values that justified special protection and that the projected increase in regional temperature would be likely to have a negative impact on future successful breeding, the United Kingdom sought the Committee's view on whether the additional protection afforded by ASPA status was still appropriate.

(134) ASOC stated that decisions to delist protected areas should not be taken lightly and suggested that the Committee should consider enhancing the protection of emperor penguin colonies at other sites, especially if ASPA 107 was delisted.

(135) The Committee thanked the United Kingdom for its comprehensive and systematic reassessment of the status of ASPA 107. It noted that the monitoring data presented by the United Kingdom had not shown any substantial recovery of the emperor colony, but also noted the observations of some emperor penguins at the site including some observations from IAATO operators.

(136) Some Members believed that, given the rigorous assessment done by the United Kingdom, there was a strong case for delisting the site. Following careful consideration, and with the support of the United Kingdom, the

Committee decided, however, that the ASPA status should be maintained for a further five years. It encouraged the United Kingdom to continue its monitoring using remote sensing techniques and other less resource intensive technologies, and to report back to the CEP. The Committee also encouraged other Members to provide any relevant monitoring data to assist with this further assessment.

(137) During discussion of WP 9, several Members highlighted the importance of taking a dynamic, science-based approach to protected area management, including de-designation processes, in order to focus attention on those areas or values that require protection additional to that already provided in the Protocol in general. Noting that the Committee should be rigorous in its consideration of these matters, several Members suggested the development of procedures or criteria to inform the Committee's consideration of proposals to de-designate ASPAs, including in the context of the framework provided by the CCRWP. The Committee welcomed Norway's offer to lead work to inform further consideration of this issue at CEP XX. Several Members expressed an interest in collaborating with Norway in this work.

(138) China introduced WP 29 *Report of the 2015/16 Intersessional Informal Discussions on the proposal for a New Antarctic Specially Managed Area at Chinese Antarctic Kunlun Station, Dome A and the follow-up work.* Following the Committee's considerations at CEP XVI, CEP XVII and CEP XVIII of China's proposal to designate an ASMA at the Chinese Antarctic Kunlun Station, Dome A, as well as the international informal discussions during the respective intersessional periods, this paper reported on further informal discussions held during the 2015/16 intersessional period. China responded to various concerns that Members had previously expressed, including: the values protected; international collaborative programmes; number of operators; overlapping activities; the appropriateness of designating an ASMA and the potential to use alternative tools; and the interpretation of Article 4, Annex V to the Protocol.

(139) China gave an overview of past, current and potential future international research activities in the area and elaborated on ongoing infrastructural developments at Kunlun Station. China also noted that it expected that, in the near future, the volume of collaborative scientific activities, number of operators, and the volume and types of other activities in the area would increase. Recalling the CEP Workshop on Marine and Terrestrial Specially Managed Areas (2011), China reiterated its view that an ASMA was the most appropriate tool to proactively manage and protect the scientific

and environmental values at Dome A. Reaffirming its commitment to the provisions of the Protocol and international scientific collaboration, China requested that the Committee note the unique scientific and environmental values in the Dome A area and encourage Members to participate in further intersessional discussions led by China.

(140) Argentina thanked China for its continuous commitment to foster debates on its proposal to establish an ASMA at Dome A. It also pointed out that a decision on this issue was needed, and it remained confident that the CEP would make best efforts to eventually find an agreement.

(141) The Committee thanked China for leading the informal intersessional discussion and for providing the report on those discussions. The Committee also expressed its appreciation to Members that participated in the intersessional discussions.

(142) The Committee recognised the scientific and environmental values of the Dome A area and its potential for more scientific research. It also noted that China was further developing its facilities and infrastructure at Dome A, and sincerely intended to promote the sharing of its facilities to promote international cooperation in scientific research. It welcomed China's aim to minimise the impacts of human activities on the Dome A environment and its desire to establish an appropriate management framework for the Dome A area.

(143) While recognising that the proposal to designate an ASMA at Dome A had been underway for some time, several Members noted that they continued to hold reservations about the proposal. They noted that international science programmes and other international activities at Dome A had not yet been realised, and that there were currently no overlapping activities between multiple operators in the area. Recognising that these views would be kept under consideration in light of possible future changes in circumstances and activities at Dome A, the Members expressed their willingness to participate in further informal discussions with China on other management options for the area.

(144) In responding to the concerns, China noted Article IV of Annex V to the Protocol permitted the designation of any area as an ASMA where activities were being conducted or may in the future be conducted. China stressed that its proposal focussed on not only current but also future pressures to the scientific and environmental values of Dome A. Referring to the current seven designated ASMAs, some of which had been proposed by single

Members, China expressed the view that the Committee had previously accepted a range of approaches to the designation of ASMAs. After considering the discussion of the Committee, China agreed to continue to lead informal intersessional work to discuss all the practical and possible management options for the Dome A area.

(145) The Committee welcomed China's offer to lead informal intersessional discussions, and encouraged interested Members to participate, with a view to considering options for achieving China's management objectives for Dome A.

(146) The United States presented IP 33 *Amundsen/Scott South Pole Station, South Pole Antarctica Specially Managed Area (ASMA No. 5). 2016 Management Report,* jointly prepared with Norway. The United States noted its progress with the review of the management plan and some of the diverse issues being addressed with Norway, including regular updates of the site maps, management of non-governmental activity and the arrangement of zones and sectors within the ASMA. It confirmed that a review would be available in the next year, following extensive stakeholder input.

(147) IAATO thanked the United States and Norway for their paper, and their work revising the ASMA Management Plan. IAATO noted that it would trial the revision of overland approaches proposed in the paper, and stood ready to participate in the management group and assist with the development of further procedures.

(148) The following papers were also submitted under this agenda item:

- IP 71 *Present zoological study at Mirny Station Area and at ASPA No. 127 "Haswell Island" (2011-2015)* (Russian Federation).

- BP 11 *Aplicación del Plan de Manejo Ambiental en la Estación Maldonado* (Ecuador).

9b) Historic Sites and Monuments

(149) The United Kingdom introduced WP 12 *Managing Antarctic Heritage: British Historic Bases in the Antarctic Peninsula*, which reported on the heritage management programme undertaken by the British Antarctic Survey (BAS) and then the United Kingdom Antarctic Heritage Trust at historic sites on the Antarctic Peninsula over the past twenty years. The United Kingdom noted three key issues in relation to managing heritage in the Antarctic area: the high costs and time commitment; the presence of hazardous materials at

many of the sites; and the management of visitor behaviour at unoccupied sites. The United Kingdom noted that it strongly supported the moratorium on the introduction of new HSMs until guidelines addressing these issues had been developed.

(150) Reflecting on lessons learned over this period, the United Kingdom recommended that CEP Members encourage greater international collaboration between those responsible for the management of Antarctic heritage and HSMs. This collaboration would include sharing and reviewing plans, and collectively ensuring Antarctic heritage was cared for to internationally recognised standards. It was also recommended that the CEP encourage Members to undertake assessments of the heritage value of HSMs and to develop management plans, particularly for new HSM designations. This included consideration of long term management and maintenance, and any plans for wider public engagement on the importance of the site. Finally, it was recommended that the CEP consider how it might communicate and share the significance of its shared Antarctic heritage more widely.

(151) The Committee thanked the United Kingdom for the paper and congratulated the United Kingdom Antarctic Heritage Trust for its comprehensive work to protect historical sites in Antarctica. Members highlighted the importance of planning and international collaboration in care and management of Antarctic sites and monuments.

(152) The Committee supported the recommendations in WP 12, and noted that the experiences and recommendations reported in the paper would be a helpful reference for others facing similar issues and for further discussion on the topic of heritage management in the Committee.

(153) Norway introduced WP 30 *Consideration of protection approaches for historic heritage in Antarctica*, which summarised approaches to historical heritage management, including discussing advantages and disadvantages to *in situ* and *ex situ* preservation approaches for historic heritage values. Aiming to reach an appropriate balance between the motivation and intentions held in Annex V and Annex III to the Environment Protocol, Norway suggested that the CEP consider developing guidance for the assessment of appropriate preservation methods for heritage elements considered for HSM listing in Antarctica.

(154) The Committee recalled its discussion on these matters at earlier meetings, and thanked Norway for the useful summary of approaches to historic

heritage management, including advantages and disadvantages of *in situ* and *ex situ* preservation.

(155) The Committee noted there was a high level of interest in this issue among Members, both from the perspective of enhancing the protection of historic sites and balancing the provisions of Annex III and Annex V, and strongly supported the recommendations presented in WP 30.

(156) Argentina stressed the need to consider the individual heritage value of items to each Member, and also expressed the need for more debate in relation to *ex situ* conservation as HSMs are a considered part of Antarctic heritage.

(157) The Committee agreed to establish an ICG led by Norway and UK with the aim of developing guidance material for Parties' assessment of conservation approaches for the management of Antarctic heritage objects. The ICG is to work during the 2016/17 and 2017/18 intersessional period(s) with the following terms of reference for the 2016/17 intersessional period:

1. Develop a work plan for the development of guidance for the consideration of the most appropriate conservation approaches to the management of historic heritage elements.

2. Identify questions that could constitute the core elements of the guidance material to be developed for the assessment of potential conservation approaches that could be used for the management of historic heritage elements as an alternative to listing of the object as an HSM, including further exploration of *inter alia* the following questions:

   • Consideration of how the age of an object in question has bearing on the management approach including its significance, current/recent usage and materials (including hazards);

   • Consideration of the national versus international significance of the heritage object in question;

   • Consideration of whether the existing suite of Antarctic HSMs already adequately covers the value of the object in question;

   • Consideration of whether an object is best maintained in situ to protect its value, or whether it can be better maintained and presented *ex situ;*

   • Consideration of whether an object would be better preserved or presented by archival methods or digitally;

   • Consideration of risks and challenges involved (resources and otherwise) in maintaining the object *in situ* and *ex situ*;

- Consideration of the state of conservation of the object at the time of designation and the potential need for rapid actions, as appropriate (short term management);
- Consideration of the medium-long term management plan for the object if kept *in situ* and the implications (expertise, costs, realisation of benefits);
- Consideration of the 'objective' of the heritage object, *ie,* will it be visited by visitors to Antarctica? Will it still be in use or part of a site still working? How does its management reflect its significance?;
- Consideration of the wider value of the object to the outside world – how will it be made accessible more widely (if no-one knows about it who will care about it?);
- Identification of resources, relevant expertise and heritage organisations to offer guidance and advice;
- Exploration of the value of implementing a model of best practice for the care of Antarctic heritage objects for all parties; and
- Identification of, when appropriate, potential international partners to aid or collaborate with in the conservation planning and execution.

3. Begin to implement the work plan as appropriate and work toward drafting of guidance material for the consideration of the CEP.

4. Develop draft terms of reference for a second intersessional period.

5. Report on progress to CEP XX.

(158) The Committee noted the desirability of engaging heritage expertise associated with ICOMOS' International Polar Heritage Committee (IPHC) in the work and encouraged Members to involve their national members of IPHC in the work.

(159) The Committee welcomed the offer from Birgit Njåstad (Norway) and Stuart Doubleday (UK) to act as ICG conveners.

(160) Argentina introduced WP 47 rev. 2 *Incorporation of a historic wooden pole to HSM No. 60 (Corvette Uruguay Cairn), in Seymour (Marambio) Island, Antarctic Peninsula*, jointly prepared with Sweden. It proposed the revision of HSM 60 to add a historic cairn and wooden pole to the description of HSM 60, following the guidelines adopted in Resolution 5 (2011) and the additional information that could be added to the description of HSMs endorsed by CEP XV, according to the outcome of the ICG held

during 2011/12 on this matter. The paper suggested a text for the proposed description.

(161) Noting the historical value of the site for both Parties, Sweden thanked Argentina for its initiative in preparing the expanded description of the site.

(162) The Committee thanked Argentina and Sweden for providing notice of the discovery of this significant historic object, consistent with the provisions of Resolution 5 (2001), and agreed to forward the modified details for HSM 60 to the ATCM for adoption by means of a Measure.

(163) Argentina introduced WP 48 rev. 1 *Notification of the location of historical pre-1958 remains in the vicinity of the Argentine Station Marambio*, jointly prepared with Norway, Sweden and the United Kingdom. The paper reported on the recent location of pre-1958 historical remains in the vicinity of the Argentine Station Marambio. The remains were linked to various well-known historical events spanning 1893 to 1945, involving Norwegian, Argentine, Swedish and British explorers. Considering the moratorium on HSM designation agreed by the Committee at CEP XVIII, Argentina, Norway, Sweden and the United Kingdom requested that the Committee either recognise the historical value of the site and recommend applying the interim protection afforded by Resolution 5 (2001) until it is ready to designate new HSMs; or, alternatively, consider HSM designation.

(164) The Committee thanked Argentina, Norway, Sweden and the United Kingdom for notifying the discovery of this significant historical site consistent with the provisions of Resolution 5 (2001), and commended the Argentinean researchers for locating the site. There was broad recognition that in future this site would very likely be worthy of HSM designation. The Committee recommended that the interim protection measures afforded by Resolution 5 (2001) be applied to the site and looked forward to further considering the HSM proposal following the development of guidance on approaches to protect historic heritage in Antarctica.

(165) The Republic of Korea introduced WP 51 *Proposal to add Antarctic King Sejong Station History Gallery (Dormitory No. 2) at the Antarctic King Sejong Station to the Historic Sites and Monuments*. It noted that Dormitory No. 2 would be renamed and conserved as the Antarctic King Sejong Station History Gallery to permanently commemorate the historical significance and scientific value of Korea's Antarctic research, and to allow Korea's scientific research and discovery to be on fuller display for both the international Antarctic community and the Korean public.

(166) The Committee thanked the Republic of Korea for its proposal. While acknowledging the Republic of Korea's initiative in putting forward the proposal, the Committee recalled its decision at CEP XVIII (CEP XVIII report paragraph 177) and decided to defer consideration of the proposal until it received further guidelines for the designation of HSMs. The Republic of Korea thanked the Committee and agreed to delay further action until the moratorium was lifted.

(167) France presented IP 1 *Reinstalling the memorial plaque of Le Pourquoi Pas? on Petermann Island (Charcot's cairn 1909, HSM 27)*, prepared jointly with IAATO. It noted that during the Antarctic summer season 2014-15, the memorial plaque of *Le Pourquoi Pas?*, was found on the ground, close to the cairn to which it was fixed. The crew of *L'Austral,* a vessel of the French company Ponant, member of IAATO, reinstalled the plaque in January 2016.

CEP advice to the ATCM on proposed modifications and additions to the List of Historic Sites and Monuments

(168) The Committee agreed to forward one proposal for a modification to the List of Historic Sites and Monuments to the ATCM for approval by means of a Measure.

#	Description
HSM 60	Wooden pole and cairn (I) and wooden plaque and cairn (II) at HSM No. 60 (Corvette Uruguay Cairn)

(169) The Committee agreed to defer two proposals for additions to the List of Historic Sites and Monuments for further consideration following the development of guidance on approaches to protection of historic heritage in Antarctica:

• *Historical pre-1958 remains in the vicinity of Marambio Station;*

• *Antarctic King Sejong Station History Gallery.*

(170) The Committee agreed that the interim protection afforded to pre-1958 sites in accordance with Resolution 5 (2001) would apply to the historical remains in the vicinity of Marambio Station.

(171) The Committee agreed to establish an ICG to work during the 2016/17 and 2017/18 intersessional periods with the aim of developing guidance material for Parties' assessment of conservation approaches for the management of Antarctic heritage objects.

9c) Site Guidelines

(172) The United Kingdom introduced WP 32 S*ite Guidelines for the Yalour Islands, Wilhelm Archipelago*, prepared jointly with Ukraine, the United States, Argentina and IAATO. It noted that the site contained one of the southernmost recorded gentoo penguin colonies as well as a number of other confirmed breeding bird species and a considerable coverage of mosses and lichens. The site had also seen a growth in visitor numbers in recent years.

(173) The Committee thanked the United Kingdom, Ukraine, the United States, Argentina and IAATO for preparing the site guidelines and, recalling its discussions at CEP XVIII on the need for guidelines at this site, agreed to forward the guidelines to the ATCM for adoption.

(174) The United Kingdom introduced WP 33 *Site Guidelines for Point Wild, Elephant Island*, prepared jointly with Chile and IAATO. This site was where Sir Ernest Shackleton's crew was rescued by the Chilean Naval vessel Yelcho, commanded by Captain Luis Alberto Pardo, in August 1916, and the location of HSM 53. The United Kingdom and Chile noted that current levels of visitation to the island were low, but it was anticipated that the historic importance of the site would continue to maintain interest in the location.

(175) The Committee agreed to forward the site guidelines for adoption by the ATCM.

(176) Ecuador introduced WP 45 *Assessment of moss communities nearby the tracks of Aitcho Island. Monitoring report*, prepared jointly with Spain. Referring to its inclusion in the Five-year Work Plan of the CEP at CEP XVI, the paper presented the results of its monitoring and recovery work at visitor trails which were closed on Barrientos Island four years ago. It reported that recolonisation of the lower track seemed to be progressing well. Ecuador and Spain advised the Committee that they would continue monitoring the recolonisation process.

(177) Based on their observations, Ecuador and Spain suggested that the lower track remain closed, since it was still vulnerable to erosion and would be greatly affected by heavy circulation of visitors. They further recommended that the upper track be opened to visitors, since it appeared to have greater stability and resistance, and that the Aitcho Islands site guidelines be revised accordingly to manage the impact visitors might have on the upper track. Spain also remarked that opening the upper track might assist in dispersing impacts elsewhere on the island.

(178) The Committee thanked Ecuador and Spain for their monitoring efforts and supported the recommendation that the lower track should remain closed.

(179) IAATO noted that, as a precautionary measure, both tracks would remain closed to its operators. Several Members and ASOC commended IAATO for its precautionary approach. Several Members commented on the desirability of ensuring a comprehensive approach that would also apply to non-IAATO operators.

(180) Recalling its earlier acknowledgement of the importance of preventing further damage to this site, the Committee agreed that it would be preferable to take a precautionary approach and keep the upper track closed as well.

(181) The Committee encouraged Ecuador and Spain to continue the long-term monitoring to assess the recovery of vegetation on both tracks and to provide future reports on their status.

CEP advice to the ATCM on new Site Guidelines

(182) The Committee agreed to forward the following new Site Guidelines to the ATCM for adoption:

- *Yalour Islands, Wilhelm Archipelago*
- *Point Wild, Elephant Island*

(183) IAATO presented IP 105 *Report on IAATO Operator Use of Antarctic Peninsula Landing Sites and ATCM Visitor Site Guidelines, 2015-16 season*. It contained data collected from its members' Post Visit Report Forms. It noted that Antarctic tourism continued to be primarily focused on traditional commercial ship-borne tourism in the Antarctic Peninsula, which accounted for about 95% of all landed activity. It also observed that though the number of visitors had increased, the number of visited sites had remained relatively stable. The total number of visitors had not yet reached the peak of 2007-2008. The total number of voyages had also increased, which was reflective of the growth of air/cruise tourism.

(184) The United Kingdom presented IP 62 *National Antarctic Programme use of locations with Visitor Site Guidelines in 2015-2016*, prepared jointly with Argentina, Australia and the United States. This paper presented an overview of information provided by Parties on visits by their National Antarctic Programme personnel to locations with ATCM Site Guidelines for Visitors in place, during the 2015/16 season. In order to improve the scope of the analysis, Parties were encouraged to continue to record information about

visits of staff of National Programmes to sites that have Site Guidelines for visitors. It was also noted that it may be valuable for the CEP to review this information again in the future. The proponents urged COMNAP to remind its members of the desirability of using Visitor Site Guidelines for National Antarctic Programme recreational visits, noting the CEP's advice in Resolution 4 (2014).

(185) The Committee thanked the United Kingdom for its efforts to lead this work as well as other Members for their contribution to this initiative to gain a fully comprehensive view of the visited sites. IAATO noted that reported use was useful in helping it understand how the ATCM Site Guidelines were used by National Antarctic Programmes. The Committee urged Members to continue to collect this information to assist in its consideration of human impacts at frequently visited sites, and the effectiveness of Site Guidelines, and noted that it may be valuable to give further consideration to these issues in the future.

(186) Argentina presented IP 101 *Analysis of Management Measures of the Tourism Management Policy for Brown Scientific Station*, which reported on the implementation of the General Guidelines for Visitors to Brown Station during the 2015/16 season. Argentina noted that the introduction of the Guidelines had contributed to the avoidance of disturbances in the performance of the scientific and logistic tasks of the station. Argentina also highlighted the benefits of the Guidelines and suggested that all Members receiving visits to their scientific stations could consider the development of guidelines.

(187) Thanking Argentina for its paper, IAATO noted that it would report on the feedback to its members through its preseason notification and welcomed feedback from Members about visitor management at stations at any time. IAATO further thanked all Members that made it possible for IAATO member operators to visit their stations, and noted the significant value these visits provided for visitors and field staff to learn about National Antarctic Programmes.

(188) The following paper was also submitted under this agenda item:

- IP 104 rev.1 *Patterns of Tourism in the Antarctic Peninsula Region: a 20-year analysis* (United States, IAATO).

9d) Marine Spatial Protection and Management

(189) Belgium introduced WP 8 *The concept of 'outstanding values in the Antarctic marine environment'*, which presented the report of the ICG on this topic established at CEP XVIII. The ICG encouraged Members to

consider outstanding values of the marine environment under Annex V of the Environment Protocol when proposing new ASPAs or ASMAs, and when revising existing ones. The ICG also encouraged Members to make more frequent use of the Guidelines annexed to Resolution 1 (2000). The ICG further recommended Members apply the concept of outstanding values to the Antarctic marine environment, including considerations of potential threats to the environment and any other issue deemed pertinent, and to provide the Committee with a short list of existing ASPAs and ASMAs where the concept could be tested. The ICG also recommended that the Committee increase its cooperation with CCAMLR to better understand its approaches to marine protection and to avoid the duplication of effort.

(190) The Committee thanked Belgium for its work leading the ICG as well as all Members who participated in the discussion. Some Members expressed their support for the recommendations of the ICG and indicated their intention to follow the practical advice contained in it.

(191) Recollecting previous discussions on the matter, China, echoed by Japan, expressed the view that matters addressed in the paper needed further consideration by the Committee. These matters referred to the following issues: the dynamics and resilience of the marine environment compared to the terrestrial environment; that other elements of the Environment Protocol and its annexes could also be considered as options for the protection of outstanding values in the Antarctic marine environment; and that area protection mechanisms could not prevent or reverse natural processes. China also considered that full and appropriate application of the Guidelines annexed to Resolution 1 (2000) is a more relevant issue than emphasising the frequency of its use. Particular consideration should be given to the robustness of the marine environment, as well as to the existing protection provided by the Antarctic Treaty system. China further noted that discussions were needed to ensure ASPAs did not impede scientific research, associated logistic support and the transit of the sea. In addition, there should be a clear understanding of how to avoid duplicating the work of CCAMLR. China also suggested that Belgium continue to lead the intersessional discussion on the above issues, and then move ahead when further agreement can be reached.

(192) Noting that ASPAs played the dual roles of protecting the values of an area and protecting scientific investigation, ASOC stressed that it did not consider that ASPAs could impede the progress of science in an area.

(193) Referring to the ICG recommendations, the Committee noted the importance of Parties considering values in the marine environment when proposing

new ASPAs or ASMAs or when revising existing management plans. The Committee agreed that values in the marine environment could appropriately be considered when applying the provisions of Article 3 of Annex V, and other provisions of the Protocol and its annexes, including for example the provisions in Annex III intended to prevent pollution of the marine environment. The Committee further recognised the benefits of increasing its cooperation with CCAMLR and the importance of avoiding any duplication of effort.

(194) ASOC presented IP 83 *ASOC's update on Marine Protected Areas in the Southern Ocean*, which reported on discussions of the establishment of Marine Protected Areas (MPAs) in CCAMLR, whose area of responsibility overlaps with the Antarctic Treaty area. Mindful of the importance of adopting a representative network of MPAs to the conservation of the Southern Ocean, and acknowledging the early substantial progress made early on by CCAMLR, ASOC noted the past several years had been characterised by delays and the erosion by negotiation of the current MPA proposals. ASOC hoped that in the year of the 25th anniversary of the signature of the Protocol, the bold, forward thinking used by the ATCM in the past could help inspire CCAMLR members in their deliberations on MPAs, and that CCAMLR would adopt the MPA proposals for East Antarctica and the Ross Sea at CCAMLR XXXV in 2016.

(195) The Committee thanked ASOC for its paper.

(196) Argentina also expressed its gratitude to ASOC for its paper, as well as for its significant contributions to the Domain 1 MPA process, in relation to capacity building on the use of systematic conservation tools.

(197) Argentina presented IP 65 *The relevance of the MPA designation process in Domain 1 in the current Climate Change context*, prepared jointly with Chile. Argentina reported on the process for the designation of a representative system of MPAs in Domain 1, highlighting that the process itself transcends the mere objective of MPA designation. Argentina highlighted that the process integrates, exposes and analyses all known information, not only contributing to the best science available but also providing an exceptional platform for data sharing further improving the decision making process. Argentina further noted the compilation of data can be of great use in monitoring climate change, identifying knowledge gaps, promoting cooperation amongst Parties, and adding transparency to MPA related processes. Finally, Argentina warmly thanked all contributors to the project, including joint proponent Chile, and the United Kingdom, the United States, and other Members who contributed data.

(198) The Committee thanked the authors for the paper. It acknowledged that the process of collecting data for the MPA in Domain 1 would be beneficial for broader conservation management.

9e) Other Annex V Matters

(199) The United Kingdom introduced WP 5 *Revision of the 'Guide to the presentation of Working Papers containing proposals for Antarctic Specially Protected Areas, Antarctic Specially Managed Areas or Historic Sites and Monuments'*. The United Kingdom recommended that the Committee acknowledge the benefit of the provision of additional information on how protected areas fit within existing systematic environmental-geographical framework tools. It further encouraged the Committee to recommend to the ATCM revisions to 'Template A: Cover sheet for a Working Paper on an ASPA or ASMA' appended to Resolution 5 (2011) concerning the provision of data on Antarctic Conservation Biogeographic Regions and Important Bird Areas within proposed protected areas.

(200) The Committee thanked the United Kingdom for the paper, and agreed that it was beneficial for ASPA proponents to provide information on how proposed protected areas fit within systematic environmental geographic framework tools.

(201) Following minor amendments to the suggested new questions presented in WP 5, and one existing question, to reflect that the concept of representativeness was not applicable to all protected areas, the Committee agreed that the *Guide to the presentation of Working Papers containing proposals for Antarctic Specially Protected Areas, Antarctic Specially Managed Areas or Historic Sites and Monuments* should be amended to include questions relating to Antarctic Conservation Biogeographic Regions and Important Bird Areas.

CEP advice to the ATCM on revision of the Guide to the presentation of Working Papers containing proposals for Antarctic Specially Protected Areas, Antarctic Specially Managed Areas or Historic Sites and Monuments

(202) The Committee agreed to advise the ATCM that it recommended revising 'Template A: Cover sheet for a Working Paper on an ASPA or ASMA' appended to the *Guide to the presentation of Working Papers containing proposals for Antarctic Specially Protected Areas, Antarctic Specially Managed Areas or Historic Sites and Monument* adopted under Resolution 5 (2011) to include the following new and revised questions:

- (6) If relevant, have you identified the main Environmental Domain represented by the ASPA/ASMA (refer to the 'Environmental Domains Analysis for the Antarctic Continent' appended to Resolution 3 (2008))? Yes/No (If yes, the main Environmental Domain should be noted here).

- (7) If relevant, have you identified the main Antarctic Conservation Biogeographic Region represented by the ASPA/ASMA (refer to the 'Antarctic Conservation Biogeographic Regions' appended to Resolution 6 (2012))? Yes/No (If yes, the main Antarctic Conservation Biogeographic Region should be noted here).

- (8) If relevant, have you identified any Antarctic Important Bird Areas (Resolution 5 (2015)) represented by the ASPA/ASMA (refer to the 'Important Bird Areas in Antarctica 2015 Summary' appended to ATCM XXXVIII - IP 27 and the full report available at: *http://www. era.gs/resources/iba/*)? Yes/No (If yes, the Important Bird Area(s) should be noted here).

---

(203) The United Kingdom introduced WP 6 *Templates to summarise the prior assessment of a proposed Antarctic Specially Protected Area (ASPA) or Antarctic Specially Managed Area (ASMA) for subsequent consideration by the CEP*, prepared jointly with Norway. This paper followed the adoption at CEP XVIII of the Guidelines: A prior assessment process for the designation of ASPAs and ASMAs (see Appendix 3 to CEP XVIII Report). In order to help proponents of new ASPA and ASMA designations summarise their findings, consistent with the Guidelines, the United Kingdom and Norway proposed that the CEP consider recommending the non-mandatory use of the two short templates included in WP 6.

(204) The Committee thanked the United Kingdom and Norway for the paper and for preparing the suggested templates. It supported the intent of the proposal, which was to provide a practical and non-mandatory means of facilitating the provision of information consistent with the Guidelines agreed at CEP XVIII, and not to delay the designation of new areas. The Committee noted that Argentina had presented a similar proposal to an earlier meeting.

(205) Argentina welcomed the fact that the Committee had considered this proposal, which goes in line with a similar initiative made by Argentina in 2010 (CEP XIII - WP 50) that could not reach consensus at that occasion.

(206) Several Members expressed a desire to contribute to the further development of the templates. Belgium considered that the templates would be very useful

for its preparatory work to designate an ASPA in the Antarctic Conservation Biogeographic Region of Dronning Maud Land.

(207) The Committee welcomed the offer by the United Kingdom and Norway to consult with interested Members during the intersessional period, and to present an updated proposal to CEP XX. The Committee noted that the templates and Guidelines could be merged into a single document.

(208) SCAR introduced WP 23 *SCAR Code of Conduct for Activity within Terrestrial Geothermal Environments in Antarctica*, which provided guidance on practical measures to minimise impacts by scientists undertaking fieldwork in terrestrial geothermal areas. SCAR highlighted that the development of the Code of Conduct had involved consultation with policy makers, environmental managers, scientific experts, SCAR Subsidiary Groups and COMNAP. It recommended that the CEP consider the Code of Conduct and, if agreed, encourage its dissemination and use when planning and undertaking activities within terrestrial geothermal environments in Antarctica.

(209) The Committee warmly thanked SCAR for its work to finalise the Code of Conduct. The Committee recognised the broad and extensive consultation that had been undertaken in the development of the Code of Conduct, and thanked all Members that had engaged in the process, as well as COMNAP, and other contributors.

(210) The Committee recognised the value of the Code of Conduct for supporting the planning and conduct of activities in terrestrial geothermal areas to minimise risks to the high scientific and environmental values of such areas. Belgium appreciated that the specific guidance for not yet visited geothermal areas will enable the safeguarding of the exceptional value for the research of these areas.

(211) The Committee agreed to encourage the dissemination and use of the Code of Conduct, noting that the guidance presented should be applied as appropriate, according to the characteristics of each geothermal area.

(212) The Committee noted that SCAR had developed several other Codes of Conduct that were also of great utility, and that it would be beneficial to similarly encourage the dissemination and use of these materials through a Resolution of the ATCM. The Committee welcomed SCAR's willingness to bring forward its other Codes of Conduct in a Working Paper to CEP XX.

CEP advice to the ATCM on the SCAR Code of Conduct for Activity within Terrestrial Geothermal Areas in Antarctica

(213) The Committee endorsed the SCAR Code of Conduct for Activity within Terrestrial Geothermal Environments in Antarctica, and agreed to forward to the ATCM for approval a draft Resolution on encouraging the dissemination and use of the Code of Conduct.

(214) Norway introduced the second part of WP 31 *Subsidiary Group on Management Plans – Report on 2015/16 Intersessional Work*, which reported on the SGMP's intersessional work in accordance with terms of reference 4 and 5. Recalling that CEP XVIII had acknowledged the need for guidance material on establishing ASMAs and for preparing and reviewing ASMA management plans, the SGMP convener presented a draft guide for assessing whether an ASMA was the most appropriate management tool for an area in question. Its aim at this stage was to gather feedback on the draft as a basis for a new round of discussion and text development during the 2016/17 SGMP intersessional period, with a view to having this document adopted by CEP XX. Norway also reported on the SGMP's proposed work plan for the 2016/17 intersessional period.

(215) The Committee thanked the SGMP for its work relating to terms of reference 4 and 5 and Birgit Njåstad (Norway) and Dr Polly Penhale (United States), for jointly leading the SGMP's discussions on developing ASMA guidance. The Committee agreed the proposed work plan for the coming intersessional period should include work to finalise the development of guidance on whether an area should be designated as an ASMA, and to initiate the development of guidance on how to present a management plan if an ASMA designation was identified as the most appropriate management tool. The Committee urged all interested Members to participate in the SGMP's further work to develop of ASMA guidance.

(216) The Committee agreed to adopt the SGMP's proposed work plan for 2016/17:

Terms of Reference	Suggested tasks
ToR 1 to 3	Review draft management plans referred by CEP for intersessional review and provide advice to proponents (including the five postponed plans from the 2015/16 intersessional period).

ToR 4 and 5	Work with relevant Parties to ensure progress on review of management plans overdue for five-yearly review.
	Continue the work to develop guidance for preparing and reviewing ASMA management plans in according with agreed work plan for the process, *ie*, finalising work on developing guidance on determining whether an area should be designated as an ASMA, and initiating work on developing guidance for the process of preparing a management plan once there is a conclusion that the ASMA tool is the most appropriate tool to manage the area under discussion.
	Review and update SGMP work plan
Working Papers	Prepare report for CEP XX against SGMP ToR 1 to 3
	Prepare report for CEP XX against SGMP ToR 4 and 5

(217) The Committee expressed its sincere thanks to Birgit Njåstad from Norway for her excellent work as convenor of the SGMP for the previous four years. It also reflected on the substantial improvement the SGMP had made to the efficiency of the CEP's consideration of new and revised management plans, and to its broader work on area protection and management.

(218) ASOC introduced IP 80 *A Systematic Approach to Designating ASPAs and ASMAs,* which provided preliminary suggestions on how to expand the protected areas system under the Environment Protocol in order to comply with the requirements of Annex V, Articles 3 and 4. It recommended that Parties consider strategically using ASPAs and ASMAs to regulate current and potential future tourism. ASOC pointed out the clear need for designation of a systematic planning process based on best practices in conservation management.

(219) SCAR noted that spatially explicit conservation planning processes, including elements of the systematic processes outlined by ASOC, have the potential to complement and build on tools that exist under the Protocol, including the Environmental Domains Analysis (Resolution 3 (2008)) and the Antarctic Conservation Biogeographic Regions (Resolution 6 (2012)). SCAR suggested that contemporary conservation planning techniques have significant potential to inform the extension of the current terrestrial protected area network and that such techniques can be utilised in a manner that is consistent with the requirements of the Protocol. SCAR indicated that it would continue to bring new research on this topic to the Committee at future meetings.

(220) The Committee thanked ASOC for its paper, which addressed an issue identified as a high priority in its Five-year Work Plan. It also welcomed

SCAR's offer to report back to a future CEP meeting on its related research activities.

(221) SCAR presented IP 31 *Antarctic Geoconservation: a review of current systems and practices*, which reported on current threats to Antarctic geological features and detailed existing systems for their protection. The paper included a list of considerations relating to the protection of Antarctica's significant geological and paleontological localities and specimens for future Antarctic study. It further noted that a comprehensive paper on the findings would be presented in 2018.

(222) The Committee thanked SCAR for its paper, and noted that the importance of enhancing the protection of geological values, including fossils, had been highlighted at previous meetings. The Committee welcomed the useful and up-to-date review of current systems and practices for Antarctic geoconservation, and looked forward to the report on these matters under preparation by the SCAR Action Group on Geological Heritage and Geoconservation, which would be submitted to the CEP meeting in 2018.

(223) The United States presented IP 39 *Inspections of Antarctic Specially Protected Areas in the Ross Sea and Antarctic Peninsula Regions by the United States Antarctic Program*, which reported on inspections conducted at eight ASPAs in the Ross Sea and Antarctic Peninsula regions. While noting that all ASPAs visited continued to protect the special values that were the basis for the original designation, the United States noted a common need for clear and adequate markings on the ground and on ASPA maps of boundaries, landing locations, entry points, and trails. The United States anticipated that its paper would be useful in future reviews of relevant ASPA Management Plans. The United States encouraged others conducting occasional inspections to ensure that the management plans are fulfilling the goal of protecting the values and to note potential changes in the areas in light of ongoing climatic and ecological changes in Antarctica.

(224) Norway presented IP 113 *Recent findings from monitoring work in ASPA 142 Svarthamaren*, which reported on significant changes in the Antarctic petrel colony in the ASPA 142. Norway noted that it had provided the report as a response to obligations arising from the Protocol on informing Parties about any important changes to ASPAs, and also noted the relevance of this information to the discussions relating to assessment of an area's continued value as a protected area.

(225) The Committee thanked Norway for the report on changes at ASPA 142, in accordance with Article 10(b) of Annex V to the Protocol.

Item 10: Conservation of Antarctic Flora and Fauna

10a) Quarantine and Non-native Species

(226) The United Kingdom introduced WP 13 *Report of Intersessional Contact Group on Revision of the CEP Non-native Species Manual*, which reported on the results of the ICG established at CEP XVIII to revise the CEP Non-native Species Manual. The United Kingdom reminded the Committee of the Priority 1 issue 'Introduction of non-native species' identified in the CEP Five-year Work Plan, and presented the CEP Non-native Species Manual in draft.

(227) The Committee thanked the ICG convener, Dr Kevin Hughes, and all participants for the comprehensive review and revision of the manual, noting the substantial body of work involved.

(228) The Committee endorsed the revised Non-native Species Manual. It agreed to continue developing the Manual with the input of SCAR and COMNAP on scientific and practical matters respectively, and also recognised the value of working more closely with SC-CAMLR on marine non-native species issues.

(229) The Committee agreed to incorporate the Non-native Species Work Plan prepared by the ICG into its Five-year Work Plan and to undertake a review of the Manual and progress against the work plan in four to five years.

(230) The Committee requested that the Antarctic Treaty Secretariat publish the Manual on its website, as an online dynamic tool to be updated in line with new developments. In response to a query from Argentina, the Antarctic Treaty Secretariat noted that it could also upload the revised Manual as a PDF file in all official languages, and could update the PDF version to reflect future revisions agreed by the Committee.

(231) Argentina noted that it was testing a manual on preventing the introduction of non-native species specially adapted to its activities in Antarctica and that it would present the manual at CEP XX for possible incorporation into the CEP Non-native Species Manual.

(232) Australia drew the Committee's attention to BP 8 *Installation of a new waste water treatment facility at Australia's Davis Station*, which reported on its

progress to develop a new waste water treatment facility at Davis station, with the objective of mitigating environmental risks to the coastal marine environment, particularly the risk of introducing non-native species and genetic material.

CEP advice to the ATCM on the revision of the CEP Non-native Species Manual

(233) The Committee endorsed a revision to the CEP Non-native Species Manual. Noting that the current version of the Manual had been adopted under Resolution 6 (2011), the Committee agreed to forward to the ATCM for adoption a draft Resolution to revise the Manual and encourage its dissemination and use.

(234) The Republic of Korea introduced WP 52 *Non-native flies in sewage treatment plants on King George Island, South Shetland Islands*, prepared jointly with the United Kingdom, Chile and Uruguay. The paper reported on non-native flies that had colonised several station sewage treatment plants on King George Island. The Republic of Korea indicated its willingness to facilitate coordinated collaborative research and management action by all affected Parties to: identify non-native flies present in the local area; determine their local distribution and origin; and identify practical and coordinated management responses for fly eradication or control.

(235) The Committee thanked the Republic of Korea, the United Kingdom, Chile and Uruguay for the advice on the presence of the non-native flies, welcomed their ongoing efforts to address this issue, and expressed support for the recommendations contained in WP 52.

(236) It was noted that some species of non-native flies only survived in milder climates and therefore would not spread beyond heated buildings. In this case, the identified species was originally pre-adapted to cold environments and therefore has the potential to spread to the local environment. China noted that the Great Wall Station had been checked and no non-native flies were found, and expressed its willingness to cooperate with other neighbouring Parties on King George Island to find out the reason for the introduction of the non-native flies.

(237) Noting that the issue of non-native species introduction was a high priority in its Five-year Work Plan, the Committee agreed that Parties with stations on King George Island should check their waste water treatment plants for non-native invertebrate infestations and, if present, should join collaborative

research efforts to identify and determine the origin of these species. Several Members offered to share their experiences on the challenges of locating and eradicating non-native species in the context of waste water treatment plants, as well as more general issues related to waste water treatment, both on King George Island and elsewhere in Antarctica. Several Members noted that they were following the management efforts on King George Island with interest.

(238) COMNAP informed the Committee that this paper had already been brought to the attention of COMNAP members, and that it would discuss the extent of waste water treatment plant infestations, as well as best practice for prevention and response, at its upcoming annual general meeting in Goa, India, from 16-18 August 2016. COMNAP agreed to report back on its discussions at the next meeting.

(239) The United Kingdom presented IP 27 *Introduction of biofouling organisms to Antarctica on vessel hulls*, which provided a summary of recent research on the levels of hull fouling on the British Antarctic Survey's RRS *James Clark Ross* between 2007 and 2014 at Rothera Research Station. It noted that better quantification of the risk of marine non-native species introductions posed by vessel hulls to Antarctic environments may inform the development of appropriate management responses. Further hull surveys, on a wider variety of vessels, throughout Antarctica may yield valuable information on the likelihood of marine species introductions.

(240) The Committee thanked the United Kingdom for the paper and noted that the information presented would be relevant to work scheduled in its updated Five-year Work Plan to address the risk of marine non-native species introductions. Spain reminded the Committee of COMNAP's previous work on anti-fouling, presented at CEP IX (ATCM XXIX - IP 83) and the conclusions therein. Portugal also remarked that further research was required regarding non-native species in the Southern Ocean.

(241) Spain presented IP 57 *Monitoring for the presence of* Poa pratensis *at Cierva Point after the eradication*, jointly prepared with the United Kingdom and Argentina. It stated that this non-native species was introduced to Antarctica in 1954-55 and that an operation to eradicate it was undertaken in 2015. No repopulation was observed when monitored in January 2016.

(242) The Committee welcomed the co-authors' preliminary findings that, following the eradication activity at Cierva Point, the monitoring activities had not detected the presence of any non-native species.

(243) Poland presented IP 60 *Next step in eradication of non-native grass Poa annua L. from ASPA No 128 Western Shore of Admiralty Bay, King George Island, South Shetland Islands* which described the outcomes of field work done in 2015-2016 to eradicate *Poa annua* grass and research conducted during the process.

(244) The United Kingdom recognised the importance of this work and encouraged Poland to provide further updates to the Committee on its eradication efforts.

(245) IAATO presented IP 119 *IAATO Procedures Upon the Discovery of a High Mortality Event*, which described the procedures IAATO used to guide field staff on the discovery of a high mortality event, and reported on a recent instance of their application. It reported that the paper would be included in the CEP Non-native Species Manual, in response to a request through the recent ICG.

10b) Specially Protected Species

(246) No papers were submitted under this agenda item.

(247) Norway noted that the Antarctic Environments Portal contained a new article on the status of the Ross seal, that the CEP could usefully refer to this article in consideration of the status of this specially protected species in the near future, and that it would be relevant to have further articles on species at risk due to climate change available through the Portal when working to follow up on the CCWRP action/task relating to the assessment of species at risk.

10c) Other Annex II Matters

(248) SCAR presented IP 38 *Antarctica and the Southern Ocean in the Context of the Strategic Plan for Biodiversity 2011-2020*. Introducing this paper, SCAR noted that to date, Antarctica and the Southern Ocean have not been adequately represented in global biodiversity assessments and efforts for its conservation. One of the most significant of these is the Strategic Plan for Biodiversity 2011-2020 and its associated 20 Aichi Targets. An assessment of progress against these targets globally will be made in 2020. SCAR, the Principality of Monaco and partners held a meeting of biodiversity, legal and policy experts to assess Antarctic and Southern Ocean biodiversity and its conservation status in the context of the Strategic Plan. The aims of the meeting and its associated activities were to ensure that the considerable

biodiversity of the Antarctic and significant collaborative efforts to ensure its conservation are not omitted from any global assessment. The initial outcomes of the meeting are presented in IP 38. Notable findings are that for some areas of conservation, in the context of the Aichi Targets, Antarctica and the Southern Ocean are in a leading position globally. The work on non-native species by the CEP Members, Parties and others, such as COMNAP, IAATO and ASOC, is a clear example of collaboration for conservation success. SCAR informed the Committee that the full outcomes of the Monaco Assessment meeting will be published in 2016 and reported to CEP XX.

(249) The Committee thanked SCAR and Monaco for this important benchmarking exercise, looked forward to receiving the full report in due course, and noted the importance of ensuring that Antarctica is included in planned global biodiversity assessments.

(250) IAATO presented IP 107 *How to be a Responsible Antarctic Visitor: IAATO's New Animated Briefings*, which introduced short animated briefings to supplement IAATO's existing Mandatory Briefing. IAATO produced the films in English with subtitles in nine other languages, and noted that the videos were designed to reinforce key messages about being a responsible visitor in a concise way easily understandable by a wide audience. IAATO also presented one of the videos to the Committee.

(251) IAATO presented IP 121 *IAATO Wildlife Watching Guidelines for Emperor Penguins and Leopard Seals*, which reported that IAATO Members have adopted two new sets of wildlife watching guidelines, one for emperor penguins and one for leopard seals, which augment existing guidelines.

(252) The Committee thanked IAATO for its useful contribution and for regularly updating the CEP on its activities.

Item 11: Environmental Monitoring and Reporting

(253) New Zealand introduced WP 16 *A methodology to assess the sensitivity of sites used by visitors: Prioritising future management attention*, prepared jointly with Australia, Norway and the United States. The paper provided an update on work towards a method for assessing the sensitivity of sites to tourist visitation, in accordance with Recommendation 3 from the 2012 CEP Tourism Study which recommended that the CEP should develop an approach that would support the more systematic assessment of the sensitive features present at visitor sites. As a practical first step, the paper sought to establish a simple method that considered the presence of values, and for

expert judgement to be applied to assess the potential for normal tourism activity to have an impact on these values. The method was not intended to be used to prescribe specific management arrangements for any particular site, but rather as a systematic approach to drawing on available information and expert judgment to assess the sensitivity of sites to tourist visitation, with a view to assisting the CEP in prioritising management attention. The authors invited Members to provide feedback on the approach outlined in the paper to inform further work in the 2016/17 intersessional period.

(254) The Committee welcomed the report on progress made by New Zealand, Norway, Australia and the United States to develop a method of assessing site sensitivity in accordance with Recommendation 3 from the 2012 CEP Tourism Study.

(255) Members raised several points for consideration in the further development of the methodology, including: the concepts of relative and inherent site sensitivity; the size of the site; likely use of the site; distribution of values on the site; temporal factors; and the importance of evaluating the methodology in the field.

(256) ASOC thanked New Zealand, Norway, Australia and the United States for starting the work, and remarked that is would be useful to develop a rapid assessment procedure for consistent assessment across sites.

(257) The Committee encouraged Members and Observers to provide feedback on the approach outlined in this paper and noted that a number of Members, IAATO and ASOC expressed an interest in contributing to intersessional work ahead of CEP XX. IAATO also noted that its field staff have expert knowledge of the most visited sites and could assist with the work if required.

(258) Portugal presented IP 8 *Assessment of trace element contamination within the Antarctic Treaty Area* jointly with Chile, Germany, the Russian Federation and the United Kingdom. The paper outlined the assessment of trace elements in soil and moss samples collected from Antarctica. It also noted the importance of sharing monitoring data from the area in order to contribute to the future monitoring research and policy development.

(259) Chile presented IP 96 *Environmental Monitoring in Fildes Bay. Coastal Environment Observation Program of Chile (P.O.A.L)*, which alerted the Committee to the programme that included data on lead, arsenic and hydrocarbon concentration at sediments in Fildes Bay. It also noted that more information was available (in Spanish) at www.directemar.cl, in the link 'Aquatic Environment/POAL Data'.

(260) SCAR presented IP 32 *Report on the 2015-2016 activities of the Southern Ocean Observing System (SOOS)*, which recounted that in 2015 SOOS finalised its Five-year Implementation Plan, which following an external review facilitated by SCAR, would be made available to the community. Other key milestones for SOOS included: significant progress in the development of regional working groups for implementing the observing system in the field; the submission of a publication on ecosystem essential ocean variables; and progress in a number of capability working groups, such as Enhancing Observations under Ice. In addition, SOOS, together with SCAR and the WCRP Climate and Cryosphere project were in the final stages of a report on Southern Ocean Satellite Requirements. SCAR also thanked Australia for supporting the secretariat of SOOS in Hobart.

Item 12: Inspection Reports

(261) China introduced WP 22 *Inspection undertaken by the People's Republic of China in accordance with Article VII of the Antarctic Treaty and Article XIV of the Protocol on Environmental Protection* and referred to IP 48 *Report of the Antarctic Treaty Inspections undertaken by the People's Republic of China in accordance with Article VII of the Antarctic Treaty and Article 14 of the Environment Protocol: April 2016*. It reported on the Antarctic Treaty inspections undertaken between 25 and 28 December 2015, which involved six research stations of the Russian Federation, Chile, Uruguay and the Republic of Korea. China noted that the stations generally complied with the Environment Protocol, and highlighted the inspected stations' appropriate environmental management processes, including the training on the Environment Protocol given to new arrivals. China also noted its specific recommendations relevant to environmental management and good practice, and warmly thanked all Parties for their cooperation and hospitality during the inspections.

(262) Chile and Uruguay thanked China for the inspections of their stations, and reported on specific actions taken or planned in the future in relation to the recommendations.

(263) Noting that the South Shetland Islands are used by the air-cruise tourism sector and that some of the stations inspected allow visitors, IAATO thanked China for its inspection report and highlighted that tourist activities were not reported as impacting on station activities or the surrounding environment.

(264) The Committee congratulated China on the conduct of the inspections and thanked China for the comprehensive inspection reports. The Committee welcomed the general findings that the inspected stations were in compliance with the Environment Protocol.

(265) Argentina introduced WP 44 *Report of the joint inspection program undertaken by Argentina and Chile under Article VII of the Antarctic Treaty and Article 14 of the Environment Protocol*, and referred to IP 72 *Report of the Joint Inspections' Program undertaken by Argentina and Chile under Article VII of the Antarctic Treaty and Article 14 of the Environment Protocol*, jointly prepared with Chile. It reported on the Antarctic Treaty inspections undertaken between 16 and 18 February 2016, which involved five Antarctic stations and one non-governmental refuge in the South Shetland Islands region. It reported that in general, the level of compliance of the Environment Protocol's requirements of the stations inspected was satisfactory.

(266) In relation to the methodology of inspection, Argentina noted that, in the majority of cases, the Checklist A annexed to Resolution 3 (2010) had been previously completed by the station staff, and that this increased the speed and efficiency of inspections. While recognising the value of prior inspection reports, Argentina noted some gaps of information in the EIES, and some inconsistencies across different ATS databases, and recommended that Members keep the databases up to date. Argentina also commended COMNAP for its "Antarctic Facilities Catalogue" hoping that when concluded, it can become a useful source of information for future inspections. In addition, Argentina noted that the issues identified in previous inspections had been addressed. However, the inspections had identified opportunities for improvement in waste management and non-native species management in relation to hydroponics. Argentina thanked all those Parties whose stations were inspected for their cooperation.

(267) Chile highlighted the utility of inspections as a tool for continual improvement, both for the personnel at the stations being inspected and for the observers who carry out the inspections.

(268) China welcomed the recommendations in the report, noting that it had responded to Argentina and Chile before the inspection report was submitted to the meeting, and also noting the follow-up progress carried out in response to the recommendations.

(269) The Czech Republic noted that it was aware of problems connected to the ECO Nelson Refuge, and that it took seriously the recommendations

suggested in Argentina and Chile's report. The Czech Republic also highlighted that its Competent Authority had not approved any permits or activity in relation to the ECO Nelson Refuge in the 2015/16 season, and that its National Antarctic Programme had no relationship with the ECO Nelson Refuge.

(270) The Committee congratulated Argentina and Chile for carrying out the inspections. It welcomed the general findings that the stations operated by National Antarctic Programmes were observed to be in satisfactory compliance with the requirements of the Environment Protocol. The Committee also welcomed the inspections team's findings that there was a growing use of renewable energies, and that all staff had received training in relation to the Environment Protocol.

(271) Noting Argentina's comments regarding the absence of some information in the EIES, the Committee reiterated its view that all Members should fully comply with their information exchange requirements. COMNAP noted that its Station Infrastructure Project would compile a range of information which may be useful for the purpose of inspections.

(272) In response to the view expressed by France that the use of the inspection checklist should be optional when conducting inspections, Argentina clarified that it was aware that the checklist was not mandatory, but that it had proven very useful in preparing for and undertaking the inspections.

(273) ASOC thanked China, and Argentina and Chile, for their inspections, and stated that expanding the range of countries conducting inspections improved the Protocol's implementation. ASOC noted that the findings of these recent inspection included "old" issues where the need for further improvement had already been reported in the past, such as waste management issues, but also advances such as the increased use of renewable energy. ASOC stated that the reported increase in fly-cruise tourism had potential environmental implications regionally.

(274) The Republic of Korea presented IP 102 *Rethinking Antarctic Treaty inspections; patterns, uses and scopes for improvements*. It highlighted that inspections were organised and conducted by leading Parties that possessed operational capabilities, and more often on stations that were easily accessed. It further noted that the undertaking of inspections and follow-ups do not necessarily follow a well-defined path of steps. It proposed the development of a new, more cooperative inspection model where inspections were conducted in a more collective manner, different Parties were permitted to

contribute in unique ways, and the outcomes of inspections were delivered and acted upon.

(275) The Committee welcomed the points raised in the paper regarding the value of improving the conduct and efficiency of inspection activities, as well as enhancing participation and international cooperation. It noted the advice from the Netherlands that the ATCM was also planning to establish an ICG to further discuss how inspections could be more effective, and encouraged interested Members to contribute to the discussions through their national processes.

Item 13: General Matters

(276) Portugal presented IP 7 *POLAR WEEKS. An Education and Outreach activity to promote Antarctic science and the Antarctic Treaty System,* prepared jointly with Brazil, Bulgaria, France, and the United Kingdom. It provided a summary of POLAR WEEKS, an education and outreach activity, and highlighted the value of education and outreach to all participants in the activity. Acknowledging the co-authors of the paper, Portugal also recognised the excellent work of co-partner organisations, the Association of Polar Early Career Scientists (APECS), Polar Educators International, COMNAP and CCAMLR.

(277) The Committee commended Portugal, Bulgaria, France, Brazil and the United Kingdom for the paper, and noted the benefits of the Polar Weeks initiative for promoting awareness of Antarctic science.

(278) South Africa presented IP 47 *Upgrade of the SANAE IV Base Systems*, which highlighted its plans to implement a comprehensive upgrade of some of the base systems at SANAE IV station.

(279) The following paper was also submitted under this agenda item:

- BP 8 *Installation of a new waste water treatment facility at Australia's Davis Station (*Australia).

Item 14: Election Officers

(280) The Committee elected Ms Patricia Ortúzar from Argentina as Vice-chair for a two-year term and congratulated her on her appointment to the role. Patricia Ortúzar was also appointed convener of the Subsidiary Group on Management Plans (SGMP).

(281) The Committee warmly thanked Ms Birgit Njåstad from Norway for her tireless efforts, productivity and leadership as CEP Vice-chair and as SGMP convener.

(282) The Committee elected Mr Ewan McIvor from Australia as Chair for a second two-year term and congratulated him on his reappointment to the role.

Item 15: Preparation for the Next Meeting

(283) The Committee adopted the Preliminary Agenda for CEP XX (Appendix 3).

(284) Noting some Members' concerns over the potential duplication of discussions in the ATCM and CEP, the Committee reaffirmed the value of strengthening cooperation with the ATCM and of taking practical steps to give effect to that cooperation.

Item 16: Adoption of the Report

(285) The CEP Chair emphasised that the process of adopting the report was not an opportunity to reopen discussions already concluded under earlier agenda items.

(286) Belarus expressed its regret that it had been unable to present IP 3 *Application of air dispersion modelling for impact assessment of construction/operation activities in Antarctica* during the Committee's consideration of Agenda Item 8b, because its sole delegate to the CEP XIX had been participating in concurrent ATCM discussions at that time. The Chair noted that the Committee had considered IP 3 to be taken as read.

(287) The CEP Chair acknowledged the practical challenges faced by small delegations and encouraged Members and Observers to consult with the Chair to ensure that, at future meetings, a suitable opportunity could be made available to present their papers to the Committee.

(288) The Committee adopted its Report.

Item 17: Closing of the Meeting

(289) The Chair closed the Meeting on Friday, 27 May 2016.

Appendix 1

CEP Five-Year Work Plan

Issue / Environmental Pressure: Introduction of non-native species	
Priority: 1	
Actions:	
1. Continue developing practical guidelines & resources for all Antarctic operators. 2. Implement related actions identified in the Climate Change Response Work Programme. 3. Consider the spatially explicit, activity-differentiated risk assessments to mitigate the risks posed by terrestrial non-native species. 4. Develop a surveillance strategy for areas at high risk of non-native species establishment. 5. Give additional attention to the risks posed by intra-Antarctic transfer of propagules.	
Intersessional period 2016/17	• Revised Manual posted on ATS website, with updates by the Secretariat, as necessary, when new material becomes available. • Initiate work to assess risks of relocation of native Antarctic species and existing non-native species between and within Antarctic biogeographic regions and identify relevant management actions.
CEP XX 2017	• Discuss the intersessional work concerning the relocation of species between biogeographic regions for inclusion in the Non-native Species Manual. • Welcome contribution of Argentina's national NNS Manual.
Intersessional period 2017/18	• Initiate work to develop a non-native species response strategy, including appropriate responses to diseases of wildlife. • To help the Committee in assessing the effectiveness of the Manual, request a report from COMNAP on the implementation of quarantine and biosecurity measures by its members.
CEP XXI 2018	• Discuss the intersessional work concerning the development of a response strategy for inclusion in the Non-native Species Manual, and the implementation of quarantine and biosecurity measures by COMNAP members. Review IMO report on biofouling guidelines.
Intersessional period 2018/19	• Ask SCAR to compile a list of available biodiversity information sources and databases to help Parties establish which native species are present at Antarctic sites and thereby assist with identifying the scale and scope of current and future introductions. • Develop generally applicable monitoring guidelines. More detailed or site-specific monitoring may be required for particular locations. • Request a report from Parties and Observers on the application of biosecurity guidelines by their members.
CEP XXII 2019	• Discuss the intersessional work concerning the development of monitoring guidelines for inclusion in the NNS Manual. Consider the reports from Parties and Observers on the application of biosecurity guidelines by their members.
Intersessional period 2019/20	• Initiate work to assess the risk of marine non-native species introductions.
CEP XXIII 2020	• Discuss the intersessional work concerning the risks of marine non-native species.

Intersessional period 2020/2021	• Develop specific guidelines to reduce non-native species release with wastewater discharge. • Review the progress and contents of the CEP Non-native Species Manual.
CEP XXIV 2021	

Issue / Environmental Pressure: Tourism and NGO activities	
Priority: 1	
Actions: 1. Provide advice to ATCM as requested. 2. Advance recommendations from ship-borne tourism ATME.	
Intersessional period 2016/17	• Further develop methodology for site sensitivity assessment (recommendation 3 of the tourism study).
CEP XX 2017	
Intersessional period 2017/18	
CEP XXI 2018	
Intersessional period 2018/19	
CEP XXII 2019	
Intersessional period 2019/20	
CEP XXIII 2020	
Intersessional period 2020/2021	
CEP XXIV 2021	

Issue / Environmental Pressure: Climate Change Implications for the Environment	
Priority: 1	
Actions: 1. Consider implications of climate change for management of Antarctic environment. 2. Advance recommendations from climate change ATME. 3. Implement the Climate Change response work programme.	
Intersessional period 2016/17	• SCAR and WMO to map research activities against CCRWP. • Chair to consult with ICED and SOOS on contributions to CCRWP. • Actions associated with recommendations arising from joint CEP/SC-CAMLR workshop, as appropriate. • Implement CCRWP in consultation with experts. • Intersessional discussion on mechanism for managing CCRWP.
CEP XX 2017	• Standing agenda item. • SCAR provides update to ACCE report, with input as appropriate from WMO and ICED, SOOS. • Consider advice from SCAR and WMO on how research priorities and programs map to CCRWP. • Establish a mechanism for managing CCRWP.
Intersessional period 2017/18	• Implement CCRWP in consultation with experts.
CEP XXI 2018	• Standing agenda item. • SCAR provides update to ACCE report, with input as appropriate from WMO and ICED, SOOS.
Intersessional period 2018/19	• Implement CCRWP in consultation with experts.

CEP XXII 2019	• Standing agenda item. • SCAR provides update to ACCE report, with input as appropriate from WMO and ICED, SOOS.
Intersessional period 2019/20	• Implement CCRWP in consultation with experts.
CEP XXIII 2020	• Standing agenda item. • SCAR provides update to ACCE report, with input as appropriate from WMO and ICED, SOOS.
Intersessional period 2020/2021	• Implement CCRWP in consultation with experts.
CEP XXIV 2021	

Issue / Environmental Pressure: Processing new and revised protected / managed area management plans

Priority: 1

Actions:
1. Refine the process for reviewing new and revised management plans.
2. Update existing guidelines.
3. Advance recommendations from climate change ATME.
4. Develop guidelines to ASMAs preparation.

Intersessional period 2016/17	• SGMP conducts work as per agreed work plan. • Continue the work on developing guidelines to ASMAs preparation. • Norway and interested Members prepare paper on guidance for delisting ASPAs. • Norway and UK, and interested Members, to develop templates for prior assessment tools for proposed ASPAs or ASMAs.
CEP XX 2017	• Consider paper by Norway and interested Members. • Consider paper by Norway, UK and interested Members. • Consider SGMP report.
Intersessional period 2017/18	
CEP XXI 2018	
Intersessional period 2018/19	
CEP XXII 2019	
Intersessional period 2019/20	
CEP XXIII 2020	
Intersessional period 2020/2021	
CEP XXIV 2021	

Issue / Environmental Pressure: Operation of the CEP and Strategic Planning

Priority: 1

Actions:
1. Keep the 5 year plan up to date based on changing circumstances and ATCM requirements.
2. Identify opportunities for improving the effectiveness of the CEP.
3. Consider long-term objectives for Antarctica (50-100 years time).
4. Consider opportunities for enhancing the working relationship between the CEP and the ATCM.

Intersessional period 2016/17	
CEP XX 2017	
Intersessional period 2017/18	
CEP XXI 2018	
Intersessional period 2018/19	

CEP XXII 2019	
Intersessional period 2019/20	
CEP XXIII 2020	
Intersessional period 2020/2021	
CEP XXIV 2021	

Issue / Environmental Pressure: Repair or Remediation of Environmental Damage	
Priority: 2	
Actions:	
1. Respond to further request from the ATCM related to repair and remediation, as appropriate. 2. Monitor progress on the establishment of Antarctic-wide inventory of sites of past activity. 3. Consider guidelines for repair and remediation. 4. Members develop practical guidelines and supporting resources for inclusion in the Clean-up Manual. 5. Continue developing bioremediation and repair practices for inclusion in the Clean-up Manual.	
Intersessional period 2016/17	
CEP XX 2017	• Consider review of the Clean-up Manual.
Intersessional period 2017/18	
CEP XXI 2018	
Intersessional period 2018/19	
CEP XXII 2019	
Intersessional period 2019/20	
CEP XXIII 2020	
Intersessional period 2020/2021	
CEP XXIV 2021	

Issue / Environmental Pressure: Human footprint / wilderness management	
Priority: 2	
Actions:	
1. Develop methods for improved protection of wilderness under Annexes I and V.	
Intersessional period 2016/17	
CEP XX 2017	
Intersessional period 2017/18	
CEP XXI 2018	
Intersessional period 2018/19	
CEP XXII 2019	
Intersessional period 2019/20	
CEP XXIII 2020	
Intersessional period 2020/2021	
CEP XXIV 2021	

Issue / Environmental Pressure: Monitoring and state of the environment reporting	
Priority: 2	
Actions:	
1. Identify key environmental indicators and tools. 2. Establish a process for reporting to the ATCM. 3. SCAR to support information to COMNAP and CEP.	
Intersessional period 2016/17	• Actions associated with recommendations arising from joint CEP/SC-CAMLR workshop, as appropriate.
CEP XX 2017	• Report from SCAR on the scientific understanding use of unmanned aerial vehicles (UAVs) on wildlife. • Establish an ICG to develop UAV guidance. • Actions associated with recommendations arising from joint CEP/SC-CAMLR workshop, as appropriate.
Intersessional period 2017/18	
CEP XXI 2018	
Intersessional period 2018/19	
CEP XXII 2019	
Intersessional period 2019/20	
CEP XXIII 2020	
Intersessional period 2020/21	
CEP XXIV 2021	• Consider monitoring report by UK on ASPA 107.

Issue / Environmental Pressure: Marine spatial protection and management	
Priority: 2	
Actions:	
1. Cooperation between the CEP and SC-CAMLR on common interest issues. 2. Cooperate with CCAMLR on Southern Ocean bioregionalisation and other common interests and agreed principles. 3. Identify and apply processes for spatial marine protection. 4. Advance recommendations from climate change ATME.	
Intersessional period 2016/17	
CEP XX 2017	
Intersessional period 2017/18	
CEP XXI 2018	
Intersessional period 2018/19	
CEP XXII 2019	
Intersessional period 2019/20	
CEP XXIII 2020	
Intersessional period 2020/2021	
CEP XXIV 2021	

Issue / Environmental Pressure: Site specific guidelines for tourist-visited sites	
Priority: 2	
Actions:	
1. Periodically review the list of sites subject to site guidelines and consider whether development of guidelines should be needed for additional sites. 2. Provide advice to ATCM as required. 3. Review the format of the site guidelines.	
Intersessional period 2016/17	
CEP XX 2017	• Standing agenda item; Parties to report on their reviews of site guidelines.
Intersessional period 2017/18	
CEP XXI 2018	• Standing agenda item; Parties to report on their reviews of site guidelines.
Intersessional period 2018/19	
CEP XXII 2019	• Standing agenda item; Parties to report on their reviews of site guidelines.
Intersessional period 2019/20	
CEP XXIII 2020	• Standing agenda item; Parties to report on their reviews of site guidelines.
Intersessional period 2020/2021	
CEP XXIV 2021	

Issue / Environmental Pressure: Overview of the protected areas system	
Priority: 2	
Actions:	
1. Apply the Environmental Domains Analysis (EDA) and Antarctic Conservation Biogeographic Regions (ACBR) to enhance the protected areas system. 2. Advance recommendations from climate change ATME. 3. Maintain and develop Protected Area database. 4. Assess the extent to which Antarctic IBAs are or should be represented within the series of ASPAs.	
Intersessional period 2016/17	• Implement related actions from the CCRWP. • Norway and UK, and interested Members, to develop templates for prior assessment tools for proposed ASPAs or ASMAs.
CEP XX 2017	• Consider paper by Norway, UK and interested Members. • Parties to provide update reports on research and management efforts to apply biogeographic tools. • Parties to provide updates on research undertaken or planned to identify climate change vulnerable biogeographic regions.
Intersessional period 2017/18	
CEP XXI 2018	• Plan for a joint SCAR/CEP workshop on Antarctic biogeography, including to: identify practical management applications of biogeographic tools and future research needs. • Provide a status report to the ATCM on the status of the Antarctic Protected Areas network.
Intersessional period 2018/19	• Joint SCAR/CEP workshop on Antarctic biogeography.
CEP XXII 2019	• Consider report from joint SCAR/CEP workshop on Antarctic biogeography.
Intersessional period 2019/20	
CEP XXIII 2020	

Intersessional period 2020/2021	
CEP XXIV 2021	

Issue / Environmental Pressure: Outreach and education

Priority: 2

Actions:
1. Review current examples and identify opportunities for greater education and outreach.
2. Encourage Members to exchange information regarding their experiences in this area.
3. Establish a strategy and guidelines for exchanging information between Members on Education and Outreach for long term perspective.

Intersessional period 2016/17	• Disseminate the 25ᵗʰ anniversary publication agreed at CEP XIX/ATCM XXXIX. • Release publication at events on 4 October 2016.
CEP XX 2017	
Intersessional period 2017/18	
CEP XXI 2018	
Intersessional period 2018/19	
CEP XXII 2019	
Intersessional period 2019/20	
CEP XXIII 2020	
Intersessional period 2020/2021	
CEP XXIV 2021	

Issue / Environmental Pressure: Implementing and Improving the EIA provisions of Annex I

Priority: 2

Actions:
1. Refine the process for considering CEEs and advising the ATCM accordingly.
2. Develop guidelines for assessing cumulative impacts.
3. Review EIA guidelines and consider wider policy and other issues.
4. Consider application of strategic environmental assessment in Antarctica.
5. Advance recommendations from climate change ATME.

Intersessional period 2016/17	• Establish ICG to review draft CEEs as required. • UK and interested Members develop paper on taking forward broader policy and other EIA related issues.
CEP XX 2017	• Consideration of ICG reports on draft CEE, as required. • Dedicated discussion on policy and other related matters on EIA.
Intersessional period 2017/18	• Establish ICG to review draft CEEs as required.
CEP XXI 2018	• Consideration of ICG reports on draft CEE, as required.
Intersessional period 2018/19	
CEP XXII 2019	
Intersessional period 2019/20	
CEP XXIII 2020	
Intersessional period 2020/2021	
CEP XXIV 2021	

Issue / Environmental Pressure: Designation and management of Historic Sites and Monuments	
Priority: 2	
Actions:	
1. Maintain the list and consider new proposals as they arise. 2. Consider strategic issues as necessary, including issues relating to designation of HSM versus clean-up provisions of the Protocol. 3. Review the presentation of the HSM list with the aim to improve information availability.	
Intersessional period 2016/17	• Secretariat update list of HSMs. • ICG on development of guidance relating to designation of HSM.
CEP XX 2017	• Standing item. • Consider ICG report .
Intersessional period 2017/18	• ICG on development of guidance relating to designation of HSM.
CEP XXI 2018	• Consider ICG report.
Intersessional period 2018/19	
CEP XXII 2019	
Intersessional period 2019/20	
CEP XXIII 2020	
Intersessional period 2020/2021	
CEP XXIV 2021	

Issue / Environmental Pressure: Biodiversity knowledge	
Priority: 3	
Actions:	
1. Maintain awareness of threats to existing biodiversity. 2. Advance recommendations from climate change ATME. 3. CEP to consider further scientific advice on wildlife disturbance.	
Intersessional period 2016/17	• Actions associated with recommendations arising from joint CEP/SC-CAMLR workshop, as appropriate.
CEP XX 2017	• Discussion of SCAR update on underwater noise.
Intersessional period 2017/18	
CEP XXI 2018	
Intersessional period 2018/19	
CEP XXII 2019	
Intersessional period 2019/20	
CEP XXIII 2020	
Intersessional period 2020/2021	
CEP XXIV 2021	

Issue / Environmental Pressure: Exchange of Information	
Priority: 3	
Actions:	
1. Assign to the Secretariat.	
2. Monitor and facilitate easy use of the EIES.	
3. Review environmental reporting requirements.	
Intersessional period 2016/17	
CEP XX 2017	• Secretariat Report.
Intersessional period 2017/18	
CEP XXI 2018	
Intersessional period 2018/19	
CEP XXII 2019	
Intersessional period 2019/20	
CEP XXIII 2020	
Intersessional period 2020/2021	
CEP XXIV 2021	

Issue / Environmental Pressure: Protection of outstanding geological values	
Priority: 3	
Actions:	
1. Consider further mechanisms for protection of outstanding geological values.	
Intersessional period 2016/17	
CEP XX 2017	
Intersessional period 2017/18	
CEP XXI 2018	• Consider advice from SCAR.
Intersessional period 2018/19	
CEP XXII 2019	
Intersessional period 2019/20	
CEP XXIII 2020	
Intersessional period 2020/2021	
CEP XXIV 2021	

Appendix 2

Climate Change Response Work Programme

CCRWP Vision: Taking into account the conclusions and recommendations from the ATME on Climate Change in 2010, the CCRWP provides a mechanism for identifying and revising goals and specific actions by the CEP to support efforts within the Antarctic Treaty System to prepare for, and build resilience to, the environmental impacts of a changing climate and the associated implications for the governance and management of Antarctica.

Climate related Issue	Gaps/needs	Response area	Action/Task	Priority	Who	IP	CEP 2017	IP	CEP 2018	IP	CEP 2019	IP	CEP 2020	IP	CEP 2021
1) Enhanced potential for non-native species (NNS) introduction/establishment	• Framework for surveillance for non-native species establishments in marine, terrestrial and freshwater environment • Response strategy for suspected NNS introductions • Assessment of whether existing regimes for preventing NNS introductions and transfer are sufficient. Analyze management tools applied in other areas.	Management	a. Continue to develop the NNS manual consistent with Resolution 6 (2011), ensuring climate change impacts are included, specifically in the • Development of surveillance approaches (p. 21) • Response strategy (p. 22) • EIA guidelines to include NNS (p. 18)	1.3	CEP / Parties	Parties to undertake preparatory work relevant to discussions on the development of NNS surveillance and response strategy. Parties to consider implementation of the guidelines contained in the revised NNS manual in planning and conducting their activities	Initiate ISW* to develop a NNS surveillance and response strategy, including identification of highest risk habitats / bioregions. Consider education initiatives around the risk from non-natives	ISW	Receive report of ISW and take action accordingly							Ensure climate change implications are sufficiently considered and appropriately incorporated in specific guidelines to reduce non-native species release with wastewater discharge. Ensure climate change implications are sufficiently considered and appropriately incorporated in review of NNS manual
			b. Review of IMO biofouling guidelines to check adequacy for Southern Ocean and vessels moving from region to region	2.6	Interested Parties, Experts and Observers				Ensure climate change implications are sufficiently considered and appropriately incorporated in discussions relating to biofouling in accordance with 5-year work plan.						
	• Improved understanding of risks associated with relocation of native terrestrial species • Assessment and mapping of Antarctic habitats at risk of invasion	Management / Research	c. Undertake a risk assessment: identification of native species at risk of relocation, and pathways for intra-continental transfer including developing regional maps / descriptions of habitats at risk of invasion	3.2	CEP, interested Parties, Experts and Observers	ISW	Receive report of ISW and take action accordingly								
	• Assessment of risks of introducing non-native marine species • Techniques for eradication and control		d. Undertake a risk assessment: identification of marine habitats at risk of invasion and pathways for introduction	1.8	CEP, interested Parties and Observers				Ensure climate change implications are sufficiently considered and appropriately incorporated in non-native species response strategy.	Parties to undertake preparatory work ahead on assessing the risks of marine NNS introductions.	Initiate ISW to assess risk of marine NNS introductions.	ISW	Receive report of ISW and take action accordingly	ISW	
	• Ongoing surveillance programme to identify status of NNS in light of climate change	Monitoring	e. Progress actions identified under "Response" in NNS manual (p. 22-23)	1.6	NAPs, SCAR	Parties to identify existing research projects relevant to surveillance and bring information to CEP 2017									
			f. Implement marine and terrestrial monitoring in accordance with established surveillance framework (pt. a) (once developed)	1.9	NAPs, SCAR	Consideration of information provided by Parties (see 1a above).					Members to report on measures taken to implement surveillance and response actions		Members to report on measures taken to implement surveillance and response actions		

175

Climate related Issue	Gaps/needs	Response areas	Action/Task	Priority	Who	IP	CEP 2017	IP	CEP 2018	IP	CEP 2019	IP	CEP 2020	IP	CEP 2021
2) Change to the terrestrial (incl. aquatic) biotic and abiotic environment due to climate change	• Understanding how terrestrial and freshwater biota will respond to a changing climate and the impacts of these changes • Understanding as to how the abiotic terrestrial environment will change and the impacts of these changes	Research	a. Support and undertake research to improve understanding of current and future climate change and to inform response	1.9	NAPs; SCAR	SCAR to assimilate current major research initiatives relevant to terrestrial and freshwater environmental change.	Ongoing. Update reports to be provided, including through the Portal.		Ongoing. Update reports to be provided, including through the Portal.		Ongoing. Update reports to be provided, including through the Portal.		Ongoing. Update reports to be provided, including through the Portal.		
			b. Support and undertake long term monitoring of change, including collaborative efforts (e.g. ANTOS).	1.8	NAPs; SCAR	SCAR to develop advisory to CEP on relevance of ANTOS findings / outcomes to CEP's management interests.	Consider questions relating to access of data for the CEP		Consider obvious gaps in monitoring network and encourage initiation where such gaps exist						
			c. Continue to develop biogeographic tools (EDA and ACBR) to provide a sound basis for informing Antarctic area protection and management at regional and continental scales in light of climate change, including identifying the need to set aside reference areas for future research and identifying areas resilient to climate change	2.1	Initiated by interested Parties and CEP		Parties to provide update reports on research and management efforts to apply biogeographic tools.	Joint SCAR/CEP workshop on Antarctic biogeography	Plan for a joint SCAR/CEP workshop on Antarctic biogeography, including to identify practical management applications of biogeographic tools and future research needs		Consider report from joint SCAR/CEP workshop on Antarctic biogeography				
			d. Identify and prioritize Antarctic biogeographic regions most vulnerable to climate change	1.6	Initiated by interested Parties and CEP		Parties to provide updates on research undertaken or planned to identify climate change vulnerable biogeographic regions.								
		Manage-ment	e. Review and review where necessary existing management tools to consider if they afford the best practical adaptation measure to areas at risk from climate change	1.9	CEP								Parties to provide information on experiences of implementing climate considerations in the EIA process.		
			f. Holistic review of existing Protected Areas network and the process for designation of such areas to ensure they take into account climate change impacts and consider how we might respond.	1.8	CEP	SGMP ASMA work. Initiate work on developing guidelines/ criteria for delisting of protected areas due to ix. climate change	SGMP work on ASMA guidelines (cf. SGMP work plan) considers and incorporates appropriately the implication of climate change	WS**	Plan for intersessional workshop on a review of the protected areas system		Review the outcomes to the Protected Areas Workshop.				
			g. Initiate action with the aim to protect representative areas of each biogeographic region and areas likely to provide refuges to species and ecosystems at risk	2.3	CEP				Provide a status report to the ATCM on the status of the Antarctic Protected Areas network						

Climate related issue	Gaps/needs	Response area	Action/Task	Priority	Who	IP	CEP 2017	IP	CEP 2018	IP	CEP 2019	IP	CEP 2020	IP	CEP 2021
3) Change to marine near-shore abiotic and biotic environment (excluding OA)***	• Understanding and have the ability to predict near-shore marine changes and impacts of the change • Have a broader understanding of what monitoring data will be required to assess climate driven changes to the marine environment	Research	a. Encourage research by national programmes and SCAR and seek regular knowledge updates from SCAR on climate impacts on marine biota	2.0	NAPs, SCAR	SCAR to assimilate current research initiatives relevant to marine environmental change.	Ongoing. Update reports to be provided, incl. through the Portal.		Ongoing. Update reports to be provided, incl. through the Portal.		Ongoing. Update reports to be provided, incl. through the Portal.		Ongoing. Update reports to be provided, incl. through the Portal.		
			b. Support and undertake collaborative long term monitoring of change (eg. SOOS, ANTOS) and seek regular state of knowledge reports from such programmes	2.0	NAPs, SCAR	SCAR to assimilate overview of how existing research programmes (such as SOOS and ANTOS) can contribute to CEP's management interests. CEP Chair to write to Steering Committees of relevant international research programmes (e.g. ICED) to request regular update reports.	Ongoing. Update reports to be provided, incl. through the Portal.		Ongoing. Update reports to be provided, incl. through the Portal.		Ongoing. Update reports to be provided, incl. through the Portal.		Ongoing. Update reports to be provided, incl. through the Portal.		
		Management	c. Review and revise where necessary existing management tools to consider if they afford the best practical adaptation measure to species or geographic areas at risk from climate change in SO	2.0	CEP										
			d. Continue to work with CCAMLR to identify the process for defining reference areas for future research	2.5	CEP;SCAR;SC-CAMLR										
			e. Maintain regular dialogue (or sharing of information) with SC-CAMLR on Climate Change and the Southern Ocean in particular on actions being taken	1.5	CEP;CCAMLR										Hold workshop as noted in CEP 5-year work plan
4) Ecosystem change due to ocean acidification	• Understanding of the impact of OA to marine biota and ecosystems	Research	a. As required, encourage further research and assessment on impact of OA informed by the SCAR report	1.9	NAPs, SCAR	SCAR report on OA released August 2016.	Ongoing. Update reports to be provided, incl. through the Portal.		Ongoing. Update reports to be provided, incl. through the Portal.		Ongoing. Update reports to be provided, incl. through the Portal.		Ongoing. Update reports to be provided, incl. through the Portal.		
		Management	b. Consider forthcoming SCAR report on OA and act accordingly (understanding some actions may be best advanced by ATCM)	1.6	CEP; CCAMLR***		Preliminary consideration of SCAR report								
			c. Review and revise where necessary existing relevant management tools to consider if they afford the best practical adaptation measure to species or geographic areas at risk from ocean acidification	2.4	CEP, CCAMLR***										

177

Climate related issue	Gaps/needs	Response area	Action/Task	Priority	Who	IP	CEP 2017	IP	CEP 2018	IP	CEP 2019	IP	CEP 2020	IP	CEP 2021
5) Climate change impact to the built (human) environment resulting in impacts on natural and heritage values	• Understanding how the antarctic terrestrial environment will change and how this might result in impacts on environmental or heritage values • Understanding of effects of climate change on contaminated sites and implications for species/ecosystems (eg. whether climate change will increase mobilization and exposure of species/ecosystems to contaminants and understanding how species/ecosystems will respond to exposure to such contaminants) • Understanding what conservation/remedial interventions might be applicable to counteract these impacts	Research	a. National operators to assess risk of change in climate (eg. permafrost) to their infrastructure and environmental consequences	3.0	NAPs, COMNAP				Encourage COMNAP to assess risk of climate change to NAP infrastructure				Receive report from COMNAP and take action accordingly		
			b. Assess risk of changes in climate change to HSM/ heritage values/ ASPA	2.9	Proponents and interested Parties								Initiate risk assessment for HSMs		
			c. Identify and specify research needs and communicate them to the research community	3.3	CEP										
		Management	d. Update the EIA guidelines to take into account the impacts of cc, eg ensuring proposed long term facilities are suitably resilient to cc and will not have an impact on species or habitats at risk.	1.9	CEP										
			e. Further development of the Clean Up Manual (ref. Resolution 2 (2013))	2.0	CEP		Ensure clean up manual revisions (informed to in 5 year plan) consider implications of climate change.								
			f. Encourage national programmes to assess which sites of their past activities (not yet cleaned up or remediated) are more likely to be more affected by climate change in order to prioritize their work.	2.3	NAPs		Members to provide a status report to CEP on which sites (not yet cleaned up or remediated) are more likely to be affected by climate change and plans to clean up or remediate those sites		Ongoing		Ongoing		Ongoing		
6) Marine and terrestrial species at risk due to climate change	• Understand population status, trends, vulnerability and distribution of key Antarctic species • Improved understanding of effect on climate on species at risk, including critical thresholds that would give irreversible impacts • Understand the effects on key species to ensure the effects on key species are identified • Framework for monitoring to ensure key species are identified • Understand relationship between species and climate change impacts in important locations/ areas	Research	a. Encourage research by national programmes, SCAR and SC-CCAMLR eg. through programmes such as AntEco and AntERA, and CCAMLR Ecosystem Monitoring Program (CEMP)	1.6	NAPs, SCAR, SC-CCAMLR	SCAR to assimilate overview of how existing research programmes (such as AntERA and AntECO) can contribute to CEP's management interests.									
		Management	b. Consider if and how the IUCN red list criteria can be applied on a regional basis for the Antarctic change*****	2.4	SCAR		Facilitate a programme of work with SCAR, SC-CAMLR, ACAP and IUCN to: 1. initiate a programme to provide regular update reports on the status of Antarctic species		Facilitate a programme of work with SCAR, SC-CAMLR, ACAP and IUCN to: 1. Progress assessments on Antarctic species not yet assessed 2. Develop an approach to applying the Red List criteria on a regional basis in Antarctica						
			c. Begin a rolling programme of status assessments for Antarctic species focusing particularly on those species not currently assessed in the IUCN Red List	1.7	CEP, SCAR, ACAP		See 6a above						Provide update report to ATCM on status, trends and vulnerability of Antarctic species		
			d. Review and revise where necessary existing management tools, to consider if they afford the best practical adaptation measure to species at risk of climate change	1.6	CEP CCAMLR consid.		See 6a above								
			e. Where necessary develop management actions to maintain or improve the conservation status of species threatened by climate change, eg. through SPS action plans.	2.0	CEP, SCAR CCAMLR consid.		Ongoing		Ongoing		Ongoing				

Climate related issue	Gaps/needs	Response area	Action/Task	Priority	Who	IP	CEP 2017	IP	CEP 2018	IP	CEP 2019	IP	CEP 2020	IP	CEP 2021
7) Marine, terrestrial and freshwater habitats at risk due to climate change	• Understand habitat status, trends, vulnerability and distribution • Improved understanding of the effects of climate change on habitat, e.g. sea ice extent and duration, snow cover, ground moisture, microclimate, changing melt flows and consequences to lake systems • Improved understanding of potential expansion of human presence in Antarctica as a result of changes resulting from climate change through e.g. changes in sea ice distribution; collapse of ice shelves; expansion of ice free area).	Research	a. Encourage research by national programmes, SCAR and SC-CCAMLR	2.4	NAPs, SCAR, SC-CCAMLR		Ongoing. Update reports to be provided, incl. through the Portal		Ongoing. Update reports to be provided, incl. through the Portal		Ongoing. Update reports to be provided, incl. through the Portal		Ongoing. Update reports to be provided, incl. through the Portal		
		Management	b. Review and review where necessary existing management tools to consider if they afford the best practical adaptation measure to habitats at risk of climate change.	2.3	CEP CCAMLR consist.										

*   ISW = Intersessional work (could be ICG, workshop, interested members, etc).

**   Workshop.

*** Noting the importance of CCAMLR consideration of climate change issues in the Southern Ocean.

**** Including in context of proposed joint workshop (pt. 3c).

***** Note that the IUCN criteria cover many aspects besides climate change, and does not necessarily identify the effects solely due to climate change. The benefit of using IUCN criteria in our response to climate change will be assessed prior to its use.

Appendix 3

Preliminary Agenda for CEP XX

1. Opening of the Meeting
2. Adoption of the Agenda
3. Strategic Discussions on the Future Work of the CEP
4. Operation of the CEP
5. Cooperation with other Organisations
6. Repair and Remediation of Environment Damage
7. Climate Change Implications for the Environment
    a. Strategic approach
    b. Implementation and Review of the Climate Change Response Work Programme
8. Environmental Impact Assessment (EIA)
    a. Draft Comprehensive Environmental Evaluations
    b. Other EIA Matters
9. Area Protection and Management Plans
    a. Management Plans
    b. Historic Sites and Monuments
    c. Site Guidelines
    d. Marine Spatial Protection and Management
    e. Other Annex V Matters
10. Conservation of Antarctic Flora and Fauna
    a. Quarantine and Non-native Species
    b. Specially Protected Species
    c. Other Annex II Matters
11. Environmental Monitoring and Reporting
12. Inspection Reports
13. General Matters
14. Election of Officers
15. Preparation for Next Meeting
16. Adoption of the Report
17. Closing of the Meeting

3. Appendices

Santiago Declaration on the Twenty Fifth Anniversary of the signing of the Protocol on Environmental Protection to the Antarctic Treaty

The Consultative Parties to the Antarctic Treaty, meeting in Santiago, Chile, in May 2016, on the occasion of the twenty fifth anniversary of the signing of the 1991 Protocol on Environmental Protection to the Antarctic Treaty (the Environmental Protocol),

Recalling the 2009 ATCM XXXII Washington Ministerial Meeting Declaration on the 50th Anniversary of the Antarctic Treaty,

Further recalling the 2011 Declaration on Antarctic Co-operation on the occasion of the 50th Anniversary of the entry into force of the Antarctic Treaty,

Recognizing the significance of the Environmental Protocol, signed in Madrid on 4 October 1991, within the Antarctic Treaty system,

Recalling the commitment of the Consultative Parties to the comprehensive protection of the Antarctic environment and dependent and associated ecosystems, and the designation of Antarctica as a natural reserve, devoted to peace and science,

Reaffirming that the comprehensive protection of the Antarctic environment and dependent and associated ecosystems is in the interests of science and mankind as a whole,

Recalling the responsibilities of the Antarctic Treaty Consultative Parties to ensure that all activities in Antarctica are consistent with the Antarctic Treaty system,

Further recalling that the comprehensive protection of the Antarctic environment and dependent and associated ecosystems is a fundamental consideration in planning activities and scientific research in the Antarctic Treaty area,

Determined to ensure full implementation of the principles and provisions of the Protocol and its Annexes to support comprehensive protection of the Antarctic environment and dependent and associated ecosystems,

Deeply concerned about the effects of global environmental change, in particular climate change, for the Antarctic environment and dependent and associated ecosystems,

Convinced that international cooperation in Antarctica is essential to effectively study global environmental changes and that the Antarctic Treaty system provides the necessary framework to enhance this cooperation,

Mindful of the need to ensure that all human activity in Antarctica is conducted in a manner that effectively promotes the continued protection of the Antarctic environment and prevents and minimizes impacts,

Reaffirming the importance of drawing upon the best available scientific and technical advice in the management of activities in Antarctica and the comprehensive protection of the Antarctic environment and dependent and associated ecosystems,

Recognizing the importance of the Committee on Environmental Protection as an advisory body to the Antarctic Treaty Consultative Meetings in connection with the implementation of the Environmental Protocol,

Hereby:

1. Reaffirm their strong and unwavering commitment to the objectives and purposes of the Antarctic Treaty and its Environmental Protocol;

2. Pledge to further strengthen their efforts to preserve and protect the Antarctic terrestrial and marine environments, bearing in mind the designation of Antarctica as a natural reserve, devoted to peace and science;

3. Reaffirm, in particular, their strong and unequivocal commitment to Articles 6 and 7 of the Environmental Protocol, which respectively set out principles on Cooperation in the planning and conduct of activities in the Antarctic Treaty area, and prohibit any activity relating to mineral resources, other than scientific research;

4. Pledge to make all necessary efforts to bring Annex VI of the Protocol on Environmental Protection on Liability Arising from Environmental Emergencies into force, as a critical step towards implementing Articles 15 and 16 of the Environmental Protocol;

5. Welcome the increase in Parties to the Environmental Protocol to thirty-seven Parties at the time of this declaration and encourage other States that are committed to the objectives and purposes of the Protocol to accede;

6. Commit to ensure that current and future tourism and non-governmental activities are effectively managed, including addressing challenges and impacts arising from potential growth and diversification of such activities, bearing in mind the provisions of the Antarctic Treaty system and in particular, those contained in the Environmental Protocol;

7. Reaffirm their intention to work together to better understand changes to the Antarctic climate and to actively seek ways to address the effects of climate change on the Antarctic environment and dependent and associated ecosystems;

8. Renew their commitment to promote co-operative programs of scientific, technical and educational value, including activities designed to protect the Antarctic environment and dependent and associated ecosystems; and to facilitate the sharing of Antarctic assets and infrastructure to support collaborative scientific projects wherever possible and practicable;

9. Reaffirm their commitment to remain vigilant and take effective and timely action to address future Antarctic environmental challenges.

Adopted at Santiago, Chile, May 30th, 2016.

Preliminary Agenda for ATCM XL, Working Groups and Allocation of Items

Plenary

1. Opening of the Meeting

2. Election of Officers and Creation of Working Groups

3. Adoption of the Agenda, Allocation of Items to Working Groups and Consideration of the Multi-year Strategic Work Plan

4. Operation of the Antarctic Treaty System: Reports by Parties, Observers and Experts

5. Report of the Committee on Environmental Protection

Working Group 1: *(Policy, Legal, Institutional)*

6. Operation of the Antarctic Treaty System: General matters

7. Operation of the Antarctic Treaty System: Matters related to the Secretariat

8. Liability

9. Biological Prospecting in Antarctica

10. Exchange of Information

11. Education Issues

12. Multi-year Strategic Work Plan

Working Group 2: *(Science, Operations, Tourism)*

13. Safety and Operations in Antarctica

14. Inspections under the Antarctic Treaty and Environmental Protocol

15. Science Issues, Scientific Cooperation and Facilitation

16. Implications of Climate Change for Management of Antarctic Treaty Area

17. Tourism and Non-governmental Activities in the Antarctic Treaty Area, including Competent Authorities Issues

Plenary

18. Appointment of the Executive Secretary

19. Preparation for the XLI Meeting

20. Any other Business

21. Adoption of the Final Report

22. Close of the Meeting

Host country communique

The XXXIX Antarctic Treaty Consultative Meeting (ATCM) was held in Santiago, Chile, from the 23 May to 1 June 2016. The Meeting was chaired by Ambassador Alfredo Labbé (Chile). The XIX Meeting of the Committee on Environmental Protection (CEP) was held from 23 – 27 May and was chaired by Ewan McIvor (Australia). The Meetings were organised by the Ministry of Foreign Affairs of Chile.

Over 340 participants from the Antarctic Treaty Parties, experts, representatives of civil society and international observers attended the annual Meeting. The Meeting was inaugurated by the Minister of Foreign Affairs of Chile, M. Heraldo Muñoz.

The following topics were discussed in the CEP: exchange of information on environmental matters, climate change implications for the Antarctic environment, area protection and management plans, conservation of Antarctic flora and fauna and environmental impact assesments. The CEP also considered the report of the Joint Meeting of the Committee on Environmental Protection and the Scientific Committee for the Conservation of Marine Living Resources (SC-CAMLR), that was held in Punta Arenas, Chile, on the 19 and 20 May.

Discussions in the ATCM focused on the following issues: promoting scientific research and consolidating the culture of international collaboration, safety and operations in Antarctica, Antarctic inspections, tourism and non-govermental activities in the Antarctic Treaty area, information exchange between competent authorities, management and protection of historical sites and general matters concerning the operation of the Antarctic Treaty system. Education issues and outreach were also widely discussed.

The Meeting also held a Special Working Group to comemorate the 25th anniversary years of the signing of the Protocol to the Antarctic Treaty on Environmental Protection, which was inaugurated by the Vice-Minister of Foreign Affairs of Chile Edgardo Riveros. This working group had the structure of a symposium, with the participation of 11 panelists and was aimed at celebrating and discussing achievements in relation to the Environmental Protocol's role as the framework for advancing environmental protection in Antarctica and to focus on ensuring that the Protocol was future-proof. The Meeting also adopted a resolution reaffirming the commitment of Parties to the mining ban under article 7 of the Protocol.

The ATCM adopted the Santiago Declaration on the twenty fifth anniversary of the signing of the Protocol on Environmental Protection to the Antarctic Treaty. The declaration reaffirms the commitment of the Consultative Parties to the protection of the Antarctic environment and its associated and dependant ecosystems. The Santiago Declaration is attached to the present communique.

Parties expressed their gratitude to the Chilean government and their appreciation for the excellent facilities provided for the Meeting.

The next ATCM will be hosted by China in 2017.

Conclusions of the ATCM on Information Exchange

1. The meeting considered WP 17 *Report of the intersessional contact group established to review information exchange requirements.* The ICG was tasked to review the items of information currently required to be exchanged and to formulate recommendations on: whether there was continued value for Parties to exchange information on these items; whether some of them needed to be modified, updated, differently described, made mandatory (where currently described as optional) or removed; the timing of information exchange for these items; and how each item would best fit into the category of pre-season, annual and permanent information; and whether the information could be better exchanged through other mechanisms.

2. Australia noted that the interessional discussions had focussed on remaining items carried over from ATCM XXXVIII. The ICG had successfully concluded its consideration of these remaining items.

3. The meeting also considered advice from the CEP on those items of information of an environmental nature.

4. The meeting noted that points were raised in the ICG discussion which were beyond the scope of the ICG terms of reference. These included:

    *   the desirability of determining what use is made by the Parties of the information that is exchanged;

    *   the level of detail of information exchanged, and whether this detail is necessary;

    *   variations in the level of detail provided by different Parties; and

    *   the different options available for exchanging information (for example through the electronic information exchange system, or via other means).

5. The ATCM took note of these issues, and encouraged Parties to give consideration as to how they might be advanced, with a view to bringing forward any proposals relating to these issues to a future meeting.

6. The meeting considered the recommendations of the ICG, and agreed to make changes to the information exchange requirements in a number of cases, and took note of a number of other issues. The conclusions of the ATCM on the items of information considered are as follows:

Scientific information	ATCM conclusion
Scientific information: Forward plans	The ATCM agreed to modify the timing for the optional provision of information on forward plans to allow provision at any time, for example when domestic plans are completed or updated.

Operational information – national expeditions	ATCM conclusion
Operational: national expeditions – Stations	The ATCM noted, given the issues raised by participants in the ICG, the desirability of making possible changes to the items of information in the Operational: national expeditions – stations' category. The ATCM requested COMNAP to consult with its members and provide advice on an appropriate set of categories for describing stations and facilities to facilitate the exchange of accurate information. The ATCM noted that there is no item of information for aviation facilities, and reaffirmed that this was appropriate, given that Resolution 1 (2013) specifies that Parties should facilitate the ongoing revision of the Antarctic Flight Information Manual maintained by COMNAP, which includes information on aviation-related facilities.
Research rockets	The ATCM noted that any changes relating to information exchange on research rocket launches be considered in the context of broader air safety management discussions in the ATCM and COMNAP.
Search and rescue information items – stations, vessels, and aircraft	The ATCM noted that it was not sufficiently clear what information should be exchanged or what reporting format is contemplated for this requirement. The ATCM further noted that COMNAP maintains information and systems in relation to search and rescue. The ATCM requested COMNAP to provide advice on whether there was any need, from an operational perspective, for Parties to exchange search and rescue information via the information exchange system. The ATCM further requested COMNAP to provide advice on whether there were benefits in having COMNAP-curated search and rescue information available publicly, by linking to it from the ATCM website, and whether there are any technical or other issues.

Operational information – non-Governmental expeditions	ATCM conclusion
Non-Governmental expeditions	The ATCM concluded that the timing of information on non-governmental expeditions should be changed to allow for it to be provided as soon as possible after completion of national processes, with the relevant timing description being: 'as soon as possible following completion of national processes, preferably by the pre-season target date of 1 October, and no later than the start of the activity'.
	The ATCM noted the desirability of Parties providing information about their domestic implementation of Measure 4 (2004) through the "relevant national legislation" item, using the existing items of information in that section.
Non-Governmental expeditions – aircraft activities (no current requirement)	The ATCM noted that there is no current requirement for non-governmental aircraft activities, and decided to add a new category for non-governmental aircraft activities, comprising the information items: name of operator, type of aircraft, number of flights, period of flights, departure date per flight, departure and arrival location per flight, route per flight, purpose per flight, and number of passengers.
	For consistency with other categories of non-Governmental expedition information, this information should be required pre-season and annually.
Vessel-based operations – Location	The ATCM noted that issues had been raised by a number of ICG participants who pointed out that pre-season information (on locations of planned activities) was in many cases different to the actual activity, and questioned whether it was necessary to provide detailed information as part of the pre-season information exchange. The ATCM encouraged interested Parties to consider this issue further, as appropriate, and bring forward any proposals to a future meeting.
Vessel-based operations – Date	The ATCM decided to add an additional optional item of information for non-Governmental vessel-based operations, namely 'duration of landing' to reflect situations where an activity will spend multiple days at one site, or multiple sites visited on the same day.

7. The ATCM considered the advice of the CEP on the items of information exchange relating to environmental matters, and agreed:

   1) changes to the items of information exchange on *Contingency plans for oil spills and other emergencies* as follows:

   - modifying the description of the item to add underlined text as follows "oil spills and other environmental emergencies";

   - adding an optional item to describe 'scope/coverage of the plan (eg. ship oil spill, station oil spill, station chemical incident etc)', in case this is not indicated in the title;

- retaining the item 'link', but making it 'optional'; and
- removing the item 'implementation report'.

2) changes to the items of information exchange on IEEs and CEEs as follows:

- the inclusion of an additional optional item of information, for indicating 'the period/length of the activity'; and
- modifying the timing for information on IEEs and CEEs to encourage provision 'as soon as domestic processes are concluded, while maintaining the existing deadline for Parties to submit the information'.

PART II

Measures, Decisions and Resolutions

1. Measures

Antarctic Specially Protected Area No 116
(New College Valley, Caughley Beach, Cape Bird, Ross Island): Revised Management Plan

The Representatives,

Recalling Articles 3, 5 and 6 of Annex V to the Protocol on Environmental Protection to the Antarctic Treaty providing for the designation of Antarctic Specially Protected Areas ("ASPA") and approval of Management Plans for those Areas;

Recalling

- Recommendation XIII-8 (1985), which designated Caughley Beach as Site of Special Scientific Interest ("SSSI") No 10 and annexed a Management Plan for the Site;

- Recommendation XIII-12 (1985), which designated New College Valley as Specially Protected Area ("SPA") No 20;

- Recommendation XVI-7 (1991), which extended the expiry date of SSSI 10;

- Recommendation XVII-2 (1992), which annexed a Management Plan for SPA 20;

- Measure 1 (2000), which expanded SPA 20 to incorporate Caughley Beach, annexed a revised Management Plan for the Area, and provided that thereupon SSSI 10 shall cease to exist;

- Decision 1 (2002), which renamed and renumbered SPA 20 as ASPA 116;

- Measures 1 (2006) and 2 (2011), which adopted revised Management Plans for ASPA 116;

Recalling that Recommendation XVI-7 (1991) and Measure 1 (2000) have not become effective, and that Recommendation XVII-2 (1992) was withdrawn by Measure 1 (2010);

Recalling that Recommendations XIII-12 (1985) and XVI-7 (1991) were designated as no longer current by Decision 1 (2011);

Noting that the Committee for Environmental Protection has endorsed a revised Management Plan for ASPA 116;

Desiring to replace the existing Management Plan for ASPA 116 with the revised Management Plan;

Recommend to their Governments the following Measure for approval in accordance with paragraph 1 of Article 6 of Annex V to the Protocol on Environmental Protection to the Antarctic Treaty:

That:

1. the revised Management Plan for Antarctic Specially Protected Area No 116 (New College Valley, Caughley Beach, Cape Bird, Ross Island), which is annexed to this Measure, be approved; and

2. the Management Plan for Antarctic Specially Protected Area No 116 annexed to Measure 1 (2011) be revoked.

Antarctic Specially Protected Area No 120
(Pointe-Géologie Archipelago, Terre Adélie): Revised Management Plan

The Representatives,

Recalling Articles 3, 5 and 6 of Annex V to the Protocol on Environmental Protection to the Antarctic Treaty providing for the designation of Antarctic Specially Protected Areas ("ASPA") and approval of Management Plans for those Areas;

Recalling

- Measure 3 (1995), which designated Pointe-Géologie Archipelago as Specially Protected Area ("SPA") No 24 and annexed a Management Plan for the Area;

- Decision 1 (2002), which renamed and renumbered SPA 24 as ASPA 120;

- Measures 2 (2005) and 2 (2011), which adopted revised Management Plans for ASPA 120;

Recalling that Measure 3 (1995) had not become effective and was withdrawn by Measure 2 (2011);

Noting that the Committee for Environmental Protection has endorsed a revised Management Plan for ASPA 120;

Desiring to replace the existing Management Plan for ASPA 120 with the revised Management Plan;

Recommend to their Governments the following Measure for approval in accordance with paragraph 1 of Article 6 of Annex V to the Protocol on Environmental Protection to the Antarctic Treaty:

That:

1. the revised Management Plan for Antarctic Specially Protected Area No 120 (Pointe-Géologie Archipelago, Terre Adélie), which is annexed to this Measure, be approved; and

2. the Management Plan for Antarctic Specially Protected Area No 120 annexed to Measure 2 (2011) be revoked.

Antarctic Specially Protected Area No 122
(Arrival Heights, Hut Point Peninsula, Ross Island): Revised Management Plan

The Representatives,

Recalling Articles 3, 5 and 6 of Annex V to the Protocol on Environmental Protection to the Antarctic Treaty providing for the designation of Antarctic Specially Protected Areas ("ASPA") and approval of Management Plans for those Areas;

Recalling

- Recommendation VIII-4 (1975), which designated Arrival Heights, Hut Point Peninsula, Ross Island as Site of Special Scientific Interest ("SSSI") No 2 and annexed a Management Plan for the Site;

- Recommendations X-6 (1979), XII-5 (1983), XIII-7 (1985), XIV-4 (1987), Resolution 3 (1996) and Measure 2 (2000), which extended the expiry date of SSSI 2;

- Decision 1 (2002), which renamed and renumbered SSSI 2 as ASPA 122;

- Measures 2 (2004) and 3 (2011), which adopted revised Management Plans for ASPA 122;

Recalling that Measure 2 (2000) was withdrawn by Measure 5 (2009);

Recalling that Recommendations VIII-4 (1975), X-6 (1979), XII-5 (1983), XIII-7 (1985), XIV-4 (1987) and Resolution 3 (1996) were designated as no longer current by Decision 1 (2011);

Noting that the Committee for Environmental Protection has endorsed a revised Management Plan for ASPA 122;

Desiring to replace the existing Management Plan for ASPA 122 with the revised Management Plan;

Recommend to their Governments the following Measure for approval in accordance with paragraph 1 of Article 6 of Annex V to the Protocol on Environmental Protection to the Antarctic Treaty:

That:

1. the revised Management Plan for Antarctic Specially Protected Area No 122 (Arrival Heights, Hut Point Peninsula, Ross Island), which is annexed to this Measure, be approved; and

2. the Management Plan for Antarctic Specially Protected Area No 122 annexed to Measure 3 (2011) be revoked.

Antarctic Specially Protected Area No 126
(Byers Peninsula, Livingston Island, South Shetland Islands): Revised Management Plan

The Representatives,

Recalling Articles 3, 5 and 6 of Annex V to the Protocol on Environmental Protection to the Antarctic Treaty providing for the designation of Antarctic Specially Protected Areas ("ASPA") and approval of Management Plans for those Areas;

Recalling

- Recommendation IV-10 (1966), which designated Byers Peninsula, Livingstone Island, South Shetland Islands as Specially Protected Area ("SPA") No 10;

- Recommendation VIII-2 (1975), which terminated SPA 10, and Recommendation VIII-4 (1975), which redesignated the Area as Site of Special Scientific Interest ("SSSI") No 6 and annexed the first Management Plan for the Site;

- Recommendations X-6 (1979), XII-5 (1983), XIII-7 (1985) and Measure 3 (2001), which extended the expiry date of SSSI 6;

- Recommendation XVI-5 (1991), which adopted a revised Management Plan for SSSI 6;

- Decision 1 (2002), which renamed and renumbered SSSI 6 as ASPA 126;

- Measures 1 (2002) and 4 (2011), which adopted revised Management Plans for ASPA 126;

Recalling that Recommendation XVI-5 (1991) and Measure 3 (2001) had not become effective and were withdrawn by Measure 4 (2011);

Recalling that Recommendations VIII-2 (1975), X-6 (1979), XII-5 (1983), XIII-7 (1985) and XVI-5 (1991) were designated as no longer current by Decision 1 (2011);

Noting that the Committee for Environmental Protection has endorsed a revised Management Plan for ASPA 126;

Desiring to replace the existing Management Plan for ASPA 126 with the revised Management Plan;

Recommend to their Governments the following Measure for approval in accordance with paragraph 1 of Article 6 of Annex V to the Protocol on Environmental Protection to the Antarctic Treaty:

That:

1. the revised Management Plan for Antarctic Specially Protected Area No 126 (Byers Peninsula, Livingston Island, South Shetland Islands), which is annexed to this Measure, be approved; and

2. the Management Plan for Antarctic Specially Protected Area No 126 annexed to Measure 4 (2011) be revoked.

Antarctic Specially Protected Area No 127
(Haswell Island): Revised Management Plan

The Representatives,

Recalling Articles 3, 5 and 6 of Annex V to the Protocol on Environmental Protection to the Antarctic Treaty providing for the designation of Antarctic Specially Protected Areas ("ASPA") and approval of Management Plans for those Areas;

Recalling

- Recommendation VIII-4 (1975), which designated Haswell Island as Site of Special Scientific Interest ("SSSI") No 7 and annexed a Management Plan for the Site;

- Recommendations X-6 (1979), XII-5 (1983), XIII-7 (1985), XVI-7 (1987) and Measure 3 (2001), which extended the expiry date of SSSI 7;

- Decision 1 (2002), which renamed and renumbered SSSI 7 as ASPA 127;

- Measure 4 (2005), which extended the expiry date of the Management Plan for ASPA 127;

- Measures 1 (2006) and 5 (2011), which adopted revised Management Plans for ASPA 127;

Recalling that Recommendations VIII-4 (1975), X-6 (1979), XII-5 (1983), XIII-7 (1985) and XVI-7 (1987) were designated as no longer current by Decision 1 (2011);

Noting that the Committee for Environmental Protection has endorsed a revised Management Plan for ASPA 127;

Desiring to replace the existing Management Plan for ASPA 127 with the revised Management Plan;

Recommend to their Governments the following Measure for approval in accordance with paragraph 1 of Article 6 of Annex V to the Protocol on Environmental Protection to the Antarctic Treaty:

That:

1. the revised Management Plan for Antarctic Specially Protected Area No 127 (Haswell Island), which is annexed to this Measure, be approved; and

2. the Management Plan for Antarctic Specially Protected Area No 127 annexed to Measure 5 (2011) be revoked.

Antarctic Specially Protected Area No 131
(Canada Glacier, Lake Fryxell, Taylor Valley, Victoria Land): Revised Management Plan

The Representatives,

Recalling Articles 3, 5 and 6 of Annex V to the Protocol on Environmental Protection to the Antarctic Treaty providing for the designation of Antarctic Specially Protected Areas ("ASPA") and approval of Management Plans for those Areas;

Recalling

- Recommendation XIII-8 (1985), which designated Canada Glacier, Lake Fryxell, Taylor Valley, Victoria Land as Site of Special Scientific Interest ("SSSI") No 12 and annexed a Management Plan for the Site;

- Recommendation XVI-7 (1987), which extended the expiry date of SSSI 12;

- Measure 3 (1997), which adopted a revised Management Plan for SSSI 12;

- Decision 1 (2002), which renamed and renumbered SSSI 12 as ASPA 131;

- Measures 1 (2006) and 6 (2011), which adopted revised Management Plans for ASPA 131;

Recalling that Measure 3 (1997) had not become effective and was withdrawn by Measure 6 (2011);

Recalling that Recommendation XVI-7 (1987) had not become effective and was designated as no longer current by Decision 1 (2011);

Noting that the Committee for Environmental Protection has endorsed a revised Management Plan for ASPA 131;

Desiring to replace the existing Management Plan for ASPA 131 with the revised Management Plan;

Recommend to their Governments the following Measure for approval in accordance with paragraph 1 of Article 6 of Annex V to the Protocol on Environmental Protection to the Antarctic Treaty:

That:

1. the revised Management Plan for Antarctic Specially Protected Area No 131 (Canada Glacier, Lake Fryxell, Taylor Valley, Victoria Land), which is annexed to this Measure, be approved; and

2. the Management Plan for Antarctic Specially Protected Area No 131 annexed to Measure 6 (2011) be revoked.

Antarctic Specially Protected Area No 149
(Cape Shirreff and San Telmo Island, Livingston Island, South Shetland Islands): Revised Management Plan

The Representatives,

Recalling Articles 3, 5 and 6 of Annex V to the Protocol on Environmental Protection to the Antarctic Treaty providing for the designation of Antarctic Specially Protected Areas ("ASPA") and approval of Management Plans for those Areas;

Recalling

- Recommendation IV-11 (1966), which designated Cape Shirreff, Livingston Island, South Shetland Islands as Specially Protected Area ("SPA") No 11;

- Recommendation XV-7 (1989), which terminated SPA 11 and redesignated the Area as Site of Special Scientific Interest ("SSSI") No 32 and annexed a Management Plan for the Site;

- Resolution 3 (1996) and Measure 2 (2000), which extended the expiry date of SSSI 32;

- Decision 1 (2002), which renamed and renumbered SSSI 32 as ASPA 149;

- Measures 2 (2005) and 7 (2011), which adopted revised Management Plans for ASPA 149;

Recalling that Recommendation XV-7 (1989) and Measure 2 (2000) have not become effective, and that Measure 2 (2000) was withdrawn by Measure 5 (2009);

Recalling that Recommendation XV-7 (1989) and Resolution 3 (1996) were designated as no longer current by Decision 1 (2011);

Noting that the Committee for Environmental Protection has endorsed a revised Management Plan for ASPA 149;

Desiring to replace the existing Management Plan for ASPA 149 with the revised Management Plan;

Recommend to their Governments the following Measure for approval in accordance with paragraph 1 of Article 6 of Annex V to the Protocol on Environmental Protection to the Antarctic Treaty:

That:

1. the revised Management Plan for Antarctic Specially Protected Area No 149 (Cape Shirreff and San Telmo Island, Livingston Island, South Shetland Islands), which is annexed to this Measure, be approved; and

2. the Management Plan for Antarctic Specially Protected Area No 149 annexed to Measure 7 (2011) be revoked.

Antarctic Specially Protected Area No 167
(Hawker Island, Princess Elizabeth Land):
Revised Management Plan

The Representatives,

Recalling Articles 3, 5 and 6 of Annex V to the Protocol on Environmental Protection to the Antarctic Treaty providing for the designation of Antarctic Specially Protected Areas ("ASPA") and approval of Management Plans for those Areas;

Recalling

- Measure 1 (2006), which designated Hawker Island, Vestfold Hills, Ingrid Christensen Coast, Princess Elizabeth Land, East Antarctica as ASPA 167 and annexed a Management Plan for the Area;

- Measure 9 (2011), which adopted a revised Management Plan for ASPA 167;

Noting that the Committee for Environmental Protection has endorsed a revised Management Plan for ASPA 167;

Desiring to replace the existing Management Plan for ASPA 167 with the revised Management Plan;

Recommend to their Governments the following Measure for approval in accordance with paragraph 1 of Article 6 of Annex V to the Protocol on Environmental Protection to the Antarctic Treaty:

That:

1. the revised Management Plan for Antarctic Specially Protected Area No 167 (Hawker Island, Princess Elizabeth Land), which is annexed to this Measure, be approved; and

2. the Management Plan for Antarctic Specially Protected Area No 167 annexed to Measure 9 (2011) be revoked.

Revised List of Antarctic Historic Sites and Monuments:

Incorporation of a historic wooden pole to Historic Site and Monument No 60 (Corvette Uruguay Cairn), in Seymour Island (Marambio), Antarctic Peninsula

The Representatives,

Recalling the requirements of Article 8 of Annex V to the Protocol on Environmental Protection to the Antarctic Treaty to maintain a list of current Historic Sites and Monuments ("HSM"), and that such sites shall not be damaged, removed or destroyed;

Recalling

- Recommendation XVII-3 (1992), which designated HSM 60 (Corvette Uruguay Cairn);

- Measure 19 (2015), which revised and updated the List of HSM;

Desiring to modify the description of HSM 60;

Recommend to their Governments the following Measure for approval in accordance with Paragraph 2 of Article 8 of Annex V to the Protocol on Environmental Protection to the Antarctic Treaty:

That:

1. the description of Historic Site and Monument No 60 (Corvette Uruguay Cairn) be modified in order to read as follows:

   "Wooden pole and cairn (I), and wooden plaque and cairn (II), both located at Penguins Bay, southern coast of Seymour Island (Marambio), James Ross Archipelago. The wooden pole and a cairn (I) were installed in 1902 during the Swedish South Polar Expedition led by Dr. Otto Nordenskjöld.

This cairn used to have attached a 4 m high wooden pole – nowadays only 44 cm high –, guy-lines and a flag, and was installed to signal the location of a well stocked deposit, composed of few wooden boxes containing food supplies, notes and letters saved inside bottles. The deposit was to be used in case the Swedish South Polar Expedition was forced to retreat on its way to the south.

The wooden plaque (II) was placed on 10 November 1903 by the crew of a rescue mission of the Argentinean Corvette Uruguay in the site where they met the members of the Swedish expedition led by Dr Otto Nordenskjöld. The text of the wooden plaque reads as follows:

"10.XI.1903 Uruguay (Argentine Navy) in its journey to give assistance to the Swedish Antarctic expedition."

In January 1990, a rock cairn (II) was erected by Argentina in memory of this event in the place where the plaque is located."

Location:

(I): 64° 17' 47.2" S, 56° 41' 30.7" W

(II): 64° 16' S, 56° 39' W

Original proposing Parties: Argentina and Sweden

Parties undertaking management: Argentina and Sweden

2. the revised and updated List of Historic Sites and Monuments be annexed to this Measure.

Revised List of Historic Sites and Monuments

No.	Description	Location	Designation/ Amendment
1.	Flag mast erected in December 1965 at the South Geographical Pole by the First Argentine Overland Polar Expedition. Original proposing Party: Argentina Party undertaking management: Argentina	90°S	Rec. VII-9
2.	Rock cairn and plaques at Syowa Station in memory of Shin Fukushima, a member of the 4th Japanese Antarctic Research Expedition, who died in October 1960 while performing official duties. The cairn was erected on 11 January 1961, by his colleagues. Some of his ashes repose in the cairn. Original proposing Party: Japan Party undertaking management: Japan	69°00'S, 39°35'E	Rec. VII-9
3.	Rock cairn and plaque on Proclamation Island, Enderby Land, erected in January 1930 by Sir Douglas Mawson. The cairn and plaque commemorate the landing on Proclamation Island of Sir Douglas Mawson with a party from the British, Australian and New Zealand Antarctic Research Expedition of 1929-31. Original proposing Party: Australia Party undertaking management: Australia	65°51'S, 53°41'E	Rec.VII-9
4.	Pole of Inaccessibility Station building. Station building to which a bust of V.I. Lenin is fixed, together with a plaque in memory of the conquest of the Pole of Inaccessibility by Soviet Antarctic explorers in 1958. As of 2007 the station building was covered by snow. The bust of Lenin is erected on the wooden stand mounted on the building roof at about 1.5 m high above the snow surface. Original proposing Party: Russia Party undertaking management: Russia	82°06'42"S, 55°01'57"E	Rec. VII-9 Measure 11 (2012)

No.	Description	Location	Designation/ Amendment
5.	Rock cairn and plaque at Cape Bruce, Mac. Robertson Land, erected in February 1931 by Sir Douglas Mawson. The cairn and plaque commemorate the landing on Cape Bruce of Sir Douglas Mawson with a party from the British, Australian and New Zealand Antarctic Research Expedition of 1929-31. Original proposing Party: Australia Party undertaking management: Australia	67°25'S, 60°47'E	Rec. VII-9
6.	Rock cairn at Walkabout Rocks, Vestfold Hills, Princess Elizabeth Land, erected in 1939 by Sir Hubert Wilkins. The cairn houses a canister containing a record of his visit. Original proposing Party: Australia[1] Party undertaking management: Australia	68°22'S, 78°33'E	Rec. VII-9
7.	Ivan Khmara's Stone. Stone with inscribed plaque erected at Buromsky island in memory of Ivan Khmara, driver-mechanic, the member of the 1st Complex Antarctic Expedition of the USSR (1st Soviet Antarctic Expedition) who perished on fast ice in the performance of duties on 21.01.1956. Initially the stone was erected at Mabus Point, Mirny observatory. In 1974, 19th SAE, the stone was moved to Buromsky Island because of construction activity Original proposing Party: Russia Party undertaking management: Russia	66°32'04"S, 92°59'57"E	Rec. VII-9 Measure 11 (2012)
8.	Anatoly Shcheglov's Monument. Metal stele with plaque in memory of Anatoly Shcheglov, driver-mechanic who perished in the performance of duties, erected on sledge on the Mirny – Vostok route, at 2 km from Mirny station. Original proposing Party: Russia Party undertaking management: Russia	66°34'43"S, 92°58'23"E	Rec. VII-9 Measure 11 (2012)
9.	Buromsky Island Cemetery. Cemetery on Buromsky Island, near Mirny Observatory in which are buried citizens of the USSR (Russian Federation), Czechoslovakia, GDR and Switzerland (members of the Soviet and Russian Antarctic Expeditions) who perished in the performance of their duties. Original proposing Party: Russia Party undertaking management: Russia	66°32'04"S, 93°00'E	Rec. VII-9 Measure 11 (2012)

No.	Description	Location	Designation/ Amendment
10.	Soviet Oasis Station Observatory. Magnetic observatory building at Dobrowolsky station (a part of the former Soviet station Oasis transferred to Poland) at Bunger Hills with a plaque in memory of the opening of Oasis station in 1956. Original proposing Party: Russia Party undertaking management: Russia	66°16'30"S, 100°45'03"E	Rec. VII-9 Measure 11 (2012)
11.	Vostok Station Tractor. Heavy tractor ATT 11 at Vostok station which participated in the first traverse to the Earth Geomagnetic Pole, with plaque in memory of the opening of the Station in 1957. Original proposing Party: Russia Party undertaking management: Russia	78°27'48"S, 106°50'06"E	Rec. VII-9 Measure 11 (2012)
12.	*Cross and plaque at Cape Denison, George V Land. (Removed from the Antarctic Treaty list of Historic Sites and Monuments subsumed with HSM 13 into HSM 77)*		
13.	*Hut at Cape Denison, George V Land, (Removed from the Antarctic Treaty list of Historic Sites and Monuments subsumed with HSM 12 into HSM 77)*		
14.	Site of ice cave at Inexpressible Island, Terra Nova Bay, constructed in March 1912 by Victor Campbell's Northern Party, British Antarctic Expedition, 1910-13. The party spent the winter of 1912 in this ice cave. A wooden sign, plaque and seal bones remain at the site. Original proposing Party: New Zealand Parties undertaking management: New Zealand/Italy/UK	74°54'S, 163°43'E	Rec. VII-9 Measure 5 (1995)
15.	Hut at Cape Royds, Ross Island, built in February 1908 by the British Antarctic Expedition of 1907-09, led by Sir Ernest Shackleton. Restored in January 1961 by the Antarctic Division of New Zealand Department of Scientific and Industrial Research. Site incorporated within ASPA 157. Original proposing Parties: New Zealand/UK Parties undertaking management: New Zealand/UK	77°33'S, 166°10'E	Rec. VII-9

No.	Description	Location	Designation/ Amendment
16.	Hut at Cape Evans, Ross Island, built in January 1911 by the British Antarctic Expedition of 1910-1913, led by Captain Robert F. Scott. Restored in January 1961 by the Antarctic Division of New Zealand Department of Scientific and Industrial Research. Site incorporated within ASPA 155. Original proposing Parties: New Zealand /UK Parties undertaking management: New Zealand/UK	77°38'S, 166°24'E	Rec. VII-9
17.	Cross on Wind Vane Hill, Cape Evans, Ross Island, erected by the Ross Sea Party, led by Captain Aeneas Mackintosh, of Sir Ernest Shackleton's Imperial Trans-Antarctic Expedition of 1914-1916, in memory of three members of the party who died in the vicinity in 1916. Site incorporated within ASPA 155. Original proposing Parties: New Zealand/UK Parties undertaking management: New Zealand/UK	77°38'S, 166°24'E	Rec. VII-9
18.	Hut at Hut Point, Ross Island, built in February 1902 by the British Antarctic Expedition of 1901-04, led by Captain Robert F. Scott. Partially restored in January 1964 by the New Zealand Antarctic Society, with assistance from the United States Government. Site incorporated within ASPA 158. Original proposing Parties: New Zealand/UK Parties undertaking management: New Zealand/UK	77°50'S, 166°37'E	Rec. VII-9
19.	Cross at Hut Point, Ross Island, erected in February 1904 by the British Antarctic Expedition of 1901-04, in memory of George Vince, a member of the expedition, who died in the vicinity. Original proposing Parties: New Zealand/UK Parties undertaking management: New Zealand/UK	77°50'S, 166°37'E	Rec. VII-9
20.	Cross on Observation Hill, Ross Island, erected in January 1913 by the British Antarctic Expedition of 1910-13, in memory of Captain Robert F. Scott's party which perished on the return journey from the South Pole in March 1912. Original proposing Parties: New Zealand/UK Parties undertaking management: New Zealand/UK	77°51'S, 166°41'E	Rec. VII-9

No.	Description	Location	Designation/ Amendment
21.	Remains of stone hut at Cape Crozier, Ross Island, constructed in July 1911 by Edward Wilson's party of the British Antarctic Expedition (1910-13) during the winter journey to collect Emperor penguin eggs. Original proposing Party: New Zealand Parties undertaking management: New Zealand/UK	77°31'S, 169°22'E	Rec. VII-9
22.	Three huts and associated historic relics at Cape Adare. Two were built in February 1899 during the British Antarctic (*Southern Cross*) Expedition, 1898-1900, led by Carsten E. Borchgrevink. The third was built in February 1911 by Robert F. Scott's Northern Party, led by Victor L.A.Campbell. Scott's Northern Party hut has largely collapsed with only the porch standing in 2002. Site incorporated within ASPA 159. Original proposing Parties: New Zealand/UK Parties undertaking management: New Zealand/UK	71°18'S, 170°12'E	Rec. VII-9
23.	Grave at Cape Adare of Norwegian biologist Nicolai Hanson, a member of the British Antarctic (*Southern Cross*) Expedition, 1898-1900, led by Carsten E. Borchgrevink. A large boulder marks the head of the grave with the grave itself outlined in white quartz stones. A cross and plaque are attached to the boulder. Original proposing Parties: New Zealand/ UK Parties undertaking management: New Zealand/ Norway	71°17'S, 170°13'E	Rec. VII-9
24.	Rock cairn, known as 'Amundsen's cairn', on Mount Betty, Queen Maud Range erected by Roald Amundsen on 6 January 1912, on his way back to *Framheim* from the South Pole. Original proposing Party: Norway Party undertaking management: Norway	85°11'S, 163°45'W	Rec. VII-9
25.	*De-listed*		
26.	Abandoned installations of Argentine Station 'General San Martin' on Barry Island, Debenham Islands, Marguerite Bay, with cross, flag mast, and monolith built in 1951. Original proposing Party: Argentina Party undertaking management: Argentina	68°08'S, 67°08'W	Rec. VII-9

No.	Description	Location	Designation/ Amendment
27.	Cairn with a replica of a lead plaque erected on Megalestris Hill, Petermann Island, in 1909 by the second French expedition led by Jean-Baptiste E. A. Charcot. The original plaque is in the reserves of the Museum National d'Histoire Naturelle (Paris). Original proposing Parties: Argentina/France/UK Parties undertaking management: France /UK	65°10'S, 64°09'W	Rec. VII-9
28.	Rock cairn at Port Charcot, Booth Island, with wooden pillar and plaque inscribed with the names of the first French expedition led by Jean-Baptiste E. A. Charcot which wintered here in 1904 aboard *Le Français*. Original proposing Party: Argentina Parties undertaking management: Argentina/France	65°03'S, 64°01'W	Rec. VII-9
29.	Lighthouse named 'Primero de Mayo' erected on Lambda Island, Melchior Islands, by Argentina in 1942. This was the first Argentine lighthouse in the Antarctic. Original proposing Party: Argentina Party undertaking management: Argentina	64°18'S, 62°59'W	Rec. VII-9
30.	Shelter at Paradise Harbour erected in 1950 near the Chilean Base 'Gabriel Gonzalez Videla' to honour Gabriel Gonzalez Videla, the first Head of State to visit the Antarctic. The shelter is a representative example of pre-IGY activity and constitutes an important national commemoration. Original proposing Party: Chile Party undertaking management: Chile	64°49'S, 62°51'W	Rec. VII-9
31.	*De-listed.*		
32.	Concrete monolith erected in 1947, near Capitán Arturo Prat Base on Greenwich Island, South Shetland Islands. Point of reference for Chilean Antarctic hydrographic surveys. The monolith is representative of an important pre-IGY activity and is currently preserved and maintained by personnel from Prat Base. Original proposing Party: Chile Party undertaking management: Chile	62°28'S, 59°40'W	Rec. VII-9

No.	Description	Location	Designation/ Amendment
33.	Shelter and cross with plaque near Capitán Arturo Prat Base (Chile), Greenwich Island, South Shetland Islands. Named in memory of Lieutenant-Commander González Pacheco, who died in 1960 while in charge of the station. The monument commemorates events related to a person whose role and the circumstances of his death have a symbolic value and the potential to educate people about significant human activities in Antarctica. Original proposing Party: Chile Party undertaking management: Chile	62°29'S, 59°40'W	Rec. VII-9
34.	Bust at Capitán Arturo Prat Base (Chile), Greenwich Island, South Shetland Islands, of the Chilean naval hero Arturo Prat, erected in 1947. The monument is representative of pre-IGY activities and has symbolic value in the context of Chilean presence in Antarctica. Original proposing Party: Chile Party undertaking management: Chile	62°50'S, 59°41'W	Rec. VII-9
35.	Wooden cross and statue of the Virgin of Carmen erected in 1947 near Capitán Arturo Prat Base (Chile), Greenwich Island, South Shetland Islands. The monument is representative of pre-IGY activities and has a particularly symbolic and architectural value. Original proposing Party: Chile Party undertaking management: Chile	62°29'S, 59°40'W	Rec. VII-9
36.	Replica of a metal plaque erected by Eduard Dallmann at Potter Cove, King George Island, to commemorate the visit of his German expedition on 1 March, 1874 on board *Grönland.* Original proposing Parties: Argentina/UK Parties undertaking management: Argentina/Germany	62°14'S, 58°39'W	Rec. VII-9

No.	Description	Location	Designation/ Amendment
37.	O'Higgins Historic Site located on Cape Legoupil, Antarctic Peninsula and comprising the following structures of historical value: • "Capitán General Bernardo O'Higgins Riquelme" Bust, erected in 1948 opposite the Base known under the same name. General O'Higgins was the first ruler of Chile to recognise the importance of Antarctica. It has a symbolic meaning in the history of Antarctic exploration since it was during his government that the vessel Dragon landed on the coast of the Antarctic Peninsula in 1820. This monument is also representative of pre-IGY activities in Antarctica. (63°19'14.3" S / 57°53'53.9"W) • Former "Capitán General Bernardo O'Higgins Riquelme" Antarctic Base, unveiled on 18th February, 1948 by the President of the Republic of Chile, Gabriel González Videla, the first President in the world to visit Antarctica. It is considered as a model pioneering base in the modern period of Antarctic exploration. (63°19' S, 57°54'W) • Plaque in memory of Lieutenants Oscar Inostroza Contreras and Sergio Ponce Torrealba, who perished in the Antarctic Continent for the sake of peace and science, on 12th August, 1957. (63°19'15.4" S / 57°53'52.9"W) Virgen del Carmen Grotto, located in the surroundings of the base, built approximately forty years ago. It has served as a place of spiritual withdrawal for the staff of the different Antarctic stations and expeditions. (63°19'15.9" S / 57°54'03.2"W). Original proposing Party: Chile Party undertaking management: Chile	63°19'S, 57°54'W	Rec. VII-9 Measure 11 (2012)
38.	Wooden hut on Snow Hill Island built in February 1902 by the main party of the Swedish South Polar Expedition led by Otto Nordenskjöld. Original proposing Parties: Argentina/ UK Parties undertaking management: Argentina/Sweden	64°22'S, 56°59'W	Rec. VII-9

No.	Description	Location	Designation/ Amendment
39.	Stone hut at Hope Bay, Trinity Peninsula, built in January 1903 by a party of the Swedish South Polar Expedition. Original proposing Parties: Argentina/UK Parties undertaking management: Argentina/Sweden	63°24'S, 56°59'W	Rec. VII-9
40.	Bust of General San Martin, grotto with a statue of the Virgin of Lujan, and a flag mast at Base 'Esperanza', Hope Bay, erected by Argentina in 1955; together with a graveyard with stele in memory of members of Argentine expeditions who died in the area. Original proposing Party: Argentina Party undertaking management: Argentina	63°24'S, 56°59'W	Rec. VII-9
41.	Stone hut on Paulet Island built in February 1903 by survivors of the wrecked vessel *Antarctic* under Captain Carl A. Larsen, members of the Swedish South Polar Expedition led by Otto Nordenskjöld, together with a grave of a member of the expedition and the rock cairn built by the survivors of the wreck at the highest point of the island to draw the attention of rescue expeditions. Original proposing Parties: Argentina/UK Parties undertaking management: Argentina/Sweden/ Norway	63°34'S, 55°45'W	Rec. VII-9 Measure 5 (1997)
42.	Area of Scotia Bay, Laurie Island, South Orkney Island, in which are found: stone hut built in 1903 by the Scottish Antarctic Expedition led by William S. Bruce; the Argentine meteorological hut and magnetic observatory, built in 1905 and known as Moneta House; and a graveyard with twelve graves, the earliest of which dates from 1903. Original proposing Party: Argentina Parties undertaking management: Argentina/UK	60°46'S, 44°40'W	Rec. VII-9
43.	Cross erected in 1955, at a distance of 1,300 metres north-east of the Argentine General Belgrano I Station (Argentina) and subsequently moved to Belgrano II Station (Argentina), Nunatak Bertrab, Confin Coast, Coats Land in 1979. Original proposing Party: Argentina Party undertaking management: Argentina	77°52'S, 34°37'W	Rec. VII-9

No.	Description	Location	Designation/Amendment
44.	Plaque erected at the temporary Indian station 'Dakshin Gangotri', Princess Astrid Kyst, Dronning Maud Land, listing the names of the First Indian Antarctic Expedition which landed nearby on 9 January 1982. Original proposing Party: India Party undertaking management: India	70°45'S, 11°38'E	Rec. XII-7
45.	Plaque on Brabant Island, on Metchnikoff Point, mounted at a height of 70 m on the crest of the moraine separating this point from the glacier and bearing the following inscription: This monument was built by François de Gerlache and other members of the Joint Services Expedition 1983-85 to commemorate the first landing on Brabant Island by the Belgian Antarctic Expedition, 1897-99: Adrien de Gerlache (Belgium) leader, Roald Amundsen (Norway), Henryk Arctowski (Poland), Frederick Cook (USA) and Emile Danco (Belgium) camped nearby from 30 January to 6 February 1898. Original proposing Party: Belgium Party undertaking management: Belgium	64°02'S, 62°34'W	Rec. XIII-16
46.	All the buildings and installations of Port-Martin base, Terre Adélie constructed in 1950 by the 3rd French expedition in Terre Adélie and partly destroyed by fire during the night of 23 to 24 January 1952. Original proposing Party: France Party undertaking management: France	66°49'S, 141°24'E	Rec. XIII-16
47.	Wooden building called 'Base Marret' on the Ile des Pétrels, Terre Adélie, where seven men under the command of Mario Marret overwintered in 1952 following the fire at Port Martin Base. Original proposing Party: France Party undertaking management: France	66°40'S, 140°01'E	Rec. XIII-16
48.	Iron cross on the North-East headland of the Ile des Pétrels, Terre Adélie, dedicated as a memorial to André Prudhomme, head meteorologist in the 3rd International Geophysical Year expedition who disappeared during a blizzard on 7 January 1959. Original proposing Party: France Party undertaking management: France	66°40'S, 140°01'E	Rec. XIII-16

No.	Description	Location	Designation/ Amendment
49.	The concrete pillar erected by the First Polish Antarctic Expedition at Dobrolowski Station on the Bunger Hill to measure acceleration due to gravity g = 982,439.4 mgal ±0.4 mgal in relation to Warsaw, according to the Potsdam system, in January 1959. Original proposing Party: Poland Party undertaking management: Poland	66°16'S, 100°45'E	Rec. XIII-16
50.	A brass plaque bearing the Polish Eagle, the national emblem of Poland, the dates 1975 and 1976, and the following text in Polish, English and Russian: In memory of the landing of members of the first Polish Antarctic marine research expedition on the vessels 'Profesor Siedlecki' and 'Tazar' in February 1976. This plaque, south-west of the Chilean and Soviet stations, is mounted on a cliff facing Maxwell Bay, Fildes Peninsula, King George Island. Original proposing Party: Poland Party undertaking management: Poland	62°12'S, 59°01'W	Rec. XIII-16
51.	The grave of Wlodzimierz Puchalski, surmounted by an iron cross, on a hill to the south of Arctowski station on King George Island. W. Puchalski was an artist and a producer of documentary nature films, who died on 19 January 1979 whilst working at the station. Original proposing Party: Poland Party undertaking management: Poland	62°13'S, 58°28'W	Rec. XIII-16
52.	Monolith erected to commemorate the establishment on 20 February 1985 by the Peoples Republic of China of the 'Great Wall Station' on Fildes Peninsula, King George Island, in the South Shetland Islands. Engraved on the monolith is the following inscription in Chinese: 'Great Wall Station, First Chinese Antarctic Research Expedition, 20 February 1985'. Original proposing Party: China Party undertaking management: China	62°13'S, 58°58'W	Rec. XIII-16

No.	Description	Location	Designation/ Amendment
53.	Bust of Captain Luis Alberto Pardo, monolith and plaques on Point Wild, Elephant Island, south Shetland Islands, celebrating the rescue of the survivors of the British ship *Endurance* by the Chilean Navy cutter *Yelcho* displaying the following words: "Here on August 30th, 1916, the Chilean Navy cutter *Yelcho* commanded by Pilot Luis Pardo Villalón rescued the 22 men from the Shackleton Expedition who survived the wreck of the 'Endurance' living for four and one half months in this Island". The Monolith and the plaques have been placed on Elephant Island and their replicas on the Chilean bases Capitan Arturo Prat (62°30'S, 59°49'W) and President Eduardo Frei (62°12'S, 62°12'W). Bronze busts of the pilot Luis Pardo Villalon were placed on the three above-mentioned monoliths during the XXIVth Chilean Antarctic Scientific Expedition in 1987-88. Original proposing Party: Chile Party undertaking management: Chile	61°03'S, 54°50'W	Rec. XIV-8 Rec. XV-13
54.	Richard E. Byrd Historic Monument, McMurdo Station, Antarctica. Bronze bust on black marble, 5ft high x 2ft square, on wood platform, bearing inscriptions describing the polar achievements of Richard Evelyn Byrd. Erected at McMurdo Station in 1965. Original proposing Party: USA Party undertaking management: USA	77°51'S, 166°40'E	Rec. XV-12
55.	East Base, Antarctica, Stonington Island. Buildings and artefacts at East Base, Stonington Island and their immediate environs. These structures were erected and used during two U.S. wintering expeditions: the Antarctic Service Expedition (1939-1941) and the Ronne Antarctic Research Expedition (1947-1948). The size of the historic area is approximately 1,000 metres in the north-south direction (from the beach to Northeast Glacier adjacent to Back Bay) and approximately 500 metres in the east-west direction. Original proposing Party: USA Party undertaking management: USA	68°11'S, 67°00'W	Rec. XIV-8

No.	Description	Location	Designation/ Amendment
56.	Waterboat Point, Danco Coast, Antarctic Peninsula. The remains and immediate environs of the Waterboat Point hut. It was occupied by the UK two-man expedition of Thomas W. Bagshawe and Maxime C. Lester in 1921-22. Only the base of the boat, foundations of doorposts and an outline of the hut and extension still exist. It is situated close to the Chilean station 'President Gabriel Gonzáles Videla'. Original proposing Party: Chile/UK Parties undertaking management: Chile/UK	64°49'S, 62°51'W	Rec. XVI-11
57.	Commemorative plaque at 'Yankee Bay' (Yankee Harbour), MacFarlane Strait, Greenwich Island, South Shetland Islands. Near a Chilean refuge. Erected to the memory of Captain Andrew MacFarlane, who in 1820 explored the Antarctic Peninsula area in the brigantine *Dragon*. Original proposing Parties: Chile/UK Parties undertaking management: Chile/UK	62°32'S, 59°45'W	Rec. XVI-11
58.	*De-listed.*		
59.	A cairn on Half Moon Beach, Cape Shirreff, Livingston Island, South Shetland Islands and a plaque on 'Cerro Gaviota' opposite San Telmo Islets commemorating the officers, soldiers and seamen aboard the Spanish vessel *San Telmo,* which sank in September 1819; possibly the first people to live and die in Antarctica. Site incorporated within ASPA 149. Original proposing Parties: Chile/Spain/Peru Parties undertaking management: Chile/Spain/Peru	62°28'S, 60°46'W	Rec. XVI-11

No.	Description	Location	Designation/ Amendment
60.	"Wooden pole and cairn (I), and wooden plaque and cairn (II), both located at Penguins Bay, southern coast of Seymour Island (Marambio), James Ross Archipelago. The wooden pole and a cairn (I) were installed in 1902 during the Swedish South Polar Expedition led by Dr. Otto Nordenskjöld. This cairn used to have attached a 4 m high wooden pole – nowadays only 44 cm high –, guy-lines and a flag, and was installed to signal the location of a well stocked deposit, composed of few wooden boxes containing food supplies, notes and letters saved inside bottles. The deposit was to be used in case the Swedish South Polar Expedition was forced to retreat on its way to the south. The wooden plaque (II) was placed on 10 November 1903 by the crew of a rescue mission of the Argentinean Corvette Uruguay in the site where they met the members of the Swedish expedition led by Dr Otto Nordenskjöld. The text of the wooden plaque reads as follows: "10.XI.1903 Uruguay (Argentine Navy) in its journey to give assistance to the Swedish Antarctic expedition." In January 1990, a rock cairn (II) was erected by Argentina in memory of this event in the place where the plaque is located. Original proposing Parties: Argentina/Sweden Parties undertaking management: Argentina/Sweden	(I): 64°17'47.2"S, 56°41'30.7"W (II): 64°16'S, 56°39'W	Rec. XVII-3 Measure 9 (2016)
61.	'Base A' at Port Lockroy, Goudier Island, off Wiencke Island, Antarctic Peninsula. Of historic importance as an Operation Tabarin base from 1944 and for scientific research, including the first measurements of the ionosphere, and the first recording of an atmospheric whistler, from Antarctica. Port Lockroy was a key monitoring site during the International Geophysical Year of 1957/58. Original Proposing Party: UK Party undertaking management: UK	64°49'S, 63°29'W	Measure 4 (1995)
62.	'Base F (Wordie House)' on Winter Island, Argentine Islands. Of historic importance as an example of an early British scientific base. Original proposing Party: UK Parties undertaking management: UK/Ukraine	65°15'S, 64°16'W	Measure 4 (1995)

No.	Description	Location	Designation/ Amendment
63.	'Base Y' on Horseshoe Island, Marguerite Bay, western Graham Land. Noteworthy as a relatively unaltered and completely equipped British scientific base of the late 1950s. 'Blaiklock', the refuge hut nearby, is considered an integral part of the base. Original proposing Party: UK Party undertaking management: UK	67°48'S, 67°18'W	Measure 4 (1995)
64.	'Base E' on Stonington Island, Marguerite Bay, western Graham Land. Of historical importance in the early period of exploration and later British Antarctic Survey (BAS) history of the 1960s and 1970s. Original proposing Party: UK Party undertaking management: UK	68°11'S, 67°00'W	Measure 4 (1995)
65.	Message post, Svend Foyn Island, Possession Islands. A pole with a box attached was placed on the island on 16 January 1895 during the whaling expedition of Henryk Bull and Captain Leonard Kristensen of the ship *Antarctic*. It was examined and found intact by the British Antarctic Expedition of 1898-1900 and then sighted from the beach by the USS *Edisto* in 1956 and USCGS *Glacier* in 1965. Original proposing Parties: New Zealand/Norway/UK Parties undertaking management: New Zealand/ Norway	71°56'S, 171°05'W	Measure 4 (1995)
66.	Prestrud's Cairn, Scott Nunataks, Alexandra Mountains, Edward VII Peninsula. The small rock cairn was erected at the foot of the main bluff on the north side of the nunataks by Lieutenant K. Prestrud on 3 December 1911 during the Norwegian Antarctic Expedition of 1910-1912. Original proposing Parties: New Zealand/ Norway/ UK Parties undertaking management: New Zealand/ Norway	77°11'S, 154°32'W	Measure 4 (1995)

No.	Description	Location	Designation/ Amendment
67.	Rock shelter, 'Granite House', Cape Geology, Granite Harbour. This shelter was constructed in 1911 for use as a field kitchen by Griffith Taylor's second geological excursion during the British Antarctic Expedition of 1910-1913. It was enclosed on three sides with granite boulder walls and used a sledge to support a seal-skin roof. The stone walls of the shelter have partially collapsed. The shelter contains corroded remnants of tins, a seal skin and some cord. The sledge is now located 50 m seaward of the shelter and consists of a few scattered pieces of wood, straps and buckles. Site incorporated within ASPA 154. Original proposing Parties: New Zealand/Norway/UK Parties undertaking management: New Zealand/UK	77°00'S, 162°32'E	Measure 4 (1995)
68.	Site of depot at Hells Gate Moraine, Inexpressible Island, Terra Nova Bay.This emergency depot consisted of a sledge loaded with supplies and equipment which was placed on 25 January 1913 by the British Antarctic Expedition, 1910-1913. The sledge and supplies were removed in 1994 in order to stabilize their deteriorating condition. Original proposing Parties: New Zealand/Norway/UK Parties undertaking management: New Zealand/UK	74°52'S, 163°50'E	Measure 4 (1995)
69.	Message post at Cape Crozier, Ross Island, erected on 22 January 1902 by Captain Robert F. Scott's *Discovery* Expedition of 1901-04. It was to provide information for the expedition's relief ships, and held a metal message cylinder, which has since been removed. Site incorporated within ASPA 124. Original proposing Parties: New Zealand/Norway/UK Parties undertaking management: New Zealand/UK	77°27'S, 169°16'E	Measure 4 (1995)
70.	Message post at Cape Wadworth, Coulman Island. A metal cylinder nailed to a red pole 8 m above sea level placed by Captain Robert F. Scott on 15 January 1902. He painted the rocks behind the post red and white to make it more conspicuous. Original proposing Parties: New Zealand/Norway/UK Parties undertaking management: New Zealand/UK	73°19'S, 169°47'E	Measure 4 (1995)

No.	Description	Location	Designation/ Amendment
71.	Whalers Bay, Deception Island, South Shetland Islands. The site comprises all pre-1970 remains on the shore of Whalers Bay, including those from the early whaling period (1906-12) initiated by Captain Adolfus Andresen of the Sociedad Ballenera de Magallanes, Chile; the remains of the Norwegian Hektor Whaling Station established in 1912 and all artefacts associated with its operation until 1931; the site of a cemetery with 35 burials and a memorial to ten men lost at sea; and the remains from the period of British scientific and mapping activity (1944-1969). The site also acknowledges and commemorates the historic value of other events that occurred there, from which nothing remains. Original proposing Parties: Chile/ Norway Parties undertaking management: Chile/Norway/UK	62°59'S, 60°34'W	Measure 4 (1995)
72.	Mikkelsen Cairn, Tryne Islands, Vestfold Hills. A rock cairn and a wooden mast erected by the landing party led by Captain Klarius Mikkelsen of the Norwegian whaling ship *Thorshavn* and including Caroline Mikkelsen, Captain Mikkelsen's wife, the first woman to set foot on East Antarctica. The cairn was discovered by Australian National Antarctic Research Expedition field parties in 1957 and again in 1995. Original proposing Parties: Australia/Norway Parties undertaking management: Australia/Norway	68°22'S 78°24'E	Measure 2 (1996)
73.	Memorial Cross for the 1979 Mount Erebus crash victims, Lewis Bay, Ross Island. A cross of stainless steel which was erected in January 1987 on a rocky promontory three kilometers from the Mount Erebus crash site in memory of the 257 people of different nationalities who lost their lives when the aircraft in which they were travelling crashed into the lower slopes of Mount Erebus, Ross Island. The cross was erected as a mark of respect and in remembrance of those who died in the tragedy. Original proposing Party: New Zealand Party undertaking management: New Zealand	77°25'S, 167°27'E	Measure 4 (1997)

No.	Description	Location	Designation/ Amendment
74.	The un-named cove on the south-west coast of Elephant Island, including the foreshore and the intertidal area, in which the wreckage of a large wooden sailing vessel is located. Original proposing Party: UK Party undertaking management: UK	61°14'S, 55°22'W	Measure 2 (1998)
75.	The A Hut of Scott Base, being the only existing Trans Antarctic Expedition 1956/1957 building in Antarctica sited at Pram Point, Ross Island, Ross Sea Region, Antarctica. Original proposing Party: New Zealand Party undertaking management: New Zealand	77°51'S, 166°46'E	Measure 1 (2001)
76.	The ruins of the Base Pedro Aguirre Cerda Station, being a Chilean meteorological and volcanological center situated at Pendulum Cove, Deception Island, Antarctica, that was destroyed by volcanic eruptions in 1967 and 1969. Original proposing Party: Chile Party undertaking management: Chile	62°59'S, 60°40'W	Measure 2 (2001)
77.	Cape Denison, Commonwealth Bay, George V Land, including Boat Harbour and the historic artefacts contained within its waters. This Site is contained within ASMA No. 3, designated by Measure 1 (2004). Part of this site is also contained within ASPA No. 162, designated by Measure 2 (2004). Original proposing Party: Australia Party undertaking management: Australia	67°00'30"S, 142°39'40"	Measure 3 (2004)
78.	Memorial plaque at India Point, Humboldt Mountains, Wohlthat Massif, central Dronning Maud Land erected in memory of three scientists of the Geological Survey of India (GSI) and a communication technician from the Indian Navy - all members of the ninth Indian Expedition to Antarctica, who sacrificed their lives in this mountain camp in an accident on 8th January 1990. Original proposing Party: India Party undertaking management: India.	71°45'08"S, 11°12'30"E	Measure 3 (2004)

No.	Description	Location	Designation/ Amendment
79.	Lillie Marleen Hut, Mt. Dockery, Everett Range, Northern Victoria Land. The hut was erected to support the work of the German Antarctic Northern Victoria Land Expedition (GANOVEX I) of 1979/1980. The hut, a bivouac container made of prefabricated fiberglass units insulated with polyurethane foam, was named after the Lillie Glacier and the song "Lillie Marleen". The hut is closely associated with the dramatic sinking of the expedition ship "Gotland II" during GANOVEX II in December 1981. Original proposing Party: Germany Party undertaking management: Germany	71°12'S, 164°31'E	Measure 5 (2005)
80.	Amundsen's Tent. The tent was erected at 90° by the Norwegian group of explorers led by Roald Amundsen on their arrival at the South Pole on 14 December 1911. The tent is currently buried underneath the snow and ice in the vicinity of the South Pole. Original proposing Party: Norway Party undertaking management: Norway	90°S	Measure 5 (2005)
81.	Rocher du Débarquement (Landing Rock), being a small island where Admiral Dumont D'Urville and his crew landed on 21 January 1840 when he discovered Terre Adélie. Original proposing Party: France Party undertaking management: France	66° 36.30'S, 140° 03.85'E	Measure 3 (2006)

No.	Description	Location	Designation/ Amendment
82.	Monument to the Antarctic Treaty and Plaque. This Monument is located near the Frei, Bellingshausen and Escudero bases, Fildes Peninsula, King George Island. The plaque at the foot of the monument commemorates the signatories of the Antarctic Treaty. This Monument has 4 plaques in the official languages of the Antarctic Treaty. The plaques were installed in February 2011 and read as follows: "This historic monument, dedicated to the memory of the signatories of the Antarctic Treaty, Washington D.C., 1959, is also a reminder of the legacy of the First and Second International Polar Years (1882-1883 and 1932-1933) and of the International Geophysical Year (1957-1958) that preceded the Antarctic Treaty, and recalls the heritage of International Cooperation that led to the International Polar Year 2007-2008." This monument was designed and built by the American Joseph W. Pearson, who offered it to Chile. It was unveiled in 1999, on the occasion of the 40th anniversary of the signature of the Antarctic Treaty." Original proposing Party: Chile Party undertaking management: Chile	62° 12' 01" S; 58° 57' 41" W	Measure 3 (2007) Measure 11 (2011)
83.	Base "W", Detaille Island, Lallemande Fjord, Loubert Coast. Base "W" is situated on a narrow isthmus at the northern end of Detaille Island, Lallemand Fjord, Loubet Coast. The site consists of a hut and a range of associated structures and outbuildings including a small emergency storage building, bitch and pup pens, anemometer tower and two standard tubular steel radio masts (one to the south west of the main hut and the other to the east). Base "W" was established in 1956 as a British science base primarily for survey, geology and meteorology and to contribute to the IGY in 1957. As a relatively unaltered base from the late 1950s, Base "W" provides an important reminder of the science and living conditions that existed when the Antarctic Treaty was signed 50 years ago. Original proposing Party: United Kingdom Party undertaking management: United Kingdom	66°52'S; 66°48'W	Measure 14 (2009)

No.	Description	Location	Designation/ Amendment
84.	Hut at Damoy Point, Dorian Bay, Wiencke Island, Palmer Archipelago. The site consists of a well-preserved hut and the scientific equipment and other artefacts inside it. It is located at Damoy Point on Dorian Bay, Wiencke Island, Palmer Archipelago. The hut was erected in 1973 and used for a number of years as a British summer air facility and transit station for scientific personnel. It was last occupied in 1993. Original proposing Party: United Kingdom Party undertaking management: United Kingdom	64°49'S; 63°31'W	Measure 14 (2009)
85.	Plaque Commemorating the PM-3A Nuclear Power Plant at McMurdo Station. The plaque is approximately 18 x 24 inches, made of bronze and secured to a large vertical rock at McMurdo Station, the former site of the PM-3A nuclear power reactor. It is approximately half way up the west side of Observation Hill. The plaque text details achievements of PM-3A, Antarctica's first nuclear power plant. Original proposing Party: United States Party Undertaking Management: United States	77°51'S, 166°41'E	Measure 15 (2010)
86.	No.1 Building at Great Wall Station. The No.1 Building, built in 1985 with a total floor space of 175 square meters, is located at the centre of the Chinese Antarctic Great Wall Station which is situated in Fildes Peninsula, King George Island, South Shetlands, West Antarctica. The Building marked the commencement of China devoting to Antarctic research in the 1980s, and thus it is of great significance in commemorating China's Antarctic expedition. Original proposing Party: China Party undertaking management: China	62°13'4"S, 58°57'44"W	Measure 12 (2011)

No.	Description	Location	Designation/ Amendment
87.	Location of the first permanently occupied German Antarctic research station "Georg Forster" at the Schirmacher Oasis, Dronning Maud Land. The original site is situated by the Schirmacher Oasis and marked by a commemorative bronze plaque with the label in German language: Antarktisstation Georg Forster 70° 46' 39" S 11° 51' 03" E von 1976 bis 1996 The plaque is well preserved and affixed to a rock wall at the southern edge of the location. This Antarctic research station was opened on 21 April 1976 and closed down in 1993. The entire site has been completely cleaned up after the dismantling of the station was successfully terminated on 12 February 1996. The site is located about 1.5 km east of the current Russian Antarctic research station Novolazarevskaya. Original proposing Party: Germany Party undertaking management: Germany	70°46'39" S, 11°51'03" E Elevation: 141 meters above sea level	Measure 18 (2013)
88.	Professor Kudryashov's Drilling Complex Building. The drilling complex building was constructed in the summer season of 1983-84. Under the leadership of Professor Boris Kudryashov, ancient mainland ice samples were obtained. Original proposing Party: Russian Federation Party undertaking management: Russian Federation	78°28' S, 106° 48' E Height above sea level 3488 m.	Measure 19 (2013)
89.	Terra Nova Expedition 1910-12, Upper "Summit Camp" used during survey of Mount Erebus in December 1912. Camp Site location includes part of a circle of rocks, which were likely used to weight the tent valences. The camp site was used by a science party on Captain Scott's Terra Nova Expedition, who undertook mapping and collected geological specimens on Mount Erebus in December 1912. Original proposing Parties: United Kingdom, New Zealand and United States Parties undertaking management: United Kingdom, New Zealand and United States	77°30.348' S, 167°10.223'E Circa 3,410m above sea level	Measure 20 (2013)

No.	Description	Location	Designation/ Amendment
90.	Terra Nova Expedition 1910-12, Lower "Camp E" Site used during survey of Mount Erebus in December 1912. Camp Site location consists of a slightly elevated area of gravel and includes some aligned rocks, which may have been used to weight the tent valences. The camp site was used by a science party on Captain Scott's Terra Nova Expedition, who undertook mapping and collected geological specimens on Mount Erebus in December 1912. Original proposing Parties: United Kingdom, New Zealand and United States Parties undertaking management: United Kingdom, New Zealand and United States	77°30.348' S, 167°9.246'E Circa 3,410 m above sea level	Measure 21 (2013)
91.	Lame Dog Hut at the Bulgarian base St. Kliment Ohridski, Livingston Island. The Lame Dog Hut was erected in April 1988, and had been the main building of St. Kliment Ohridski base until 1998. It is presently the oldest preserved building on Livingston Island, used as radio shack and post office, and hosting a museum exhibition of associated artefacts from the early Bulgarian science and logistic operations in Antarctica. Original proposing Party: Bulgaria Party undertaking management: Bulgaria	62°38'29"S, 60°21'53"W	Measure 19 (2015)
92.	Oversnow heavy tractor "Kharkovchanka" that was used in Antarctica from 1959 to 2010. The oversnow heavy tractor "Kharkovchanka" was designed and produced at the Malyshev Transport Machine-Building Plant in Kharkov specially for organizing inland sledge-tractor traverses in Antarctica. This was the first non-serial transport vehicle of the Soviet machine-building produced exclusively for operations in Antarctica. This tractor was not used outside Antarctica. Thus, the STT "Kharkovchanka" is a unique historical sample of engineering-technical developments made for exploration of Antarctica. Original proposing Party: the Russian Federation Party undertaking management: the Russian Federation	69°22'41,0" S, 76°22'59,1" E.	Measure 19 (2015)

237

2. Decisions

Observers to the Committee for Environmental Protection

The Representatives,

Acting upon the advice of the Committee for Environmental Protection ("CEP");

Recalling Decision 1 (2000) confirming certain organisations as observers;

Decide to confirm as observers to the CEP according to Rule 4c of the Rules of Procedure for the Committee for Environmental Protection the following organisations: ASOC, IAATO, IHO, IPCC, IUCN, UNEP and WMO, until such time as the Antarctic Treaty Consultative Meeting decides otherwise.

Revised Rules of Procedure for the Antarctic Treaty Consultative Meeting

The Representatives,

Recalling Decision 1 *(2015) Revised Rules of Procedure for the Antarctic Treaty Consultative Meeting (2015), Revised Rules of Procedure for the Committee for Environmental Protection (2011) and Procedures for the Submission, Translation and Distribution of documents for the ATCM and the CEP*;

Recognising the need to provide clear guidance to the Secretariat of the Antarctic Treaty ("the Secretariat") about which contact persons each Antarctic Treaty Consultative Party considers appropriate to contact during a formal intersessional consultation;

Further recognising the continued utility of the contact points for dissemination of both Antarctic Treaty and scientific information as envisaged in Recommendation XIII-1 (1985);

Noting, however, that the contact points designated under Recommendation XIII-1 (1985) are not necessarily the appropriate individuals to contact during a formal intersessional consultation;

Considering that awareness of the work of the Antarctic Treaty Consultative Meeting ("ATCM") would be enhanced through the public release of its report within three months following each ATCM;

Noting the need to update the *Revised Rules of Procedure for the Antarctic Treaty Consultative Meeting (2015)* including its Annex *Procedures for the Submission, Translation and Distribution of documents for the ATCM and the CEP*;

Decide:

1. that the Revised Rules of Procedure for the Antarctic Treaty Consultative Meeting annexed to this Decision shall replace the Revised Rules of Procedure for the Antarctic Treaty Consultative Meeting (2015); and

2. that the Secretariat shall make the list of Representatives and Alternate Representatives designated under the revised Rule 46(a) of the Rules of Procedure of the Antarctic Treaty Consultative Meeting available to the public on its website under the heading "ATCM Intersessional Representatives" on a page separate from that listing the CEP and Recommendation XIII-1 (1985) contact points.

Revised Rules of Procedure for the Antarctic Treaty Consultative Meeting (2016)

1. Meetings held pursuant to Article IX of the Antarctic Treaty shall be known as Antarctic Treaty Consultative Meetings. Contracting Parties entitled to participate in those Meetings shall be referred to as "Consultative Parties"; other Contracting Parties which may have been invited to attend those Meetings shall be referred to as "non-Consultative Parties". The Executive Secretary of the Secretariat of the Antarctic Treaty shall be referred to as the "Executive Secretary".

2. The Representatives of the Commission for the Conservation of Antarctic Marine Living Resources, the Scientific Committee on Antarctic Research and the Council of Managers of National Antarctic Programs, invited to attend those Meetings in accordance with Rule 31, shall be referred to as "Observers".

Representation

3. Each Consultative Party shall be represented by a delegation composed of a Representative and such Alternate Representatives, Advisers and other persons as each State may deem necessary. Each non-Consultative Party which has been invited to attend a Consultative Meeting shall be represented by a delegation composed of a Representative and such other persons as it may deem necessary within such numerical limit as may from time to time be determined by the Host Government in consultation with the Consultative Parties. The Commission for the Conservation of Antarctic Marine Living Resources, the Scientific Committee on Antarctic Research and the Council of Managers of National Antarctic Programs shall be represented by their respective Chairman or President, or other persons appointed to this end. The names of members of delegations and of the observers shall be communicated to the Host Government prior to the opening of the Meeting.

4. The order of precedence of the delegations shall be in accordance with the alphabet in the language of the Host Government, all delegations of non-Consultative Parties following after those of Consultative Parties, and all delegations of observers following after non-Consultative Parties.

Officers

5. A Representative of the Host Government shall be the Temporary Chairman of the Meeting and shall preside until the Meeting elects a Chairman.

6. At its inaugural session, a Chairman from one of the Consultative Parties shall be elected. The other Representatives of Consultative Parties shall serve as Vice-Chairmen of the Meeting in order of precedence. The Chairman normally shall preside at all plenary sessions. If he is absent from any session or part thereof, the Vice-Chairmen, rotating on the basis of the order of precedence as established by Rule 4, shall preside during each such session.

Secretariat

7. The Executive Secretary shall act as Secretary to the Meeting. He or she shall be responsible, with the assistance of the Host Government, for providing secretariat services for the meeting, as provided in Article 2 of Measure 1 (2003), as provisionally applied by Decision 2 (2003) until Measure 1 becomes effective.

Sessions

8. The opening plenary session shall be held in public, other sessions shall be held in private, unless the Meeting shall determine otherwise.

Committees and Working Groups

9. The Meeting, to facilitate its work, may establish such committees as it may deem necessary for the performance of its functions, defining their terms of reference.

10. The committees shall operate under the Rules of Procedure of the Meeting, except where they are inapplicable.

11. Working Groups may be established by the Meeting, or its committees to deal with various agenda items. The Meeting will determine the provisional arrangements for Working Groups at the end of each Consultative Meeting, when it approves the preliminary agenda for the subsequent Meeting (under Rule 36). These arrangements will include

   a.   the establishment of Working Group(s) for the subsequent Meeting;

   b.   the appointment of Working Group Chair(s); and

   c.   the allocation of agenda items to each Working Group.

Where the Meeting decides that a Working Group should be continued for more than one year, the Chair(s) of those Working Group(s) may be appointed for a period of one or two consecutive Meetings in the first instance. Working Group Chairs may subsequently be appointed for further terms of one or two years, but will not serve for more than four consecutive years in the same Working Group.

Should the Meeting be unable to appoint a Working Group Chair(s) for the subsequent Meeting, a Chair(s) shall be appointed at the beginning of the subsequent Meeting.

Conduct of Business

12. A quorum shall be constituted by two-thirds of the Representatives of Consultative Parties participating in the Meeting.

13. The Chairman shall exercise the powers of his office in accordance with customary practice. He shall see to the observance of the Rules of Procedure and the maintenance of proper order. The Chairman, in the exercise of his functions, remains under the authority of the Meeting.

14. Subject to Rule 28, no Representative may address the Meeting without having previously obtained the permission of the Chairman and the Chairman shall call upon speakers in the order in which they signify their desire to speak. The Chairman may call a speaker to order if his remarks are not relevant to the subject under discussion.

15. During the discussion of any matter, a Representative of a Consultative Party may rise to a point of order and the point of order shall be decided immediately by the Chairman in accordance with the Rules of Procedure. A Representative of a Consultative Party may appeal against the ruling of the Chairman. The appeal shall be put to a vote immediately, and the Chairman's ruling shall stand unless over-ruled by a majority of the Representatives of Consultative Parties present and voting. A Representative of a Consultative party rising to a point of order shall not speak on the substance of the matter under discussion.

16. The Meeting may limit the time to be allotted to each speaker, and the number of times he may speak on any subject. When the debate is thus limited and a Representative has spoken his allotted time, the Chairman shall call him to order without delay.

17. During the discussion of any matter, a Representative of a Consultative Party may move the adjournment of the debate on the item under discussion. In addition to the proposer of the motion, Representatives of two Consultative Parties may speak in favour of, and two against, the motion, after which the motion shall be put to the vote immediately. The Chairman may limit the time to be allowed to speakers under this Rule.

18. A Representative of a Consultative Party may at any time move the closure of the debate in the item under discussion, whether or not any other Representative has signified his wish to speak. Permission to speak on the closure of the debate shall be accorded only to Representatives of two Consultative Parties opposing the closure, after which the motion shall be put to the vote immediately. If the Meeting is in favour of the closure, the Chairman shall declare the closure of the debate. The Chairman may limit the time to be allowed to speakers under this Rule. (This Rule shall not apply to debate in committees.)

19. During the discussion of any matter, a Representative of a Consultative Party may move the suspension or adjournment of the Meeting. Such motions shall not be debated, but shall be put to the vote immediately. The Chairman may limit the time to be allowed to the speaker moving the suspension or adjournment of the Meeting.

20. Subject to Rule 15, the following motions shall have precedence in the following order over all other proposals or motions before the Meeting:

    a.   to suspend the Meeting;

    b.   to adjourn the Meeting;

    c.   to adjourn the debate on the item under discussion;

    d.   for the closure of the debate on the item under discussion.

21. Decisions of the Meeting on all matters of procedure shall be taken by a majority of the Representatives of Consultative Parties participating in the Meeting, each of whom shall have one vote.

Languages

22. English, French, Russian and Spanish shall be the official languages of the Meeting.

23. Any Representative may speak in a language other than the official languages. However, in such cases he shall provide for interpretation into one of the official languages.

Measures, Decisions, and Resolutions and Final Report

24. Without prejudice to Rule 21, Measures, Decisions and Resolutions, as referred to in Decision 1 (1995), shall be adopted by the Representatives of all Consultative Parties present and will thereafter be subject to the provisions of Decision 1 (1995).

25. The final report shall also contain a brief account of the proceedings of the Meeting. It will be approved by a majority of the Representatives of Consultative Parties present and shall be transmitted by the Executive Secretary to Governments of all Consultative and non-Consultative Parties which have been invited to take part in the Meeting for their consideration.

26. Notwithstanding Rule 25, the Executive Secretary, immediately following the closure of the Consultative Meeting, shall notify all Consultative Parties of all Measures, Decisions and Resolutions taken and send them authenticated copies of the definitive texts in an appropriate language of the Meeting. In respect to a Measure adopted under the procedures of Article 6 or 8 of Annex V of the Protocol, the respective notification shall also include the time period for approval of that Measure.

Non-Consultative Parties

27. Representatives of non-Consultative Parties, if invited to attend a Consultative Meeting, may be present at:

    a.   all plenary sessions of the Meeting; and

    b.   all formal Committees or Working Groups, comprising all Consultative Parties, unless a Representative of a Consultative Party requests otherwise in any particular case.

28. The relevant Chairman may invite a Representative of a non-Consultative Party to address the Meeting, Committee or Working group which he is attending, unless a Representative of a Consultative Party requests otherwise. The Chairman shall at any time give priority to Representatives of Consultative Parties who signify their desire to speak and may, in inviting Representatives of non-Consultative Parties to address the Meeting, limit the time to be allotted to each speaker and the number of times he may speak on any subject.

29. Non-Consultative Parties are not entitled to participate in the taking of decisions.

30.

    a.   Non-Consultative Parties may submit documents to the Secretariat for distribution to the Meeting as information documents. Such documents shall be relevant to matters under Committee consideration at the Meeting.

b.   Unless a Representative of a Consultative Party requests otherwise such documents shall be available only in the language or languages in which they were submitted.

Antarctic Treaty System Observers

31. The observers referred to in Rule 2 shall attend the Meetings for the specific purpose of reporting on:

a.   in the case of the Commission for the Conservation of Antarctic Marine Living Resources, developments in its area of competence.

b.   in the case of the Scientific Committee on Antarctic Research:

    i)   the general proceedings of SCAR;

    ii)   matters within the competence of SCAR under the Convention for the Conservation of Antarctic Seals;

    iii)   such publications and reports as may have been published or prepared in accordance with Recommendations IX-19 and VI-9 respectively.

c.   in the case of the Council of Managers of National Antarctic Programs, the activities within its area of competence.

32. Observers may be present at:

a.   the plenary sessions of the Meeting at which the respective Report is considered;

b.   formal committees or working groups, comprising all Contracting Parties at which the respective Report is considered, unless a Representative of a Consultative Party requests otherwise in any particular case.

33. Following the presentation of the pertinent Report, the relevant Chairman may invite the observer to address the Meeting at which it is being considered once again, unless a Representative of a Consultative Party requests otherwise. The Chairman may allot a time limit for such interventions.

34. Observers are not entitled to participate in the taking of decisions.

35. Observers may submit their Report and/or documents relevant to matters contained therein to the Secretariat, for distribution to the Meeting as working papers.

Agenda for Consultative Meetings

36. At the end of each Consultative Meeting, the Host Government of that Meeting shall prepare a preliminary agenda for the next Consultative Meeting. If approved by the Meeting, the preliminary agenda for the next Meeting shall be annexed to the Final Report of the Meeting.

37. Any Contracting Party may propose supplementary items for the preliminary agenda by informing the Host Government for the forthcoming Consultative Meeting no later than 180

days before the beginning of the Meeting; each proposal shall be accompanied by an explanatory memorandum. The Host Government shall draw the attention of all Contracting Parties to this Rule no later than 210 days before the Meeting.

38. The Host Government shall prepare a provisional agenda for the Consultative Meeting. The provisional agenda shall contain:

   a.   all items on the preliminary agenda decided in accordance with Rule 36; and

   b.   all items the inclusion of which has been requested by a Contracting Party pursuant to Rule 37.

Not later than 120 days before the Meeting, the Host Government shall transmit to all the Contracting Parties the provisional agenda, together with explanatory memoranda and any other papers related thereto.

Experts from International Organisations

39. At the end of each Consultative Meeting, the Meeting shall decide which international organisations having a scientific or technical interest in Antarctica shall be invited to designate an expert to attend the forthcoming Meeting in order to assist it in its substantive work.

40. Any Contracting Party may thereafter propose that an invitation be extended to other international organisations having a scientific or technical interest in Antarctica to assist the Meeting in its substantive work; each such proposal shall be submitted to the Host Government for that Meeting not later than 180 days before the beginning of the Meeting and shall be accompanied by a memorandum setting out the basis for the proposal.

41. The Host Government shall transmit these proposals to all Contracting Parties in accordance with the procedure in Rule 38. Any Consultative Party which wishes to object to a proposal shall do so not less than 90 days before the Meeting.

42. Unless such an objection has been received, the Host Government shall extend invitations to international organisations identified in accordance with Rules 39 and 40 and shall request each international organisation to communicate the name of the designated expert to the Host Government prior to the opening of the Meeting. All such experts may attend the Meeting during consideration of all items, except for those items relating to the operation of the Antarctic Treaty System which are identified by the previous Meeting or upon adoption of the agenda.

43. The relevant Chairman, with the agreement of all the Consultative Parties, may invite an expert to address the meeting he is attending. The Chairman shall at any time give priority to Representatives of Consultative Parties or non-Consultative Parties or Observers referred to in Rule 31 who signify their desire to speak, and may in inviting an expert to address the Meeting limit the time to be allotted to him and the number of times he may speak on any subject.

44. Experts are not entitled to participate in the taking of decisions.

45.

    a.   Experts may, in respect of the relevant agenda item, submit documents to the Secretariat for distribution to the Meeting as information documents.

    b.   Unless a Representative of a Consultative Party requests otherwise, such documents shall be available only in the language or languages in which they were submitted.

Intersessional Consultations

46. Intersessionally, the Executive Secretary shall, within his/her competence as established under Measure 1 (2003) and associated instruments that govern the operation of the Secretariat, consult the Consultative Parties, when legally required to do so under relevant instruments of the ATCM and when the exigencies of the circumstances require action to be taken before the opening of the next ATCM, using the following procedure:

    a.   Each Consultative Party shall keep the Executive Secretary advised on an ongoing basis of its Representative and any Alternate Representatives, who shall have authority to speak for their Consultative Party for the purposes of intersessional consultations.

    b.   The Executive Secretary shall maintain a list of the Representatives and Alternate Representatives and ensure that it remains current.

    c.   When intersessional consultations are required, the Executive Secretary shall transmit the relevant information and any proposed action to all Consultative Parties through their Representatives and any Alternate Representatives designated under paragraph (a) above, indicating an appropriate date by which responses are requested.

    d.   The Executive Secretary shall ensure that all Consultative Parties acknowledge the receipt of such transmission.

    e.   Each Consultative Party shall consider the matter and communicate its reply, if any, to the Executive Secretary through its Representative or an Alternate Representative by the specified date.

    f.   The Executive Secretary after informing the Consultative Parties of the result of the consultations, may proceed to take the proposed action if no Consultative Party has objected.

    g.   The Executive Secretary shall keep a record of the intersessional consultations, including results of those intersessional consultations and the actions taken by him/her and shall reflect these results and actions in his/her report to the ATCM for its review.

47. Intersessionally, when a request for information about the activities of the ATCM is received from an international organisation having a scientific or technical interest in Antarctica, the Executive Secretary shall coordinate a response, using the following procedure:

a.   The Executive Secretary shall transmit the request and a first draft response to all Consultative Parties through their Representatives and any Alternate Representatives designated under Rule 46 (a), proposing to answer the request, and including an appropriate date by which Consultative Parties should either (1) indicate that it would not be appropriate to answer, or (2) provide comments to the first draft response. The date shall give a reasonable amount of time to provide comments, taking into account any deadlines set by the initial requests for information. If a Consultative Party indicates that a response would not be appropriate, the Executive Secretary shall send only a formal response, acknowledging the request without going into the substance of the matter.

b.   If there is no objection to proceeding and if comments are provided before the date specified in the transmission referred to in paragraph (a) above, the Executive Secretary shall revise the response in light of the comments and transmit the revised response to all Consultative Parties, including an appropriate date by which reactions are requested.

c.   If any further comments are provided before the date specified in the transmission referred to in paragraph (b) above, the Executive Secretary shall repeat the procedure referred to in paragraph (b) above until no further comments are provided.

d.   If no comments are provided before the date specified in a transmission referred to in paragraph (a), (b) or (c) above, the Executive Secretary shall circulate a final version and shall request both an active digital "read"-confirmation and an active digital "accept"-confirmation from each Consultative Party, suggesting a date by which the "accept"-confirmation should be received. The Executive Secretary shall keep the Consultative Parties informed about the progress of received confirmations. After receipt of "accept"-confirmations from all Consultative Parties the Executive Secretary shall sign and send the response to the international organisation concerned, on behalf of all Consultative Parties, and shall provide a copy of the signed response to all Consultative Parties.

e.   Any Consultative Party may, at any stage of this process, ask for more time for consideration.

f.   Any Consultative Party may, at any stage of this process, indicate that it would not be appropriate to respond to the request. In this case the Executive Secretary shall send only a formal response, acknowledging the request without going into the substance of the matter.

Meeting Documents

48. Working Papers shall refer to papers submitted by Consultative Parties that require discussion and action at a Meeting and papers submitted by Observers referred to in Rule 2.

49. Secretariat Papers shall refer to papers prepared by the Secretariat pursuant to a mandate established at a Meeting, or which would, in the view of the Executive Secretary, help inform the Meeting or assist in its operation.

50. Information Papers shall refer to:

- Papers submitted by Consultative Parties or Observers that provide information in support of a Working Paper or that are relevant to discussions at a Meeting;
- Papers submitted by Non-Consultative Parties that are relevant to discussions at a Meeting; and
- Papers submitted by Experts that are relevant to discussions at a Meeting.

51. Background Papers shall refer to papers submitted by any participant that will not be introduced in a Meeting, but that are submitted for the purpose of formally providing information.

52. Procedures for the submission, translation and distribution of documents are annexed to these Rules of Procedure.

Amendments

53. These Rules of Procedure may be amended by a two-thirds majority of the Representatives of Consultative Parties participating in the Meeting. This Rule shall not apply to Rules 24, 27, 29, 34, 39-42, 44, and 46, amendments of which shall require the approval of the Representatives of all Consultative Parties present at the Meeting.

Annex

Procedures for the Submission, Translation and Distribution of Documents for the ATCM and the CEP

1. These procedures apply to the submission, translation and distribution of official papers for the Antarctic Treaty Consultative Meeting (ATCM) and for the Committee on Environmental Protection (CEP) as defined in their respective Rules of Procedure. These papers consist of Working Papers, Secretariat Papers, Information Papers and Background Papers.

2. Papers that are submitted to both the ATCM and the CEP should indicate, where feasible, what portions or elements of the paper should, in the opinion of the submitter, be discussed in each forum.

3. Documents to be translated are Working Papers, Secretariat Papers, reports submitted to the ATCM by ATCM Observers and invited Experts according to the provisions of Recommendation XIII-2, reports submitted to the ATCM in relation to Article III-2 of the Antarctic Treaty, and Information Papers that a Consultative Party requests be translated. Background Papers will not be translated.

4. Papers that are to be translated, with the exception of the reports of Intersessional Contact Groups (ICG) convened by the ATCM or CEP, Chair Reports from Antarctic Treaty Meetings of Experts, and the Secretariat's Report and Programme, should not exceed 1500 words. When calculating the length of a paper, proposed Measures, Decisions and Resolutions and their attachments are not included.

5. Papers that are to be translated should be received by the Secretariat no later than 45 days before the Consultative Meeting. If any such paper is submitted later than 45 days before the Consultative Meeting, it may only be considered if no Consultative Party objects.

6. The Secretariat should receive Information Papers for which no translation has been requested and Background Papers that participants wish to be listed in the Final Report no later than 30 days before the Meeting.

7. The Secretariat will indicate on each document submitted by a Contracting Party, an Observer, or an Expert the date it was submitted.

8. When a revised version of a Paper made after its initial submission is resubmitted to the Secretariat for translation, the revised text should indicate clearly the amendments that have been incorporated.

9. The Papers should be transmitted to the Secretariat by electronic means and will be uploaded to the ATCM Home Page established by the Secretariat. Working Papers received before the 45 day limit should be uploaded as soon as possible and in any case not later than

30 days before the Meeting. Papers will be uploaded initially to the password protected portion of the website, and moved to the non-password protected part once the Meeting has concluded.

10. Parties may agree to present any paper for which a translation has not been requested to the Secretariat during the Meeting for translation.

11. No paper submitted to the ATCM should be used as the basis for discussion at the ATCM or at the CEP unless it has been translated into the four official languages.

12. Within three months of the end of the Consultative Meeting, the Secretariat will post on the ATCM Home Page a preliminary version of the Final Report of the Meeting in the four official languages. This version of the report shall be clearly marked "PRELIMINARY" and shall indicate that it is subject to final formatting, editing, and publishing processes.

13. Within six months of the end of the Consultative Meeting, the Secretariat will circulate to Parties and also post on the ATCM Home Page the Final Report of that Meeting in the four official languages.

Secretariat Report, Programme and Budget

The Representatives,

Recalling Measure 1 (2003) on the establishment of the Secretariat of the Antarctic Treaty ("the Secretariat");

Recalling Decision 2 (2012) on the establishment of the open-ended Intersessional Contact Group ("ICG") on Financial Issues to be convened by the host country of the next Antarctic Treaty Consultative Meeting ("ATCM");

Bearing in mind the Financial Regulations for the Secretariat of the Antarctic Treaty annexed to Decision 4 (2003);

Decide:

1. to approve the audited Financial Report for 2014/15, annexed to this Decision (Annex 1);

2. to take note of the Secretariat Report 2015/16, which includes the Provisional Financial Report for 2015/16 annexed to this Decision (Annex 2);

3. to take note of the Five Year Forward Budget Profile 2016-2020 and approve the Secretariat Programme 2016/17, including the Budget for 2016/17, annexed to this Decision (Annex 3); and

4. to invite the host country for the next ATCM to request that the Executive Secretary open the ATCM forum for the ICG on Financial Issues, and provide assistance to it.

Audited Financial Report for 2014/2015

AUDITOR'S REPORT

To: Head of the Antarctic Treaty Secretariat

Maipú 757, 4th floor

CUIT 30-70892567-1

Subject: ATCM XXXIX - CEP XIX Antarctic Treaty Consultative Meeting, 2016 - Santiago, Chile

1. Report on Financial Statements

We have audited the attached Financial Statements of the Antarctic Treaty Secretariat, which include the following: Statement of Income and Expenditure, Statement of Financial Position, Statement of Net Capital Assets, Cash Flow Statement and Explanatory Notes for the period commencing 1st April 2014 and ending 31st March 2015.

2. Management Responsibility for Financial Statements

The Antarctic Treaty Secretariat, organised under Argentine Act No. 25.888 of 14 May 2004, is responsible for the preparation and reasonable presentation of these Financial Statements according to International Accounting Standards and the specific standards for Antarctic Treaty Consultative Meetings. Such responsibility includes the design, implementation and maintenance of internal controls on the preparation and presentation of the Financial Statements, such that they are free of misstatements due to error or fraud; selection and implementation of appropriate accounting policies, and preparation of accounting estimates which are reasonable under the circumstances.

3. Auditor's Responsibility

Our responsibility is to express an opinion on these Financial Statements based on our audit.

The audit was conducted in accordance with International Auditing Standards and the Annexe to Decision 3 (2012) of the XXXI Antarctic Treaty Consultative Meeting, which describes the tasks to be carried out by the external audit.

These standards require compliance with ethical requirements, and planning and execution of the audit so as to provide reasonable assurance that the Financial Statements are free of material misstatements.

An audit includes the execution of procedures in order to obtain evidence on the amounts and the exposure reflected in the Financial Statements. The procedures selected depend on the auditor's judgement, including an assessment of the risks of material misstatement in the Financial Statements.

On conducting such assessment of risks, the auditor considers the internal control relevant to the preparation and reasonable presentation of the Financial Statements by the organisation, in order to design suitable procedures that are appropriate to the circumstances.

An audit also includes an assessment of appropriateness, of the accounting principles used, an opinion on whether the accounting estimates made by management are reasonable, as well as an assessment of the general presentation of the Financial Statements.

We believe that the audited evidence we have obtained is sufficient and appropriate to provide a basis for our opinion as auditors.

4. Opinion

In our opinion, the Financial Statements audited reasonably reflect, in all material aspects, the financial position of the Antarctic Treaty Secretariat as at 31st March 2015 and its financial performance for the period ending on such date in accordance with International Accounting Standards and the specific standards for Antarctic Treaty Consultative Meetings.

5. Additional Information Required by Law

Pursuant to the analysis described in point 3, I report that the abovementioned Financial Statements arise from accounting records that are not transcribed into books in accordance with current Argentine standards.

We also report that, according to bookkeeping as at 31 March 2015, the liabilities accrued for the Argentine Single Social Security System in Argentine pesos and pursuant to calculations made by the Secretariat amounted to $124,004.85 (US$ 14,059.51), none of which was due and payable in Argentine pesos as at that date.

It is worth noting that labour relationships are governed by Antarctic Treaty Secretariat Staff Regulations.

Dr Gisela Algaze
Public Accountant
CPCECABA Volume N°. 300, Folio N°· 169

Buenos Aires, 8 April 2016
Sindicatura General de la Nación
Av. Corrientes 389, Buenos Aires, Argentina

1. Statement of Income and Expenditure for all funds for the period 1ˢᵗ April 2014 to 31ˢᵗ March 2015, comparatively with the prior year.

INCOME	31/03/2014	Budget 31/03/2015	31/03/2015
CONTRIBUTIONS (Note 10)	1,339,600	1,379,710	1,379,710
Other Income (Note 2)	3,811	1,000	6,162
Total Income	1,343,411	1,380,710	1,385,872
EXPENDITURE			
Salaries and wages	650,000	678,600	677,760
Translation and interpreting services	249,671	325,780	294,318
Travel an accommodation	81,093	110,266	104,207
Information technology	41,919	44,000	33,224
Printing, editing and copying	12,823	23,640	18,910
General services	32,943	72,052	73,382
Communications	17,623	19,700	15,254
Office expenses	11,589	18,200	12,471
Administration	11,780	20,300	8,582
Representation expenses	2,211	3,500	4,267
Other	0	0	0
Financing	16,290	11,000	7,986
Total Expenses	1,127,942	1,327,038	1,250,361
FUND APPROPRIATION			
Staff Termination Fund	29,369	29,820	30,314
Staff Replacement Fund	0	0	0
Working Capital Fund	0	6,685	6,685
Contingency fund	0	0	0
Total Fund Appropriation	29,369	36,505	36,999
Total Expenses & Appropriation	1,157,311	1,363,543	1,287,360
(Deficit) / Surplus for the period	186,100	17,167	98,512

This statement should be read together with Notes 1 to 10 attached

2. Statement of Financial Position as at 31ˢᵗ March 2015, comparatively with the prior year

ASSETS	31/03/2014	31/03/2015
Current Assets		
Cash and cash equivalents (Note 3)	1,231,803	1,057,170
Contributions owed (Notes 9 and 10)	108,057	196,163
Other debtors (Note 4)	37,687	39,306
Other current assets (Note 5)	99,947	146,018
Total Current Assets	1,477,494	1,438,657
Non-Current Assets		
Fixed Assets (Notes 1,3 and 6)	79,614	79,614
Total Non-Current Assets	79,614	79,614
Total Assets	1,557,108	1,548,091
LIABILITIES		
Current Liabilities		
Accounts payable (Note 7)	25,229	30,462
Contributions received in advance (Note 10)	626,595	467,986
Special voluntary fund for specific purposes (Note 1,9)	0	13,372
Remuneration and payable contributions (Note 8)	64,507	30,163
Total Current Liabilities	716,331	541,983
Non-Current Liabilities		
Staff Termination Fund (Note 1,4)	176,880	207,194
Staff Replacement Fund (Note 1,5)	50,000	50,000
Contingency fund (Note 1,7)	30,000	30,000
Fixed assets replacement fund (Note 1,8)	13,318	43,138
Total Non-Current Liabilities	270,198	330,332
Total Liabilities	986,529	872,315
NET ASSETS	570,579	675,776

This statement should be read together with Notes 1 to 10 attached

3. Statement of Changes in Net Assets as at 31st March 2013 and 2014

Represented by	Net Assets 31/03/2014	Income	Expenses and appropriation	Earned interest	Net Assets
General Fund	347,312	1,379,710	-1,287,360	6,162	445,824
Working Capital Fund (Note 1,6)	223,267		6,685		229,952
Net Assets	570,579				675,776

This statement should be read together with Notes 1 to 10 attached

4. Cash Flow Statement for the period 1st April 2014 as at 31st March 2015, comparatively with the prior year

Variation in cash & cash equivalents		31/03/2015	31/03/2014
Cash & cash equivalent at beginning of the year	1,231,803		
Cash & cash equivalent at year end	1,057,170		
Net increase in cash and cash equivalents		-174,633	342,716
Causes for variations in Cash & Cash Equivalents			
Operating Activities			
Contributions received	665,014		
Payment of salaries and wages	-732,513		
Payment of translation services	-291,846		
Payment of travel and accommodation	-114,420		
Printing, editing and copying payment	-18,910		
General services payment	-56,338		
Other payments to providers	-36,290		
Net Cash & Cash Equivalents from Operating Activities		-585,303	-262,333
Investment Activities			

Purchase of Fixed Assets	-35,719		
Special voluntaryFund	0		
Net Cash & Cash Equivalents from Investment Activities		-35,719	-3,393
Financing Activities			
Contributions received in advance	467,986		
Collection pt. 5,6 Staff Regulations	151,897		
Payment pt. 5,6 Staff Regulations	-152,962		
Lease prepayment	24,400		
Net AFIP reimbursement	-42,934		
Net Cash & Cash Equivalents from Financing Activities		454,379	624,732
Foreign currency activities			
Net loss	-7,991		
Net cash & cash equivalents from foreign currency activities		-7,991	-16,290
Net increase in cash and cash equivalents		-174,632	342,716

This statement should be read together with Notes 1 to 10 attached

Notes to the Financial Statements
as at 31ˢᵗ March 2014 and 2015

1. Basis for Preparation of Financial Statements

These financial statements are presented in US dollars, following the guidelines established in Financial Regulations, annexed to Decision 4 (2003). These financial statements have been prepared in accordance with International Financial Reporting Standards (IFRS), as issued by the International Accounting Standards Board (IASB).

1.1. Historical Cost

The accounts are prepared in accordance with the historical cost rule, except where otherwise indicated.

1.2. Premises

The Secretariat Offices are provided by the Ministry of Foreign Affairs, International Trade and Cult of the Argentine Republic. Premises are free of rent and common expenses.

1.3. Fixed Assets

All items are valued at historical cost, less accumulated depreciation. Depreciation iscalculated on a straight-line basis at annual rates appropriate to their estimated useful life. The aggregate residual value of fixed assets does not exceed their use value.

1.4. Executive Staff Termination Fund

Pursuant to Section 10.4 of the Staff Regulations, this fund shall be sufficiently funded to compensate executive staff members at a rate of one month base pay for each year of service.

1.5. Staff Replacement Fund

This fund is used to cover Secretariat executive staff travel expenses to and from the Secretariat Head Office.

1.6. Working Capital Fund

Pursuant to Financial Regulations 6.2 (a), the fund shall stand at one-sixth (1/6) of the budget for the current financial year.

1.7. Contingency fund

Pursuant to Decision 4 (2009), this Fund was created to cover the translation expenses arising from the unexpected increase in the volume of documentation filed with the ATCM for translation purposes.

1.8. Fixed Assets Replacement Fund

Pursuant to IAS, assets with a useful life beyond the current financial year shall be reflected as an asset in the Statement of Financial Position. Up to March 2010, the balancing entry was an adjustment to the General Fund. As from April 2010, the balancing entry shall be reflected as a liability under such heading.

1.9. Voluntary Special Fund for Specific Purposes

Pt (82) of the XXXV ATCM Final Report, to receive voluntary contributions by the parties. The voluntary fund refers to money to pay lease rents and common expenses for the fiscal year.

1.10. Contributions not received

At the end of each year, there are unsettled contributions. This causes the General Fund to increase by an amount equal to unsettled contributions. Based on Financial Regulations 6.(3), "... notify Consultative Parties about any cash surplus in the General Fund...", during the year ended 31 March 2015 an amount of $196,163 should be deducted and, as at 31 March 2014, the deduction would amount to $108,057.

Notes to the Financial Statements
as at of 31st March 2014 and 2015

		31/03/2014	31/03/2015
2	**Other Income**		
	Earned interest	3,740	6,162
	Discounts obtained	71	0
	Total	3,811	6,162
3	**Cash and Cash Equivalents**		
	Cash US Dollars	1,185	61
	Cash Argentine Pesos	382	480
	BNA special US Dollar account	411,565	539,324
	BNA Argentine Peso account	15,557	17,077
	Santander Rio checking account in ARS	0	58
	Investments	803,114	500,170
	Total	1,231,803	1,057,170
4	**Other Receivables**		
	Staff Regulation pt 5,6.	37,687	39,306
5	**Other Current Assets**		
	Advance Payments	80,561	86,992
	VAT Receivable	14,771	54,250
	Other Recoverable Expenses	4,615	4,776
	Total	99,947	146,018
6	**Fixed Assets**		
	Books & Subscriptions	8,104	8,667
	Office Equipment	11,252	37,234
	Furniture	45,466	45,466
	IT Equipment and Software	95,025	120,262
	Total Original Cost	159,847	211,629
	Accumulated Depreciation	-80,233	-102,195
	Total	79,614	109,434

Notes to the Financial Statements
as at of 31st March 2014 and 2015

7 Accounts Payables

	Business	3,764	8,670
	Accrued Expenses	20,854	18,287
	Others	611	3,504
	Total	25,229	25,229

8 Remuneration and payable contributions

	Remuneration	45,479	9,274
	Contributions	19,028	20,889
	Total	64,507	30,163

Notes to the Financial Statements
as at of 31st March 2014 and 2015

9 Contributions owed, committed, settled and prepaid.

Contributions Parties	Owed 31/03/2014	Committed	Settled $	Owed 31/03/2015	Prepaid 31/03/2015
Argentina		60,346	60,346	0	0
Australia	25	60,346	60,346	25	60,347
Belgium	68	40,110	40,128	50	0
Brazil	866	40,110	708	40,268	0
Bulgaria		34,038	34,038	0	33,923
Czech Republic		40,110	40,110	0	0
Chile		46,181	46,181	0	46,119
China	25	46,181	46,181	25	0
Ecuador	34,039	34,038	34,038	34,039	0
Finland		40,110	40,110	0	40,021
France		60,346	60,346	0	60,347
Germany	23	52,250	52,262	11	0
India	74	46,181	46,143	112	0
Italy		52,250	52,250	0	0
Japan		60,346	60,346	0	0
Korea		40,110	40,110	0	0
Netherlands		46,181	46,181	0	0
New Zealand		60,346	60,321	25	60,391
Norway	35	60,346	60,321	60	60,372
Peru	32,692	34,038	65,643	1,087	0
Poland		40,110	40,110	0	0
Russia		46,181	46,181	0	0
South Africa		46,181	46,181	0	46,119
Spain	25	46,181	46,181	25	0
Sweden		46,181	46,151	30	0
Ukraine	40,110	40,110	0	80,220	0
United Kingdom		60,346	60,346	0	0
United States of America	25	60,346	60,346	25	60,347
Uruguay	50	40,110	0	40,160	0
Total	108,057	1,379,710	1,291,605	196,163	467,986

Dr. Manfred Reinke
Executive Secretary

Roberto A. Fennell
Finance Officer

Provisional Financial Report for 2015/16

**Estimate of Income and Expenditure for all Funds
for the Period 1 April 2015 to 31 March 2016**

APPROPRIATION LINES	Audited Statement 2014/15	Budget 2015/16	Prov. Statement 2015/16
INCOME			
CONTRIBUTIONS pledged	$ -1,379,710	$ -1,378,097	$ -1,378,099
Other Income	$ -6,162	$ -1,000	$ -13,577
Total Income	**$ -1,385,872**	**$ -1,379,097**	**$ -1,391,676**
EXPENDITURE			
SALARIES			
Executive	$ 322,658	$ 331,680	$ 331,679
General Staff	$ 318,417	$ 330,098	$ 330,359
ATCM Support Staff	$ 16,496	$ 18,192	$ 16,398
Trainee	$ 6,837	$ 10,600	$ 3,667
Overtime	$ 13,351	$ 16,000	$ 12,552
	$677,760	**$ 706,570**	**$ 694,656**
TRANSLATION AND INTERPRETATION			
Translation and Interpretation	**$ 294,318**	**$ 323,000**	**$ 301,634**
TRAVEL			
Travel	**$ 104,207**	**$ 99,000**	**$ 88,741**
INFORMATION TECHNOLOGY			
Hardware	$ 8,315	$ 10,815	$ 13,306
Software	$ 4,468	$ 3,500	$ 1,940
Development	$ 13,104	$ 24,000	$ 17,693
Support	$ 5,451	$ 9,500	$ 11,009
	$ 33,224	**$ 47,815**	**$ 43,949**
PRINTING, EDITING & COPYING			
Final report	$ 13,473	$ 17,850	$ 6,510
Compilation	$ 639	$ 3,500	$ 2,000
Site guidelines	$ 3,396	$ 3,500	$ 0
	$ 18,910	**$ 24,850**	**$ 8,995**

APPROPRIATION LINES	Audited Statement 2014/15	Budget 2015/16	Prov. Statement 2015/16
GENERAL SERVICES			
Legal advice	$ 1,036	$ 4,200	$ 2,008
External audit	$ 9,345	$ 10,500	$ 9,539
Cleaning, maintenance & security	$ 50,820	$ 19,011	$ 12,829
Training	$ 4,401	$ 6,880	$ 4,275
Banking	$ 5,276	$ 6,300	$ 5,143
Rental of equipment	$ 2,504	$ 2,556	$ 2,543
	$ 73,382	**$ 49,447**	**$ 36,335**
COMMUNICATION			
Telephone	$ 5,201	$ 5,460	$ 6,535
Internet	$ 2,487	$ 3,150	$ 2,574
Web hosting	$ 6,731	$ 9,450	$ 6,846
Postage	$ 834	$ 2,625	$ 5,437
	$ 15,254	**$ 20,685**	**$ 21,393**
OFFICE			
Stationery & supplies	$ 4,562	$ 4,515	$ 4,084
Books & subscriptions	$ 1,299	$ 3,150	$ 1,994
Insurance	$ 2,558	$ 3,675	$ 3,603
Furniture	$ 0	$ 7,945	$ 4,535
*Office equipment	$ 4,053	$ 21,200	$ 21,416
Maintenance	$ 0	$ 2,625	$ 0
	$ 12,471	**$ 43,110**	**$ 35,632**
ADMINISTRATIVE			
Supplies	$ 3,749	$ 4,725	$ 2,618
Local transport	$ 318	$ 840	$ 483
Miscellaneous	$ 3,477	$ 4,200	$ 1,481
Utilities (Energy)	$ 1,038	$ 6,550	$ 3,199
	$ 8,582	**$ 16,315**	**$ 7,781**
REPRESENTATION			
Representation	**$ 4,267**	**$ 4,000**	**$ 3,950**

APPROPRIATION LINES	Audited Statement 2014/15	Budget 2015/16	Prov. Statement 2015/16
FINANCING			
Exchange loss	**$ 7,986**	**$ 11,393**	**$ 10,540**
SUBTOTAL APPROPRIATIONS	**$ 1,250,361**	**$ 1,346,185**	**$ 1,253,605**
ALLOCATION TO FUNDS			
Translation Contingency Fund	$ 0	$ 0	$ 0
Staff Replacement Fund	$ 0	$ 0	$ 0
Staff Termination Fund	$ 30,314	$ 32,912	$ 32,912
Working Capital Fund	$ 6,685	$ 0	$ 0
	$ 36,999	**$ 32,912**	**$ 32,912**
TOTAL APPROPRIATIONS	**$ 1,287,360**	**$ 1,379,097**	**$ 1,286,517**
** Unpaid Contributions	**$ 40,325**	**$ 0**	**$ 81,547**
BALANCE	**$ 58,187**	**$ 0**	**$ 23,612**
Summary of Funds			
Translation Contingency Fund	$ 30,000	$ 30,000	$ 30,000
Staff Replacement Fund	$ 50,000	$ 50,000	$ 50,000
Staff Termination Fund	$ 207,194	$ 240,101	$ 237,489
***Working Capital Fund	$ 229,952	$ 229,952	$ 229,952

* Transfer from appropriation line "Translation and Interpretation" to Office Equiment" in Budget 15/16 (see SP 3)

** Unpaid contributions as of 31 March 2016

*** Maximum Required Amount Working Capital Fund (Fin Reg. 6,2)

	$ 229,683	$ 229,683	$ 229,683

Secretariat Programme 2016/17

Introduction

This work programme outlines the activities proposed for the Secretariat in the Financial Year 2016/17 (1 April 2016 to 31 March 2017). The main areas of activity of the Secretariat are treated in the first four parts, followed by a section on management and a forecast of the programme for the Financial Year 2017/18.

The Budget for the Financial Year 2016/17, the Forecast Budget for the Financial Year 2017/18, and the accompanying contribution and salary scales are included in the appendices.

The programme and the accompanying budget figures for 2016/17 are based on the Forecast Budget for the Financial Year 2016/17 (Decision 3 (2015), Annex 3, Appendix 1).

The programme focuses on the regular activities, such as the preparation of the ATCM XXXIX and ATCM XL, the publication of Final Reports, and the various specific tasks assigned to the Secretariat under Measure 1 (2003).

Contents:

1. ATCM/CEP support
2. Information Technology
3. Documentation
4. Public Information
5. Management
6. Forecast Programme for the Financial Year 2016/17
   - Appendix 1: Provisional Report for the Financial Year 2015/16, Budget for the Financial Year 2016/17, Forecast Budget for the Financial Year 2017/18
   - Appendix 2: Contribution Scale for the Financial Year 2017/18
   - Appendix 3: Salary Scale

1. ATCM/CEP Support

ATCM XXXIX

The Secretariat will support the ATCM XXXIX by gathering and collating the documents for the meeting and publishing them in a restricted section of the Secretariat website. The Secretariat will also provide, in a USB flash drive distributed to all delegates, an application that allows offline browsing of all documents and automatic synchronization with the online database for the latest updates. The Delegates section will provide online registration for delegates and a downloadable, up-to-date list of delegates.

The Secretariat will support the functioning of the ATCM through the production of Secretariat Papers, a Manual for Delegates, and summaries of papers for the ATCM, the CEP, and the ATCM Working Groups.

The Secretariat will organise the services for translation and interpretation. It is responsible for pre- and post-sessional translation and for the translation services during the ATCM. It maintains contact with the provider of interpretation services, ONCALL.

The Secretariat will organise the note-taking services in cooperation with the secretariat of the host country and is responsible for the compilation and editing of the Reports of the CEP and ATCM for adoption during the final plenary meetings.

The Secretariat will also support the Joint CEP/SC-CAMLR Workshop to be held in May 2016 in Punta Arenas by providing a restricted meeting document section, handling paper submission and assisting the registration process.

ATCM XL

The Host Country Secretariat of China and the Secretariat of the Antarctic Treaty will jointly prepare the ATCM XL, which will take place in China in May/June 2017.

The Secretariat will support the functioning of the ATCM through the production of Secretariat Papers, a Manual for Delegates, and summaries of papers with annotated agendas for the ATCM, the CEP, and the ATCM Working Groups.

Coordination and contact

Aside from maintaining constant contact via email, telephone and other means with the Parties and international institutions of the Antarctic Treaty System, attendance at meetings is an important tool to maintain coordination and communication.

The travelling to be undertaken is as follows:

- COMNAP Annual General Meeting (AGM) XXVII, Goa, India, 16 - 18 August 2016. Attendance to the meeting will provide an opportunity to further strengthen the connections and interaction with COMNAP.

- XXXIV SCAR Delegates Meeting, Kuala Lumpur, Malaysia, 29-30 August 2016. Attendance to the meeting will provide an opportunity to further strengthen the connections and interaction with SCAR.

- CCAMLR, Hobart, Australia, 19 - 30 October 2015. The CCAMLR meeting, which takes place roughly halfway between succeeding ATCMs, provides an opportunity for the Secretariat to brief the ATCM Representatives, many of whom attend the CCAMLR meeting, on developments in the Secretariat's work. Liaison with the CCAMLR Secretariat is also important for the Antarctic Treaty Secretariat, as many of its regulations are modelled after those of the CCAMLR Secretariat.

- Coordination Meetings with China as Host Country of ATCM XL in August 2015 and March 2016.

Support of intersessional activities

During recent years both the CEP and the ATCM have produced an important amount of intersessional work, mainly through Intersessional Contact Groups (ICGs). The Secretariat will provide technical support for the online establishment of the ICGs agreed at the ATCM XXXIX and CEP XIX, and will produce specific documents if required by the ATCM or the CEP.

The Secretariat will update its website with the measures adopted by the ATCM and with the information produced by the CEP and the ATCM.

The Secretariat will produce for each ATCM a Secretariat Paper, based on information received from the Depository Government, stating which Measures are current and not yet in force, as well as which Consultative Parties have approved a particular Measure and which have not yet done so.

The Secretariat will update the website to show a list of all stations, the date of last inspection and separately a list of those stations that have never been inspected.

Printing

The Secretariat will translate, publish and distribute the Final Report and its Annexes of the ATCM XXXIX in the four Treaty languages. The text of the Final Report will be published on the website of the Secretariat and will be printed in book form. The full text of the Final Report will be available in book form (two volumes) through online retailers and also in electronic book form.

2. Information Technology

Information Exchange

The Secretariat will continue to assist Parties in posting their information exchange materials, as well as processing information uploaded using the File Upload functionality.

The Secretariat will continue to provide advice, if requested, to the ongoing ICG on reviewing information exchange requirements.

Electronic Information Exchange System

During the next operational season and depending on the decisions of the ATCM XXXIX, the Secretariat will continue to make the adjustments necessary to facilitate the use of the electronic system for the Parties, as well as develop tools to compile and present summarised reports.

Contacts Database

The Secretariat plans to carry out a complete redesign of this tool, introducing new technologies which will make its interface more user friendly and improve usability on multiple devices.

Additionally, improved internal procedures for contact and communications management, including development of required software, will be implemented.

Development of the Secretariat website

The website will continue to be improved to make it more concise and easier to use, and to increase the visibility of the most relevant sections and information.

3. Records and documents

Documents of the ATCM

The Secretariat will continue its efforts to complete its archive of the Final Reports and other records of the ATCM and other meetings of the Antarctic Treaty System in the four Treaty languages. Assistance from Parties in searching for their files will be essential in order to achieve a complete archive at the Secretariat. The project will continue in the Financial Year 2016/17. A complete and detailed list of missing papers in our database is available to all delegations interested in collaborating.

Glossary

The Secretariat will continue to further develop the Secretariat's glossary of terms and expressions of the ATCM to generate a nomenclature in the four Treaty languages. It will further improve the implementation of the electronically-controlled vocabulary server to manage, publish and share these ATCM ontologies, thesauri, and lists.

Antarctic Treaty database

The database of Recommendations, Measures, Decisions and Resolutions of the ATCM is at present complete in English and almost complete in Spanish and French, although the Secretariat still lacks various Final Report copies in those languages. In Russian, further Final Reports are lacking.

4. Public Information

The Secretariat and its website will continue to function as a clearinghouse for information on the Parties' activities and relevant developments in Antarctica.

5. Management

Personnel

On 1 April 2016 the Secretariat staff consisted of the following personnel:

Executive staff

Name	Position	Since	Rank	Step	Term
Manfred Reinke	Executive Secretary (ES)	01-09-2009	E1	7	31-08-2017
José María Acero	Assistant Executive Secretary (AES)	01-01-2005	E3	12	31-12-2018

General staff

José Luis Agraz	Information Officer	1-11-2004	G1	6	
Diego Wydler	Information Technology Officer	01-02-2006	G1	6	
Roberto Alan Fennell	Finance Officer (part time)	01-12-2008	G2	6	
Pablo Wainschenker	Editor	01-02-2006	G2	2	
Violeta Antinarelli	Librarian (part time)	01-04-2007	G3	6	
Anna Balok	Communications Specialist (part time)	01-10-2010	G5	6	
Viviana Collado	Office Manager	15-11-2012	G5	5	
Margarita Tolaba	Cleaning Professional	01-07-2015	G7	1	

The ATCM XXXVI decided to reappoint the Executive Secretary for a term of four years starting on 1 September 2013 (see Decision 2 (2013)). The ATCM may wish to commence consideration of his replacement at this ATCM.

The Executive Secretary asks for approval to advance Ms Anna Balok to salary level G4(1) and Ms. Viviana Collado to salary level G4(1) pursuant to Regulation 5.5 of the Staff Regulations.

Ms Balok has conferred responsibly for external and internal communication and editing processes in the Secretariat supporting the Information Officer, the Editor and the Executive staff. She has proven to work independently and responsibly in a wide range of tasks including, inter alia, support to Chairs during ATCMs, active participation in the editing processes of reports, and general management of the Secretariat.

Ms Collado has conferred, besides her tasks as Office Manager, wide responsibility in organising the complex banking issues with Banco de la Nación Argentina concerning exemptions of the Secretariat from certain financial restrictions according to Article 12 of the Headquarters Agreement. Furthermore, she conferred more responsibilities in the Secretariat's accounting processes to implement a secure system of segregation of duties this area.

The Secretariat will invite international trainees from Parties for internships with the Secretariat. It has extended an invitation to China as host of the ATCM XL to send one member of its organisational team for an internship in Buenos Aires.

Financial Matters

The Budget for the Financial Year 2016/17 and the Forecast Budget for the Financial Year 2017/18 are shown in Appendix 1.

Salaries

Costs of living continued to rise considerably in Argentina in the year 2015. Due to changes in the methodology of the calculation of cost rises by the Argentine National Office of Statistics and Census (INDEC), final statistical data for the year 2015 are not yet available. An estimation by the Secretariat determined that the rise in costs of living was probably compensated by the several small devaluations and one large devaluation of the Argentine Peso against the US$.

The Executive Secretary proposes not to compensate for the rise in the cost of living to the General Staff and the Executive Staff.

Regulation 5.10 of the Staff Regulations requires the compensation of General Staff members when they are required to work more than 40 hours during one week. Overtime is requested during the ATCM Meetings.

Funds

Working Capital Fund

According to Financial Regulation 6.2 (a), the Working Capital Fund must be maintained at 1/6 of the Secretariat's budget of 229,952 US$ in the upcoming years. The contributions of the Parties form the basis of the calculation of the level of the Working Capital Fund.

Further Details of the Draft Budget for the Financial Year 2016/17

The Chilean government and the Secretariat agreed that the Secretariat would contract the international rapporteurs for ATCM XXXIX and that the Chilean government would reimburse the costs incurred through a voluntary contribution.

The allocation to the appropriation lines follows the proposal from last year. Some smaller adjustments have been implemented according to the foreseen expenses of the Financial Year 2016/2017.

- *Translation and Interpretation:* Extra funds for the maintenance of the glossary are included.
- *Office:* Some further expenditures are foreseen concerning the replacement of some furniture in the Secretariat.

Appendix 1 shows the Budget for the Financial Year 2016/2017 and the Forecast Budget for the Financial Year 2017/2018. The salary scale is given in Appendix 3.

Contributions for the Financial Year 2017/18

The contributions for the Financial Year 2017/18 will not rise.

Appendix 2 shows the contributions of the Parties for the Financial Year 2017/18.

6. Forecast Programme for the Financial Year 2017/18 and the Financial Year 2018/19

It is expected that most of the ongoing activities of the Secretariat will be continued in the Financial Year 2017/18 and the Financial Year 2018/2019, and therefore, unless the programme undergoes major changes, no change in staff positions is foreseen for the following years.

Appendix 1

Provisional Statement FY 2015/16, Forecast FY 2016/17, Budget FY 2016/17 and Forecast FY 2017/18

APPROPRIATION LINES	Prov. Statement 2015/16*	Forecast 2016/17	Budget 2016/17	Forecast 2017/18
INCOME				
CONTRIBUTIONS pledged	$ -1,378,099	$ -1,378,097	$ -1,378,097	$ -1,378,097
**Voluntary Contributions			$ -53,207	
Interest Investments	$ -13,577	$ -3,000	$ -2,000	$ -2,000
Total Income	**$ -1,391,676**	**$ -1,381,097**	**$ -1,433,304**	**$ -1,380,097**
EXPENDITURE				
SALARIES				
Executive	$ 331,679	$ 336,377	$ 336,376	$ 326,636
General Staff	$ 330,359	$ 341,392	$ 336,801	$ 345,666
ATCM Support Staff	$ 16,398	$ 18,092	$ 18,092	$ 18,092
Trainee	$ 3,667	$ 9,600	$ 9,600	$ 9,600
Overtime	$ 12,552	$ 16,000	$ 16,000	$ 16,000
	$ 694,656	**$ 721,461**	**$ 716,869**	**$ 715,994**
TRANSLATION AND INTERPRETATION				
Translation and Interpretation	**$ 301,634**	**$ 338,505**	**$ 326,326**	**$ 331,518**
TRAVEL				
Travel	**$ 88,741**	**$ 90,000**	**$ 99,000**	**$ 99,000**
INFORMATION TECHNOLOGY				
Hardware	$ 13,306	$ 11,356	$ 11,000	$ 11,000
Software	$ 1,940	$ 3,605	$ 9,000	$ 3,500
Development	$ 17,693	$ 21,630	$ 21,500	$ 21,500
Hardware and Software Maintenance	$ 2,587	$ 0	$ 2,000	$ 2,040
Support	$ 8,422	$ 9,785	$ 9,500	$ 10,000
	$ 43,949	**$ 46,376**	**$ 53,000**	**$ 48,040**

APPROPRIATION LINES	Prov. Statement 2015/16*	Forecast 2016/17	Budget 2016/17	Forecast 2017/18
PRINTING, EDITING & COPYING				
Final report	$ 6,510	$ 18,386	$ 18,386	$ 18,937
Compilation	$ 2,000	$ 3,412	$ 3,412	$ 3,271
Site guidelines	$ 0	$ 3,396	$ 3,396	$ 3,497
	$ 8,995	**$ 25,194**	**$ 25,194**	**$ 25,705**
GENERAL SERVICES				
Legal advice	$ 2,008	$ 4,326	$ 3,500	$ 3,605
**Rapporteur Services			$ 53,207	
External audit	$ 9,539	$ 10,815	$ 10,815	$ 11,139
Cleaning, maintenance & security	$ 12,829	$ 17,845	$ 15,000	$ 16,480
Training	$ 4,275	$ 7,086	$ 6,500	$ 7,298
Banking	$ 5,143	$ 6,489	$ 6,489	$ 6,683
Rental of equipment	$ 2,543	$ 3,245	$ 3,245	$ 3,342
	$ 36,335	**$ 49,806**	**$ 98,756**	**$ 48,547**
COMMUNICATION				
Telephone	$ 6,535	$ 5,624	$ 7,000	$ 7,210
Internet	$ 2,574	$ 3,245	$ 3,000	$ 3,000
Web hosting	$ 6,846	$ 9,734	$ 8,500	$ 8,500
Postage	$ 5,437	$ 2,704	$ 2,704	$ 2,785
	$ 21,393	**$ 21,307**	**$ 21,204**	**$ 21,495**
OFFICE				
Stationery & supplies	$ 4,084	$ 4,650	$ 4,650	$ 4,789
Books & subscriptions	$ 1,994	$ 3,245	$ 3,245	$ 3,342
Insurance	$ 3,603	$ 3,785	$ 4,200	$ 4,326
Furniture	$ 4,535	$ 973	$ 4,565	$ 1,255
Office equipment	$ 21,416	$ 4,326	$ 4,326	$ 4,455
Maintenance	$ 0	$ 2,704	$ 2,704	$ 2,785
	$ 35,632	**$ 19,683**	**$ 23,690**	**$ 20,952**
ADMINISTRATIVE				
Supplies	$ 2,618	$ 4,867	$ 4,867	$ 5,013
Local transport	$ 483	$ 865	$ 865	$ 890
Miscellaneous	$ 1,481	$ 4,326	$ 4,326	$ 4,455
Utilities (Energy)	$ 3,199	$ 11,897	$ 11,897	$ 12,253
	$ 7,781	**$ 21,955**	**$ 21,955**	**$ 22,611**

APPROPRIATION LINES	Prov. Statement 2015/16*	Forecast 2016/17	Budget 2016/17	Forecast 2017/18
REPRESENTATION				
Representation	**$ 3,950**	**$ 3,500**	**$ 4,000**	**$ 4,000**
FINANCING				
Exchange loss	$ 7,518	$ 7,519	$ 7,520	$ 7,521
	$ 10,540	**$ 11,893**	**$ 11,893**	**$ 12,249**
SUBTOTAL APPROPRIATIONS	**$ 1,253,605**	**$ 1,349,680**	**$ 1,401,887**	**$ 1,350,111**
ALLOCATION TO FUNDS				
Translation Contingency Fund	$ 0	$ 0	$ 0	$ 0
Staff Replacement Fund	$ 0	$ 0	$ 0	$ 0
Staff Termination Fund	$ 32,912	$ 31,417	$ 31,417	$ 29,986
Working Capital Fund	$ 0	$ 0	$ 0	$ 0
	$ 32,912	**$ 31,417**	**$ 31,417**	**$ 29,986**
TOTAL APPROPRIATIONS	**$ 1,286,517**	**$ 1,349,680**	**$ 1,401,887**	**$ 1,381,097**
***Unpaid Contributions	**$ 81,547**	**$ 0**	**$ 0**	**$ 0**
BALANCE	**$ 23,612**	**$ 0**	**$ 0**	**$ 0**
Summary of Funds				
Translation Contingency Fund	$ 30,000	$ 30,000	$ 30,000	$ 30,000
Staff Replacement Fund	$ 50,000	$ 50,000	$ 50,000	$ 50,000
Staff Termination Fund	$ 237,489	$ 237,489	$ 237,489	$ 174,066
**** Working Capital Fund	$ 229,952	$ 229,952	$ 229,952	$ 229,952

*	Provisional Statement as of 31 Mar 2016			
**	Rapporteur services contracted by the Secretariat and reembursed by the Host Country of ATCM XXXIX			
***	Unpaid contributions as of 31 March 2016			
****	Maximum Required Amount Working Capital Fund (Fin. Reg. 6,2)	$ 229,683	$ 229,683	$ 229,683	$ 229,683

Appendix 2

Contribution Scale FY 2017/18

2017/18	Cat.	Mult.	Variable	Fixed	Total
Argentina	A	3.6	$ 36,587	$ 23,760	$ 60,347
Australia	A	3.6	$ 36,587	$ 23,760	$ 60,347
Belgium	D	1.6	$ 16,261	$ 23,760	$ 40,021
Brazil	D	1.6	$ 16,261	$ 23,760	$ 40,021
Bulgaria	E	1	$ 10,163	$ 23,760	$ 33,923
Chile	C	2.2	$ 22,359	$ 23,760	$ 46,119
China	C	2.2	$ 22,359	$ 23,760	$ 46,119
Czech Republic	D	1.6	$ 16,261	$ 23,760	$ 40,021
Ecuador	E	1	$ 10,163	$ 23,760	$ 33,923
Finland	D	1.6	$ 16,261	$ 23,760	$ 40,021
France	A	3.6	$ 36,587	$ 23,760	$ 60,347
Germany	B	2.8	$ 28,456	$ 23,760	$ 52,216
India	C	2.2	$ 22,359	$ 23,760	$ 46,119
Italy	B	2.8	$ 28,456	$ 23,760	$ 52,216
Japan	A	3.6	$ 36,587	$ 23,760	$ 60,347
Republic of Korea	D	1.6	$ 16,261	$ 23,760	$ 40,021
Netherlands	C	2.2	$ 22,359	$ 23,760	$ 46,119
New Zealand	A	3.6	$ 36,587	$ 23,760	$ 60,347
Norway	A	3.6	$ 36,587	$ 23,760	$ 60,347
Peru	E	1	$ 10,163	$ 23,760	$ 33,923
Poland	D	1.6	$ 16,261	$ 23,760	$ 40,021
Russian Federation	C	2.2	$ 22,359	$ 23,760	$ 46,119
South Africa	C	2.2	$ 22,359	$ 23,760	$ 46,119
Spain	C	2.2	$ 22,359	$ 23,760	$ 46,119
Sweden	C	2.2	$ 22,359	$ 23,760	$ 46,119
Ukraine	D	1.6	$ 16,261	$ 23,760	$ 40,021
United Kingdom	A	3.6	$ 36,587	$ 23,760	$ 60,347
United States	A	3.6	$ 36,587	$ 23,760	$ 60,347
Uruguay	D	1.6	$ 16,261	$ 23,760	$ 40,021

Budget					$ 1,378,097

Appendix 3

Salary Scale FY 2016/17

Schedule A
SALARY SCALE FOR THE EXECUTIVE STAFF
(United States Dollar)

2014/15 Level		I	II	III	IV	V	VI	VII	VIII	IX	X	XI	XII	XIII	XIV	XV
E1	A	$135,302	$137,819	$140,337	$142,855	$145,373	$147,890	$150,407	$152,926							
E1	B	$169,127	$172,274	$175,421	$178,569	$181,716	$184,863	$188,009	$191,158							
E2	A	$113,932	$116,075	$118,218	$120,359	$122,501	$124,642	$126,783	$128,926							
E2	B	$142,415	$145,093	$147,772	$150,449	$153,126	$155,802	$158,479	$161,158							
E3	A	$95,007	$97,073	$99,140	$101,207	$103,275	$105,341	$107,408	$109,476	$111,542	$113,608	$115,675	$116,915	$118,154	$120,193	$122,231
E3	B	$118,758	$121,341	$123,925	$126,509	$129,094	$131,676	$134,260	$136,845	$139,427	$142,010	$144,594	$146,143	$147,693	$150,242	$152,788
E4	A	$78,779	$80,693	$82,609	$84,518	$86,435	$88,347	$90,257	$92,174	$94,089	$96,000	$97,915	$98,448	$100,336	$102,223	$104,110
E4	B	$98,474	$100,866	$103,262	$105,648	$108,044	$110,434	$112,822	$115,217	$117,611	$119,999	$122,393	$123,060	$125,419	$127,778	$130,137
E5	A	$65,315	$67,029	$68,739	$70,452	$72,162	$73,873	$75,586	$77,293	$79,007	$80,719	$82,427	$82,981			
E5	B	$81,644	$83,786	$85,924	$88,065	$90,203	$92,342	$94,482	$96,617	$98,759	$100,899	$103,034	$103,726			
E6	A	$51,706	$53,351	$54,994	$56,641	$58,284	$59,928	$61,575	$63,219	$64,862	$65,862	$66,508				
E6	B	$64,632	$66,689	$68,742	$70,801	$72,855	$74,910	$76,969	$79,024	$81,078	$82,328	$83,135				

Note: Row B is the base salary (shown in Row A) with an additional 25% for salary on-costs (retirement fund and insurance premiums, installation and repatriation grants, education allowances etc.) and is the total salary entitlement for executive staff in accordance with regulation 5.

Schedule B
SALARY SCALE FOR THE GENERAL STAFF
(United States Dollar)

Level	I	II	III	IV	V	VI	VII	VIII	IX	X	XI	XII	XIII	XIV	XV
G1	$61,102	$63,952	$66,804	$69,653	$72,624	$75,722									
G2	$50,918	$53,293	$55,670	$58,044	$60,520	$63,102									
G3	$42,430	$44,410	$46,390	$48,370	$50,434	$52,587									
G4	$35,360	$37,010	$38,659	$40,309	$42,029	$43,822									
G5	$29,210	$30,574	$31,936	$33,301	$34,723	$36,207									
G6	$23,944	$25,059	$26,177	$27,294	$28,460	$29,675									
G7	$11,000	$11,512	$12,026	$12,539	$13,075	$13,633									

Decision 4 (2016)

Procedure for Selection and Appointment of the Executive Secretary of the Secretariat of the Antarctic Treaty

The Representatives,

Recalling Article 3 of Measure 1 (2003) regarding the appointment of an Executive Secretary of the Secretariat of the Antarctic Treaty ("Executive Secretary");

Recalling Decision 4 (2008) on the Selection and Appointment of the Executive Secretary;

Noting Regulation 6.1 of the Staff Regulations for the Secretariat of the Antarctic Treaty ("the Secretariat");

Noting that the term of appointment of the current Executive Secretary ends on 31 August 2017;

Decide: that the Executive Secretary of the Secretariat shall be selected and appointed in accordance with the following procedure:

Advertisement

The Secretariat will advertise the vacancy on its website using the Draft Advertisement (Annex 1) and the Standard Application Form (Annex 2).

Antarctic Treaty Consultative Parties may advertise, at their own cost, the vacancy in publications, websites and other media they consider appropriate.

Eligible Applicants

Applicants must satisfy the following selection criteria:

1) Demonstrated experience or detailed knowledge of the operations of international meetings or intergovernmental organisations.

2) Demonstrated high level managerial and leadership experience and competence in areas including:

   a) selection and supervision of professional, administrative and technical staff;

   b) preparation of financial budgets and the management of expenditures;

   c) organisation of meetings and provision of secretariat support for high level committees; and

   d) oversight and management of computer services and information technology.

3) Familiarity with Antarctic affairs, including the principles of the Antarctic Treaty and the scope of activities in the region.

4) Fluency in one of the four official working languages of the Antarctic Treaty Consultative Meeting, *i.e.* English, French, Russian or Spanish.

5) Hold a university degree, academic degree, or equivalent qualification.

6) Be a national of an Antarctic Treaty Consultative Party.

Submission of Eligible Applications

Nationals of a Consultative Party may apply for the post of Executive Secretary only to their national authority, who will be responsible for forwarding the applications to the Secretariat, no later than 180 days before the Antarctic Treaty Consultative Meeting at which the selection of the Executive Secretary will be considered. Applications received after this date will not be considered. Applications must be submitted electronically using the Standard Application Form (Annex 2) and providing a curriculum vitae.

Receipt of Applications

The Secretariat will notify Consultative Parties of the receipt of applications.

Distribution of Applications

A copy of each application received by the Secretariat no later than 180 days before the relevant Antarctic Treaty Consultative Meeting will be forwarded electronically without delay by the Secretariat to the Representative of each Consultative Party.

Ranking of Applicants

Each Consultative Party will notify the Depositary Government of up to ten preferred candidates in order of preference, no later than 120 days before the relevant Antarctic Treaty Consultative Meeting. In relation to those rankings received by the deadline, the Depositary Government will aggregate individual applicants' rankings, awarding ten points for a first preference, nine points for a second preference, etc.

Shortlisting

The candidates with the five highest aggregate scores will form the shortlist for selection. Should the application of any shortlisted candidate/s be withdrawn, the next ranking candidate/s will be substituted.

Interview Process

The Depositary Government will notify, through the Secretariat the names of the short-listed candidates to Consultative Parties no later than 60 days before the relevant Antarctic Treaty Consultative Meeting. The Secretariat will invite the shortlisted candidates to attend an interview at that Antarctic Treaty Consultative Meeting.

The shortlisted candidates invited for interview are required to meet the costs of their travel and expenses. Each relevant Consultative Party is encouraged to assume these costs.

Shortlisted candidates will be interviewed by those Heads of Delegation wishing to participate in the selection process at the relevant Antarctic Treaty Consultative Meeting.

The outcome of the selection process will be notified to shortlisted candidates at the conclusion of the first week of the relevant Antarctic Treaty Consultative Meeting by the Chair of that meeting.

Selection

The relevant Antarctic Treaty Consultative Meeting will take a Decision regarding the appointment of the selected candidate.

The chosen candidate will be required to enter into a contract outlining the terms of employment.

Start Date

The chosen candidate will report to the Secretariat headquarters in Buenos Aires for commencement of duties no later than the date agreed by the relevant Antarctic Treaty Consultative Meeting.

Draft Advertisement Executive Secretary of the Secretariat of the Antarctic Treaty

The Antarctic Treaty Consultative Meeting (ATCM) invites applications for the position of Executive Secretary of the Secretariat of the Antarctic Treaty.

The ATCM, consisting of 29 Consultative Parties, meets annually to consult on the application and implementation of the Antarctic Treaty. The Secretariat of the Antarctic Treaty is located in Buenos Aires, Argentina. Further information is available at *www.ats.aq*.

The Executive Secretary manages a small administrative staff to carry out the duties of the Secretariat assigned to it by the ATCM. The Executive Secretary presents and manages the Secretariat's budget, supports the organisation of the ATCM, and performs other duties identified by the ATCM.

Selection Criteria

Applicants must satisfy the following selection criteria:

1) Demonstrated experience or detailed knowledge of the operations of international meetings or intergovernmental organisations.

2) Demonstrated high level of managerial and leadership experience and competence in areas including:

   a) selection and supervision of professional, administrative and technical staff;

   b) preparation of financial budgets and the management of expenditures;

   c) organisation of meetings and provision of secretariat support for high level committees; and

   d) oversight and management of computer services and information technology.

3) Familiarity with Antarctic affairs, including the principles of the Antarctic Treaty and the scope of activities in the region.

4) Fluency in one of the four official working languages of the ATCM, i.e. English, French, Russian or Spanish.

5) Hold a university degree, academic degree, or equivalent qualification.

6) Be a national of an Antarctic Treaty Consultative Party.

Salary and Allowances

Details of remuneration and allowances are available from the Secretariat of the Antarctic Treaty on request.

The appointment will be for a term of four years with the possibility of one additional four year appointment.

Interview

The Depositary Government will draw up a short list of applicants by DD MM 2017. Interviews of the short listed candidates will occur during ATCM XL to be held in XXXXXX, China, on DD-DD MM 2017. The successful candidate will be announced at that meeting.

Availability

The individual chosen for the post of Executive Secretary should be available to commence duties no later than 1 September 2017.

Additional Information

Please consult the Secretariat of the Antarctic Treaty website: *www.ats.aq* for complete information on remuneration and allowances; duties; selection criteria; the application process; staff regulations; and other relevant documents.

Closing Date

Applicants should check the national closing date for applications with their own Consultative Party government.

Please consult the Secretariat of the Antarctic Treaty website: *www.ats.aq* for the national government contact details of the relevant Consultative Party.

Each Consultative Party government will accept applications from its own nationals on the Standard Application Form together with a curriculum vitae and submit them to the Secretariat of the Antarctic Treaty no later than DD MM 2016.

Standard application form

Personal Details

Name:

Address:

Phone:

Facsimile:

Email:

Nationality:

Selection Criteria

(Include additional information elaborating on these criteria and attach a curriculum vitae)

1) Demonstrated experience or detailed knowledge of the operations of international meetings or intergovernmental organisations.

2) Demonstrated high level of managerial and leadership experience and competence in areas including:

   a) selection and supervision of professional, administrative and technical staff;

   b) preparation of financial budgets and the management of expenditures;

   c) organisation of meetings and provision of secretariat support for high level committees; and

   d) oversight and management of computer services and information technology.

3) Familiarity with Antarctic affairs, including the principles of the Antarctic Treaty and the scope of activities in the region.

4) Fluency in one of the four official working languages of the ATCM, i.e. English, French, Russian or Spanish.

5) Hold a university degree, academic degree, or equivalent qualification.

6) Be a national of an Antarctic Treaty Consultative Party.

Liability arising from Environmental Emergencies

The Representatives,

Recalling Articles III(1)(a) and VII(5) of the Antarctic Treaty;

Conscious of the obligations within the Protocol on Environmental Protection to the Antarctic Treaty ("the Protocol") and its Annexes to exchange information;

Conscious also of decisions of the Antarctic Treaty Consultative Meeting ("ATCM") in relation to the information to be exchanged by Parties;

Desiring to ensure that the exchange of information by Parties is conducted in the most efficient and timely manner;

Desiring also that the information to be exchanged by Parties can be readily identified;

Recalling Decision 4 (2012), which made mandatory the use of the Electronic Information Exchange System ("EIES") as the means for Parties to fulfil their information exchange obligations under the Antarctic Treaty and the Protocol and specified that Parties shall continue to work with the Secretariat of the Antarctic Treaty ("the Secretariat") to refine and improve the EIES;

Noting that Decision 4 (2012) requires Parties to update relevant sections of the EIES regularly throughout the year, and at a minimum in accordance with Resolution 6 (2001), in order that such information be available and accessible to Parties as soon as practicable;

Decide:

1. that the Annex to this Decision represents a consolidated list of the information agreed to be exchanged by Parties;

2. that the Secretariat shall modify the EIES to reflect the information contained in the Annex attached to this Decision, and make available, as soon as practicable, information submitted by Parties; and

3. that the Annex to Decision 6 (2015) and Appendix 1 to the Final Report of ATCM XXXVIII are no longer current.

Information Exchange Requirements

1. Pre-season Information

The following information should be submitted as early as possible, preferably by 1 October, and in any event no later than the start of the activities being reported.

1.1 Operational information

1.1.1 National Expeditions

A. Stations

Names of wintering stations (giving region, latitude and longitude), maximum population and medical support available.

Names of summer stations/bases and field camps (giving region, latitude, longitude), operating period, maximum population and medical support available.

Names of refuges (region, latitude and longitude) medical facilities and accommodation capacity. Other major field activities, e.g. scientific traverse (giving locations).

B. Vessels

Name of vessels, country of registry of vessels, number of voyages, planned departure dates, areas of operation, ports of departure and arrival to and from Antarctica, and purpose of voyage (e.g. science deployment, resupply, change-over, oceanography, etc).

Maximum Crew, Maximum Passengers.

C. Aircraft

Category (Intercontinental Flights, Intracontinental Flights, Local Helicopter Flights), type of aircraft, planned number of flights, period of flights or planned departure dates, routes and purpose.

D. Research Rockets

Coordinates of the place of launching, time and date/period, direction of launching, planned maximum altitude, impact area, type and specifications of rockets, purpose and title of research project.

E. Military

- Number of military personnel in expeditions, and rank of any officers.
- Number and types of armaments possessed by personnel.

- Number and types of armaments of ships and aircraft and information on military equipment, if any, and its location in the Antarctic Treaty Area.

1.1.2 Non-governmental Expeditions*

A. Vessel-based Operations

Name of operator, name of vessel, Maximum crew, Maximum Passengers, country of registry of vessel, number of voyages, expedition leader, planned departure dates, ports of departure and arrival to and from Antarctica, areas of operation including the names of proposed visited sites and the planned dates at which these visits will take place, type of activity, whether these visits include landing, (optionally) duration of landing and the number of visitors that participate in each of the specific activities.

B. Land-based Operations

Name of expedition, name of the operator, method of transportation to, from and within Antarctica, type of adventure/activity, location/s of activities and/or routes, dates of expedition, number of personnel involved, contact address, web-site address.

C. Aircraft Activities

Name of operator, type of aircraft, number of flights, period of flights, departure date per flight, departure and arrival location per flight, route per flight, purpose per flight, and number of passengers.

D. Denial of Authorizations

Name of Vessel and/or Expedition, Name of Operator, Date, Reason for Denial.

1.2 Visits to Protected Areas

Name and number of protected area, number of people permitted to visit, date/period and purpose.

2. Annual Report

The following information should be submitted as early as possible after the end of the austral summer season, but in all cases before 1 October, with a reporting period of 1 April to 30 March.

---

* Provision of information on Non-governmental expeditions will be allowed for it to be provided as soon as possible after completion of national processes, with the relevant timing description being: 'as soon as possible following completion of national processes, preferably by the pre-season target date of 1 October, and no later than the start of the activity'.

2.1 Scientific Information

2.1.1 Forward Plans*

Details of strategic or multi-year science plans or contact point for printed version. List of planned participations in major, international, collaborative science programs/projects.

2.1.2 Science Activities in Previous Year

List of research projects undertaken in previous year under science discipline (giving location/s, principal investigator, project name or number, discipline and main activity/remarks).

2.2 Operational information

2.2.1 National expeditions

Update of information given under 1.1.1.

2.2.2 Non-governmental expeditions

Update of information given under 1.1.2.

2.3 Permit Information

2.3.1 Visits to Protected Areas

Update of information provided under 1.2.

2.3.2 Taking and harmful interference with flora and fauna

Permit number, permit period, Species, location, amount, sex, age and purpose.**

2.3.3 Introduction of non-native species

Permit number, permit period, species, location, amount, purpose,*** removal or disposal.

2.4 Environmental Information

2.4.1 Compliance with the Protocol****

Description of measure, date of effect.

---

* Optional provision of information on Forward plans will be allowed at any time, for example when domestic plans are completed or updated.
** Purpose with reference to Article 4 of Annex II of the Protocol.
*** Purpose with reference to Article 4 of Annex II of the Protocol.
**** New measures adopted during past year in accordance with Article 13 of the Protocol on Environmental Protection to the Antarctic Treaty including the adoption of laws and regulations, administrative actions and enforcement measures.

2.4.2 Contingency Plans

Title of Contingency Plan(s) for Oil Spills and other environmental emergencies, copies (PDFs) or contact point for printed versions.

2.4.3 List of IEEs and CEEs[*]

List of IEEs/CEEs undertaken during year giving proposed activity, (optionally) period/ length, location, level of assessment and decision taken.

2.4.4 Monitoring activities report[**]

Name of activity, location, procedures put in place, significant information obtained, action taken in consequence thereof.

2.4.5 Waste Management Plans

Title, name of site/vessel, copy (PDF) or contact point for printed version. Report on implementation of waste management plans during the year.

2.4.6 Measures taken to implement the provisions of Annex V[***]

Description of measures.

2.4.7 Procedures relating to EIAs

Description of appropriate National Procedures.

2.4.8 Prevention of marine pollution[****]

Description of measures.

3. Permanent Information

The following information should be submitted in accordance with the requirements of the Antarctic Treaty and Protocol on Environmental Protection to the Antarctic Treaty. The information can be updated at any time.

---

[*] Information on IEEs and CEEs is encouraged to be provided 'as soon as domestic processes are concluded, while maintaining the existing deadline for Parties to submit the information'.

[**] Monitoring activities connected with activities subject to initial and comprehensive environmental evaluations (referred to in Protocol Annex I, Art. 6.1 c).

[***] Information on measures taken to implement Annex V including site inspections and any steps taken to address instances of activities in contravention of the provisions of ASPA or ASMA management plans.

[****] Measures to ensure that any warship, naval auxiliary or other ship owned or operated by a State and used, for the time being, only on government non-commercial service acts in a manner consistent, so far as is reasonable and practicable, with the Annex.

3.1. Science Facilities

3.1.1 Automatic Recording Stations/Observatories

Site name, co-ordinates (latitude and longitude), elevation (m), parameters recorded, observation frequency, reference number (e.g. WMO no.).

3.2 Operational Information

A. Stations

Name of wintering stations (giving region, latitude and longitude, and maximum population), date established and accommodation and medical facilities.

Name of summer stations/bases and field camps (giving region, latitude, longitude, operating period and maximum population).

Names of refuges (region, latitude and longitude) medical facilities and accommodation capacity.

Search and Rescue Information.

B. Vessels

Name of vessels, Flag State, ice strength, length, beam and gross tonnage (a link may be provided to COMNAP data). Maximum crew, Maximum Passengers.

Search and Rescue Information.

C. Aircraft

Quantity and type of aircraft operated. Search and Rescue Information.

3.3 Environmental Information

3.3.1 Waste Management Plans

Title of Plan, site/vessel, copy (PDF) or contact point for printed version.

3.3.2 Contingency Plans

Title of Contingency Plan(s) for Oil Spills and other environmental emergencies, copies (PDFs) or contact point for printed versions.

3.3.3 Inventory of Past Activities

Name of station/base/field camp/traverse/crashed aircraft/etc, co-ordinates (latitude and longitude) period during which activity undertaken; description/purpose of activities undertaken; description of equipment or facilities remaining.

3.3.4 Compliance with the Protocol*

Description of measure, date of effect. 3.3.5 Procedures relating to EIAs

3.3.5 Procedures relating to EIAs

Same as 2.4.7

3.3.6 Prevention of marine pollution

Same as 2.4.8

3.3.7 Measures taken to implement the provisions of Annex V

Same as 2.4.6

3.4 Other Information

3.4.1 Relevant National Legislation

Description of law, regulation, administrative action or other measure, date of effect/ enacted, giving copy (PDF) or contact point for printed version.

---

* Measures adopted in accordance with Article 13 of the Protocol on Environmental Protection to the Antarctic Treaty including the adoption of laws and regulations, administrative actions and enforcement measures.

Multi-Year Strategic Work Plan for the Antarctic Treaty Consultative Meeting

The Representatives,

Reaffirming the values, objectives and principles contained in the Antarctic Treaty and its Protocol on Environmental Protection;

Recalling Decision 3 (2012) on the Multi-Year Strategic Work Plan ("the Plan") and its principles;

Bearing in mind that the Plan is complementary to the agenda of the Antarctic Treaty Consultative Meeting ("ATCM") and that the Parties and other ATCM participants are encouraged to contribute as usual to other matters on the ATCM agenda;

Decide:

1. to adopt the Plan annexed to this Decision; and

2. that the Plan annexed to Decision 4 (2015) is no longer current.

ATCM Multi-year Strategic Work Plan

	Priority	ATCM 39 (2016)	Intersessional	ATCM 40 (2017)	ATCM 41 (2018)	ATCM 42 (2019)
1.	Conduct a comprehensive review of existing requirements for information exchange and of the functioning of the Electronic Information Exchange System, and the identification of any additional requirements	• WG1 considered the report of the ICG on Information Exchange • WG1 agreed Decision F (2016) *Exchange of Information*		• WG1 to review functioning of the EIES.		
2.	Consider coordinated outreach to non-party states whose nationals or assets are active in Antarctica and states that are Antarctic Treaty Parties but not yet to the Protocol	• WG1 requested WG2 to provide input on non-Party states whose nationals are active in Antarctica		• ATCM to identify and reach out to non-party states whose nationals are active in Antarctica		
3.	Contribute to nationally and internationally coordinated education and outreach activities from an Antarctic Treaty perspective	• WG1 considered the report of the ICG on Education and Outreach and agreed the ICG should continue its work	• ICG on Education and Outreach	• WG1 to consider the report of the ICG on Education and Outreach		
4.	Share and discuss strategic science priorities in order to identify and pursue opportunities for collaboration as well as capacity building in science, particularly in relation to climate change	• WG2 to collate and compare strategic science priorities with a view to identify cooperation opportunities		• WG2 to collate and compare strategic science priorities with a view to identify cooperation opportunities		

	Priority	**ATCM 39 (2016)**	**Intersessional**	**ATCM 40 (2017)**	**ATCM 41 (2018)**	**ATCM 42 (2019)**
5.	Enhance effective cooperation between Parties (e.g. joint inspections, joint scientific projects and logistic support) and effective participation in meetings (e.g. consideration of effective working methods in meetings)	• WG2 agreed to establish an ICG on Joint Inspections • WG1 considered working methods in Meetings	• ICG on Joint Inspections • Working Groups and CEP Chairs to coordinate on basis of annotated agendas	• WG2 to consider the report of the ICG on Joint Inspections		
6.	Strengthening cooperation between the CEP and the ATCM	• ATCM received advice from the CEP • ATCM agreed need to better sequence next CEP and ATCM meetings		• ATCM to consider issues raised in CEP report at ATCM 39 and 40 • ATCM to receive advice from CEP that requires follow-up action		
7.	To bring Annex VI in to force and to continue to gather information on repair and remediation of environmental damage and other relevant issues to inform future negotiations on liability	• ATCM evaluated progress made towards Annex VI becoming effective in accordance with Article IX of the Antarctic Treaty, and what action may be necessary and appropriate to encourage Parties to approve Annex VI in a timely manner	• Parties to work towards the approval of Annex VI and to share with one another information and experience • Parties to upload their Annex VI legislation to the EIES • Secretariat to invite IOPC Funds and P & I Club to provide advice on issues relating to insurance under Annex VI	• ATCM to evaluate progress made towards Annex VI becoming effective in accordance with Article IX of the Antarctic Treaty, and what action may be necessary and appropriate to encourage Parties to approve Annex VI in a timely manner		

	Priority	ATCM 39 (2016)	Intersessional	ATCM 40 (2017)	ATCM 41 (2018)	ATCM 42 (2019)
8.	Assess the progress of the CEP on its ongoing work to reflect best practices and to improve existing tools and develop further tools for environmental protection, including environmental impact assessment procedures (and consider, if appropriate, further development of the tools)	• ATCM received advice from CEP • ATCM adopted Resolution A (2016)		• WG1 to consider advice of the CEP and discuss the policy considerations of the review of Environmental Impact Assessment (EIA) Guidelines		
9.	Address the recommendations of the Antarctic Treaty Meeting of Experts on Implications of Climate Change for Antarctic Management and Governance (CEP-ICG)	• WG2 considered recommendations 7 and 8		• WG2 to consider recommendations 4-6 • WG2 to consider outcomes of the SC-CCAMLR and CEP workshop		
10.	Discuss implementation of the Climate Changes Response Work Programme (CCRWP)			• WG2 to consider annual update from CEP on implementation of CCRWP	• WG2 to consider annual update from CEP on implementation of CCRWP	• WG2 to consider annual update from CEP on implementation of CCRWP
11.	Modernisation of Antarctic Stations in context of climate change			• WG2 to discuss exchange of information and COMNAP advice		
12.	Strengthen cooperation among Parties on current Antarctic specific air and marine operations and safety practices, and identify any issues that may be brought forward to the IMO and ICAO, as appropriate	• ATCM received advice from CEP	• Secretariat to write to ICAO and IMO to advise them of ATCM concerns about air and maritime safety in Antarctica and to invite them to present their views for discussion at next ATCM	• WG2 to consider any advice from CEP and COMNAP on UAVs • WG2 to consider any views presented on air and maritime safety issues by ICAO and IMO	• Dedicated discussion on UAVs	
13.	Hydrographic surveying in Antarctica				• Consideration of hydrographic surveying in Antarctica	

	Priority	ATCM 39 (2016)	Intersessional	ATCM 40 (2017)	ATCM 41 (2018)	ATCM 42 (2019)
14.	Review and assess the need for additional actions regarding area management and permanent infrastructure related to tourism, as well as issues related to land based and adventure tourism, and address the recommendations of the CEP tourism study			• Consider a report from the Secretariat concerning progress against recommendation 1 of 2012 CEP Tourism Study.		
15.	Develop a strategic approach to environmentally managed tourism and non-governmental activities in Antarctica	• ATCM considered ICG report on Strategic Approach to Environmentally Managed Tourism and non-governmental Activities in Antarctica	• Secretariat to provide an update on current state of recommendations of the 2012 CEP Tourism Study	• WG2 to consider Secretariat update • Develop a strategic vision for tourism and non-governmental activities in Antarctica		
16.	Visitor site monitoring				• Discuss the advice of the CEP regarding improvement of visitor site monitoring arising from recommendation 7 of the CEP Tourism Study.	

Note: The ATCM Working Groups mentioned above are not permanent but are established by consensus at the end of each Antarctic Treaty Consultative Meeting.

3. Resolutions

Revised Guidelines for Environmental Impact Assessment in Antarctica

The Representatives,

Recalling the requirements under Article 8 of the Protocol on Environmental Protection to the Antarctic Treaty ("the Protocol") and its Annex I regarding environmental impact assessments for proposed activities in the Antarctic Treaty area;

Recognising that Parties should already have in place national procedures for implementation of the Protocol in accordance with Article 1 of Annex I thereof;

Noting that under Resolution 1 (1999) the Antarctic Treaty Consultative Meeting ("ATCM") adopted Guidelines for Environmental Impact Assessment in Antarctica ("Guidelines");

Noting also that under Resolution 4 (2005) the ATCM adopted revised Guidelines for Environmental Impact Assessment in Antarctica;

Noting that the Committee for Environmental Protection has endorsed revised Guidelines;

Desiring to update the Guidelines to reflect current best practice in the revised environmental impact assessment of proposed activities in Antarctica;

Recommend that:

1. the Guidelines for Environmental Impact Assessment in Antarctica annexed to this Resolution replace the Guidelines annexed to Resolution 4 (2005); and

2. the Secretariat of the Antarctic Treaty post the text of Resolution 4 (2005) on its website in a way that makes clear that it is no longer current.

Guidelines for Environmental Impact Assessment in Antarctica

1. Introduction

Article 3 of the Protocol on Environmental Protection to the Antarctic Treaty (the Protocol) establishes a number of environmental principles which can be considered a guide to environmental protection in Antarctica and its dependent and associated ecosystems. It states that "the protection of the Antarctic environment and dependent and associated ecosystems and the intrinsic value of Antarctica, including its wilderness and aesthetic values and its value as an area for the conduct of scientific research, in particular research essential to understanding the global environment, shall be fundamental considerations in the planning and conduct of all activities in the Antarctic Treaty area."

To give effect to the above over-arching principle, Article 3.2(c) requires that 'activities in the Antarctic Treaty area shall be planned and conducted on the basis of information sufficient to allow prior assessments of, and informed judgements about, their possible impacts on the Antarctic environment and dependent and associated ecosystems and on the value of Antarctica for the conduct of scientific research'. In addition, it states that 'such judgements shall take account of:

i)   the scope of the activity, including its area, duration and intensity;

ii)   the cumulative impacts of the activity, both by itself and in combination with other activities in the Antarctic Treaty Area;

iii)   whether the activity will detrimentally affect any other activity in the Antarctic Treaty Area;

iv)   whether technology and procedures are available to provide for environmentally safe operations;

v)   whether there exists the capacity to monitor key environmental parameters and ecosystem components so as to identify and provide early warning of any adverse effects of the activity and to provide for such modification of operating procedures as may be necessary in the light of the results of monitoring or increased knowledge of the Antarctic environment and dependent and associated ecosystems; and

vi)   whether there exists the capacity to respond promptly and effectively to accidents, particularly those with potential environmental effects'.

Article 8 of the Protocol introduces the term *Environmental Impact Assessment* and provides three categories of environmental impacts (*less than a minor or transitory impact, a minor or transitory impact* and *more than a minor or transitory impact*), according to their significance. The Article also requires that activities proposed to be undertaken in Antarctica shall be subject to the prior assessment procedures set out in Annex I to the Protocol.

317

Annex I provides a more comprehensive explanation of the different environmental impact categories and establishes a set of basic principles to conduct an EIA for planned activities in Antarctica.

In addition, it sets up a preliminary stage for assessing the environmental impact of Antarctic activities, which is intended to determine if an impact produced by a certain activity is less than minor or transitory or not. Such determination must be accomplished through the appropriate national procedures.

According to the results of the preliminary stage, or subsequent evaluations if required, the activity can either:

- proceed (if the predicted impacts of the activity are likely to be less than minor or transitory); or

- be preceded by an Initial Environmental Evaluation (IEE), if predicted impacts are likely to be no more than minor or transitory; or

- be preceded by a Comprehensive Environmental Evaluation (CEE), if the predicted impacts are to be more than minor or transitory.

Although the key to decide whether an activity shall be preceded by an IEE or a CEE is the concept of *"minor or transitory impact"*, no agreement on this term has so far been reached. The difficulty with defining *"minor or transitory impact"* appears to be due to the dependence of a number of variables associated with each activity and each environmental context. Therefore the interpretation of this term will need to be made on a case by case site specific basis. As a consequence, this document does not focus on seeking a clear definition of *"minor or transitory impact"*, but rather is an attempt to provide basic elements for the development of the EIA process.

Article 8 and Annex I of the Protocol set out the requirements for Environmental Impact Assessments (EIAs) for proposed activities in Antarctica. These Guidelines to EIA in Antarctica do not amend, modify or interpret the requirements set out in Article 8 and Annex I of the Protocol, or the requirements of national legislation which may include procedures and guidelines for the preparation of EIAs in Antarctica. These Guidelines have been produced to assist those preparing EIAs for proposed activities in Antarctica.

2. Objectives

The general objective of these guidelines is to achieve transparency and effectiveness in assessing environmental impacts during the planning stages of possible activities in Antarctica, as well as consistency of approach in fulfilling the obligations of the Protocol.

Specifically, the guidelines aim to:

- assist proponents of activities who may have little experience of EIA in Antarctica;

- assist in determining the proper level of EIA document (according to the Protocol) to be prepared;

- facilitate co-operation and co-ordination in EIA for joint activities;
- facilitate comparison of EIAs for similar activities and/or environmental conditions;
- provide advice to both government and non-government operators;
- where appropriate, assist proponents to give consideration to the possible implications of climate change for proposed activities and their associated environmental impacts;
- where appropriate, assist proponents to give consideration to the possible risks of introduction or dissemination of non-native species associated with proposed activities;
- assist in the consideration of cumulative impacts relevant to the proposal; and
- initiate a process of continuous improvement of EIA.

3. The EIA Process

The EIA is a process having the ultimate objective of providing decision makers with an indication of the likely environmental consequences of a proposed activity (Figure 1).

The *process* of predicting the environmental impacts of an activity and assessing their significance is the same regardless of the apparent magnitude of the activity. Some activities require no more than a cursory examination to determine impacts, although it must be remembered that the level of assessment is relative to the significance of the environmental impacts, not to the scale or complexity of the activity. The process of preparing the EIA will result in an improved understanding of the likely environmental impacts. Thus, the picture that emerges with respect to the impacts of the activity will determine how much further the EIA process needs to be taken, and how complex it should be.

Those persons responsible for an Environmental Impact Assessment Process need to ensure that they consult as widely as is reasonably necessary and possible in order that the best available information and professional advice contribute to the outcome. A number of different participants may be involved throughout this process, ranging from those who are involved in the details of nearly all parts of the process (e.g. environmental officer, proponent of the activity) to those who are the technical experts who provide input in particular subjects of the process (e.g. researchers, logistic personnel, others with experience at the location or in a particular activity).

In addition, previous EIAs undertaken for proposed activities in Antarctica may represent a valuable source of information. *Resolution 1(2005)* recommends that Parties report annually to the Secretariat of the Antarctic Treaty on IEEs and CEEs prepared by or submitted to them (e.g. a short description of the development or activity; the type of environmental impact assessment undertaken (IEE or CEE); the location (name, latitude, and longitude) of the activity; the organisation responsible for the EIA; and any decision taken following consideration of the Environmental Impact Assessment). These details, including an electronic copy of the EIA document where possible, are available from the

EIA Database on the ATS website. The *Antarctic Master Directory* can also represent a helpful source of metadata.

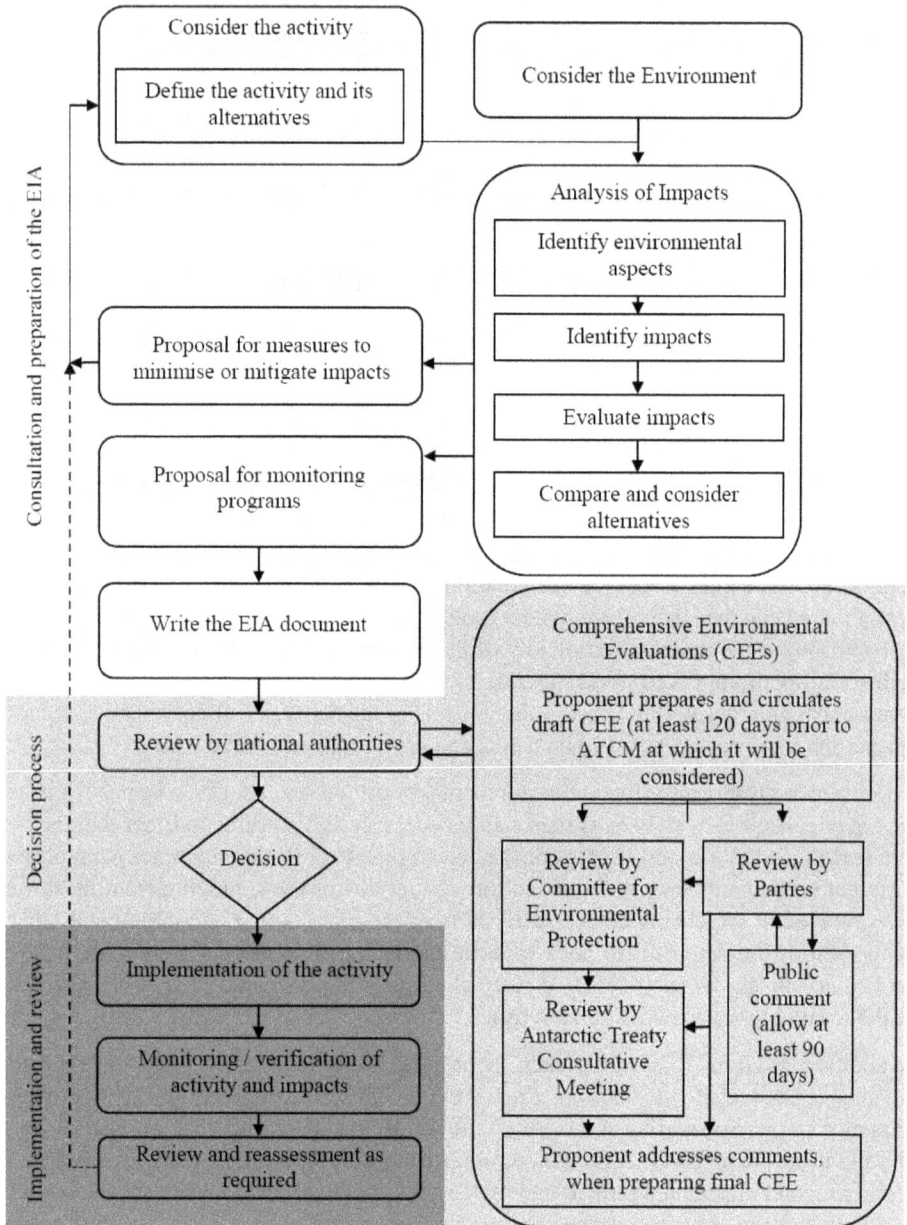

Figure 1: Steps of the EIA process for Antarctic activities

Comprehensive Environmental Evaluations (CEEs)

Under Annex I, a draft CEE must be prepared if the Party proposing an activity, or to which a proposal has been submitted, determines that an activity that is likely to have more than a minor or transitory impact. This determination will be made in accordance with appropriate national procedures, and with reference to the provisions and objectives of the Protocol.

The draft CEE shall be made publicly available and shall be circulated to all Parties, which shall also make it publicly available, for comment (Figure 1). A period of 90 days shall be allowed for the receipt of comments. It shall be forwarded to the CEP at the same time as it is circulated to the Parties, and at least 120 days before the next ATCM, for consideration as appropriate.

In accordance with the *Procedures for intersessional CEP consideration of draft CEEs*, the CEP Chair will establish an open-ended intersessional contact group (ICG) to consider the draft CEE, and will consult with CEP Members to identify a suitable convener and to agree the terms of reference. The ICG will report to the next CEP meeting, which will discuss the draft CEE and provide advice to the ATCM.

Article 3.5 of Annex I states that no final decision shall be taken to proceed with the proposed activity in the Antarctic Treaty area unless there has been an opportunity for consideration of the draft CEE by the ATCM on the advice of the CEP, provided that no decision to proceed with a proposed activity shall be delayed for longer than fifteen months from the day of circulation of the draft CEE.

A final CEE shall address and shall include or summarise comments received on the draft CEE. The final CEE, notice of any decision relating thereto, and any evaluation of the significance of the predicted impacts in relation to the advantages of the proposed activity, shall be circulated to all Parties, which shall also make them publicly available, at least 60 days before the commencement of the proposed activity in the Antarctic Treaty area.

3.1. Considering the activity

3.1.1 Defining the activity

An activity is an event or process resulting from (or associated with) the presence of humans in the Antarctic, and/or which may lead to the presence of humans in Antarctica. An activity may consist of several *actions*, e.g. an ice drilling *activity* may require *actions* such as the transport of equipment, establishment of a field camp, power generation for drilling, fuel management, drilling operation, waste management, etc. An activity should be analysed by considering all actions involved over every phase of the activity (e.g. construction, operational and decommissioning phases).

The activity and the individual actions should be defined through a planning process which considers the physical, technical and economic and other elements of the proposed project and its alternatives. Consultation with relevant experts to identify all these elements is an important part of this initial scoping process. It is important to accurately define all elements of the activity which could interact with the environment and result in impacts. The rest of the EIA process relies on this initial description, which should occur during the planning process.

The following elements of the proposed activity and its alternatives should be clearly identified:

- the purpose of and the need for the activity. The rationale for a proposed activity is an important component of any EIA and, where appropriate, should consider how the activity will contribute to advancing the objectives of the Antarctic Treaty and Protocol. In particular, where the activity is expected to result in benefits to the environment or science, this should be highlighted. Where appropriate, a description of proposed scientific activities could usefully include reference to broader national or international strategic science plans;

- the principal characteristics of the activity that might cause impact on the environment. For instance: design characteristics; construction requirements (types of material, technologies, energy, size of any installation, personnel, temporary constructions, etc.); transportation requirements (types, numbers and frequency of use of vehicles, fuel types); type and quantity of wastes generated through different phases of the activity and their final disposition (with reference to Annex III of the Protocol); dismantling of temporary constructions; decommissioning the activity if necessary; as well as those aspects that will result from the operational phase of the activity;

- the relationship of the proposed activity to relevant previous, current or reasonably foreseeable activities. In this respect, and where appropriate, the EIA should clearly explain the anticipated outcomes of the proposed activity, taking into account similar activities carried out in the area (e.g. how the proposed science or science support facilities will complement activities at existing nearby facilities, or how an activity proposed for educational purposes will promote the value and importance of Antarctica);

- a description of the activity's location and geographical area, including means of access and associated infrastructure. This should include a description of any characteristics that will have a bearing on the full geographic extent of the activity's impacts, including physical, visible and audible elements. Using maps will ease the evaluation process and, therefore, will be useful in the EIA documentation;

- timing of the activity (including range of calendar dates for construction time, as well as overall duration, periods of operation of the activity and decommissioning. This may be important with respect to wildlife breeding cycles, for example); and

- location of the activity with regard to areas with special management requirements (ASPA, ASMA, HSM, CCAMLR CEMP sites, proposed ASPAs and/or ASMAs, etc.) Such information is readily available in the *Antarctic Protected Areas Database* maintained by the Antarctic Treaty Secretariat.

To ensure the EIA presents an accurate and comprehensive description of the activity, and potentially significant environmental aspects are addressed, particular attention should be given to:

- taking a holistic approach to defining the scope of the activity. Careful consideration is required to determine the full scope of the activity so that the impacts can be properly assessed. This is necessary to avoid preparing a number of separate EIAs on actions which indicate an apparent low impact, when in fact, taken in its entirety, the activity actually has potential for impacts of much greater significance. For example, a proposal to construct a new station should also discuss in detail the associated logistics, major scientific infrastructure, and ancillary facilities beyond the main station building (e.g. roads, helipads / airstrips, communication facilities etc.). This is particularly common where a number of activities take place at the same site either spatially and/or temporally. Where activities are to be undertaken at sites which are visited repeatedly by one or more operators the cumulative effects of past, current, and reasonably foreseeable activities should be taken into consideration;

• considering, and to the extent possible providing details of, the decommissioning phase, including the duration, costs and probable impacts. From an environmental perspective, and consistent with Annex III to the Protocol, the complete removal of infrastructure is preferable, although it is recognised there may be situations where this is not possible or may result in greater adverse environmental impacts. The EIA should describe whether any items will be left in place following decommissioning and, if so, clearly explain why they will not be removed. It should also be noted that, depending on the circumstances (e.g. elapsed time, changes in the activity/ use of the installation, changes in the environment) a new EIA may need to be prepared at the time for decommissioning activities; and

• describing in detail activities relevant to the possible transfer of non-native species into and between locations in Antarctica (e.g. transport of vehicles / equipment / supplies / personnel). In this respect, the transport of equipment and heavy machinery from locations with a similar climate, such as the Arctic region or sub-Antarctic islands, may be of particular relevance.

In identifying spatial and temporal boundaries for the EIA proponents should identify other activities occurring in the region within the EIA framework.

When defining an Antarctic activity, experience gained in similar projects undertaken within and outside the Antarctic Treaty area (e.g. the Arctic region or sub-Antarctic islands) may be an additional and valuable source of information.

Once the activity is defined, any subsequent changes to the activity must be clearly identified and addressed according to when they occur in the EIA process (e.g. if the change occurs once the EIA document is completed, then an amendment to the EIA or a rewrite of the document may be necessary depending on how significant the change is). In every case it is important that the change and its implications (in terms of impacts) is assessed in the same manner as other impacts previously identified in the EIA process (Figure 1)

3.1.2 Alternatives to the activity

Both the proposed activity and possible alternatives should be examined in concert so that a decision maker can more easily compare the potential impacts on the Antarctic environment and dependent and associated ecosystems; in accordance with Article 3 of the Protocol, this should include consideration of impacts on the intrinsic value of Antarctica, including its wilderness and aesthetic values and its value as an area of the conduct of scientific research.

Examples of alternatives for consideration include:

- use of different locations or sites for the activity. Overall impacts can be minimised by selecting a location that will avoid adverse interactions between the activity and the environment (e.g. away from wildlife colonies, vegetated areas, locations of scientific projects, pristine sites important for microbiology, historic sites). For similar reasons, consideration should be given to the alternative of undertaking the activity in a location that has already been modified as a result of previous human activity;

- alternative arrangements for use of a proposed location, including the layout of facilities. For example, a multi-story building might minimise the area disturbed by footings. However, the visibility of structures should also be considered;

- opportunities for international cooperation on facilities, research and logistics. Where appropriate, there can be scientific and cost benefits, as well as environmental benefits, from cooperative arrangements with other nations, such as the shared use of existing research stations or other infrastructure, joining existing or planned scientific programs, or making arrangements to utilise established shipping, air and ground transport;

- use of different technologies, in order to reduce the outputs (or the intensity of the outputs) of the activity. For example, the use of renewable energy sources, energy efficient equipment, and building management systems that will help minimise atmospheric emissions, waste water treatment plants that may allow the re-use of treated water, the use of unmanned aerial vehicles (UAVs) that may minimise direct human impact in fragile environments, or alternative survey equipment that may minimise underwater noise;

- use of pre-existing facilities. For example, this may involve sharing or expanding operational facilities, including international collaboration, or the re-opening, rehabilitation and re-use of abandoned or temporarily closed facilities;

- alternatives that may avoid / minimise the cost and effort of decommissioning, as well as environmental impacts. If possible, the EIA should consider a combination of alternatives identified above, including location, layouts, international cooperation or technologies; and

- different timing for the activity (e.g. to avoid vehicle access during the breeding season of native birds or mammals, or during times of year when temporarily snow/ice-free ground may be susceptible to vehicle traffic).

The alternative of not proceeding with the proposed activity (i.e. the "no-action" alternative) should always be included in any analysis of environmental impacts of the proposed activity.

The EIA should describe the factors / criteria considered when assessing alternatives (e.g. environmental impact, logistical considerations, safety considerations, cost), and clearly explain the rationale and process for assessing and identifying the preferred option.

3.2. Considering the environment

A thorough understanding of the pre-activity state of the environment is an essential basis for predicting and evaluating impacts, and for identifying relevant and effective mitigation measures. If it is proposed that the activity will take place in multiple locations, consideration should be given to all locations in question.

Consideration of the environment requires the characterisation of all relevant physical, biological, chemical and anthropic values or resources in a given area, where and when an activity is proposed. Relevant means all those elements of the environment that the proposed activity might influence or which might influence the activity, including dependent and associated ecosystems.

Such information should be quantitative (e.g. heavy metal concentration on organisms or on river flows, a bird population size) where available and appropriate. The recording of metadata (i.e. important information about a dataset, such as where, when and how such data were collected) can be valuable for future comparisons, including monitoring and verification of predicted impacts. In many cases qualitative descriptions may have to be used, such as when describing the aesthetic value of a landscape. Maps, publications, research results and researchers are different sources of information to be identified and taken into account.

Consideration of the existing environment should include, where appropriate:

- recognition of the special status accorded to Antarctica by the ATS, including its status as a natural reserve devoted to peace and science;
- the physical and biological features that could be affected directly or indirectly, including:
  - the physical characteristics, such as topography, bathymetry, geology, geomorphology, soils, hydrology, meteorology, glaciology;
  - the biota. For example inventories of terrestrial, freshwater and marine plant and animal species, populations and communities, other important features such as the presence of breeding grounds, and microbial communities and habitats); and
  - any dependent populations. For example. bird nesting areas related to feeding areas;
- an assessment, to the extent possible, of the pre-activity wilderness state of the location of the proposed activity. While the Antarctic Treaty Parties have not agreed a definition for the term wilderness, it is generally understood to represent a measure of the relative absence of evidence of, or impacts from, human activity;
- an assessment of the value of the location as an area for the conduct of scientific research;
- natural variations in environmental conditions that could occur on a diurnal, seasonal, annual and/or interannual timescale;
- information about the spatial and temporal variability of the environmental sensitivity. For example, differences in impacts when an area is snow covered, or covered by sea ice, compared to when it is not;
- identification and consideration of any particular vulnerabilities associated with the locations where the activity will take place, or any dependent or associated ecosystems, including any unique characteristics and vulnerabilities

of the biogeographic region. It may be useful to have reference to the Antarctic Conservation Biogeographic Regions and the Environmental Domains Analysis of Antarctica);

- current trends in natural processes such as population growth or spread of particular species, geological or hydrological phenomena;
- the reliability of the data (e.g. anecdotal, historical, scientific, etc.);
- elements of the environment which have been changed, or may be changing as the result of other current or previous activities;
- special values of the area (if previously identified). This may include, but is not necessarily limited to, the presence of ASPAs, ASMAs or HSMs – see the *Antarctic Protected Areas Database*;
- the existence of areas potentially subject to indirect and cumulative impacts;
- the influence that the activity may exert on dependent and associated ecosystems;
- existing activities being carried out in the area or at the site, or planned to be carried out at the site, particularly scientific activities, given their intrinsic importance as a value to be protected in Antarctica; and
- specific parameters against which predicted changes are to be monitored.

A thorough consideration of the environment before starting the activity (baseline information) is essential to ensure a valid prediction of impacts and to define monitoring parameters, if required. If such baseline information is not available, field research may be necessary to obtain reliable data about the state of the environment before beginning the activity. Remotely sensed data, such as satellite or aerial imagery, can also be a useful source of information. An example checklist to help guide the process of obtaining and recording baseline information is presented at Appendix 1. The Resources section at the end of this document provides direction to a range of sources of information that may also be of use when considering the environment.

As far as possible, consideration should be given to anticipated / potential environmental consequences of climate changes in the location of the proposed activity, and over the timeframe of the proposed activity, including the decommissioning phase where relevant. For this purpose, relevant sources of general information would include, but would not be limited to, SCAR's 2009 Antarctic Climate Change and Environment report, and subsequent regular updates produced by SCAR. Proponents should also investigate sources of information that can give insight into observed or anticipated climate-related changes at the particular location in question.

It is also important to clearly identify gaps in knowledge and uncertainties encountered in compiling the information. The EIA should consider the extent to which any limitations in the understanding of the environment will affect the accuracy and relevance of the impact assessment and, where appropriate, indicate the means by which any gaps and uncertainties will be addressed (e.g. by further site surveys, field research, remote sensing etc.).

When an operator plans an activity which will be undertaken at several sites, each one of those sites should be described according to the methodology above.

3.3. Analysis of Impacts

3.3.1 Identification of environmental aspects

Understanding the ways in which a proposed activity can interact with the environment (i.e. its environmental *aspects*) is an important step in identifying and addressing the potential environmental impacts.

An environmental aspect may involve an output or addition to the environment (e.g. emission of pollutants / noise / light, human presence, transfer of native or non-native species, direct contact with wildlife / vegetation, leak or spill of hazardous substances etc.) or a removal from the environment (e.g. use of lake water, collection of moss samples, removal of rocks). Identifying environmental aspects involves determining the type of interaction (e.g. emission, discharge, extraction) and which component or components of the environment may be involved in interactions with the activity (e.g. discharge of waste water to the ocean / discharge of waste water into ice, or emission of noise to air / emission of noise to water).

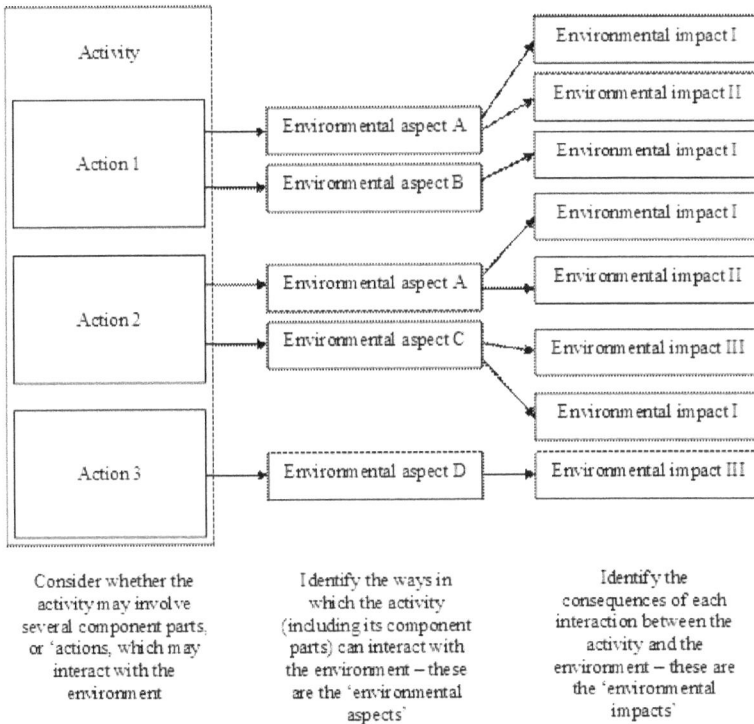

Figure 2: Conceptual model for the process of identifying environmental aspects and impacts

A single activity may involve several component parts or *actions*, each of which may have several associated environmental aspects (see Figure 2). For example, the overall activity of constructing and operating a research station may involve the use of vehicles, which may interact with the environment by directly compacting soil, emitting atmospheric emissions, emitting noise, etc.). Constructing and operating a research station may also involve other actions, such as the management of waste and the management of fuel, each of which may interact with the environment. Similarly, different activities or actions may have similar environmental aspects. For example in an ice drilling activity the aspect 'atmospheric emissions' may be associated with the use of vehicles, use of the drilling rig itself or power generation. In turn, each environmental aspect may potentially result in one or more environmental impact (see Section 3.3.2).

The identification of aspects should include not only normal operating conditions but should also consider, to the extent possible, abnormal conditions (e.g. such as start-up or shut-down) and emergency situations.

Systematising actions and aspects in a matrix format may be helpful in this process. As an example, the table below identifies some environmental aspects that may arise from some of the various actions associated with the construction of a new research station; this draws on an earlier example presented in *"Monitoring of Environmental Impacts from Science and Operations in Antarctica" (SCAR/COMNAP, 1996)*, and is not intended to be representative of all actions and aspects of all potential activities in Antarctica.

ACTIONS	POTENTIAL ENVIRONMENTAL ASPECTS									
	Air emissions (incl. Dust)	Presence	Wastes	Noise	Fuel spills	Mechanical action on land	Mechanical action in water	Heat	Light	Transfer of species
Vehicles										
- Land	X	X	-	X	X	X	-	X	X	X
- Aircraft	X	X	-	X	X	X	-	-	-	X
- Watercraft	X	X	-	X	X	-	X	-	-	X
Power generation	X	-	-	X	X	-	-	X	-	-
Construction of buildings	X	X	X	X	X	X	-	-		
Fuel storage	-	X	-	-	X	-	-	-		-
Waste treatment	X	-	X	X	-	-	-	-	-	X

Aspects may vary across different alternatives, because some alternatives may involve a particular type of interaction with the environment while others do not. An appropriate way to avoid impacts arising is to modify the proposed activity so that the potential interaction with the environment (the environmental aspect) does not occur. For example, recycling waste water for use on station may avoid discharges to the marine environment and, in turn, avoid impacts to near shore marine species and habitats.

The geographical spread of an aspect has to be accurately estimated in order to determine to what extent the environment may be impacted.

3.3.2 Impact identification

In the context of environmental impact assessment, an environmental *impact* (synonym: *effect*) is a change in environmental values or resources that is attributable to a human activity. It is the consequence of an interaction between an activity and the environment, not the interaction itself. Impact may also be defined as the result of the interaction between an activity and an environmental value or resource. For example, the environmental aspect of 'trampling' may result in the impact of 'reduced plant cover'.

Identifying potential impacts means determining which component(s) of the environment are susceptible to be affected by an activity or action. An activity will not result in an impact to an environmental value or resource if there is no process of interaction, or 'exposure'. Following the example in the previous section, wastewater management will not result in impacts to the near shore marine species or habitats environment if all wastewater is recycled for use on station, because there is no interaction between the activity and the near shore marine environment.

Overlaying spatial information (e.g. use of a geographic information system, or GIS) can be a valuable tool to assist in this determination. For example, an activity that has the environmental aspect 'discharge of hazardous liquids' might result in impacts on freshwater invertebrates if the activity is undertaken in location where lakes are present, but not if the activity is undertaken at a location remote from any lakes.

Correct identification of the intensity of exposure of an activity is a crucial step in making a reliable prediction of impacts. Some elements contributing to that identification are:

- Temporal variation. The interactions between an activity and an environmental value or resource may change with the timing of the activity, because of climate cycles, breeding patterns etc. For example, noise generated by an activity might cause wildlife disturbance if the activity is undertaken during the breeding season, but not if the activity is undertaken when no wildlife are present.

- Cause-effect relationships between the activity and environmental values or resources must be determined, especially in cases where the relationships are indirect, where the activity has numerous types of interactions with a value or resource, or where a single type of interaction occurs repeatedly.

It should also be noted that a single environmental aspect might have several related environmental impacts (Figure 2). For example, discharge of untreated wastewater to the marine environment might result in impacts on benthic communities, seals and water quality. Appendix 2 presents an illustrative list of aspects and potential impacts of Antarctic activities. It is not intended to be comprehensive, or prescriptive, but may be a useful reference when planning an activity.

The identification of environmental impacts consists of the characterisation of all changes in environmental values or resources resulting from the activity. Only when the impact is identified can an evaluation be made of its significance.

The identification of impacts should consider whether the impacts might change over the planned duration or the proposed activity. For example, the environmental impacts of a long-term activity may vary over time due to interaction with environmental responses to climate changes, or due to changes to the activity to respond or adapt to climate changes.

An impact may be identified by its nature, spatial extent, intensity, duration, reversibility and lag time.

Nature: type of change imposed on the environment due to the activity (e.g. contamination, erosion, mortality).

Spatial extent: area or volume where changes are likely to be detectable.

Intensity: a measure of the amount of change imposed on the environment due to the activity.(it can be measured, or estimated, through, e.g. number of species or individuals effected, concentration of a given pollutant in a waterbody, rates of erosion, rates of mortality, etc.).

Duration: period of time during which changes in the environment are likely to occur.

Reversibility / resilience: possibility of the system to return to its initial environmental conditions once an impact is produced.

Lag time: time span between the moment an environmental interaction takes place and the moment impacts occur.

In addition, a proper impact identification should also identify direct, indirect and cumulative impacts, as well as unavoidable impacts.

A *direct impact* is a change in environmental values or resources that results from direct cause-effect consequences of interaction between the exposed environment and an activity or action (e.g. decrease of a limpet population due to an oil spill, or a decrease of a freshwater invertebrate population due to lake water removal). An *indirect impact* is a change in environmental values or resources that results from interactions between the environment and other impacts - direct or indirect - (e.g. alteration in seagull population due to a decrease in limpet population which, in turn, was caused by an oil spill).

A *cumulative impact* is the combined impact of past, present, and reasonably foreseeable activities. These activities may occur over time and space and can be additive or interactive/synergistic (e.g. decrease of limpet population due to the combined effect of oil discharges by base and ship operations). See also the section below on 'Considering Cumulative Impacts'.

An *unavoidable impact* is an impact for which no further mitigation is possible. For example, it may be possible to reduce the area from which proposed new infrastructure will be visible, but it is unavoidable that the infrastructure will be visible over some area.

3.3.3 Consideration of cumulative impacts

The environmental aspects and impacts of a proposed activity should be considered together with those of past, present, and reasonably foreseeable future. Therefore, potential for additive, synergistic or antagonistic interactions (thus resulting in possible significant environmental impacts) has to be considered. As noted in Section 3.3.2, the identification of impacts may also need to consider the effects of climate changes, particularly for long-term activities.

Cumulative impacts can often be one of the hardest impact categories to adequately identify in the EIA process. When attempting to identify cumulative impacts it is important to consider both spatial and temporal aspects and to identify other activities which have occurred, are occurring, or could occur at the same site or within the same area. When considering spatial aspects, thought should be given to the distribution of that environment type across the wider Antarctic environment, particularly when that environment type might be unique to certain locations or limited in geographical extent (e.g. geothermal sites or unique geological formations). It is also important to identify and consider the activities or actions of other proponents that can contribute to cumulative effects. In some instances, the potential cumulative impacts of activities by multiple operators might best be considered through the joint preparation of an EIA.

The accurate assessment of actual or predicted cumulative impacts is still an emerging field. However, several methods exist to identify impacts such as: overlay maps, checklists, matrices, etc. The choice of the methodology will depend on the character of the activity and the environment that is likely to be affected. Recognition should be given to relevant scientific data, where this exists, and to the results of monitoring programs. Spatial data relating to other past, ongoing or future activities, where available, is particularly relevant. Such data might be available from databases, such as the *EIA Database*, or accessible through direct consultation with relevant other operators.

In summary, important questions when considering the potential cumulative impacts of a proposed activity include:

- What activities have been undertaken, are currently being undertaken or are likely to be undertaken at the area of the proposed activity?

- Is there a temporal or spatial overlap (or a combination) with other activities in the area that might result in particular impacts?

- What are the likely pathways or processes of accumulation for the assessed impacts of the proposed activity?

- What effects may result from the proposed activity that may contribute to cumulative impacts?

- What are the likely cumulative impacts that could occur in the area?

3.3.4 Impact Evaluation

The purpose of impact evaluation is to assign relative significance to predicted impacts associated with an activity (and the various identified alternatives).

Significance: it is a value judgment about the severity and importance of a change in a given environment or environmental value or resource.

According to the Protocol and Annex I, impacts shall be evaluated by taking into account three levels of significance:

- less than a minor or transitory impact;
- no more than a minor or transitory impact; or
- more than a minor or transitory impact.

The interpretation of these terms should be made on a case by case site specific basis. However it may be useful to consider how similar impacts have been judged in earlier EIAs at similar sites and/or for similar types of activities (as noted above, details of previous IEEs and CEEs are readily accessible from the *EIA Database*).

An inherent consideration to judging significance is that it may have a rather subjective component and this fact should be acknowledged. Where an impact has the possibility of being significant, several experts should be consulted to achieve an informed and broadly-agreed judgment. This is particularly important either if there is a reliance on incomplete data or if there are gaps in the knowledge.

Judging significance should not be based solely on direct impacts, but must also take account of possible indirect and cumulative impacts. This evaluation should determine the magnitude and significance of cumulative effects.

The significance of the unavoidable impacts (those impacts for which no further mitigation is possible) represents an important consideration for the decision maker in deciding whether, on balance, an activity is justified.

Some problems can arise when evaluating impacts, due to misunderstanding or overlooking some aspects of the process of evaluating impacts. These can include for example:

- confusing duration of the impact with duration of the activity;
- confusing environmental aspects (i.e. interactions between an activity and the environment) of activities with impacts (i.e. the changes to the environment that result from those interactions); and
- limiting the analysis to direct impacts, without consideration of indirect and cumulative impacts.
- To enable independent verification / assessment of the evaluation, the EIA document should clearly describe the methods and criteria used to assess the significance of predicted impacts.

3.4. Comparison of impacts

When the project has been assessed with respect to environmental impacts it is necessary to summarise and aggregate the significant impacts for the various alternatives in a form suitable for communication to the decision makers. From such an aggregation of information a comparison among alternatives can be easily made.

3.5. Measures to minimise or mitigate impacts

The EIA process should consider measures to decrease, avoid, or eliminate any of the components of an impact on the environment, or on the conduct of scientific research and on other existing uses and values. This can be considered a process of feedback, and should occur throughout the EIA process, not simply as a final step. Such measures include mitigation and remediation actions.

Mitigation is the use of practice, procedure or technology to minimise or to prevent impacts associated with proposed activities. The modification of any component of the activity (and hence the consideration of the environmental aspects and impacts) as well as the establishment of supervision procedures represent effective ways of mitigation.

Mitigation measures will vary according to the activity and the characteristics of the environment, and may include, for example:

- selecting an appropriate location (e.g. avoiding environmentally sensitive sites, where possible) and identifying sub-areas within the location that may require additional protection or management;
- developing on site control procedures (e.g. arrangements for fuel storage and handling, use of renewable energy systems and other means of minimising atmospheric emissions, water supply, appropriate methods for waste disposal and management, approaches to minimising noise and light emissions);
- applying appropriate methods to prevent the transfer of species to, or between locations within, Antarctica (e.g. with reference to the guidelines and resources presented in the *CEP Non-Native Species Manual*);
- establishing the best time for the activity (e.g. to avoid the breeding season of penguins);
- taking steps to limit the spatial and temporal extent of impacts (e.g. utilising temporary rather than permanent infrastructure, locating facilities in already modified locations, minimising the spread of individual items of infrastructure, or considering the setting of infrastructure in the landscape to minimise visibility);
- providing environmental education and training to personnel, or contractors, involved in the activity;
- measures to prevent, and where necessary respond to, emergencies that may cause environmental impacts (e.g. oil spills, fires); and
- ensuring adequate on site supervision of the activity by senior project staff or environmental specialists.

Remediation consists of the steps taken after impacts have occurred to promote, as much as possible, the return of the environment to its original condition.

The final version of the activity to be assessed should describe both planned mitigation and remediation measures. Impact avoidance, as a form of mitigation, may contribute to minimising monitoring, reducing remediation costs and generally contribute also to maintaining the existing state of the environment.

When considering mitigation and remediation measures, the following issues should be addressed:

- making a clear distinction between mitigation and remediation measures;
- clearly defining the state of the environment that is being aimed for through such measures;
- considering that new, unforeseen impacts may appear as a result of inadequate implementation of proposed mitigation measures;
- recognising that mitigation and remediation measures may also need to take into account the cumulative impacts of past, present and reasonably foreseeable activities;
- considering the extent to which decommissioning efforts could return the site to its pre-activity environmental state;
- noting that the environment may not always be capable of returning to its original condition, even when remediation actions are implemented; and
- considering that a given corrective measure may interact antagonistically or synergistically with other corrective measures.

Where the EIA refers to separate documents (e.g. waste management plans, oil spill contingency plans etc.) a link to such documents should be provided, where possible, or sufficient information should be included in the EIA to allow an assessment of the likely effectiveness of the planned arrangements.

The Resources section at the end of this document identifies several sources of guidance and information, including guidelines endorsed by the CEP, which may be of assistance in identifying mitigation and remediation measures.

3.6. Monitoring

Monitoring consists of standardised measurements or observations of key parameters (outputs/removals and environmental variables) over time, their statistical evaluation and reporting on the state of the environment in order to define quality and trends. For the EIA process, monitoring should be oriented towards confirming the accuracy of predictions about environmental impacts of the activity (e.g. impacts arising from planned waste discharges, noise generation or atmospheric emissions), including cumulative impacts, and to detect unforeseen impacts or impacts more significant than expected. Given this, it may be useful to set environmental thresholds or standards for an activity that monitoring results are assessed against. If these thresholds are exceeded, then a review or re-analysis would be required of assumptions made regarding the environmental impacts or of management systems related to the activity.

Monitoring may also include any other procedures that can be used to assess and verify the predicted impacts of the activity. Where measurement of specific parameters is not necessary or appropriate, assessment and verification procedures could include maintaining a log of the activity that actually occurred, and of changes in the nature of the activity where they were significantly different from those described in the EIA. This information can be useful for further minimising or mitigating impacts, and, where appropriate, for modifying, suspending or even cancelling all or part of the activity.

Monitoring is about precise measurement of a few target species, processes, or other indicators, carefully selected on the basis of scientifically sound predetermined criteria. Where a number of proponents are conducting activities at the same sites they should give consideration to establishing joint regional monitoring programs.

The process of selecting key indicators should be accomplished during the activity's planning stage, once environmental aspects have been identified, the environment has been considered and associated impacts have been assessed (including impacts on dependent and associated ecosystems, where relevant), while monitoring environmental parameters generally should start before the commencement of the activity if adequate baseline information is not available.

Monitoring should be designed, wherever possible, to accommodate and account for climate-related changes during the period of the activity. This will be of particular relevance for activities with a lengthy duration, and activities occurring in locations known or expected to be subject to rapid change.

Where the EIA identifies the potential for the proposed activity to result in the introduction of non-native species, monitoring arrangements should seek to verify the effectiveness of planned preventive measures.

Planning or undertaking monitoring activities may be hindered by a number of situations including, for example:

- leaving the planning of monitoring programs until the activity is in progress;
- monitoring activities can be costly, especially for multi-year projects and activities;
- some assumptions about the environmental impacts of an activity cannot be tested;
- failure to follow through with monitoring;
- failure to adequately scope the monitoring program, so that it does not encompass all elements of the environment that may be impacted or does not cover a broad enough geographic area; and
- failure to distinguish between natural and human-induced variability in environmental parameters.

Guidance for designing monitoring programs relevant to the environmental characteristics of Antarctica can be found in:

- COMNAP Practical Guidelines for Developing and Designing Environmental Monitoring Programmes in Antarctica
- COMNAP-SCAR Antarctic Environmental Monitoring Handbook
- CEP Clean-Up Manual
- CEP Non-Native Species Manual

4. Writing the EIA Document

The outcome of an EIA is a formal document, which presents all the relevant information about the EIA process. The EIA document represents a fundamental link between the EIA process and decision makers seeing that conclusions stemming from the EIA process will assist decision makers to consider the environmental aspects of the proposed activity.

Four bodies of information arise from an EIA process: *methodology, data, results* and *conclusions* derived from them. Since *results* and *conclusions* are of particular interest for decision makers, these chapters should be written in an accessible language, avoiding very technical terms. The use of graphical information, such as maps, tables and graphs, is an effective way of improving communication.

The size and level of detail in the document will depend on the significance of the environmental impacts that have been identified throughout the EIA process. Thus, Annex I to the Protocol establishes two formats to document it: Initial Environmental Evaluation (IEE) and Comprehensive Environmental Evaluation (CEE), for which the Protocol requires the presentation of different volumes of information (Annex I, Articles 2 and 3).

Unless it has been determined that an activity will have less than a minor or transitory impact or it has already been determined that a Comprehensive Environmental Evaluation is needed, an Initial Environmental Evaluation (IEE) shall be prepared. If the EIA process indicates that a proposed activity is likely to have more than a minor or transitory impact a Comprehensive Environmental Evaluation must be prepared.

According to Annex I requirements a draft CEE shall be prepared first, which shall be circulated to all Parties as well as to CEP for comments. Once comments and suggestions have been incorporated, a final CEE is circulated to all Parties.

The following table summarises the steps to be considered throughout the EIA process (which are explained in Section 3 of the present guidelines). It also lists the requirements stemming from Annex I that should be included in an EIA document. In the case of IEE, some of the marked items are not specifically mentioned in Annex I, Article 2. However, their inclusion in the IEE document is often useful to communicate the results of the process in a transparent manner. These items were distinguished in the table with an X.

EIA Contents and Annex I Requirements	IEE	CEE
Cover sheet		X
Index	X	X
Preparers and advisors	X	√
Non-technical summary	X	√
Description of the proposed activity, including its purpose, location, duration and intensity	√	√
Description of the possible alternatives to the proposed activity	√	√
• Alternative of not proceeding with the activity	X	√
Description of the initial environmental reference state and prediction of the environmental state in absence of the proposed activity	X	√
Description of methods and data used to forecast the impacts of the proposed activity	X	√
Estimation of nature, extent, duration and intensity of direct impacts	√	√
Consideration of possible indirect or second order impacts	X	√
Consideration of cumulative impacts	√	√
Identification of unavoidable impacts	X	√
Effects of the activity on scientific research and other uses or values	X	√
Mitigation measures	X	√
• Monitoring programs	X	√
Identification of gaps in the knowledge	X	√
Conclusions	X	X
References	X	X
Glossary		X

√ Required by annex I.
X Often useful.

The following text focuses briefly on how the items listed above should be referred to in the text of any EIA. Further technical information is already described in previous chapters.

Description of the purpose and need for the proposed activity (see also Section 3.1)

This section should include a brief description of the proposed activity and an explanation of the intent of the activity, including any benefits that will arise (e.g. environmental protection, scientific understanding, education). It should include sufficient detail to make it clear why the activity is being proposed including the need for the activity to proceed (e.g. reference to national or international strategic science plans). It should also provide details on the process by which the scope of the activity was defined. This will help ensure that the full scope of the activity has been included so that impacts can be properly assessed. If a formal process was used to accomplish this (a formal meeting or solicitation of input from the public or other groups), that process and its results should be discussed here.

Description of the proposed activity and possible alternatives and the consequences of those alternatives (See also Sections 3.1.1 and 3.1.2)

This section should include a detailed description of the proposed activity as well as reasonable alternatives. The first alternative to be described would be the proposed activity. The description should be as comprehensive and detailed as possible (see section 3.1).

It may be useful to provide a comparison of alternatives in this section. For instance, for a new research station, alternatives might include differences in the size of the station and the number of persons that could be accommodated. These differences would mean different quantities of materials required, fuels consumed and emissions or wastes generated. Tables showing appropriate comparisons can be very helpful to the reader of the document.

Alternative of not proceeding with the activity (see also Section 3.1.2)

The alternative of not proceeding with the proposed activity (i.e. the "no-action" alternative) should be described to highlight the pros and cons of not conducting the activity. Although the Protocol only requires its inclusion in CEEs, it is useful to also include the "no-action" alternative in the text of IEEs in order to better justify the need for proceeding with the activity.

Description of the initial environmental reference state and prediction of the environmental state in absence of the activity (see also Section 3.2)

Such a description should not be limited to a characterisation of the relevant physical, biological, chemical and anthropic elements of the environment, but should also take into account the existence and behaviour of dynamic trends and processes in order to predict the state of the environment in absence of the activity. For example, modelling tools may assist with considering climate related changes to the environment with, and in the absence of, the proposed activity (e.g. future projections of wildlife, flora and ice retreat/increase). A proper description of the initial environmental reference state provides elements against which changes are to be compared.

Description of methods and data used to forecast the impacts (see also Section 3.3)

The purpose of this section is to explain and, if necessary, defend the design of the assessment and then provide enough detail that a further evaluator can understand and reproduce the procedure. Careful writing of the methodology is critically important because it determines that results can be reproducible and/or comparable.

Estimation of nature, extent, duration and intensity of impacts (including consideration of possible indirect and cumulative impacts) (see also Sections 3.3.2 and 3.3.3)

This section should include a clear description of identified environmental aspects and impacts. It must clearly establish the significance assigned to each impact and the justification for such assignment. In addition, and to summarise this section, the inclusion of a table showing the environmental impacts on each environmental component can be very helpful.

Special attention must be paid to the consideration of possible indirect and cumulative impacts, since cause-effect relationship determining the existence of such impacts usually exhibit a higher degree of complexity.

Monitoring programs (see also Section 3.6)

When necessary, this section should clearly define monitoring objectives, set testable hypotheses, choose key parameters to be monitored, assess data collection methods, design statistical sampling program, and decide on frequency and timing of data collection/recording. Implementation of such monitoring programs is a further step that may begin after the planning of the activity has been completed, even though the activity has not actually been initiated.

Mitigation and remediation measures (see also Section 3.5)

An important purpose of the EIA process is to take steps to avoid or minimise likely impacts through the application of mitigation and remediation measures. For this reason, a description of planned mitigation measures (commensurate with the nature of the activity and the level of EIA) is a fundamental part of the EIA document. Since such measures usually aim to correct some aspects of the activity, communication of these measures must be concrete, pointing out the proposed actions and their timing, as well as the benefits associated to each individual measure.

Identification of unavoidable impacts (see also Section 3.3.2)

Recognition of the existence of unavoidable impacts should be included within any impact analysis. Consideration of such impacts is of great importance given that the occurrence of unavoidable impacts may affect the decision on whether to proceed with the proposed activity.

Effects of the activity on scientific research and other uses or values (see also Section 3.3)

Taking into account that the Protocol designates Antarctica as an area devoted to peace and science, the effects of the proposed activity on ongoing scientific research, or on the potential of a site to future scientific research (e.g. as a scientific reference site), must be a fundamental consideration when the impact analysis is carried out. Where appropriate, it is also important to consider the effects of the proposed activity on other existing uses and values.

Identification of gaps in the knowledge (see also Section 3.2)

Existing bodies of knowledge (i.e. empirical, theoretical, or anecdotal data and information) are used to support the assessment process. Nonetheless, these bodies of knowledge may be incomplete or may be surrounded by varying degrees of uncertainty. It is critical to identify explicitly in the assessment where such incompleteness or uncertainty exists; and how this has been factored into the assessment process. This disclosure can be useful in assessment by clearly identifying where more knowledge is needed. Where relevant, plans to address gaps and uncertainties should also be described.

Conclusions

Although not an explicit requirement of Annex I, an EIA should briefly describe the conclusion of the EIA process, reflecting the language of Article 8 and Annex I of the Protocol (e.g. is the proposed activity assessed as likely to have: less than a minor or transitory impact; no more than a minor or transitory impact; or more than a minor or transitory impact). The conclusion should also include a clear statement of why the proposed activity, with the likely environmental impacts, should proceed.

Preparers and advisers

This section provides a list of those experts who were consulted in preparing the assessment, their areas of expertise, and appropriate contact information. It should also list the persons who were responsible for the actual preparation of the document. This information is useful to reviewers and decision makers to ensure that the appropriate expertise was brought to bear on the analyses needed to assess the type and degree of impact from the proposed activity. It is also useful information for future assessments on similar activities or issues.

References

This section should list any references used in preparing the evaluation. They may include research or other scientific papers used in the analysis of impacts or monitoring data used to establish baseline conditions in the area where the activity is proposed. They may also include other environmental assessments of similar activities at other or similar locations.

Index

As an EIA document may be fairly large, an index is a very helpful aid to the reader.

Glossary

This section provides a list of terms and definitions as well as abbreviations that are helpful to the reader, especially if the terms are not commonly understood.

Cover Sheet

A CEE should contain a title page or cover sheet that lists the name and address of the person or organization who prepared the CEE and the address to which comments should be sent (for the draft document only).

Non-Technical Summary

A CEE must contain a non-technical summary of the contents of the document. This summary should be written in an accessible language and include pertinent information on the purpose and need for the proposed activity, the issues and alternatives considered, the existing environment, and the impacts associated with each alternative. A non-technical summary might also be useful for an IEE.

Finally, in either case (IEE or CEE) a number of considerations about writing the EIA document should be taken into account, such as:

- avoidance of including irrelevant descriptive information;
- documenting all relevant steps of the process;
- clearly describing the impact identification methodology;

- clearly distinguishing between results (identification of impacts, mitigation measures, etc.) and final value judgement of significance; and
- properly connecting results and conclusions.

5. EIA feedback processes

It is important to recognise that the EIA process does not stop once the EIA document has been approved and the activity commences. There remains a need to verify the predicted impacts of the activity and assess the effectiveness of mitigation measures, including to consider whether it is necessary to make any changes to the activity or prepare a new EIA. There are three principal components of the feedback process that should be considered during the undertaking of the activity in question and upon its completion. These relate to: monitoring; changes to the activity, and review.

5.1. Monitoring

As recorded in Section 3.6 above and in Figure 1, monitoring of key parameters will often be required and is an important part of the EIA process so as to: verify the scale of predicted impacts; provide early warning of any un-predicted impacts; and assess the effectiveness of mitigation measures.

Such monitoring effort should form part of the EIA feedback process. Information that is gathered through monitoring can be assessed against the planned mitigation measures and the activity adjusted accordingly to maintain the actual impacts within the accepted or approved constraints.

This approach is consistent with the provisions of Article 3 of the Protocol, which provides for monitoring "*so as to identify and provide early warning of any adverse effects of the activity and to provide for such modification of operating procedures as may be necessary in the light of the results of monitoring*" (Article 3(c)(v)), and that "*regular and effective monitoring shall take place to allow assessment of the impacts of ongoing activities, including the verification of predicted impacts*" (Article 3(d)).

If information obtained from the monitoring programme identifies a significant departure from the predicted impacts, either in their nature/type or scale, or significant un-predicted impacts are observed, a review of the EIA may be required, and additional mitigation measures may need to be identified.

5.2. Changes to the activity

As noted in Section 3.1.1 above, changes to the activity may also require a reconsideration or review of the EIA. This is consistent with Article 8(3) of the Protocol which provides that "*the assessment procedures set out in Annex I shall apply to any change in an activity whether the change arises from an increase or decrease in the intensity of an existing activity, from the addition of an activity, the decommissioning of a facility, or otherwise*".

Changes to an activity that may require an amendment to an EIA, or a new EIA, might include, for example:

- changes to the timing and duration of an activity;
- changes to the methods and materials to be used;
- changes in the size of a facility;
- changes in the primary use of a facility;
- the establishment of nearby facilities or protected areas;
- a noticeable increase or decrease in the population of a facility from one year to the next or over a few years;
- an expansion of surface area of a facility or activity;
- an increase or decrease in the number of buildings, or the replacement of buildings;
- increasing intensity or diversity of tourism or national Antarctic programme activities at particular sites; and
- projects that did not go to plan and encountered significant delays.

It is important therefore that the implications of any such changes are reassessed to identify changes to the predicted impacts and the mitigation measures that need to be applied. If significant changes to an activity are proposed, the EIA process may need to be repeated in full.

In situations where monitoring suggests that an EIA review is required, and when a significant change occurs to an activity, which may also prompt a review of the EIA or a new EIA, it will be important to consult with other stakeholders and interested parties. Such stakeholders might include, for example:

- the proponents of the project or activity who will need to consider: the environmental impacts associated with the operational and financial implications of adjusting the programme; and the need to accommodate additional mitigation measures that might arise from the EIA review;
- the relevant national authority who will need to be consulted on the extent to which an EIA needs to be amended or reviewed and the process to be followed; and
- third parties, including other national Antarctic programmes with interests in the activity, or who may be affected by changes to the activity, and independent reviewers seconded to provide an assessment of the activity against the EIA (see below).

In many cases the need to review or modify an EIA will need to be communicated to all those with an interest in the activity and its regulation.

5.3. Review

There is significant benefit in considering a review of the EIA process at an appropriate point, for example on completion of the activity in question. A review process will provide an opportunity to assess the effectiveness of the EIA process, and identify where opportunities for improvement might be made for future EIAs.

Such reviews might be based on the EIA process described in these guidelines and consider each part in turn to determine what went well and what improvements might be made when undertaking future EIA processes.

For activities assessed at the level of a CEE the Antarctic Treaty Parties have encouraged such reviews to be undertaken. By means of Resolution 2 (1997), the ATCM has encouraged Parties to:

1)   Include in their procedures for assessing the environmental impacts of their activities in Antarctica, provision for review of the activities undertaken following the completion of a CEE.

2)   Adopt the following process for CEE follow-up:

   a)   Review activities carried out following completion of CEE, including analysis of whether the activities were conducted as proposed, whether applicable mitigation measures were implemented, and whether the impacts of the activity were as predicted in the assessment;

   b)   Record any changes to the activities described in the CEE, the reasons for the changes, and the environmental consequences of those changes; and

   c)   Report to the Parties on the outcomes of (a) and (b) above.

6. Definition of terms in the EIA process

Action: any step taken as a part of an activity.

Activity: an event or process resulting from (or associated with) the presence of humans in the Antarctic, and/or which may lead to the presence of humans in Antarctica. (Adapted from *SCAR/COMNAP Monitoring Workshop*).

Aspect: any element of an activity or action that can interact with the environment (*i.e.* through an output or addition to the environment, or through a removal from the environment).

Comprehensive Environmental Evaluation (CEE): an environmental impact document required for proposed activities that may have more than a minor or transitory impact on the Antarctic environment (from *Protocol, Annex I, Article 3*).

Cumulative Impact: the combined impact of past, present, and reasonably foreseeable activities. These activities may occur over time and space and can be additive or interactive/synergistic (adapted from *IUCN Cumulative Impacts Workshop*). These activities may involve visits by multiple operators or repeated visits to the same site by the same operator.

Direct Impact: a change in environmental components that results from direct cause-effect consequences of interaction between the exposed environment and an activity or action.

Environmental Impact Assessment (EIA): a process for identifying, predicting, evaluating and mitigating the biophysical, social and other relevant impacts of proposed activities prior to major decisions and commitments being made. (Adapted from *Guidelines for Environmental Impact Assessment (EIA) in the Arctic*).

Exposure: the process of interaction between an output/input and an environmental value or resource. (Adapted from *SCAR/COMNAP Monitoring Workshop*).

Impact: a change in the values or resources attributable to a human activity. It is the consequence (e.g. reduced plant cover) of an agent of change, not the agent itself (e.g. increase of trampling). Synonym: effect. (From *SCAR/COMNAP Monitoring Workshop*).

Indirect Impact: a change in environmental components that results from interactions between the environment and other impacts (direct or indirect). (From *Guidelines EIA in the Arctic.*)

Initial Environmental Evaluation (IEE): an environmental impact document required for proposed activities that may have no more than a minor or transitory impact on the Antarctic environment (from *Protocol, Annex I, Article 2*).

Mitigation: the use of practice, procedure or technology to minimise or to prevent impacts associated with proposed activities. (*COMNAP Practical Guidelines.*)

Monitoring: consists of standardised measurements or observations of key parameters (outputs and environmental variables) over time, their statistical evaluation and reporting on the state of the environment in order to define quality and trends (adapted from *SCAR/COMNAP Monitoring Workshop*).

Operator: individuals or organisations undertaking activities to or within Antarctica from which impacts arise.

Output: a physical change (e.g. movement of sediments by vehicle passage, noise) or an entity (e.g. emissions, an introduced species) imposed on or released to the environment as the result of an *action* or an *activity*. (*SCAR/COMNAP Monitoring Workshop.*)

Preliminary Stage (PS): a process that considers the level of environmental impacts of proposed activities -before their commencement- referred to in Article 8 of the Protocol , in accordance with appropriate national procedures (from *Protocol, Annex I, Article 1*).

Proponent: an individual or a national program advocating the activity and responsible for the preparation of the EIA document.

Remediation: consists of the steps taken after impacts have occurred to promote, as much as possible, the return of the environment to its original condition.

Unavoidable Impact: an impact for which no further mitigation is possible.

7. References

ATCM XXXV / IP23, CEP Tourism Study. Tourism and Non-Governmental Activities in the Antarctic: Environmental Aspects and Impacts, submitted by New Zealand.

ATCPs. 1991. Protocol on Environmental Protection to the Antarctic Treaty (plus annexes). 11th. Antarctic Treaty Special Consultative Meeting. Madrid, 22-30 April, 17-23 June 1991.

COMNAP. 1992. The Antarctic Environmental Assessment Process, Practical Guidelines. Bologna (Italy) June 20, 1991, revised Washington D.C. (USA), March 4, 1992.

IUCN - The World Conservation Union. 1996. Cumulative Environmental Impacts in Antarctica. Minimisation and Management. Edited by M. de Poorter and J.C. Dalziell. Washington, D.C., USA. 145 pp.

SCAR/COMNAP. 1996. Monitoring of Environmental Impacts from Science and Operations in Antarctica. Workshop report. 43 pp and Annexes, 1996 Workshops.

8. Acronyms

ASMA: Antarctic Specially Managed Area

ASPA: Antarctic Specially Protected Area

ATCM: Antarctic Treaty Consultative Meeting

ATCP: Antarctic Treaty Consultative Party

ATS: Antarctic Treaty System

CCAMLR: Commission for the Conservation of Antarctic Marine Living Resources

CEE: Comprehensive Environmental Evaluation

CEMP: CCAMLR Ecosystem Monitoring Program

CEP: Committee for Environmental Protection

COMNAP: Council of Managers of National Antarctic Programmes

EIA: Environmental Impact Assessment

GIS: Geographical Information System

HSM: Historic Sites and Monuments

IEE: Initial Environmental Evaluation

IUCN: International Union for the Conservation of Nature (World Conservation Union)

SCAR: Scientific Committee of Antarctic Research

9. Resources

It is not practical to refer to all guidelines and resources that may be of relevance to the EIA process, and proponents should identify and draw on sources of information that are relevant to the proposed activity in question. The following list provides direction to guidance materials that may be of general relevance. While the list was accurate at the time of preparation of the EIA Guidelines, it also would be important to check for additional or updated materials. In addition, there is an extensive academic literature on EIA, including in the Antarctic context.

- *Website of the Antarctic Treaty Secretariat*: the Antarctic Treaty Secretariat maintains a comprehensive website that contains a variety of information that may be useful for persons involved in an EIA process, including:
    - *Antarctic Protected Areas Database*: contains the texts of the management plans for Antarctic Specially Protected Areas and Antarctic Specially Managed Areas, their legal status, location in the Antarctic continent and a brief summary of the purpose of designation. The database also contains information related to the list and location of Historic Sites and Monuments in Antarctica.
    - *Antarctic Treaty database*: contains the text of all Recommendations, Measures, Decisions and Resolutions and other measures adopted by the ATCM together with their attachments and information on their legal status.
    - *EIA Database*: contains details of IEEs and CEE undertaken in accordance with Annex I of the Protocol, where possible including an electronic version of the EIA document.
    - *Electronic Information Exchange System*: allows parties to fulfil the Antarctic Treaty exchange of information requirements and acts as a central repository for this information.
    - *CEP Handbook*: a compilation of key references, for use by CEP representatives when attending meetings or undertaking CEP-related work. It contains the Antarctic Treaty System instruments that guide the Committee's work, copies of procedures and approved guidelines that explain how the CEP conducts its business, other documents the CEP has produced or endorsed to help Treaty Parties protect the Antarctic environment, plus links to other useful references
    - *CEP Clean-Up Manual:*[*] provides guidance, including key guiding principles and links to practical guidelines and resources, that operators can apply and use, as appropriate to assist with addressing the requirements of the Protocol, in particular Annex III.
    - *CEP Non-Native Species Manual:*[**] provides guidance to Antarctic Treaty

---

[*] Resolution 2 (2013).
[**] Resolution 6 (2011).

Parties in order to conserve Antarctic biodiversity and intrinsic values by preventing the unintended introduction to the Antarctic region of species not native to that region, and the movement of species within Antarctica from one biogeographic zone to any other. Includes key guiding principles and links to recommended practical guidelines and resources that operators can apply and use, as appropriate, to assist with meeting their responsibilities under Annex II to the Protocol.

- *General Guidelines for Visitors to the Antarctic:*[*] provide general advice for visiting any location, with the aim of ensuring visits do not have adverse impacts on the Antarctic environment, or on its scientific and aesthetic values.

- *Guidance for Visitors to the Antarctic:*[**] intended to ensure that all visitors are aware of, and are therefore able to comply with, the Treaty and the Protocol.

- *Site Guidelines for Visitors*: the guidelines aim to provide specific instructions on the conduct of activities at the most frequently visited Antarctic sites. This includes practical guidance for tour operators and guides on how they should conduct visits in those sites, taking into account their environmental values and sensitivities.

• *Scientific Committee on Antarctic Research (SCAR) data and products*: for the benefit of SCAR scientists and the wider community, SCAR provides several products that support the work of SCAR scientists but are also made widely available to others. SCAR promotes free and unrestricted access to Antarctic data and information by promoting open and accessible archiving practices. SCAR aims to be a portal to data repositories of Antarctic scientific data and information.

• *Council of Managers of National Antarctic Programs (COMNAP) publications*: contains links to operational guidelines developed by COMNAP's Expert Groups and Networks with the aim of assisting National Programs implementing common procedures and practices to enhance operational effectiveness and safety, as well as manual and handbooks that provide National Programs and others with guidance in specialist fields of activity.

• *International Association of Antarctica Tour Operators (IAATO) guidelines and resources*: contains links to information and guidance materials relevant to tourism and non-governmental activities.

• *Antarctic Environments Portal:* provides an important link between Antarctic science and Antarctic policy. All scientific information available through the Portal is based on published, peer-reviewed science and has been through a rigorous editorial review process.

---

[*] Resolution 3 (2011).
[**] Recommendation XVIII-1 (1994).

Appendix 1

Example checklist for collecting and recording of baseline information about the state of the environment in the location of a proposed activity

(Modified from the CEP Clean-Up Manual, Annex 1: Checklist for Preliminary Site Assessment)

ASSESSMENT AND REPORTING INFORMATION				
Title of Report/Assessment				
Date of Report		Prepared by:		Contact details:
Date of site visit (if applicable)		Assessor(s):		Contact details:

GENERAL CHARACTERISTICS OF SITE				
Place name				
Intended site use (e.g. building, storage area, wastewater disposal, road, location of vehicle use etc.)				
Location (coordinates of point)				
Location (coordinates of bounding polygon)	North:	South:	East:	West:
Nearest Operational Antarctic Station		Distance from Station:	Accessibility:	
General Description of Site				
Human health and safety considerations				
Site Type (seasonally ice- free land, lake, permanent snow/ ice, marine)				
Sea ice (if applicable)				
Glaciology (if applicable)				
Geomorphology (slope, aspect, landscape features etc.)				

GENERAL CHARACTERISTICS OF SITE	
Geology (rock type, rock fracturing etc.)	
Regolith (depth and type of soil/sediment if present, depth to permafrost etc.)	
Protected area status (list ASMAs and ASPAs in the vicinity)	
Biogeographic region (after Terauds et al. 2012)	
Fauna/flora present	

FLORA AND FAUNA INVENTORY				
Type	Species	Location	Timing of presence (*i.e.*, constant, seasonal, etc.)	Other information
Breeding birds				
Breeding mammals				
Transient birds				
Transient mammals				
Coastal species				
Marine species				
Flora				

MICROBIAL COMMUNITIES INVENTORY			
Location	Date	Species recorded	Other information

CLIMATE AND WEATHER	
Indicator	Data
Weather patterns	
Temperature data (seasonal average, min/max)	
Snowfall/precipitation data (frequency, total accumulation)	
Cloud cover (%)	
Wind (average speed, min/max, direction)	
Other relevant information	

HUMAN ACTIVITIES				
Type	Number of persons involved	Duration	Frequency	Other details
Research				
Tourism				
Other				

HISTORY OF SITE USE AND CONTAMINATION EVENTS	
History of Site Use and Activities	
Information Sources (Station/Voyage Leader Reports, people interviewed, photographs etc.)	
Contamination History (operational activities and events, such as spills and spill responses if applicable – see CEP Clean-Up Manual for detailed guidance on site assessment for contaminated sites)	

VALUES/RECEPTORS POTENTIALLY OR ACTUALLY IMPACTED BY ACTIVITY			
Values/Receptor	Site-Specific Information on Values/ Receptors and Exposure Pathways (include estimates of distance from contaminants)	Actual or Potential Impacts?	Cumulative or one-time?
Fauna and flora			
Scientific			
Historic			
Aesthetic			
Wilderness			
Geological and geomorphological			
Other environments (atmospheric, terrestrial (including glacial)			
Marine environment (if applicable)			
Protected areas			
Other values/receptors (such as station water supply)			

PREDICTION OF FUTURE ENVIRONMENTAL STATUS IF ACTIVITY DOES NOT PROCEED	
Site Aspect	Prediction
Flora	
Fauna	
Terrestrial environment	
Marine environment	

351

Appendix 2

Aspects and potential impacts of Antarctic activities

(Modified from ATCM XXXV/IP23 CEP Tourism Study. Tourism and Non-Governmental Activities in the Antarctic: Environmental Aspects and Impacts, Table 2. Aspects and potential impacts of Antarctic tourism. Note: this table presents examples for illustrative purposes only, and is not intended to be an exhaustive list.)

Environmental aspect	Potential impact
1. Presence • The presence of people and human-made objects in the Antarctic.	• Modification of, or risk to, the intrinsic value of Antarctica, including its wilderness and aesthetic values and its value as an area for the conduct of scientific research.
2. Atmospheric emissions • Discharge of emissions to the atmosphere (including greenhouse gases and particulates) from engines, generators and incinerators, signalling or marking devices.	• Pollution of marine, terrestrial, freshwater and atmospheric environments.
3. Anchoring • Interaction with the seafloor or coastal mooring sites from deploying and retrieving anchors and anchor chains.	• Disturbance and damage of benthic marine species, communities and habitats.
4. Light emission • Discharge / escape of light from windows and other sources during dark hours.	• Injury or death of seabirds striking vessels (see interaction with wildlife).
5. Generation of noise • Sound arising from activities in water, on land or in the air from the operation of vessels, small boats, aircraft, equipment or from individuals or groups of people.	• Disturbance to wildlife.
6. Release of waste • Release or loss of any garbage, sewage, chemicals, noxious substances, pollutants, equipment or presence of toxic coatings (e.g. antifouling on hulls).	• Pollution of marine, terrestrial and freshwater environments. • Introduction of pathogens. • Toxicity and other chronic impacts at the species, habitat and ecosystem level.
7. Release of fuel, oil or oily mixtures • Leak or spill of oil or oily wastes to the environment, including the subsequent movement of such substances.	• Pollution of marine, terrestrial and freshwater environments. • Toxicity and other chronic impacts at the species, habitat and ecosystem level.

Environmental aspect	Potential impact
8. Interaction with water and ice • Disturbance to the water column, by vessel movement or propulsion. • Altered wave action. • Direct breaking of sea ice with a vessel.	• Mixing of the water column resulting in sediment disturbance or ecosystem disruptions. • Coastal erosion from wave action. • Enhanced breakout of sea ice.
9. Interaction with ice-free ground • Direct or indirect contact with land by foot traffic, vehicles, camp equipment, etc.	• Physical changes to the landscape (e.g. erosion, tracks) • Physical changes to watercourses. • Alien species introductions. • Modification in the distribution, abundance or biodiversity of species or populations of species of fauna and flora. • Altered ecosystem performance.
10. Interaction with wildlife • Direct or indirect contact with, or approach to, wildlife.	• Changes to wildlife behaviour, physiology and breeding success. • Increased risk to endangered or threatened species or populations of such species.
11. Interaction with vegetation • Direct or indirect contact with vegetation or controls on vegetation abundance (e.g. altered water availability).	• Physical damage to flora. • Modification in the distribution, abundance or productivity of species or populations of species of flora. • Increased risk to endangered or threatened species or populations of such species.
12. Interaction with historic sites • Direct or indirect contact with historic sites, monuments or artefacts and taking of artefacts.	• Detrimental changes to the historic values of the areas or items of historic significance. • Enhanced deterioration of or damage to historic sites and monuments through physical contact.
13. Interaction with scientific stations or scientific research • Direct or indirect contact with science equipment, monitoring or research sites and with station activities.	• Degradation of scientific values. • Interruption of station activity. • Interruption of, or interference with experimentation.
14. Transfer of non-native species or propagules (via ballast water, vessel hulls, anchors, clothing, footwear, non-sterile soil) • Unintended introduction to the Antarctic region of species not native to that region, and the movement of species within Antarctica from one biogeographic zone to any other.	• Alien species introduced. • Modification in the distribution, abundance or biodiversity of species or populations of species of fauna and flora. • Altered ecosystem performance. • Increased risk to endangered or threatened species or populations of such species.

353

Site Guidelines for visitors

The Representatives,

Recalling Recommendations 5 (2005), 2 (2006), 1 (2007), 2 (2008), 4 (2009), 1 (2010), 4 (2011), 2 (2012), 3 (2013) and 4 (2014) which adopted lists of sites subject to Site Guidelines for visitors ("Site Guidelines");

Believing that Site Guidelines enhance the provisions set out in Recommendation XVIII-1 (1994) Guidance for those organising and conducting tourism and non-Governmental activities in the Antarctic;

Confirming that the term "visitors" does not include scientists conducting research within such sites, or individuals engaged in official governmental activities;

Noting that Site Guidelines have been developed based on the current levels and types of visits at each specific site, and aware that Site Guidelines would require review if there were any significant changes to the levels or types of visits to a site;

Believing that the Site Guidelines for each site must be reviewed and revised promptly in response to changes in the levels and types of visits, or in response to any demonstrable or likely environmental impacts;

Desiring to keep the list of sites subject to Site Guidelines and the Site Guidelines up to date;

Recommend that:

1. Point Wild, Elephant Island and Yalour Islands, Wilhelm Archipelago be added to the list of sites subject to Site Guidelines annexed to this Resolution, and that the Site Guidelines for those sites, as adopted by the Antarctic Treaty Consultative Meeting, be added to the Site Guidelines;

2. the Secretariat of the Antarctic Treaty ("the Secretariat") update its website accordingly;

3. their Governments urge all potential visitors to ensure that they are fully conversant with and adhere to the relevant Site Guidelines; and

4. the Secretariat post the text of Resolution 4 (2014) on its website in such a way that makes clear that it is no longer current.

List of sites subject to Site Guidelines:

Site Guidelines	First Adopted	Latest Version
1. Penguin Island (Lat. 62° 06' S, Long. 57° 54' W)	2005	2005
2. Barrientos Island - Aitcho Islands (Lat. 62° 24' S, Long. 59° 47' W)	2005	2013
3. Cuverville Island (Lat. 64° 41' S, Long. 62° 38' W)	2005	2013
4. Jougla Point (Lat 64° 49' S, Long 63° 30' W)	2005	2013
5. Goudier Island, Port Lockroy (Lat 64° 49' S, Long 63° 29' W)	2006	2006
6. Hannah Point (Lat. 62° 39' S, Long. 60° 37' W)	2006	2013
7. Neko Harbour (Lat. 64° 50' S, Long. 62° 33' W)	2006	2013
8. Paulet Island (Lat. 63° 35' S, Long. 55° 47' W)	2006	2006
9. Petermann Island (Lat. 65° 10' S, Long. 64° 10' W)	2006	2013
10. Pleneau Island (Lat. 65° 06' S, Long. 64° 04' W)	2006	2013
11. Turret Point (Lat. 62° 05' S, Long. 57° 55' W)	2006	2006
12. Yankee Harbour (Lat. 62° 32' S, Long. 59° 47' W)	2006	2013
13. Brown Bluff, Tabarin Peninsula (Lat. 63° 32' S, Long. 56° 55' W)	2007	2013
14. Snow Hill (Lat. 64° 22' S, Long. 56° 59' W)	2007	2007
15. Shingle Cove, Coronation Island (Lat. 60° 39' S, Long. 45° 34' W)	2008	2008
16. Devil Island, Vega Island (Lat. 63° 48' S, Long. 57° 16.7' W)	2008	2008

Site Guidelines	First Adopted	Latest Version
17. Whalers Bay, Deception Island, South Shetland Islands (Lat. 62° 59' S, Long. 60° 34' W)	2008	2011
18. Half Moon Island, South Shetland Islands (Lat. 60° 36' S, Long. 59° 55' W)	2008	2013
19. Baily Head, Deception Island, South Shetland Islands (Lat. 62° 58' S, Long. 60° 30' W)	2009	2013
20. Telefon Bay, Deception Island, South Shetland Islands (Lat. 62° 55' S, Long. 60° 40' W)	2009	2009
21. Cape Royds, Ross Island (Lat. 77° 33' 10.7" S, Long. 166° 10' 6.5" E)	2009	2009
22. Wordie House, Winter Island, Argentine Islands (Lat. 65° 15' S, Long. 64° 16' W)	2009	2009
23. Stonington Island, Marguerite Bay, Antarctic Peninsula (Lat. 68° 11' S, Long. 67° 00' W)	2009	2009
24. Horseshoe Island, Antarctic Peninsula (Lat. 67° 49' S, Long. 67° 18' W)	2009	2014
25. Detaille Island, Antarctic Peninsula (Lat. 66° 52' S, Long. 66° 48' W)	2009	2009
26. Torgersen Island, Arthur Harbour, Southwest Anvers Island (Lat. 64° 46' S, Long. 64° 04' W)	2010	2013
27. Danco Island, Errera Channel, Antarctic Peninsula Lat. 64° 43' S, Long. 62° 36' W)	2010	2013
28. Seabee Hook, Cape Hallett, Northern Victoria Land, Ross Sea, Visitor Site A and Visitor Site B (Lat. 72° 19' S, Long. 170° 13' E)	2010	2010
29. Damoy Point, Wiencke Island, Antarctic Peninsula (Lat. 64° 49' S, Long. 63° 31' W)	2010	2013
30. Taylor Valley Visitor Zone, Southern Victoria Land (Lat. 77° 37.59' S, Long. 163° 03.42' E)	2011	2011
31. North-east beach of Ardley Island (Lat. 62° 13' S; Long. 58° 54' W)	2011	2011
32. Mawson's Huts and Cape Denison, East Antarctica (Lat. 67° 01' S; Long. 142 ° 40' E)	2011	2014

Site Guidelines	First Adopted	Latest Version
33. D'Hainaut Island, Mikkelsen Harbour, Trinity Island (Lat. 63° 54' S, Long. 60° 47' W)	2012	2012
34. Port Charcot, Booth Island (Lat. 65° 04'S, Long. 64 °02'W)	2012	2012
35. Pendulum Cove, Deception Island, South Shetland Islands (Lat. 62°56'S, Long. 60°36' W)	2012	2012
36. Orne Harbour, Southern arm of Orne Harbour, Gerlache Strait (Lat 64° 38'S, Long. 62° 33'W)	2013	2013
37. Orne Islands, Gerlache Strait (Lat. 64° 40'S, Long. 62° 40'W)	2013	2013
38. Point Wild, Elephant Island (Lat. 61° 6'S, Long. 54°52'W)	2016	2016
39. Yalour Islands, Wilhelm Archipelago (Lat. 65° 14'S, 64°10'W)	2016	2016

Code of Conduct for Activity within Terrestrial Geothermal Environments in Antarctica

The Representatives,

Recalling Article 3 of the Protocol on Environmental Protection to the Antarctic Treaty ("the Protocol"), which requires that activities in the Antarctic Treaty area shall be planned and conducted so as to limit adverse impacts on the Antarctic environment and dependent and associated ecosystems;

Recognising that terrestrial geothermal sites in Antarctica may contain exceptional glaciological and geological features and support unique and diverse biological communities, and consequently may be of high scientific value to a wide range of disciplines;

Recognising also that some sites have already been subjected to relatively high levels of visitation,visitation and the focus of the guidelines in the Code of Conduct for Activity within Terrestrial Geothermal Environments of the Scientific Committee on Antarctic Research ("SCAR Code of Conduct") is on unvisited or relatively undisturbed sites;

Acknowledging that these environments may be at risk from impacts associated with human activities, including the introduction of non-native species;

Welcoming the development by the SCAR, through broad consultation, including with the Council of Managers of National Antarctic Programmes ("COMNAP"), of the SCAR Code of Conduct that Parties can apply and use, as appropriate, to assist with meeting their obligations under the Protocol;

Recommend that their Governments:

1. endorse the non-mandatory SCAR Code of Conduct as representing current best practice for planning and undertaking activities, as appropriate, in terrestrial geothermal environments in Antarctica;

2. consider the SCAR Code of Conduct during the environmental impact assessment process for activities within terrestrial geothermal areas and urge all potential visitors to consider the contents of this Code of Conduct in their planning; and

3. encourage all visitors to terrestrial geothermal environments to be fully conversant with and adhere to the guidelines in the SCAR Code of Conduct.

SCAR Code of Conduct for Activity within Terrestrial Geothermal Environments in Antarctica

Background

1. This SCAR Code of Conduct provides guidance when planning or undertaking field activities within terrestrial geothermal environments.[*]

2. This Code of Conduct was prepared following discussions held at the August 2014 Auckland Workshop which focused on the need to develop guidelines for working in terrestrial geothermal areas in Antarctica (see ATCM XXXVIII (2015) IP024 and ATCM XXXVIII (2015) WP035) and has been finalised through broad consultation, including with the Council of Managers of National Antarctic Programs (COMNAP).

3. The *SCAR Environmental Code of Conduct for Terrestrial Scientific Research in Antarctica* (2009) continues to provide guidance on practical measures to minimize impacts by scientists undertaking fieldwork in terrestrial environments, generally applicable across all of Antarctica.

4. This Code of Conduct for activities within terrestrial geothermal environments was developed in recognition of a specific need for guidelines for operations and scientific activities beyond those generally applicable guidelines, since terrestrial geothermal environments in Antarctica represent a unique case where more specific and customized guidance is needed because safeguarding the values of these sites requires measures that extend beyond those required in most areas in which activities are undertaken.

5. This Code of Conduct will be updated and refined as new scientific results and environmental impact reports become available from future research in terrestrial geothermal environments.

Introduction

6. Terrestrial geothermal environments in Antarctica are of high scientific value to a wide range of disciplines, for example to geologists, glaciologists, biologists and atmospheric scientists.

7. Recent studies provide evidence that terrestrial geothermal sites in Antarctica support unique and diverse biological communities, and have played an important role as biological refugia in some regions of the continent, where indigenous species survived glacial cycles and from which regional recolonization took place.

8. These environments, particularly those that to date have not been subjected to a high number of visits, may be at risk from introduced species or other damage through human

---

[*] 'Geothermal' is defined as 'of or relating to the natural internal heat of the earth', and 'terrestrial geothermal environments' are defined as 'non-marine ice, land, water or atmospheric environments at or near the earth's surface that are detectably influenced by geothermal heat'.

activity. Microbiological communities in these environments are highly vulnerable to disturbance, and require specialized and rigorous measures of protection.

9. Fragile soils, plant and microfaunal communities, and/or delicate geological or ice structures (e.g. steam vents, fumaroles), may exist on geothermally heated ground, and these may be particularly susceptible to damage by trampling.

10. It is recognised that some terrestrial geothermal sites in Antarctica have already been subjected to relatively high levels of various human activity, for example, at some sites on Deception Island or near the summit of Mount Erebus, and may already have permanent installations that are needed to monitor geothermal activity for reasons of safety, and these require regular visits and maintenance. For such sites, responsible stewardship during subsequent visits to those sites should proceed in a manner that is consistent with the Protocol to the Antarctic Treaty, that minimizes possible future impact and protect, as far as possible, their value.

11. The application of this Code of Conduct should be considered prior to visiting any terrestrial geothermal environment. At geothermal sites that have already been subjected to relatively high levels of various human activity, the general rules under the Protocol on Environmental Protection to the Antarctic Treaty and guidance as provided in the *SCAR Code of Conduct for Terrestrial Scientific Field Research in Antarctica* should be sufficient. At geothermal sites that are presently unvisited or relatively undisturbed by human activities, there are important scientific (e.g. microbiological, geochemical and geological) and environmental reasons why extra precautions should be taken before values are degraded or lost. In such cases, this Code of Conduct should be taken into consideration. This is especially the case for geothermal environments that are known to be previously unvisited and, for this reason, more stringent recommendations that apply to previously unvisited terrestrial geothermal sites are made at the end of this Code of Conduct.

12. At this time, geothermal sites in Antarctica have not been assessed or classified according to their level of disturbance or in terms of their scientific value. For practical reasons it is therefore recommended that National Programs consult with each other, and with appropriate experts, about the extent to which, and where, this Code of Conduct should be applied, and that these decisions and the site locations should be made publicly available.

Guiding Principles

13. Careful planning is required before undertaking research within a terrestrial geothermal environment, and appropriate measures need to be considered to help maintain the integrity of sites. These should include:

- Careful selection of the site to be visited. Geothermal sites that are known to have been previously visited should be used, unless use of a previously unvisited site is essential to meet scientific needs;
- Coordinating planned activities with other researchers interested in the area to the maximum extent practicable.

14. In accordance with the provisions of Annex I to the Protocol on Environmental Protection to the Antarctic Treaty, and as part of the planning process, decisions on the level of environmental impact assessment (EIA) to be applied should take full account of the extent of previous visits to the geothermal site, as well as the anticipated impacts arising from planned activities at the site.

15. Decisions on whether to implement aseptic measures* should be assessed as part of the EIA and should take into account the likelihood of any conservation or scientific benefit to maintaining a sterile regime at a particular geothermal site that has been previously visited. If such benefits are considered likely, then aseptic measures should be implemented.

16. The locations of sites visited and nature of activities undertaken should be documented and maintained in publicly available records, and include accurate locations recorded with GPS, so that visited and unvisited sites may be more easily distinguished by future researchers.

Code of Conduct

Access

17. Movement to a terrestrial geothermal environment should be by way of designated access routes and landing sites where these are known or have been used previously, and this should be discussed with all personnel in the group, including pilots or vehicle drivers, prior to departure.

18. All overland movement of visitors within terrestrial geothermal sites should be on foot.

19. To the fullest extent practicable, vehicles and crewed aircraft should not be operated close to, or within, terrestrial geothermal environments due to the risks of damaging sensitive vegetation and introducing non-native species. As a guideline, it is recommended that crewed aircraft should avoid landing or overflying within 100 m of geothermal sites.

20. Areas of visible vegetation or moist soil both on ice-free ground and among ice hummocks and, as far as practicable, areas of geothermally heated ground, should be avoided.

21. The number of visitors entering a geothermal site should be minimised without compromising safety and the ability to undertake planned research. Visitors should follow established trails/routes where available and be aware that geothermal environments are dynamic and may be subject to frequent change; sites that were safe for access or travel when visited on a previous occasion may not necessarily remain so.

22. Pedestrian movement within the terrestrial geothermal area should be kept to the minimum necessary consistent with the objectives of the visit and every reasonable effort should be made to minimise the effects of walking activity, including by educating members of the group visiting the site, because:

---

* 'Aseptic measures' are measures that 'aim to exclude microorganisms not native to the local geothermal environment'.

- Fragile plant and/or microbial communities may be present, including beneath snow or ice surfaces. Be alert and avoid walking on, or close to, such features;
- Walking can also compact soil, alter temperature gradients (which may change rates of steam release), and break thin ice crusts which may form over geothermally heated ground, resulting in changes to soil and biota below;
- The presence of snow or ice surfaces is not a guaranteed indication of a suitable pathway.

23. Remotely operated vehicles, including Unmanned Aerial Systems (UAS) (also known as Unmanned Aerial Vehicles (UAVs), Remotely Piloted Aircraft (RPA), drones, etc.), may have useful scientific and other applications in terrestrial geothermal environments in Antarctica, and potentially may reduce environmental impacts. Such use of UAS should be carried out within relevant guidelines and given adequate consideration to national Antarctic programme operations procedures, including procedures to be implemented in the case of a malfunction of the UAS.

Camps

24. When a field camp is necessary to support activities, where practicable, this should be located at least 100 m from the geothermal site.

25. To minimize contamination of geothermal sites from camping activities (e.g. from stove gases, food particles etc.), where practicable, locate camps downwind from geothermal sites, although not where there is a risk of noxious gases drifting downwind from geothermal sites.

26. Where possible, designated, former or existing camp sites should be used.

Clothing, footwear and equipment

Prior to access

27. All clothing, footwear and personal equipment (including bags or backpacks, and safety equipment such as ropes and ice screws) brought to geothermal sites should, as a minimum, be thoroughly cleaned and maintained in this condition before use within the geothermal site. Consideration should be given to changing into clean* clothing and footwear immediately prior to entry into a geothermal site.

28. Consideration should always be given to the use of sterile protective over-clothing and sterile footwear prior to working at geothermal sites. The over-clothing should be suitable for working at a wide range of temperatures and comprise, as a minimum, overalls to cover arms, legs, and body, a hat to cover the head and gloves (which may need to be suitable for placing over the top of cold-weather clothing). At sites where sterilization of footwear is deemed appropriate, this should be achieved by washing exposed surfaces in a 70% ethanol solution in water. Disposable sterile / protective foot coverings that can disintegrate under field conditions should *not* be used.

* 'Clean' is defined as 'free from visible particles of biological material, soil, dirt, debris, food, mould or fungi'

29. To the maximum extent practicable, select clothing and equipment that are in good condition and are made of tightly woven or knitted fabrics that do not shed fibres.

Following access:

30. To the maximum extent practicable, visitors should remain covered by their clean or sterile protective clothing, including head covers, while conducting activities within geothermal sites where this Code of Conduct has been determined to apply.

31. Precautions should be taken to prevent human-mediated transfer of biota from one geothermal area to another. Footwear should be cleaned to remove all soil and biological material, preferably using a 70% ethanol solution in water. New, clean or just laundered outer clothing should be put on before entering the new geothermal location. Equipment used must be at least thoroughly cleaned, but ideally sterilized, before use at another geothermal site.

Food

32. Where practicable, depending on site size and duration of visit, avoid eating or drinking while within geothermal sites.

33. Where food and drink are necessary for health and safety, foods such as gels, compressed dried fruit bars, or bite-sized chocolates, etc. will help minimize dispersal of powders, crumbs and flakes. Foods containing yeasts, moulds (e.g. cheese) or other microbes must be avoided. Food and drink should be securely contained when not being consumed.

34. Where appropriate, establish food and drink staging points within larger geothermal sites and restrict consumption to these sites only. Ensure accurate location of these points is recorded. Where practicable, cover the floor of the staging point while in use and remove the cover (carefully containing any crumbs, etc.) at the conclusion of the work.

Waste

35. All waste, including liquid and solid human waste, must be removed from geothermal sites.

Fuel / energy

36. The use of fossil-fuel-powered tools at geothermal sites should be avoided where possible because exhaust emissions and / or spills can impact the microbial environment.

37. If power tools are necessary to support science within a geothermal site, electric machines powered by batteries, or by a generator or renewable source of energy located at least 100 m away and preferably downwind from the site, are preferred.

Materials / chemicals

38. Activities that could result in spills or dispersal of materials should be avoided within geothermal sites (e.g. use of fuels, glycols, chemicals and isotopes, unpacking of boxes,

sprays, etc.). Where such activities are necessary, they should be carried out at least 100 m away from geothermal sites and preferably inside a tent or structure so that materials are not dispersed towards geothermal sites by wind.

39. Materials liable to shatter at low temperatures (e.g. polyethylene plastic products) should be avoided, as should those liable to melt at the high temperatures that can occur at geothermal sites.

40. Materials / chemicals should not be stored within geothermal sites, except as required for scientific or management purposes.

41. Explosives should not be used within geothermal sites.

42. Smoking may introduce contaminants and should therefore be prohibited within geothermal sites.

Installations / equipment

43. Except where essential for safety and / or long-term scientific or monitoring programmes, permanent installations (e.g. sensors, antennae, shelters, etc.) should be avoided within geothermal sites owing to risks associated with deterioration of materials that may compromise the microbial environment.

44. All installations and other scientific equipment brought to geothermal sites should, as a minimum, be thoroughly cleaned in advance and maintained in this condition before use on site. Consideration should always be given to sterilizing equipment prior to installation at geothermal sites.

45. Installations should be sited carefully and securely, and be easily retrievable when no longer required. Installations and equipment should be made of durable materials capable of withstanding the conditions at geothermal sites and, to the maximum extent practicable, pose minimal risk of harmful emissions to the environment (e.g. gel cells or other non-spill batteries).

46. Any long-term installations or markers should be clearly identified by country, name of principal investigator, year of installation, and intended duration of deployment. Installations and equipment should be removed by the installer or other appropriate authority at, or before, the conclusion of the activity for which they were intended.

Sampling

47. At sites where the implementation of aseptic measures is deemed appropriate, all sampling equipment, probes or markers must be cleaned appropriately and maintained in that condition before being used within geothermal sites.

48. If samples are collected from a terrestrial geothermal area, ensure sample sizes are the minimum necessary to meet scientific requirements and that any permit required for their collection has been given by an appropriate national authority.

Additional guidance for previously unvisited terrestrial geothermal sites

49. Terrestrial geothermal sites in Antarctica that are known, or suspected, to be previously unvisited are expected to be almost pristine (with the exception of low levels of contaminants transported via the atmosphere or perhaps by birds), and are considered to have exceptional value for science, especially for microbiological and geochemical studies. More stringent controls are therefore required to maintain their environmental and scientific values. Aseptic measures should always be implemented at previously unvisited geothermal sites.

Access

50. The interior *and* exterior of crewed aircraft, vehicles and boats should be inspected and cleaned thoroughly before being used for access to previously unvisited geothermal sites.

51. Where practicable, crewed aircraft, vehicles and boats should approach no closer than 200 m from previously unvisited geothermal sites.

Clothing, food and waste

52. Sterile protective over-clothing and footwear should always be worn at previously unvisited geothermal sites.

53. Food should not be brought into or consumed within previously unvisited geothermal sites, unless it is essential for safety because of the visit length, or the size or nature of the site.

54. All wastes, including all human wastes, should be removed from the area.

Equipment, materials / chemicals, installations and sampling

55. When accessing a previously unvisited geothermal site, it is strongly recommended that only new equipment, materials and installations be used within that site.

56. If moving between specific locations within a single previously unvisited geothermal site, only new or sterile materials / chemicals should be used at the subsequent locations.

Non-native Species Manual

The Representatives,

Conscious that the increasing introduction of non-native species to the Antarctic region, including the movement of species between locations in the region, is presenting a serious risk to biodiversity and to the intrinsic values of Antarctica;

Recognising the enhanced potential for non-native species introduction and establishment with a changing Antarctic climate;

Recalling that the overall objective for Parties' actions to address risks posed by non-native species is to protect Antarctic biodiversity and intrinsic values by preventing the unintended introduction to the Antarctic region of species not native to that region, and the movement of species within Antarctica from one biogeographic zone to any other;

Noting that under Resolution 6 (2011) the Antarctic Treaty Consultative Meeting ("ATCM") agreed to disseminate and encourage, as appropriate, the use of the Non-native Species Manual ("the Manual") developed by the Committee for Environmental Protection ("CEP");

Welcoming the revision of the Manual by the CEP, as well as the CEP's advice that it will continue to refine and develop the Manual to reflect improvements in the understanding of the risks posed by non-native species and best practice measures for prevention, surveillance and response;

Recommend that their Governments:

1. encourage the dissemination of the Manual, annexed to this Resolution, and its use by those organising, conducting and participating in Antarctic activities;

2. encourage the CEP to continue to develop the Manual with the input of the Scientific Committee on Antarctic Research ("SCAR") and the Council of Managers of National Antarctic Programs ("COMNAP") on scientific and practical matters, respectively; and

3. request the Secretariat to post the Manual on its website.

Non-Native Species Manual

Committee for Environmental Protection (CEP)

EDITION 2016

Committee for Environmental Protection (CEP)

Non-native Species Manual. – 2nd ed. – Buenos Aires: Secretariat for the Antarctic Treaty, 2016.

XX p.

ISBN XXX-XXX-XXXX-XX-X

Environmental Protection. 2. International Law. 3. Antarctic Treaty system

DDC XXX.X

The first edition of this manual was adopted by the Antarctic Treaty Consultative Meeting through Resolution 6 (2011). The manual was compiled and prepared by an Intersessional Contact Group (ICG) of the Committee for Environmental Protection (CEP) between 2009 and 2011. The second edition of the manual was developed by an ICG of the CEP between 2015 and 2016.

Content

1. Introduction

a) Objective

The overall objective for Parties' actions to address risks posed by non-native species is:

To protect Antarctic biodiversity and intrinsic values by preventing the unintended introduction to the Antarctic region of species not native to that region, and the movement of species within Antarctica from one biogeographic zone to any other.

Preventing unintended introductions is an ambitious goal, consistent with the principles of the Protocol on Environmental Protection to the Antarctic Treaty (1991). In practice, measures should be put in place to minimise the risk of impacts from non-native species in the Antarctic, taking all possible steps towards prevention.

b) Purpose and background

The purpose of this manual is to provide guidance to Antarctic Treaty Parties in order to meet the objective (above), i.e. minimise the risk of accidental or unintentional introduction of non-native species and respond effectively, should an introduction occur. This manual includes key guiding principles and links to recommended practical guidelines and resources that operators can apply and use, as appropriate, to assist with meeting their responsibilities under Annex II to the Protocol. The guidelines are recommendatory, not all guidelines will apply to all operations, and it is a 'living' document that will be updated and added to as new work, research and best practice develops to support further guidance. These measures are recommended as appropriate to assist Parties' efforts to prevent such accidental or unintended introductions or manage established non-native species and they should not be considered as mandatory.

This manual is focused on the unintended or accidental introduction of non-native species. The introduction of non-native species under permit (in accordance with Article 4 of Annex II to the Protocol) is not included within the scope of this work. However, guidelines for response to unintentional introductions can be applied to responding to any dispersal of species intentionally introduced under permits.

Due to a substantial amount of scientific research on non-native species within Antarctica in recent years (see References and supporting information) there is an improved understanding of the risks related to non-native species introductions although additional information will be of benefit. Further studies on impacts on Antarctic ecosystems, and research to underpin effective rapid response are also needed. Another objective of this manual is to support and encourage further work to fill the gaps in our knowledge. Parties, in applying their environmental assessment and authorisation processes, should consider methods to ensure proponents of Antarctic activities are aware of this manual and associated resources, and that they implement prevention practices to minimise the risk of introduction of non-native species.

c) Context[*]

Biological invasions are amongst the most significant threats to biodiversity worldwide, threatening species survival and being responsible for major changes to ecosystem structure and functioning. Despite Antarctica's isolation and harsh climatic conditions, invasions are now recognised as a serious risk to the region: the ice-free areas of Antarctica and the surrounding sub-Antarctic Islands support a large proportion of the world's seabird species, and their terrestrial biotas, though species-poor, include a high proportion of endemic and well-adapted taxa. Species richness in the Southern Ocean is higher than in the Antarctic terrestrial environment, and there is a high level of endemism. With rapid climate change occurring in some parts of Antarctica, increased numbers of introductions and enhanced success of colonisation by non-native species are likely, with consequent increases in impacts on ecosystems, as is already visible in the sub-Antarctic islands. In addition to introduction of species from outside Antarctica, cross-contamination between ice-free areas including isolated nunataks, or between different marine areas, also threatens the biological and genetic diversity of the biogeographic regions and the risk must be addressed. Further development of human activity in these regions (including science, logistics, tourism, fisheries and recreation) will increase the risk of unintentional introductions of organisms, which have a suite of life history traits that benefit them during transport, establishment and expansion phases of invasion, and are likely to be favored by warming conditions and potentially other effects of climate change. Reducing the risk of the transfer of species between sites in Antarctica has been a recent focus of work to manage non-native species risks. In 2012 CEP XV endorsed 15 distinct Antarctic Conservation Biogeographic Regions. The delineation of these biologically distinct regions supports the management of non-native species risks associated with moving between regions within Antarctica.

The vast majority of global non-native species do not become invasive, but those that do are one of the main threats to global diversity. Sequentially, the prevention of an introduction of a non-native species is the key. If prevention fails, then early detection and rapid response to remove the species becomes very important. It is easier to fight invasiveness if the discovery of the non-native species is made early. In addition, the presence of non-native species that are only "transient" or "persistent" but not yet "invasive" is also highly undesirable in terms of protecting the environmental and scientific values of Antarctica, especially as such species may become invasive. The current environmental changes that occur in Antarctica, as in other parts of the world, may result in alteration of the local biodiversity during the next decades or centuries. It is the responsibility of the Parties and others active in the region to minimise the chance of humans being a direct vector for change through introduction of non-native species and/or spread of diseases in the terrestrial and marine ecosystems of the Antarctic Treaty area.

[*] This section was written with the contribution of several scientists involved in the IPY "Aliens in Antarctica" project (D. Bergstrom, S. Chown, P. Convey, Y. Frenot, N. Gremmen, A. Huiskes, K. A. Hughes, S. Imura, M. Lebouvier, J. Lee, F. Steenhuisen, M. Tsujimoto, B. van de Vijver and J. Whinam) and adapted according to the ICG Members' comments.

The 2010 Antarctic Treaty Meeting of Experts on Implications of Climate Change for Antarctic Management emphasised the importance of actions towards reducing the risk and impact of non-native species to Antarctic ecosystems. The meeting:

- Acknowledged that the greatest effort should be placed on preventing the introduction of non-native species, and on minimising the risk of human assisted introductions through national programmes and tourism activities. It stressed the importance of ensuring comprehensive implementation of new measures to address this risk (Para. 111, Co-chair's report).

- Recommended that the CEP 'consider using established methods of identifying a) Antarctic environments at high risk from establishment by non-natives and b) non-native species that present a high risk of establishment in Antarctica' (Recommendation 22).

- Recommended that Parties be encouraged to comprehensively and consistently implement management measures to respond to the environmental implications of climate change, particularly measures to avoid introduction and translocation of non-native species, and to report on their effectiveness (Recommendation 23).

In 2015, the CEP agreed the Climate Change Response Work Programme (CCRWP) that seeks to advance these and other environment-related ATME recommendations (Resolution 4 (2015)). The CCRWP describes the issues facing the CEP as a result of the changing Antarctic climate, the actions/tasks required to address these issues, their prioritisation, and suggestions as to how, when, and by whom, the actions are best delivered. One of the climate-related issues identified is the enhanced potential for non-native species introduction and establishment. The CCRWP recommends that CEP Members continue to develop the CEP Non-native Species Manual, ensuring climate change impacts are included, specifically in the development of surveillance approaches, a response strategy, and the inclusion of non-native species in the EIA guidelines (see also the Annex to this manual).

The CEP 5-year Work Plan is a 'living' document that is updated annually with the work priorities of the Committee. Non-native species issues are identified in the work plan as a top priority for the CEP's attention and the work plan and may guide further work on this topic.

The Environments Portal (*www.environments.aq*) is a source of peer-reviewed Antarctic environmental information and includes topic summaries on non-native species (e.g. Newman et al., 2014; Hughes and Frenot, 2015).

d) Glossary

Terminology for non-native and invasive species has not been standardised internationally and some of the terms below are defined in the specific context of Antarctica:

Biogeographic region: a region of Antarctica that is biologically distinct from other regions. Non-native species risks to biodiversity and intrinsic values may arise if (1) native Antarctic species are moved by human activities between biogeographic regions, or (2) non-native species established in one Antarctic biogeographic region are distributed to other regions by human or natural mechanisms.

Containment: Application of management measures to prevent spread of a non-native species.

Control: Use of practical methods to contain and/or reduce the viability of a non-native species.

Endemic: native species restricted to a specified region or locality in Antarctica.

Eradication: The permanent elimination of a non-native species.

Introduction/introduced: direct or indirect movement by human agency, of an organism outside its natural range. This term may be applied to intercontinental or intracontinental movement of species.

Invasive/invasion: non-native species that are extending their range in the colonised Antarctic region, displacing native species and causing significant harm to biological diversity or ecosystem functioning.

Non-native/alien species: an organism occurring outside its natural past or present range and dispersal potential, whose presence and dispersal in any biogeographic region of the Antarctic Treaty area is due to unintentional human action.

Persistent/established: non-native species that have survived, established and reproduced for many years in a restricted locality in Antarctica, but which have not expanded their range from a specific location.

Transient: non-native species that have survived in small populations for a short period in Antarctica, but which have either died out naturally or have been removed by human intervention.

2. Key guiding principles

In order to provide greater focus on the environmental risk related to the unintentional introduction of non-native species in Antarctica and to guide Parties' actions in accordance with the overall objective, 11 key guiding principles have been developed. They are categorised according to the three major components of a non-native species management framework: prevention, monitoring and response. Many of the key guiding principles are equally applicable to the prevention of introduction and spread of pathogens that may cause diseases in Antarctic wildlife.

Prevention

Prevention is the most effective means of minimising the risks associated with the introduction of non-native species and their impacts, and is the responsibility of all who travel to Antarctica.

1. Raising awareness at multiple levels for different audiences is a critical component of management. All people travelling to the Antarctic should take appropriate steps to prevent the introduction of non-native species.

2. The risk of non-native species introductions should be identified and addressed in the planning of all activities, including through the environmental impact assessment (EIA) process under Article 8 and Annex I to the Protocol.

3. In the absence of sound scientific baseline data, a precautionary approach should be applied to minimise the risk of human-mediated introduction of non-native species, as well as the risk of inter-regional and local transfer of propagules to pristine regions.

4. Preventive measures are most likely to be implemented and effective if they are:

- focused on addressing activities and areas of highest risk;
- developed to suit the particular circumstances of the activity or area in question, and at the appropriate scale;
- technically and logistically simple;
- easily applicable;
- cost effective and not exceedingly time consuming.

5. Prevention should focus on pre-departure measures within the logistics and supply chain:

- at the point of origin outside Antarctica (e.g., cargo, personal gear, packages),
- at gateways to Antarctica (ports, airports),
- on means of transport (vessels, aircraft),
- at Antarctic stations and field camps that are departure points for activities within the continent.

6. Particularly close attention should be given to ensuring the cleanliness of items previously used in cold climates (e.g., Arctic, sub-Antarctic, mountainous areas), which may be a means for transporting species with 'pre-adaptations' that may aid establishment in the Antarctic environment.

Monitoring

Monitoring can be passive observation (i.e., waiting for non-native species to appear) or targeted (i.e., an active programme of identifying potential non-native species). Having good baseline data on native fauna and flora is important to support monitoring of non-native species.

7. Regular/periodic monitoring, with a frequency appropriate to potential risk, of high-risk sites (e.g., including, but not restricted to the area around research stations) should be encouraged.

8. Preventive measures should be periodically reviewed and revised.

9. Information and best practice related to non-native species should be exchanged between Parties and other stakeholders.

Response

The key factor will be to respond quickly and to assess the feasibility and desirability of eradicating non-native species. If eradication is not a feasible or desirable option then control and/or containment measures need to be considered.

10. To be effective, responses to introductions should be undertaken as a priority, to prevent an increase in the species' distribution range and to make eradication simpler, cost effective and more likely to succeed.

11. Efficacy of control or eradication programmes must be regularly assessed, including follow-up surveys.

3. Guidelines and resources to support prevention of the introduction of non-native species

(Including the transfer of species between sites in the Antarctic and the detection of and response to established non-native species)

In line with the objective for Parties' actions to address risks posed by non-native species and the key guiding principles (Sections 1 and 2), the following voluntary guidelines and resources have been developed that operators can apply and use, as appropriate, to assist with meeting their responsibilities under Annex II to the Protocol.

Prevention

1. The environmental impact assessment process is a key component in the prevention of non-native species introductions and their further dispersal.

Guidelines

Guidelines for Environmental Impact Assessment in Antarctica
http://www.ats.aq/documents/ATCM39/att/atcm39_att013_rev1_e.doc

2. Prevention is the most effective means of minimizing the risks associated with the introduction of non-native species.

Guidelines

The following list provides general guidance on preventing non-native species introductions to Antarctica, with more specific information detailed later:

- Unless new, ensure clothing supplied for use in Antarctica is cleaned using normal laundry procedures prior to sending to Antarctica. Pre-worn footwear should be cleaned thoroughly before arrival in Antarctica or between sites in Antarctica.

- Consider equipping research stations with the means to clean and maintain clothing and equipment that is to be used in the field, particularly in distinct or multiple locations.

- Check cargo to ensure it is clean of visible contamination (soil, mud, vegetation, propagules) before loading on board the aircraft or vessels.

- Clean vehicles in order to prevent transfer of non-native species into and around the Antarctic.

- Confirm vessels as being rodent-free before departure to the Antarctic.

- Pack, store and load cargo in an area with a clean, sealed surface (e.g., bitumen or concrete that is free from weedy plants, soil, rodents and remote from waste ground). These areas should be cleaned and inspected regularly.

- Containers, including ISO containers and boxes/crates, should not be moved from one Antarctic site to another, unless they are cleaned before arrival at the new location.

- Ensure intercontinental aircraft are checked and treated as necessary, where applicable, to ensure they are insect-free before departure to the Antarctic.

- Foods and food wastes are strictly managed to prevent them entering the environment (e.g. secured from wildlife and removed from the Antarctic or incinerated).

At CEP XV, the Committee recognised the relevance of the Antarctic Conservation Biogeographic Regions (ACBRs) to its work to address non-native species risks, particularly the risk of transfer of species between biologically distinct locations in Antarctica. Descriptions of the Antarctic Conservation Biogeographic Regions can be found at: *http://www.ats.aq/documents/recatt/Att500_e.pdf.* The Antarctic Environments Portal Map shows in detail the extent of the Antarctic Conservation Biogeographic Regions and is available from: *https://environments.aq/map/*

Procedures for vehicle cleaning to prevent transfer of non-native species into and around Antarctica (ATCM XXXIII – WP 08).
http://www.ats.aq/documents/ATCM33/wp/ATCM33_wp008_e.doc

Guidelines to minimise the risks of non-native species and disease associated with Antarctic hydroponics facilities (ATCM XXXV – WP 25 rev.1)
http://www.ats.aq/documents/ATCM35/wp/ATCM35_wp025_rev1_e.doc
http://www.ats.aq/documents/ATCM35/att/ATCM35_att103_e.doc

Resources

Checklists for supply chain managers of National Antarctic Programmes for the reduction in risk of transfer of non-native species (COMNAP, SCAR 2010)
https://www.comnap.aq/Shared%20Documents/nnschecklists.pdf

SCAR's environmental code of conduct for terrestrial scientific field research in Antarctica (ATCM XXXII - IP 04)
http://www.ats.aq/documents/ATCM32/ip/ATCM32_ip004_e.doc

SCAR's code of conduct for activities within terrestrial geothermal environments in Antarctica Resolution 3 (2016)
http://www.ats.aq/documents/ATCM39/att/atcm39_att018_e.doc

SCAR's code of conduct for the exploration and research of subglacial aquatic environments (ATCM XXXIV- IP 33)
http://www.ats.aq/documents/ATCM34/ip/ATCM34_ip033_e.doc

Raising awareness of non-native species introductions: Workshop results and checklists for supply chain managers (ATCM XXXIV – WP 12)
http://www.ats.aq/documents/ATCM34/wp/ATCM34_wp012_e.doc
http://www.ats.aq/documents/ATCM34/att/ATCM34_att014_e.pdf
http://www.ats.aq/documents/ATCM34/att/ATCM34_att015_e.pdf

Reducing the risk of inadvertent non-native species introductions associated with fresh fruit and vegetable importation to Antarctica (ATCM XXXV – WP 06)
http://www.ats.aq/documents/ATCM35/wp/ATCM35_WP006_e.doc

Biosecurity and quarantine guidelines for ACAP breeding sites
http://acap.aq/en/resources/acap-conservation-guidelines/2180-biosecurity-guidelines/file

Outcomes of the International Polar Year Programme: Aliens in Antarctica (ATCM XXXV – WP 05)
http://www.ats.aq/documents/ATCM35/wp/ATCM35_wp005_e.doc

Continent-wide risk assessment for the establishment of nonindigenous species in Antarctica (ATCM XXXV – BP 01)
http://www.ats.aq/documents/ATCM35/bp/ATCM35_bp001_e.pdf

3. Develop and deliver awareness programmes for all people travelling to and working in the Antarctic on the risks of inter and intra-continental movements of non-native species and on the measures required to prevent their introduction, including a standard set of key messages for awareness programmes. Education and training programmes should be tailored, in some case using relevant elements of the information listed above, to the activities and risks associated with the target audience, including:

- Managers of national programmes
- Logisticians/crew/contractors
- Tour operators/staff/crew
- Scientists
- Tourists
- Private expedition organisers
- Fishing vessel operators/staff/crew

- Staff at suppliers/vendors/warehouses
- Other visitors

Guidelines

General guidelines for visitors to the Antarctic
http://www.ats.aq/documents/recatt/Att483_e.pdf

Resources

Instructional video on cleaning (Aliens in Antarctica Project, 2010).
http://academic.sun.ac.za/cib/video/Aliens_cleaning_video%202010.wmv

'Don't pack a pest' pamphlet (United States).
*http://www.usap.gov/usapgov/travelAndDeployment/documents/PackaPest_brochure_
Final.pdf*

'Don't pack a pest' pamphlet (IAATO).
http://iaato.org/en_GB/dont-pack-a-pest

Boot, clothing and equipment decontamination guidelines (IAATO).
*http://iaato.org/documents/10157/14310/Boot_Washing07.pdf/2527fa99-b3b9-4848-bf0b-
b1b595ecd046*

'Know before you go' pamphlet (ASOC).
*http://www.asoc.org/storage/documents/tourism/ASOC_Know_Before_You_Go_tourist_
pamphlet_2009_editionv2.pdf*

COMNAP Practical training modules: Module 2 – non-native species (ATCMXXXVIII
– IP 101)
http://www.ats.aq/documents/ATCM38/ip/ATCM38_ip101_e.doc
http://www.ats.aq/documents/ATCM38/att/ATCM38_att102_e.pdf

4. Include consideration of non-native species in future ASPA and ASMA Management
Plans and in the review of current and future management plans.

Guidelines

Guide to the preparation of Management Plans for Antarctic Specially Protected Areas
(Resolution 2 (2011)).
http://www.ats.aq/documents/ATCM34/att/ATCM34_att004_e.doc

5. Manage ballast water in accordance with the 'Practical guidelines for ballast water
exchange in the Antarctic Treaty Area' (Resolution 3 (2006)).

Guidelines

Practical guidelines for ballast water exchange in the Antarctic Treaty Area (Resolution
3 (2006)).
http://www.ats.aq/documents/recatt/Att345_e.pdf

Monitoring

6. Record non-native species introductions and submit records to the 'Biodiversity database: aliens species in the Antarctica or subAntarctic', managed by the Australian Antarctic Data Centre (AADC), as agreed by the CEP.

Database for entering records

Alien species database (ATCM XXXIV – IP 68)
http://data.aad.gov.au/aadc/biodiversity/index_aliens.cfm

Resources

Colonisation status of known non-native species in the Antarctic terrestrial environment: a review. (ATCM XXXVIII IP 46)
http://www.ats.aq/documents/ATCM38/ip/ATCM38_IP046_e.doc

Biological invasions in terrestrial Antarctica: what is the current status and how can we respond? (ATCM XXXVIII - IP 46 Attachment A)
http://www.ats.aq/documents/ATCM38/att/ATCM38_att090_e.pdf

Supplementary information (ATCM XXXVIII - IP 46 Attachment B)
http://www.ats.aq/documents/ATCM38/att/ATCM38_att091_e.doc

Monitoring biological invasion across the broader Antarctic: a baseline and indicator framework (ATCM XXXVIII – IP 93)
http://www.ats.aq/documents/ATCM38/ip/ATCM38_IP093_e.doc

Status of known non-native species introductions and impacts (Environments Portal)
https://www.environments.aq/information-summaries/status-of-known-non-native-species-introductions-and-impacts/

Response

A species apparently new to the Antarctic may be (i) a recent natural colonist (e.g. introduced by wind or bird transport), (ii) a recent human introduction (e.g. associated with cargo, clothing or personal belongings) or (iii) a long-term inhabitant that has never before been identified by science. It is important to know the colonisation history of a new species as this will affect how it is managed.

7. Develop or employ assessment metrics to help determine whether a newly discovered species is likely to have arrived through natural colonisation pathways or through human means.

8. Expert advice should be sought as quickly as possible when potential non-native species (including any diseases of wildlife) are detected.

Guidelines

Guidance *for visitors* and environmental managers following the discovery of a suspected non-native species in the terrestrial and freshwater Antarctic environment (ATCM XXXIII - WP 15).
http://www.ats.aq/documents/ATCM33/att/ATCM33_att010_e.doc
http://www.ats.aq/documents/ATCM33/att/ATCM33_att011_e.doc

Resource

SCAR is well placed to assist with the identification of experts that could provide appropriate advice in a timely manner. SCAR has agreed to identify a group of experts who could be consulted in the event that a suspected non-native species is detected. If a non-native species is detected, contact with the group could be facilitated through the Chief Officer of the SCAR Standing Committee on the Antarctic Treaty System (SCATS), who would then co-ordinate and collate the response from the experts.

Suggested framework and considerations for scientists attempting to determine the colonisation status of newly discovered terrestrial or freshwater species within the Antarctic Treaty Area (ATCM XXXIII – IP 44).
http://www.ats.aq/documents/ATCM33/ip/ATCM33_ip044_e.doc

Annex: Guidelines and resources requiring further attention or development

In addition to the measures, guidelines and resources that have been developed (Section 3) the following non-native species issues have been identified as requiring further attention and policy development. The use of existing guidelines, resources and information and the development of more detailed guidance under these items for inclusion in the Manual are encouraged.

No.	Guidelines and resources requiring further attention or development	Existing guidelines, resources or information
	Prevention	
1.	Reducing the distribution of native Antarctic species between distinct biogeographic regions within the continent: • Identify regions of highest risk of introduction. • Identify activities, vectors and pathways that present a high risk to different biogeographical regions. • Provide guidance on what constitutes a gateway between Antarctic biogeographical regions (according to organism type). • Develop practical measures to address risks associated with the transport of personnel and equipment between locations in Antarctica. • Develop baseline studies.	Antarctic Conservation Biogeographic Regions (ACBRs) *http://www.ats.aq/documents/recatt/Att500_e.pdf* The Antarctic Environments Portal Map shows the extent of the Antarctic Conservation Biogeographic Regions and is available from: *https://environments.aq/map/* Current knowledge for reducing risks posed by terrestrial non-native species: towards an evidence-based approach (ATCM XXXIII - WP 06). *http://www.ats.aq/documents/ATCM33/wp/ATCM33_wp006_e.doc* A framework for analysing and managing non-native species risks in Antarctica (ATCM XXXII - IP 36). *http://www.ats.aq/documents/ATCM32/ip/ATCM32_ip036_e.doc* ATCM XXXIII - WP 14 (United Kingdom) 2010 - Intra-regional transfer of species in terrestrial Antarctica. *http://www.ats.aq/documents/ATCM33/wp/ATCM33_wp014_e.doc*
2.	Preventing further distribution of existing non-native species to other Antarctica locations: • Provide guidance, and develop practical biosecurity measures, to reduce anthropogenic transfer of non-native species within Antarctica. • Provide guidance on reducing natural transfer of non-native species within Antarctica.	Colonisation status of known non-native species in the Antarctic terrestrial environment: a review. Attachment A: Biological invasions in terrestrial Antarctica: what is the current status and how can we respond? Attachment B: Supplementary information (ATCM XXXVIII – IP 46) *http://www.ats.aq/documents/ATCM38/ip/ATCM38_IP046_e.doc* *http://www.ats.aq/documents/ATCM38/att/ATCM38_att090_e.pdf* *http://www.ats.aq/documents/ATCM38/att/ATCM38_att091_e.doc*

385

3.	Identifying potential non-native species that present a high risk to Antarctic environments: • Generate a list, with suitable descriptions, of potential non-native species based on the experience of the sub-Antarctic Islands (or other relevant environments) and the biological characteristics and adaptability of the "effective" colonisers.	Current knowledge for reducing risks posed by terrestrial non-native species: towards an evidence-based approach. Appendix 1 – Risk assessment protocol for springtails developed by Greenslade (2002: page 341) (ATCM XXXIII - WP 06) *http://www.ats.aq/documents/ATCM33/wp/ATCM33_wp6_e.doc* *http://www.ats.aq/documents/ATCM33/att/ATCM33_att005_e.doc*
4.	Preventing non-native species introductions to the Antarctic marine environment: • Improve understanding of risks and pathways for introduction. • Undertake a risk assessment to identify marine habitats at risk of invasion. • Develop specific guidelines.	
5.	Addressing non-native species (including microorganisms) risk associated with wastewater discharge, including disease risk to local wildlife (see later section on Diseases): • Improve understanding of risks and pathways for introduction. • Develop specific guidelines to reduce non-native species release with wastewater discharge.	New records of the presence of human associated microorganisms in the Antarctic marine environment (ATCM XXXV – WP 55) *http://www.ats.aq/documents/ATCM35/wp/ATCM35_wp055_e.doc* Discharge of sewage and grey water from vessels in Antarctic Treaty waters (ATCM XXXVI – IP 66) *http://www.ats.aq/documents/ATCM36/ip/ATCM36_ip066_e.doc* Assessment of environmental impacts arising from sewage discharge at Davis Station (ATCM XXXV – BP10) *http://www.ats.aq/documents/ATCM35/bp/ATCM35_bp010_e.doc* Reducing sewage pollution in the Antarctic marine environment using a sewage treatment plant (ATCM XXVIII – IP37) *http://www.ats.aq/documents/ATCM28/ip/ATCM28_ip037_e.doc* Wastewater treatment in Antarctica: challenges and process improvements (ATCM XXIX – IP60) *http://www.ats.aq/documents/ATCM29/ip/ATCM29_ip060_e.doc*

6.	Limiting introductions or redistribution of microorganisms that might impact upon existing microbial communities in the Antarctic environment: • Improve understanding of risks and pathways for introductions. • Develop more specific guidelines for preventing introductions and/or redistribution of microorganisms in the Antarctic environment.	Human footprint in Antarctica and the long-term conservation of terrestrial microbial habitats (ATCM XXXVI - WP 39) *http://www.ats.aq/documents/ATCM36/wp/ATCM36_wp039_e.doc* SCAR's code of conduct for the exploration and research of subglacial aquatic environments (ATCM XXXIV- IP 33) *http://www.ats.aq/documents/ATCM34/ip/ATCM34_ip033_e.doc*
	Monitoring	
7.	Monitoring for non-native species in the Antarctic marine and terrestrial environments: • Develop generally applicable monitoring guidelines. More detailed or site-specific monitoring may be required for particular locations. • Implement marine and terrestrial monitoring following the development of a monitoring framework. • Identify who will undertake the monitoring and with what frequency. • A status report on established monitoring should be submitted regularly to the CEP.	Summary of environmental monitoring and reporting discussions (ATCM XXXI – IP 07) *http://www.ats.aq/documents/ATCM31/ip/ATCM31_ip007_e.doc*
8.	Establishing which native species are present at Antarctic sites to assist with identifying scale and scope of current and future introductions (because it is not practical to conduct surveys everywhere, priority should be given to sites of high human activity (i.e. stations, most frequently visited scientific field sites and visitor sites), high value and/or high sensitivity): • Compile existing biodiversity data (including from terrestrial, aquatic and marine ecosystems). • Develop guidelines on undertaking baseline biodiversity surveys.	Final report on the research project 'The impact of human activities on soil organisms of the maritime Antarctic and the introduction of non-native species in Antarctica' (ATCM XXXVI – IP 55) *http://www.ats.aq/documents/ATCM36/ip/ATCM36_ip055_e.doc* *http://www.umweltbundesamt.de/uba-info-medien/4416.html*

	Response	
9.	Responding rapidly to non-native species introductions: • Develop guidelines on rapid response, including information on practical eradication or containment/control of plants, invertebrates and other biological groups.	Eradication of a vascular plant species recently introduced to Whalers Bay, Deception Island (United Kingdom, Spain 2010) *http://www.ats.aq/documents/ATCM33/ip/ATCM33_ip043_e.doc* The successful eradication of *Poa pratensis* from Cierva Point, Danco Coast, Antarctic Peninsula (Argentina, Spain and the United Kingdom, 2015) *http://www.ats.aq/documents/ATCM38/ip/ATCM38_ip029_e.doc* Eradication of a non-native grass *Poa annua* L. from ASPA No 128 Western Shore of Admiralty Bay, King George Island, South Shetland Islands (Poland, 2015) *http://www.ats.aq/documents/ATCM38/ip/ATCM38_ip078_e.doc*
	Preventing, detecting and responding to diseases in Antarctic wildlife resulting from human activities	
10.	Taking steps to reduce the risk of introducing plant and animal pathogens to Antarctica and their subsequent dispersal within the region by human activity: • Develop (or formally adopt existing) guidance for responding to disease events. • Introduce preventive measures to diminish risks of introduction of diseases to Antarctic wildlife, for example, specific guidance for handling field and station waste to minimise introduction of non-native species. • Develop specific cleaning requirements that may be needed if there is reason to think that people, clothing, equipment or vehicles have been in contact with diseased animals, disease causing agents or have been in an area of known disease risk.	Report on the open-ended intersessional contact group on diseases of Antarctic wildlife. Report 2 – Practical measures to diminish risk (draft) (Australia, 2001) *http://www.ats.aq/documents/ATCM24/wp/ATCM24_wp011_e.pdf* Study to determine occurrence of non-native species introduced into Antarctica through natural pathways (Argentina, 2015) *http://www.ats.aq/documents/ATCM38/wp/ATCM38_wp046_e.doc* Health of Antarctic Wildlife: A challenge for science and policy (Kerry and Riddle, 2009). Although unusual animal mortality events may occur for a variety of reasons, disease may be a likely cause. Therefore the following resources may be relevant: Mass animal mortality event response plan (British Antarctic Survey). Available from BAS. *https://www.bas.ac.uk/* Unusual mortality response plan (Australia), referred to in: *http://www.ats.aq/documents/ATCM27/ip/ATCM27_ip071_e.doc* Procedures for reporting a high mortality event (IAATO): Available from IAATO. *http://iaato.org/* *http://www.ats.aq/documents/ATCM39/ip/ATCM39_ip119_e.doc*

References and supporting information

Note: The Environments Portal (*www.environments.aq*) is a source of peer-reviewed Antarctic environmental information and includes topic summaries on non-native species (e.g. Newman et al., 2014; Hughes and Frenot, 2015).

ATCM XXII - IP 04 (Australia) 1998 - Introduction of diseases to Antarctic wildlife: Proposed workshop.

ATCM XXIII - WP 32 (Australia) 1999 - Report to ATCM XXIII on outcomes from the Workshop on diseases of Antarctic wildlife.

ATCM XXIV - WP 10 (Australia) 2001 - Report on the open-ended intersessional contact group on diseases of Antarctic wildlife: Report 1 - Review and risk assessment.

ATCM XXIV - WP 11 (Australia) 2001 - Report on the open-ended intersessional contact group on diseases of Antarctic wildlife: Report 2 - Practical measures to diminish risk (draft).

ATCM XXV - IP 62 (Australia) 2002 - Draft response plan in the event that unusual animal deaths are discovered.

ATCM XXVII - IP 71 (Australia) 2004 - Australia's Antarctic quarantine practices.

ATCM XXVIII - WP 28 (Australia) 2005 - Measures to address the unintentional introduction and spread of non-native biota and disease to the Antarctic Treaty Area.

ATCM XXVIII - IP 37 (United Kingdom) 2005 - Reducing sewage pollution in the Antarctic marine environment using a sewage treatment plant.

ATCM XXVIII - IP 97 (IAATO) 2005 - Update on boot and clothing decontamination guidelines and the introduction and detection of diseases in Antarctic wildlife: IAATO's perspective.

ATCM XXIX - WP 05 Rev. 1 (United Kingdom) 2006 - Practical guidelines for ballast water exchange in the Antarctic Treaty Area.

ATCM XXIX - IP 44 (Australia) 2006 - Principles underpinning Australia's approach to Antarctic quarantine management.

ATCM XXIX - IP 60 (United States) 2006 - Wastewater treatment in Antarctica: challenges and process improvements.

ATCM XXX - IP 49 (Australia, SCAR) 2007 - Aliens in Antarctica.

ATCM XXXI - WP 16 (Australia) - Antarctic alien species database.

ATCM XXXI - IP 07 (Australia) 2008 - Summary of environmental monitoring and reporting discussions.

ATCM XXXI - IP 17 (Australia, China, India, Romania, Russian Federation) 2008 - Measures to protect the Larsemann Hills, East Antarctica, from the introduction of non-native species.

ATCM XXXI - IP 98 (COMNAP) - Survey on existing procedures concerning introduction of non native species in Antarctica.

ATCM XXXII - WP 05 (Australia, France, New Zealand) 2009 - A work program for CEP action on non-native species.

ATCM XXXII - WP 23 (South Africa) 2009 - Propagule transport associated with logistic operations: a South African appraisal of a regional issue.

ATCM XXXII - WP 32 (United Kingdom) 2009 - Procedures for vehicle cleaning to prevent transfer of non-native species into and around Antarctica.

ATCM XXXII - WP 33 (United Kingdom) 2009 - Review of provisions relating to non-native species introductions in ASPA and ASMA management plans.

ATCM XXXII - IP 04 (SCAR) 2009 - SCAR's environmental code of conduct for terrestrial scientific field research in Antarctica.

ATCM XXXII - IP 12 (United Kingdom) 2009 - ASPA and ASMA management plans: review of provisions relating to non-native species introductions.

ATCM XXXII - SP 11 (ATS) 2009 - Topic summary of CEP discussions on non-native species (NNS) in Antarctica.

ATCM XXXIII - WP 04 (SCAR) 2010 - Preliminary results from the International Polar Year Programme: Aliens in Antarctica.

ATCM XXXIII - WP 06 (SCAR, Australia) 2010 - Current knowledge for reducing risks posed by terrestrial non-native species: towards an evidence-based approach.

ATCM XXXIII - WP 08 (United Kingdom) 2010 - Draft procedures for vehicle cleaning to prevent transfer of non-native species into and around Antarctica.

ATCM XXXIII - WP 09 (France) 2010 - Open-ended Intersessional Contact Group on "Non-native species" (NNS) - 2009-2010 report.

ATCM XXXIII - WP 14 (United Kingdom) 2010 - Intra-regional transfer of species in terrestrial Antarctica.

ATCM XXXIII - WP 15 (United Kingdom) 2010 - Guidance for visitors and environmental managers following the discovery of a suspected non-native species in the terrestrial and freshwater Antarctic environment.

ATCM XXXIII - IP 43 (United Kingdom, Spain) 2010 - Eradication of a vascular plant species recently introduced to Whaler's Bay, Deception Island.

ATCM XXXIII - IP 44 (United Kingdom) 2010 - Suggested framework and considerations for scientists attempting to determine the colonisation status of newly discovered terrestrial or freshwater species within the Antarctic Treaty Area.

ATCM XXXIV - WP 12 (COMNAP and SCAR) 2011 - Raising awareness of non-native species introductions: Workshop results and checklists for supply chain managers.

ATCM XXXIV - WP 34 (New Zealand) 2011 – Report of the Intersessional Contact Group on non-native species 2010-2011.

ATCM XXXIV - WP 53 (SCAR) 2011 - Measures to reduce the risk of non-native species introductions to the Antarctic region associated with fresh foods.

ATCM XXXIV - IP 26 (Germany) 2011 - Progress report on the research project "The role of human activities in the introduction of non-native species into Antarctica and in the distribution of organisms within the Antarctic".

ATCM XXXIV - IP 32 (France) 2011 – Report on the IPY Oslo Science Conference session on non-native species.

ATCM XXXIV - IP 50 (United Kingdom and Uruguay) 2011 – Colonisation status of known non-native species in the Antarctic terrestrial environment (update 2011).

ATCM XXXIV - IP 68 (Australia and SCAR) 2011 - Alien species database.

ATCM XXXV - WP 05 (SCAR) 2012 – Outcomes of the International Polar Year programme: Aliens in Antarctica.

ATCM XXXV - WP 06 (SCAR) 2012 – Reducing the risk of inadvertent non-native species introductions associated with fresh fruit and vegetable importation to Antarctica.

ATCM XXXV - WP 25 rev.1 (Australia and France) 2012 – Guidelines to minimise the risks of non-native species and disease associated with Antarctic hydroponics facilities.

ATCM XXXV - WP 55 (Chile) 2012 – New records of the presence of human associated microorganisms in the Antarctic marine environment.

ATCM XXXV - IP 13 (Spain, Argentina and the United Kingdom) 2012 – Colonisation status of the non-native grass *Poa pratensis* at Cierva Point, Danco Coast, Antarctic Peninsula.

ATCM XXXV - IP 29 (United Kingdom) 2012 – Colonisation status of known non-native species in the Antarctic terrestrial environment (update 2012).

ATCM XXXV - BP 01 (SCAR) 2012 – Continent-wide risk assessment for the establishment of nonindigenous species in Antarctica.

ATCM XXXV - BP 010 (Australia) 2012 – Assessment of environmental impacts arising from sewage discharge at Davis Station.

ATCM XXXVI - WP 19 (Germany) 2013 - Report on the research project "The impact of human activities on soil organisms of the maritime Antarctic and the introduction of non-native species in Antarctica".

ATCM XXXVI - WP 39 (Belgium, SCAR, South Africa and the United Kingdom) 2013 - Human footprint in Antarctica and the long-term conservation of terrestrial microbial habitats.

ATCM XXXVI - IP 28 (United Kingdom) 2013 – Colonisation status of known non-native species in the Antarctic terrestrial environment (update 2013).

ATCM XXXVI - IP 35 (Argentina, Spain and the United Kingdom) 2013 - The non-native grass *Poa pratensis* at Cierva Point, Danco Coast, Antarctic Peninsula – on-going investigations and future eradication plans.

ATCM XXXVI - IP 55 (Germany) 2013 - Final report on the research project "The impact of human activities on soil organisms of the maritime Antarctic and the introduction of non-native species in Antarctica".

ATCM XXXVI - IP 66 (ASOC) 2013 - Discharge of sewage and grey water from vessels in Antarctic Treaty waters.

ATCM XXXVII - WP 04 (Germany) 2014 - Report on the informal discussion on tourism and the risk of introducing non-native organisms.

ATCM XXXVII - IP 23 (United Kingdom) 2014 - Colonisation status of known non-native species in the Antarctic terrestrial environment (update 2014).

ATCM XXXVII - IP 83 (Argentina) 2014 - Record of two species of non-native birds at 25 de Mayo Island, South Shetland Islands.

ATCM XXXVIII - WP 37 (Norway and the United Kingdom) 2015 – Report from ICG on climate change.

ATCM XXXVIII - WP 46 (Argentina) 2015 - Study to determine occurrence of non-native species introduced into Antarctica through natural pathways.

ATCM XXXVIII - IP 29 (Argentina, Spain and the United Kingdom) 2015 - The successful eradication of *Poa pratensis* from Cierva Point, Danco Coast, Antarctic Peninsula.

ATCM XXXVIII - IP 46 (United Kingdom, Chile and Spain) 2015 - Colonisation status of known non-native species in the Antarctic terrestrial environment: a review. Attachment A: Biological invasions in terrestrial Antarctica: what is the current status and how can we respond? Attachment B: Supplementary information.

ATCM XXXVIII - IP 78 (Poland) 2015 - Eradication of a non-native grass *Poa annua* L. from ASPA No. 128 Western Shore of Admiralty Bay, King George Island, South Shetland Islands.

ATCM XXXVIII - IP 93 (SCAR) Monitoring biological invasion across the broader Antarctic: a baseline and indicator framework.

ATCM XXXVIII - IP 101 (COMNAP) 2015 - COMNAP practical training modules: Module 2 - Non-native species.

Augustyniuk-Kram, A., Chwedorzewska, K.J., Korczak-Abshire, M., Olech, M., Lityńska–Zając, M. 2013 - An analysis of fungal propagules transported to the *Henryk Arctowski* Station. Pol. Polar Res. 34, 269–278.

Chown, S.L., Convey, P. 2007 - Spatial and temporal variability across life's hierarchies in the terrestrial Antarctic. Phil. Trans. R. Soc. B, 362, 2307–2331.

Chown, S.L., Lee, J.E., Hughes, K.A., Barnes, J., Barrett, P.J., Bergstrom, D.M., Convey, P., Cowan, D.A., Crosbie, K., Dyer, G., Frenot, Y., Grant, S.M., Herr, D., Kennicutt, M.C., Lamers, M., Murray, A., Possingham, H.P., Reid, K., Riddle, M.J., Ryan, P.G., Sanson, L., Shaw, J.D., Sparrow, M.D., Summerhayes, C., Terauds, A., Wall, D.H. 2012 - Challenges to the future conservation of the Antarctic. Science, 337, 158-159.

Chown, S.L., Huiskes, A.H.L., Gremmen, N.J.M., Lee, J.E, Terauds, A., Crosbie, K., Frenot, Y., Hughes, K.A., Imura, S., Kiefer, K., Lebouvier, M., Raymond, B., Tsujimotoi, M., Ware, C., Van de Vijver, B., Bergstrom, D.M. 2012 - Continent-wide risk assessment for the establishment of nonindigenous species in Antarctica. Proc. Nat. Acad. Sci. USA, 109, 4938-4943.

Chwedorzewska, K J., Korczak, M. 2010 - Human impact upon the environment in the vicinity of Arctowski Station, King George Island, Antarctica. Pol. Polar Res., 31, 45-60.

Chwedorzewska, K.J., Bednarek, P.T. 2012. - Genetic and epigenetic variation in a cosmopolitan grass *Poa annua* from Antarctic and Polish populations. Pol. Polar Res., 33, 63-80.

COMNAP, SCAR. 2010 - Checklists for supply chain managers of National Antarctic Programmes for the reduction in risk of transfer of non-native species. Available at: *https://www.comnap.aq/Shared%20Documents/nnschecklists.pdf*

Convey, P. 2011 - Antarctic terrestrial biodiversity in a changing world. Polar Biol., 34, 1629-1641.

Convey, P., Frenot, Y., Gremmen, N. & Bergstrom, D.M. 2006 - Biological Invasions. In Convey P., Huiskes A. & Bergstrom D.M. (eds) Trends in Antarctic Terrestrial and Limnetic Ecosystems. Springer, Dordrecht pp. 193-220.

Convey, P., Hughes, K. A., Tin, T. 2012 - Continental governance and environmental management mechanisms under the Antarctic Treaty System: sufficient for the biodiversity challenges of this century? Biodiversity. 13, 1–15.

Cowan, D.A., Chown, S. L., Convey, P., Tuffin, M., Hughes, K.A., Pointing, S., Vincent, W.F. 2011 - Non-indigenous microorganisms in the Antarctic - assessing the risks. Trends Microbiol., 19, 540-548.

Cuba-Díaz, M., Troncoso, J. M., Cordero, C., Finot, V.L., Rondanelli-Reyes, M. 2012 - *Juncus bufonius* L., a new alien vascular plant in King George Island, South Shetland Archipelago. Antarct. Sci., 25, 385–386.

Curry, C. H., McCarthy, J.S., Darragh, H.M., Wake, R.A., Todhunter, R., Terris, J. 2002. Could tourist boots act as vectors for disease transmission in Antarctica? J. Travel Med., 9, 190-193.

Dartnall, H.J.G. 2005 – Are Antarctic planktonic rotifers anthropogenic introductions? Quekett J. Microscopy, 40, 137-143.

De Poorter, M., Gilbert, N., Storey, B., Rogan-Finnemore, M. 2006 Final Report of the Workshop on "Non-native Species in the Antarctic", Christchurch, New Zealand, 10-12 April 2006.

Everatt, M.J., Worland, M.R., Bale, J.S., Convey, P., Hayward, S.A. 2012 - Pre-adapted to the maritime Antarctic? - Rapid cold hardening of the midge, *Eretmoptera murphyi*. J. Insect Physiol., 58, 1104-1111.

Falk-Petersen, J., Bohn, T., Sandlund, O.T. 2006. On the numerous concepts in invasion biology. Biological Invasions, 8, 1409-1424.

Frenot, Y., Chown S.L., Whinam, J., Selkirk P.M., Convey, P, Skotnicki, M., Bergstrom D.M. 2005 - Biological invasions in the Antarctic: extent, impacts and implications. Biological Rev., 80, 45-72.

Gielwanowska, I., Kellmann-Sopyla, W. 2015 – Generative reproduction of Antarctic grasses, the native species *Deschampsia antarctica* Desv. and the alien species *Poa annua*. Polish Polar Res. 36, 261-279.

Greenslade, P., Potapov, M., Russell, D., Convey, P. 2012 - Global Collembola on Deception Island. J. Insect Sci., 12, 111.

Headland, R. K. 2012 - History of exotic terrestrial mammals in Antarctic regions. Polar Rec., 48, 123-144.

Houghton, M., McQuillan, P.B., Bergstrom, D.M., Frost, L., Van Den Hoff, J., and Shaw, J. 2014 - Pathways of alien invertebrate transfer to the Antarctic region. Polar Biol., 39, 23-33.

Hughes, K.A., Convey, P. 2010 - The protection of Antarctic terrestrial ecosystems from inter- and intra-continental transfer of non-indigenous species by human activities: a review of current systems and practices. Global Environmental Change, 20, 96-112. DOI:10.1016/j.gloenvcha.2009.09.005.

Hughes, K.A., Worland, M.R. 2010 - Spatial distribution, habitat preference and colonisation status of two alien terrestrial invertebrate species in Antarctica. Antarct. Sci., 22, 221-231.

Hughes, K.A., Convey, P. 2012 - Determining the native/non-native status of newly discovered terrestrial and freshwater species in Antarctica - current knowledge, methodology and management action. J. Environ. Man., 93, 52-66.

Hughes, K.A., Convey, P. 2014 - Alien invasions in Antarctica – is anyone liable? Polar Res., *33*, 22103. *http://dx.doi.org/10.3402/polar.v33.22103*

Hughes, K.A., Frenot, Y. 2015 - Status of known non-native species introductions and impacts. Antarctic Environments Portal Information Summary Version 1.0. *https://environments.aq/information-summaries/status-of-known-non-native-species-introductions-and-impacts/*

Hughes, K.A., Ashton, G.V. 2016 – Breaking the ice: the introduction of biofouling organisms to Antarctica on vessel hulls. Aquat. Conserv. DOI: 10.1002/aqc.2625.

Hughes, K.A., Walsh, S., Convey, P., Richard, S., Bergstrom, D. 2005 – Alien fly populations established at two Antarctic research stations. Polar Biol., 28, 568-570.

Hughes, K.A., Convey, P., Maslen, N.R., Smith, R.I.L. 2010 - Accidental transfer of non-native soil organisms into Antarctica on construction vehicles. Biological Invasions, 12, 875-891. DOI:10.1007/s10530-009-9508-2.

Hughes, K.A., Lee, J.E., Ware, C., Kiefer, K., Bergstrom, D.M. 2010 - Impact of anthropogenic transportation to Antarctica on alien seed viability. Polar Biol., 33, 1123-1130.

Hughes, K.A., Lee, J.E., Tsujimoto, M., Imura, S., Bergstrom, D.M., Ware, C., Lebouvier, M., Huiskes, A.H.L., Gremmen, N.J.M., Frenot, Y., Bridge P.D., Chown, S. L. 2011 - Food for thought: risks of non-native species transfer to the Antarctic region with fresh produce. Biological Conservation, 144, 1682–1689.

Hughes, K.A., Fretwell, P., Rae, J. Holmes, K., Fleming, A. 2011 - Untouched Antarctica: mapping a finite and diminishing environmental resource. Antarct. Sci., 23, 537-548.

Hughes, K.A., Worland, M.R., Thorne, M., Convey, P. 2013 - The non-native chironomid *Eretmoptera murphyi* in Antarctica: erosion of the barriers to invasion. Biological Invasions, 15, 269-281.

Hughes, K.A., Huiskes, A.H.L, Convey, P. 2014 - Global movement and homogenisation of biota: challenges to the environmental management of Antarctica? In T. Tin, D. Liggett, P. Maher, and M. Lamers (eds). The Future of Antarctica: Human impacts, strategic planning and values for conservation. Springer, Dordrecht. DOI: 10.1007/978-94-007-6582-5_5

Hughes, K.A., Cowan, D.A., and Wilmotte, A. 2015 - Protection of Antarctic microbial communities – 'Out of sight, out of mind'. Front. Microbiol. DOI: 10.3389/fmicb.2015.00151

Hughes, K.A., Pertierra, L.R., Molina-Montenegro, M., Convey, P. 2015. Biological invasions in Antarctica: what it the current status and can we respond? Biodivers. Conserv., 24, 1031-1055.

Huiskes, A.H.L., Gremmen, N.J.M., Bergstrom, D.M., Frenot, Y., Hughes, K.A., Imura, S., Kiefer, K., Lebouvier, M., Lee, J.E., Tsujimoto, M., Ware, C., Van de Vijver, B., Chown, S.L. 2014 - Aliens in Antarctica: Assessing transfer of plant propagules by human visitors to reduce invasion risk. Biol. Conserv., 171, 278-284.

Kerry, K.R., Riddle, M. (Eds.) 2009 - Health of Antarctic Wildlife: A Challenge for Science and Policy, Springer Verlag, ISBN-13: 9783540939221.

Lee, J.E., Chown, S.L. 2009 – *Mytilus* on the move: transport of an invasive bivalve to the Antarctic. Mar. Ecol. Prog. Ser., 339, 307-310.

Lee, J.E., Chown, S.L. 2009 – Breaching the dispersal barrier to invasion: quantification and management. Ecol. Appl., 19, 1944-1959.

Lee, J.E., Chown, S.L. 2009 – Temporal development of hull-fouling assemblages associated with an Antarctic supply vessel. Mar. Ecol. Prog. Ser., 396, 97-105.

Lee, J.E., Chown, S.L. 2011 - Quantification of intra-regional propagule movements in the Antarctic. Antarct. Sci., 23, 337-342.

Lewis, P.N., Bergstrom, D.M., Whinam, J. 2006 – Barging in: A temperate marine community travels to the subantarctic. Biol. Invasions, 8, 787-795.

Lewis, P.N., Hewitt, C.L., Riddle, M., McMinn, A. 2003. Marine introductions in the Southern Ocean: an unrecognised hazard to biodiversity. Mar. Pollut. Bull., 46, 213-223.

Litynska-Zajac, M., Chwedorzewska, K., Olech, M., Korczak-Abshire, M., Augustyniuk-Kram, A. 2012 - Diaspores and phyto-remains accidentally transported to the Antarctic Station during three expeditions. Biodivers. Conserv., 21, 3411-3421.

McGeoch, M.A., Shaw, J.D., Terauds, A., Lee, J.E., Chown, S.L. 2015 - Monitoring biological invasion across the broader Antarctic: A baseline and indicator framework. Glob. Environ. Change. DOI: 10.1016/j.gloenvcha.2014.12.012

Molina-Montenegro, M., Carrasco-Urra, F., Rodrigo, C., Convey, P., Valladares, F., Gianoli, E. 2012 - Occurrence of the non-native annual bluegrass (*Poa annua*) on the Antarctic mainland and its negative effects on native plants. Conserv. Biol., 26, 717-723.

Molina-Montenegro, M., Carrasco-Urra, F., Acuna-Rodriquez, I., Oses, R., Torres-Díaz, C., Chwedorzewska, K.J. 2014 - Assessing the importance of human activities for the establishment of the invasive *Poa annua* in Antarctica. Polar Res., 33, 21425. *http://dx.doi.org/10.3402/polar.v33.21425*

Molina-Montenegro, M.A., Pertierra, L.R., Razeto-Barry, P., Díaz, J., Finot, V.L., Torres-Díaz, C. 2015 - A recolonization record of the invasive *Poa annua* in Paradise Bay, Antarctic Peninsula: modeling of the potential spreading risk. Polar Biol., 38, 1091-1096. DOI: 10.1007/s00300-015-1668-1

Newman, J., Coetzee, B.W.T., Chown, S.L., Terauds, A., McIvor, E. 2014 - The introduction of non-native species to the Antarctic. Antarctic Environments Portal Information Summary Version 1.0. *http://environments.aq/information-summaries/the-introduction-of-non-native-species-to-antarctica/*

Nielsen, U.N., Wall, D.H. 2013 - The future of soil invertebrate communities in polar regions: different climate change responses in the Arctic and Antarctic? Ecol. Lett., 16, 409-419.

Olech, M., Chwedorzewska, K.J. 2011 - The first appearance and establishment of an alien vascular plant in natural habitats on the forefield of a retreating glacier in Antarctica. Antarct. Sci., 23, 153-154.

Osyczka, P. 2010 - Alien lichens unintentionally transported to the "Arctowski" station (South Shetlands, Antarctica). Polar Biol., 33, 1067-1073.

Osyczka, P., Mleczko, P., Karasinski, D., Chlebicki, A. 2012 - Timber transported to Antarctica: a potential and undesirable carrier for alien fungi and insects. Biol. Invasions, 14, 15-20.

Pearce, D.A., Hughes, K.A., Lachlan-Cope, T., Harangozo, S.A., Jones, A.E. 2010 - Biodiversity of air-borne microorganisms at Halley station, Antarctica. Extremophiles, 14, 145-159.

Pertierra, L.R., Lara, F., Benayas, J., Hughes, K.A. 2013. *Poa pratensis* L., current status of the longest-established non-native vascular plant in the Antarctic. Polar Biol., 36, 1473-1481.

Potter, S. 2006 - The Quarantine Management of Australia's Antarctic Program. Australasian. J. Environ. Man., 13, 185-195.

Potter, S. 2009 - Protecting Antarctica from Non-Native Species: The Imperatives and the Impediments. In G. Alfredsson and T. Koivurova (eds), D. Leary sp. ed. The Yearbook of Polar Law, vol. 1, pp. 383-400.

Ranjith, L., Shukla, S.P., Vennila, A., Gashaw, T.D. 2012 - Bioinvasion in Antarctic Ecosystems. Proc. Nat. Acad. Sci. India Sect. B – Biol. Sci., 82, 353-359.

Reisinger, R. R., McIntyre, T., Bester, M. N. 2010 - Goose barnacles hitchhike on satellite-tracked southern elephant seals. Polar Biol., 33, 561-564.

Russell, D.J., Hohberg, K., Otte, V., Christian, A., Potapov, M., Brückner, A., McInnes, S.J. 2013 - The impact of human activities on soil organisms of the maritime Antarctic and the introduction of non-native species in Antarctica. Federal Environment Agency (Umweltbundesamt). *http://www.uba.de/uba-info-medien-e/4416.html*

Russell, D. J., Hohberg, K., Potapov, M., Brückner, A., Otte, V., Christian, A. 2014 - Native terrestrial invertebrate fauna from the northern Antarctic Peninsula: new records, state of current knowledge and ecological preferences – Summary of a German federal study. Soil Org., 86, 1-58.

SATCM XII - WP 6 (Australia) 2000 - Diseases of Antarctic Wildlife.

Smith, R.I.L. 1996 - Introduced plants in Antarctica: potential impacts and conservations issues. Biol. Conserv., 76, 135–146.

Smith, R.I.L., Richardson, M. 2011 - Fuegian plants in Antarctica: natural or anthropogenically assisted immigrants? Biol. Invasions, 13, 1-5.

Tavares, M., De Melo, G.A.S. 2004 – Discovery of the first known benthic invasive species in the Southern Ocean: the North Atlantic spider crab Hyas araneus found in the Antarctic Peninsula. Antarct. Sci., 16, 129-131.

Terauds, A., Chown, S.L., Morgan, F., Peat, H.J., Watts, D.J., Keys, H., Convey, P., Bergstrom, D.M. 2012 - Conservation biogeography of the Antarctic. Divers. Distrib., 18, 726-741.

Tin, T., Fleming, Z.L., Hughes, K.A., Ainley, D.G., Convey, P., Moreno, C.A., Pfeiffer, S., Scott, J., Snape, I. 2009 - Impacts of local human activities on the Antarctic environment. Antarct. Sci., 21, 3-33.

Tsujimoto, M., Imura, S. 2012 - Does a new transportation system increase the risk of importing non-native species to Antarctica? Antarct. Sci., 24, 441-449.

Tsujimoto, M., Imura, S. 2013 - Biosecurity measures being implemented at Australian Antarctic Division against non-native species introduction into Antarctica. Antarct. Rec., 57, 137-150.

Walther, G.-R., Roques, A., Hulme, P.E., Sykes, M.T., Pysek, P., Kühn, I., Zobel, M. 2009. Alien species in a warmer world: risks and opportunities. Trends Ecol. Evol., 24, 686-693. DOI:10.1016/j.tree.2009.06.008.

Whinam, J., Chilcott, N., Bergstrom, D.M. 2005 – Subantarctic hitchhikers: expeditioners as vectors for the introduction of alien organisms. Biol. Conserv., 21, 207-219.

Whinam, J. 2009 - Aliens in the Sub-Antarctic - Biosecurity and climate change. Papers and Proceedings of the Royal Society of Tasmania, 143, 45-52.

Wódkiewicz, M., Galera, H., Chwedorzewska, K.J., Gielwanowska, I., Olech, M. 2013 - Diaspores of the introduced species *Poa annua* L. in soil samples from King George Island (South Shetlands, Antarctica). Arct. Antarct. Alp. Res. 45: 415-419.

Wódkiewicz, M., Ziemianski, M., Kwiecien, K., Chwedorzewska, K.J., Galera, H. 2014 - Spatial structure of the soil seed bank of *Poa annua* L.- alien species in the Antarctic. Biodivers. Conserv., 23, 1339-1346.

Volonterio, O., de León, R.P., Convey, P., Krzeminska, E. 2013 - First record of Trichoceridae (Diptera) in the maritime Antarctic. Polar Biol., 36, 1125-1131.

Secretariat of the Antarctic Treaty

Maipú 757 Piso 4 (C1006ACI) - Buenos Aires - Argentina

http://www.ats.aq

ats@ats.aq

Revised Guide to the presentation of Working Papers containing proposals for Antarctic Specially Protected Areas, Antarctic Specially Managed Areas or Historic Sites and Monuments

The Representatives,

Noting that Annex V to the Protocol on Environmental Protection to the Antarctic Treaty ("the Protocol") provides for the Antarctic Treaty Consultative Meeting ("ATCM") to adopt proposals to designate an Antarctic Specially Protected Area ("ASPA") or an Antarctic Specially Managed Area ("ASMA"), to adopt or amend a Management Plan for such an area, or to designate an Historic Site or Monument ("HSM"), by a Measure in accordance with Article IX(1) of the Antarctic Treaty;

Conscious of the need to ensure clarity concerning the current status of each ASPA and ASMA and its Management Plan, and each HSM;

Recalling Resolution 3 (2008), which recommended that the Environmental Domains Analysis for the Antarctic Continent annexed to it, be used consistently and in conjunction with other tools agreed within the Antarctic Treaty system as a dynamic model for the identification of areas that could be designated as ASPA within the systematic environmental-geographical framework referred to in Article 3(2) of Annex V to the Protocol;

Recalling also Resolution 6 (2012), which recommended that the Antarctic Conservation Biogeographic Regions, annexed to it, be used in conjunction with the Environmental Domains Analysis for the Antarctic Continent and other tools agreed within the Antarctic Treaty system to support activities relevant to the interests of the Parties, including as a dynamic model for the identification of areas that could be designated as ASPA within the systematic environmental-geographic framework referred to in Article 3(2) of Annex V to the Protocol;

Recalling also Resolution 5 (2015), and the report on identified Important Birds Areas in Antarctica;

Recalling also Resolution 1 (2008), which recommended that the Guide to the presentation of Working Papers containing proposals for Antarctic Specially Protected Areas, Antarctic Specially Managed Areas or Historic Sites and Monuments ("the Guide"), annexed to it, be used by those engaged in the preparation of such Working Papers;

Desiring to update the current version of the Guide annexed to Resolution 5 (2011), to reflect the further tools that could be used to identify protected areas within a systematic environmental-geographical framework;

Recommend that:

1. the revised Guide to the presentation of Working Papers containing proposals for Antarctic Specially Protected Areas, Antarctic Specially Managed Areas or Historic Sites and Monuments annexed to this Resolution be used by those engaged in the preparation of such Working Papers; and

2. the Secretariat of the Antarctic Treaty post the text of Resolution 5 (2011) on its website in a way that makes clear that it is no longer current.

Guide to the presentation of Working Papers containing proposals for Antarctic Specially Protected Areas, Antarctic Specially Managed Areas or Historic Sites and Monuments

A. Working Papers on ASPA or ASMA

It is recommended that the Working Paper contain two parts:

i) a **COVER SHEET** explaining the intended effects of the proposal and the history of the ASPA/ASMA, using Template A as a guide. **This cover sheet will NOT form part of the Measure** adopted by the ATCM, so will not be published in the Final Report nor on the ATS website. Its sole purpose is to facilitate consideration of the proposal and the drafting of the Measures by the ATCM.

and

ii) a **MANAGEMENT PLAN,** written as a final version as it is intended to be published. **This will be annexed to the Measure and published** in the Final Report and on the ATS website.

It would be helpful if the plan is written *as final*, ready for publication. Of course, when it is first submitted to the CEP it is a draft and may be amended by the CEP or ATCM. However, the version adopted by the ATCM should be in final form for publication, and should not require further editing by the Secretariat, other than to insert cross-references to other instruments adopted at the same meeting.

For example, in its final form, the plan should not contain expressions such as:

- "this *proposed* area";
- "this *draft* plan";
- "this plan, *if adopted*, would…";
- accounts of discussions in the CEP or ATCM or details of intersessional work (unless this covers important information eg about the consultation process or activities that have occurred within the Area since the last review);
- views of individual delegations on the draft or intermediate versions of it;
- references to other protected areas using their pre-Annex V designations.

Please use the "Guide to the Preparation of Management Plans for Antarctic Specially Protected Areas" if the proposal concerns an ASPA. (The current version of this Guide is appended to Resolution 2 (2011) and is contained in the CEP Handbook).

There are several high quality management plans, including that for ASPA No.109: Moe Island, that could be used as a model for the preparation of new and revised plans.

B. Working Papers on Historic Sites and Monuments (HSM)

HSMs do not have management plans, unless they are also designated as ASPAs or ASMAs. All essential information about the HSM is included in the Measure. The rest of the Working Paper will not be annexed to the Measure; if it is desired to keep any additional background information on the record, this material may be annexed to the report of the CEP for inclusion in the Final Report of the ATCM. To ensure that all the information required for inclusion in the Measure is provided, it is recommended that Template B below is used as a guide when drafting the Working Paper.

C. The tabling of draft Measures on ASPA, ASMA and HSM to the ATCM

When a draft Measure to give effect to the advice of the CEP on an ASPA, ASMA or HSM is submitted to the Secretariat for tabling at the ATCM, the Secretariat is requested also to provide to the ATCM copies of the cover sheet from the original Working Paper setting out the proposal, subject to any revisions made by the CEP.

The sequence of events is as follows:

- A Working Paper consisting of a draft management plan and an explanatory cover sheet is prepared and submitted by the proponent.
- The Secretariat prepares a draft Measure before the ATCM;
- Draft Management Plan is discussed by CEP and any revisions made (by the proponent in liaison with the Secretariat);
- If CEP recommend adoption, the Management Plan (as agreed) plus the cover sheet (as agreed) are passed from the CEP Chair to the Chair of the Legal and Institutional Working Group;
- Legal and Institutional Working Group reviews the draft Measure;
- Secretariat formally table the draft measure plus the agreed cover sheet;
- ATCM consider and make decision.

TEMPLATE A: COVER SHEET FOR A WORKING PAPER ON AN ASPA OR ASMA

Please ensure that the following information is provided on the cover sheet:

1) Is a new ASPA proposed? Yes/No
2) Is a new ASMA proposed? Yes/No
3) Does the proposal relate to an existing ASPA or ASMA?

If so, list all Recommendations, Measures, Resolutions and Decisions pertaining to this ASPA/ASMA, including any previous designations of this area as an SPA, SSSI or other type of protected area:

In particular, please include the date and relevant Recommendation/Measure for the following:

- First designation:
- First adoption of management plan:
- Any revisions to management plan:
- Current management plan:
- Any extensions of expiry dates of management plan:
- Renaming and renumbering as ………..... by Decision 1 (2002).

(Note: this information may be found on the ATS website in the Documents database by searching under the name of the area. While the ATS has made every effort to ensure the completeness and accuracy of the information in the database, occasional errors or omissions may occur. The proponents of any revision to a protected area are best placed to know the history of that area, and are kindly requested to contact the Secretariat if they notice any apparent discrepancy between the regulatory history as they understand it and that displayed on the ATS database.)

1) If the proposal contains a revision of an existing management plan, please indicate the types of amendment:

   i) Major or minor?

   ii) Any changes to the boundaries or co-ordinates?

   iii) Any changes to the maps? If yes, are the changes in the captions only or also in the graphics?

   iv) Any change to the description of the area that is relevant to identifying its location or its boundaries?

   v) Any changes that affect any other ASPA, ASMA or HSM within this area or adjacent to it? In particular, please explain any merger with, incorporation of or abolition of any existing area or site.

   vi) Other - brief summary of other types of changes, indicating the paragraphs of the management plan in which these are located (especially helpful if the plan is long).

2) If a new ASPA or ASMA is proposed, does it contain any marine area? Yes/No

3) If yes, does the proposal require the prior approval of CCAMLR in accordance with Decision 9 (2005)? Yes/No

4) If yes, has the prior approval of CCAMLR been obtained? Yes/No (If yes, the reference to the relevant paragraph of the relevant CCAMLR Final Report should be given).

5) If the proposal relates to an ASPA, what is the primary reason for designation (i.e. which part under Article 3.2 of Annex V)?

6) If relevant, have you identified the main Environmental Domain represented by the ASPA/ASMA (refer to the 'Environmental Domains Analysis for the Antarctic Continent' appended to Resolution 3 (2008))? Yes/No (If yes, the main Environmental Domain should be noted here).

7) If relevant, have you identified the main Antarctic Conservation Biogeographic Region represented by the ASPA/ASMA (refer to the 'Antarctic Conservation Biogeographic Regions' appended to Resolution 6 (2012))? Yes/No (If yes, the main Antarctic Conservation Biogeographic Region should be noted here).

8) If relevant, have you identified any Antarctic Important Bird Areas (Resolution 5 (2015)) represented by the ASPA/ASMA (refer to the 'Important Bird Areas in Antarctica 2015 Summary' appended to ATCMXXXVIII IP27 and the full report available at: *http://www.era.gs/resources/iba/*)? Yes/No (If yes, the Important Bird Area(s) should be noted here).

The above format may be used as a template or as a check-list for the cover sheet, to ensure that all the requested information is provided.

TEMPLATE B: COVER SHEET FOR A WORKING PAPER ON A HISTORIC SITE OR MONUMENT

Please ensure that the following information is provided on the cover sheet:

1) Has this site or monument been designated by a previous ATCM as a Historic Site or Monument? Yes/No (If yes, please list the relevant Recommendations and Measures).

2) If the proposal is for a new Historic Site or Monument, please include the following information, worded for inclusion in the Measure:

   i) Name of the proposed HSM, to be added to the list annexed to Measure 2 (2003);

   ii) Description of the HSM to be included in the Measure, including sufficient identifying features to enable visitors to the area to recognize it;

   iii) Co-ordinates, expressed in degrees, minutes and seconds;

   iv) Original proposing Party;

   v) Party undertaking management.

3) If the proposal is to revise an existing designation of an HSM, please list the relevant past Recommendations and Measures.

The above format may be used as a template or as a check-list for the cover sheet, to ensure that all the requested information is provided.

Confirming ongoing commitment to the prohibition on Antarctic mineral resource activities, other than for scientific research; support for the Antarctic Mining Ban

The Representatives,

Recognising that the Protocol on Environmental Protection to the Antarctic Treaty ("the Protocol"), which was signed twenty-five years ago, is an essential element of current efforts to protect the Antarctic environment;

Noting that Article 7 of the Protocol provides that in the Antarctic Treaty area any activity relating to mineral resources, other than scientific research, shall be prohibited;

Taking into account that outside the Antarctic Treaty system there are many in the public and media who incorrectly believe that the Protocol expires in 2048;

Recalling that in accordance with its Article 25, the Protocol does not expire in 2048;

Recalling that in paragraph 5 of the Washington Ministerial Declaration on the Fiftieth Anniversary of the Antarctic Treaty the Consultative Parties reaffirmed their commitment to Article 7 of the Protocol;

Recommend that their Governments:

1. acknowledge the benefits to the Antarctic environment and dependent and associated ecosystems that have resulted from the prohibition on activities relating to mineral resources, other than scientific research, under Article 7 of the Protocol;

2. reaffirm their commitment to Article 7 of the Protocol; and

3. declare their firm commitment to retain and continue to implement this provision as a matter of highest priority to achieve the comprehensive protection of the Antarctic environment and dependent and associated ecosystems.

XXXIX REUNIÓN CONSULTIVA
DEL TRATADO ANTÁRTICO

SANTIAGO · CHILE 2016

www.ingramcontent.com/pod-product-compliance
Lightning Source LLC
Chambersburg PA
CBHW051332200326
41519CB00026B/7401